PEAK DISTRICT BOULDERING

Rupert Davies   John Coefield   Jon Barton

www.v-publishing.co.uk

Peak District Bouldering Contents

VG Copyright© 2011 Vertebrate
Graphics Ltd, Rupert Davies,
John Coefield & Jon Barton
VP Published by Vertebrate Publishing

ISBN: 9781906148270

Cover photo: Dave Norton on *Low Rider*,
Stanage Far Left. Photo: Dave Parry.
All other photos as credited.

Designed & produced by Nathan Ryder
www.v-graphics.co.uk

Printed in China.

Foreword

At the end of 1988, while my attempts to climb *Agincourt* floundered, I recalled the story Marc Le Menestrel had told me a few years earlier when he had experienced similar problems trying to climb *Le Minimum*: "*I quit the south of France and went bouldering in Fontainebleau for a month.*" Shortly after this month of bouldering Marc had climbed the hardest route in France. I didn't have Fontainebleau, but I did have the Peak District, and during the winter of 1988/89 I bouldered as hard as I possibly could. Whether it was obscure problems on Burbage South edge, the technical wall right of *Valkyrie* at Froggatt, or the fingery problems down at Rubicon and Raven Tor, weather-permitting I would be there. If the weather was bad, often the case, then it was down into someone's damp and poorly lit cellar for a session on one of the recently built boards. In late January 1989 I headed back out to France and bagged the first ascent of *Agincourt*, the hardest route in France. Marc's recipe for success had worked a treat.

Since those early days climbing in France I have been lucky enough to climb in many amazing places, yet I always end up coming home to Sheffield and it's been the Peak which has been my true stomping ground these past 25 years. The scene of soulful days alone on remote edges, training days in a big group with high motivation, training days alone when I haven't felt like training, first ascents, repeats and failures and – more recently – leisurely walks with my two-year-old daughter.

Although there are many bouldering venues around the world, I have yet to come across one that stirs up such feelings in both locals and foreigners as the Peak District. Whether you are looking for a technical masterpiece like *Crescent Arête* or *West Side Story*, or something slightly less subtle like *The Ace*, or perhaps the more brutal bouldering style found on the limestone, the Peak has it all. And, as if this wasn't enough, it's all to be found in an area of outstanding natural beauty. What more can I say, except that I feel very fortunate to have lived on its doorstep these past 25 years.

Ben Moon
Sheffield, January 2011

BEN MOON ON *VOYAGER*, BURBAGE NORTH **PHOTO:** BEN PRITCHARD

Introduction

Development has continued at a rapid pace since the last guide. Many new areas have been discovered, old areas have been reappraised, much-talked-about-but-never-tried projects have been climbed and there are more people bouldering than ever before. Over the last five years limestone bouldering in the Peak has seen a resurgence of interest, but perhaps the biggest change in the small, introverted, world of bouldering has been the increased development of 'highballing'. Many grit routes that were once regarded as ankle-breaking solos are now regularly approached ground-up above a pile of mats and a group of spotters, and the line between bouldering and short solos has been truly blurred. In this guide there's more to do in all styles and at all grades than in the last one. As long as you remain keen and uninjured, weather permitting, there's a lifetime's worth of bouldering in this guide to waste your time on.

Rupert Davies
Marple Bridge, January 2011

A legal bit

Every effort has been made to achieve accuracy of information in this guidebook. The authors, publishers and copyright owners can take no responsibility for: loss or injury (including fatal) to persons; loss or damage to property or equipment; trespass, irresponsible behaviour or any other mishap that may be suffered as a result of following descriptions or advice offered in this guidebook. The inclusion of a bouldering area or approach to a bouldering area does not guarantee a right to climb there or a Right of Way to reach it – if conflict with landowners arises, we advise that you act politely and leave by the shortest route available. If the matter needs to be taken further, please take it up with the Peak Park or other relevant authority.

For up to date information on access please visit **www.thebmc.co.uk**

Acknowledgements

Like the first edition, this guide builds upon previous works that documented bouldering in the Peak, notably Allen William's two guides and Jason Myers' Peak Plus guide – these were the first guides to document the bouldering in the Peak District from two of the area's keenest developers.

Andy Harris was responsible for compiling and writing the *Minus 10*, *Tom's Roof* and *Carl's Wark* sections of the *Stoney Middleton* chapter of the first edition of the guide. These sections are largely unchanged and special thanks go to him. Andy is also the main repository of the history of limestone bouldering in the Peak and he has given invaluable input into the other limestone chapters.

Thanks to Niall Grimes and the BMC for consenting to share information regarding names, to allow consistency between this guide and the definitive BMC guides which now also include boulder problems. Thanks also to the BMC's Henry Folkard for offering invaluable access advice.

A huge thanks to Ben Moon for writing such an inspirational foreword – Ben you are a true legend.

Thanks to our incredible photographers, without whose stunning images this book couldn't have been all we hope it is: Adam Long, Dave Parry, Tim Russon, Pete O'Donovan, Nick Brown, Ben Pritchard, Simon Wilson, Stu Littlefair, Ian Parnell, Keith Sharples, Robin Mueller, Dawid Skoczylas, James Pearson, Paul Bennett, Jon Fullwood, Stuart Brooks, Jerry Moffatt, Heinz Zak and Chris Lockyer.

Mark Hundleby, John Coefield, Adam Long and Jon Fullwood helped check the scripts for the first guide: John Coefield has of course now joined the team of authors. This time around much help was again received from Adam and Jon, and also from Andy Banks, Dave Parry, Steve Clark, Simon Wilson and Adam Coefield. Jim Hilliard provided invaluable 'local knowledge' for *Hobson Moor*, and Paul Worsdale and Ben Tetler helped too; and Ben Humphris helped fill in the gaps at the 3D lime of *Nuda's Tartan*. Thanks also to Mike Adams for giving us info on the circuits at *Black Tor* and *Tintwistle Knarr*. Stuart Brooks and Rob Mirfin provided invaluable 'local knowledge' for *The Churnet*.

The following proof readers, climbers and photographers have been of great assistance in helping us produce this edition and the last: Mike Adams, Zaff Ali, Lee Anderson, Mike Annesley, Andy Banks, Robin Barker, Percy Bishton, Stuart Brooks, Dave Buchanan, Steve Clark, Adam Coefield, Matthew Coutts, Nik Crawshaw, Sarah Davies, Chris Doyle, Iain Farrar, Ned Feehally, Jon Fullwood, Niall Grimes, Andy Harris, Richard Heap, Jim Hilliard, Andy Higginson, John Houlihan, Simon Hudson, Mark Hundleby, Paul Ingham, Alan James, Carl Kelsall, Neil Kershaw, Jamie Lilleman, Stuart Littlefair, Adam Long, Graham Lynch, Dave Mason, Alex Messenger, Jerry Moffatt, Ben Moon, Robin Mueller, Jason Myers, Dave Norton, Pete O'Donovan, Simon Panton, Dave Parry, Gareth Parry, Richie Patterson, Chris Plant, Dave Kettle, Richie Brooks, Mark Pretty, Ben Pritchard, Tom Randall, Simon Richardson, Dan Warren, Lynn Robinson, Nikki Skinner at Podsacs, Dawid Skoczylas, Rob Smith, Ben Tetler, Kim Thompson, Andi Turner, Martin Veale, Ian Vickers, Sam Whittaker, John Welford, Allen Williams, Simon Wilson, Ray Wood, Paul Worsdale, Dan Varian and the community at ukbouldering.com.

Finally, a huge thanks to Nathan at Vertebrate for his outstanding design and production work, his patience when we added and removed problems, tweaked grades, moved crags, or generally just mucked around with his design.

Apologies to anyone we've missed out.

EVOLUTION IN ACTION

ARC'TERYX

What's in and what's not

This edition of the guide is more balanced in terms of grade spread than the last one. No bias has been made towards including harder problems at the expense of easier ones and several areas of predominantly low-grade problems have been included that were omitted from the first edition. These areas aren't in to make up the numbers, they're in on merit.

Every major and most minor grit and limestone crags that have had documented development are included in this guide. Space is now at a premium and fitting all the bouldering in the Peak into one guidebook is not practical and so the guide is not definitive. We have been a little selective about which problems have been included at all venues with priority going to pure lines and the better/more historical eliminates. That said, the guide probably has over 95% coverage and is certainly the most comprehensive guide to Peak District bouldering ever published.

The Derwent Edges, omitted from the first edition, are now included on the basis that they are documented elsewhere and they offer a great day out on good problems on good rock. Through popular consensus in the bouldering community the *Grinah Stones* on Bleaklow are not included, and the bouldering on the fragile *Woolpacks* at Kinder has again been left out, as the rock is too soft to withstand anything beyond the occasional visitor. We'll leave you to discover these two areas for yourself.

The increased popularity of highballing means that more routes have made it in under the guise of boulder problems, but a line still had to be drawn and only the more popular or famous routes have been included. Some, such as those on *The Block* at *Black Rocks*, are included primarily to demonstrate the state-of-the-art with Peak highballing.

Safety statement

Climbing, bouldering and spotting are activities that carry a risk of personal injury or death. Participants must be aware of and accept that these risks are present and they should be responsible for their own actions and involvement. Nobody involved in the writing and production of this guidebook accepts any responsibility for any errors that it contains, nor are they liable for any injuries or damage that may arise from its use. All climbing, bouldering and spotting is inherently dangerous and the fact that individual descriptions in this volume do not point out such dangers does not mean that they do not exist. **Take care.**

Access

The inclusion of a crag in this guide is not a guarantee of a right of access. Seasonal restrictions may apply. Respect the wishes of any landowners you may meet and any signs you may see. Up to date access information is available from the *British Mountaineering Council* – visit: **www.thebmc.co.uk** for further information.

Behaviour

We boulderers share the rocks with many other interested parties. Our behaviour is paramount not only to other's enjoyment but also to maintaining access. *Eagle Tor*, a beautiful venue with many classic problems has had access permission removed by the landowner due to the actions of people that were probably climbers. Keep to footpaths, remove litter, do not leave chalk tick marks on the boulders, do not climb drystone walls or fences, close any gates you open, do not damage vegetation, keep dogs on leads if they might disturb sheep or wildlife, park sensibly, keep noise to a minimum and moderate your language.

Respecting the rocks

Rocks are often very big and compared to us they are very hard. Because of this, many people are under the impression that they don't wear out. Not true. Please minimise damage by not using wire brushes, keeping cleaning to a minimum, not attempting to climb when the rock is damp or wet and keeping the soles of your shoes clean.

Names and first ascents

Effort has been made to establish the correct first ascentionist and the original name for every problem. There are often competing claims however and inaccuracies will arise. Apologies if you feel you have been denied your name in print or your place in history.

climbing • bouldering • packs
www.podsacs.com

Stars

This edition of the guide features a star system to highlight problems of particular quality or classic status. The absence of a star doesn't mean that a problem is not of very good quality – we've just highlighted some of the best.

✳ A very good or minor classic problem. Worth seeking out.
★ A superb or classic problem. One of the best in the area, if not the country.

Grades

Since the first edition, the *Fontainebleau* system of grading has become established in the Peak, and we retain its use for this guide. (This system is also rightly becoming commonplace at other venues in the UK.) Similarly we have retained the principle of grading traverses using the same system as the 'up' problems, unlike in Fontainebleau where a separate and confusing system is used. This is now the norm throughout the majority of Europe. A 7a 'up' problem should therefore be of the same difficulty as a 7a traverse.

The Fontainebleau grade is one that aims to rank the absolute difficulty of getting from bottom to top of a problem by the easiest method, and the grade of any given problem is established by consensus. The grade therefore generally reflects the difficulty that would be encountered by an average climber, of average height, of average strength and ability (for the grade) with an average life. Newer, harder, or less popular problems will have had fewer ascents and therefore the grade is less likely to be correct (on average). New methods are sometimes found making the grade given for a harder method redundant. Add into mix the fact that you are unlikely to be average yourself and there are a whole host of reasons why the grade may not be right or you may not agree with it.

Map Key

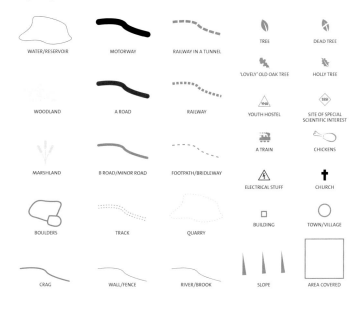

WATER/RESERVOIR — MOTORWAY — RAILWAY IN A TUNNEL — TREE — DEAD TREE

WOODLAND — A ROAD — RAILWAY — 'LOVELY' OLD OAK TREE — HOLLY TREE

MARSHLAND — B ROAD/MINOR ROAD — FOOTPATH/BRIDLEWAY — YOUTH HOSTEL — SITE OF SPECIAL SCIENTIFIC INTEREST

BOULDERS — TRACK — QUARRY — A TRAIN — CHICKENS

CRAG — WALL/FENCE — RIVER/BROOK — ELECTRICAL STUFF — CHURCH

BUILDING — TOWN/VILLAGE — SLOPE — AREA COVERED

Grade Comparison Table

Font	3	3+	4	4+	5	5+	6a	6a+	6b	6b+	6c	6c+	7a	7a+	7b	7b+	7c	7c+	8a	8a+	8b	8b+	8c
V	V0-		V0	V0+	V1		V2	V3		V4		V5	V6	V7	V8		V9		V10	V11	V12	V13	V14 V15
UK Tech	4c		5a	5b		5c		6a			6b			6c			7a				7b		

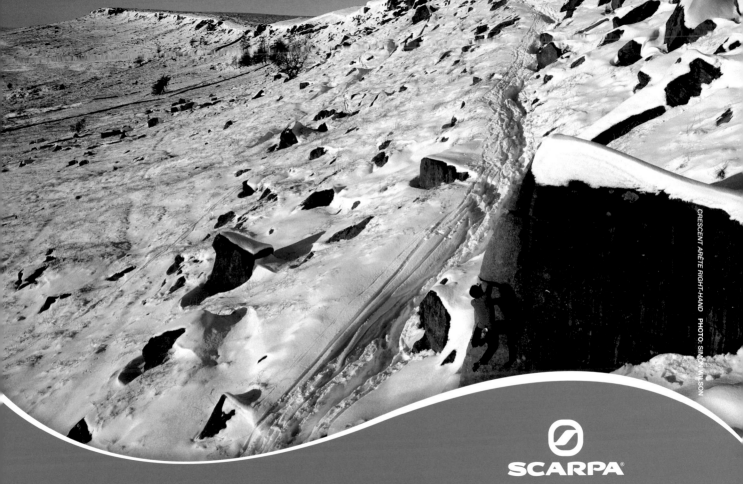

CRESCENT ARÊTE RIGHT-HAND   PHOTO: SIMON WILSON

FOR LIVES LESS ORDINARY

SCARPA®

www.scarpa.co.uk   0191 296 0212

Useful information

Here's a few pointers to places to eat, drink, sleep and shop in and around the Peak, plus some useful websites and other resources.

Tourist Information Centres

www.visitpeakdistrict.com – Official tourism website for the Peak District & Derbyshire.
www.peakdistrict.org – Official website of the Peak District National Park Authority.

Ashbourne	01335 343 666
Bakewell	01629 816 558
Buxton	01298 251 06
Castleton	01629 816 558
Edale	01433 670 207
Fairholmes, Upper Derwent Valley	01433 650 953
Glossop	01457 869 176
Manifold Valley (nr Dove Dale)	01298 846 79
Matlock	01629 583 388

Cafés & Pubs

Eastern and Limestone Crags

Outside Café, Hathersage	01433 651 936
Outside Café, Calver	01433 631 111
Grindleford Station Café	01433 631 920
Lovers Leap Bistro, Stoney Middleton	01433 630 300
Fox House Inn, on the A6187 nr Burbage South	01433 630 374
The Grouse Inn, on the A625	01433 698 132
The Norfolk Arms, Ringinglow	0114 230 2197
The Moon, Stoney Middleton	01433 630 203
Three Stags Heads, Wardlow Mires, A623	01298 872 268
The Monsal Head Hotel, nr Ashford in the Water on the B6465	01629 640 250
The Café, Elton (Sundays only)	01629 650 217
The Druid Inn, Birchover	01629 650 302
The Old Bowling Green, Winster, nr Cratcliffe Area	01629 650 219

Western Crags

Flash Bar Stores, Flash on the A53	01298 227 63
The Roaches Tearoom	01538 300 345
Ye Olde Rock Inn, Upper Hulme	01538 300 324
The Lazy Trout, Meerbrook, nr Tittesworth Reservoir	01538 300 385
The King William IV, Greenfield	01457 873 933
The Crown Inn, Glossop	01457 862 824
The Rambler's Retreat, Dimmings Dale, The Churnet	01538 702 730

Campsites & Accommodation

North Lees Campsite, Hathersage	01433 650 838
Hardhurst Farm Campsite, nr Hope	01433 620 001
Barn Farm Campsite, Birchover	01629 650 245
Sladen Cottage Self Catering, Hathersage	01433 650 104
Woodbine B&B, Hope	07778 113 882

Also try the local Tourist Information Centres for full details of accommodation, or try one of the trusty Youth Hostels dotted around the Peak: www.yha.org.uk

Gear Shops

CragX at *The Foundry*, Sheffield	0114 276 9741
Outside, Hathersage	01433 651 936
Outside, Calver	01433 631 111
The Square, Hathersage	01433 698 109
Hitch n Hike, Bamford (at the garden centre)	01433 651 013
Cotswold Outdoor, Bakewell	01629 812 231
Jo Royle Outdoor, Buxton	01298 258 24
Go Outdoors, Sheffield	0114 272 9733
Climbing Works, Sheffield	0114 250 9990

www.**evolve**sports.com

www.**prana**.com

BEN BRANSBY ON COURTESY OF JONBOY   PHOTO: ADAM LONG

Climbing Walls

There are many climbing walls within easy driving distance of the Peak. Leeds, Manchester, Nottingham, Sheffield and Birmingham all have excellent plastic pulling potential. Check out the BMC's Climbing Wall Directory. The closest walls for when it turns wet are:

The Foundry, Mowbray St, Sheffield	0114 275 4802	foundryclimbing.com
The Climbing Works, Sheffield	0114 250 9990	climbingworks.com
The Edge, John Stt, Sheffield	0114 275 8899	sheffieldclimbing.com
The Matrix, Northumberland Rd, Sheffield	0114 222 6999	
The Rope Race, Hibbert Lane, Marple	0161 426 0226	roperace.co.uk
Awesome Walls, Stockport	0161 494 9949	awesomewalls.co.uk
Awesome Walls, Stoke-on-trent	01782 341 919	awesomewalls.co.uk
Manchester Climbing Centre, Manchester	0161 230 7006	manchesterclimbingcentre.com

Useful Websites

www.bmc.co.uk/bmccrag – the British Mountaineering Council's Regional Access Database.
www.peakbouldering.info – Boulderer-run database of pretty much every problem and associated eliminates and variations. Includes photos and videos.
www.ukbouldering.com – Lively bouldering forum and essential resource for problem beta, crag conditions reports, gear help and pretty much anything else bouldering related.
www.ukclimbing.com – UK's biggest climbing website.
www.chewvalley.bravehost.com – More info on some of the other esoteric bouldering areas near Wimberry in the Chew Valley.
www.kirkleesclimbing.co.uk – Info on some of the esoteric bouldering areas just outside the Peak near Huddersfield.
www.metoffice.gov.uk – The Met Office. Dedicated Peak forecasts, plus plot the rainfall, check wind direction and much more.
www.mwis.org.uk/pd.php – Mountain Weather Information Service forecast for the Peak District.
www.buxtonweather.co.uk – Useful for checking the weather on the western side of the Peak.
www.raintoday.co.uk
www.outside.co.uk/latest/weather – Outside webcam: check the weather on the eastern side of the Peak.
www.maccinfo.com/Flash – Flash Bar Stores webcam: check the weather on the western side of the Peak.
www.matlockbathcam.co.uk – Webcam in Matlock Bath for the southern Peak.
www.peakdistrictonline.co.uk – All kinds of info about the Peak.

Other publications

Peak District Climbing, pb Vertebrate Publishing 2008
Easy climbing (up to E1) and bouldering (up to 7a) all over the Peak.
ISBN 978-1-906148-06-5   www.v-publishing.co.uk

The BMC has produced four outstanding guidebooks documenting the bulk of the popular climbing in the Peak District. These modern definitive route guides now feature bouldering too. Additional guides are in the pipeline, including one for the Moorland Grit of the northern Peak.

Burbage, Millstone and Beyond, pb BMC 2005
Includes Burbage, Millstone Area, Sheffield Area, Derwent Edges.
ISBN 978-0-903908-77-1   www.thebmc.co.uk

Stanage – The Definitive Guide, pb BMC 2007
ISBN 978-0-903908-08-5   www.thebmc.co.uk

The Roaches, pb BMC 2009
Includes The Roaches, Ramshaw, Newstones, Baldstones and The Churnet.
ISBN 978-0-903908-18-4   www.thebmc.co.uk

Froggatt to Black Rocks, pb BMC 2010
Includes Froggatt, Curbar, Baslow, Gardom's, Birchen, Cratcliffe Area and Matlock Area.
ISBN 978-0-903908-77-1   www.thebmc.co.uk

High Over Buxton – A boulderer's guide, pb Raven Rock 2003
Dan and Graham Warren's guide to the bouldering in the Buxton area.
Available from Jo Royle Outdoor in Buxton.
ISBN 0-953035-21-2

MOON
100% CLIMBING

CLOTHING AND HARD GOODS
VISIT: WWW.MOONCLIMBING.COM

BEN MOON
VOYAGER (V14)
BURBAGE NORTH

moon

"IT HAS BEEN QUITE A BATTLE, I MUST SAY, AND I'VE LOST TRACK OF THE NUMBER OF
DAYS I HAVE SPENT ON THIS PARTICULAR CLIMB... I FELT SO UNMOTIVATED OVER THE
SUMMER AND WONDERED IF I WOULD EVER START THE BATTLE AGAIN... IT'S AMAZING
HOW A FEW COLD DAYS CAN TURN YOUR MOOD AROUND!"

BEN WRITES ON THE MOON BLOG ABOUT HIS ASCENT
OF VOYAGER (V14), BURBAGE NORTH, PEAK DISTRICT.

Peak District Area Map

EASTERN CRAGS

JON BARTON ON BLUNTED PHOTO: JOHN COEFIELD

Wharncliffe

In 2001 Foot and Mouth disease hit the UK, closing many of the country's most popular crags. Few crags remained open, *Wharncliffe* was one of them. The crag experienced a new wave of popularity and, with it, development. In the space of a few months it was transformed from a routes-only venue into an equally extensive bouldering crag. It lacks the popularity of some Peak venues, but there are some good problems here.

Wharncliffe can be divided into five main areas, spread out along almost a mile of edge: *The Belle Vue Boulders*, *Long John's Stride*, *The Upper Tier*, *The Outlook* and *The Lodge/Dragon's Den* areas. The best climbing is at the *Dragon's Den* and *The Outlook* areas.

The bouldering here was developed in the main by Jon Fullwood, Kim and Yan Thompson and Iain Farrar, and much of the original information here comes from the subsequent documentation by Jon Fullwood.

Access and Approach

Leave Grenoside along Woodhead Road and pass the public parking for Wharncliffe Woods on the left. Continue, passing a large farm on the left after emerging from the trees. About 2½ miles out of Grenoside, look for a small lay-by on the left, opposite the lane to a stone yard. Park here and walk on the road for 20m to a lane: take this.

At the right-hand bend, pick up a small path straight ahead into the woods. Pass the big tree and bear left to pick up the path at the wood edge: from here you can either pass through the gate and follow paths across *Wharncliffe Chase* (access land) towards *Dragon's Den/The Lodge*, or follow the path down the wood edge to the crag, which emerges just north of *Long John's Stride* by a fenced area. Follow the edge-top path south to get to *Dragon's Den* from here. Navigation can be confusing on a first visit. During lambing season, there's no access across the *Chase*, so you'll need to approach towards *Long John's Stride*.

Access was previously direct from the lane up to *Chase Lodge*, but the owners have now blocked off the parking spaces there and it's a bit dangerous walking back up the road from the lay-by.

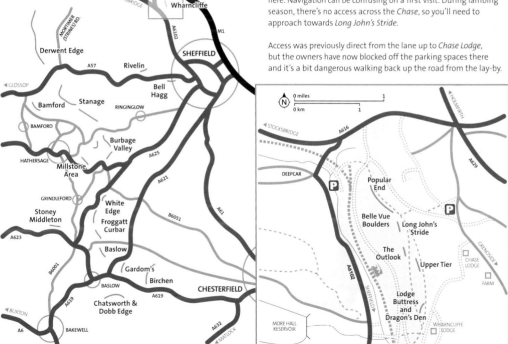

Lodge Buttress Right

Lodge Buttress and the *Dragon's Den* have the best bouldering at Wharncliffe.

The Slab

1 **4**
The right arête of the slab.

2 **4+**
The narrow slab left of the arête.

3 **3**
The centre of the slab.

Crazy Legs Boulder

4 **The Parson's Finch** *7b*
The rounded prow climbed directly on slopers, starting with feet in the back.

5 **Crazy Legs Crane** *6b*
The left wall starting from the slot and trending left to an exciting top-out.

Ewden Wall Buttress

6 **5**
The steep finger crack.

7 **6a+**
Climb the steep arête to the ledge – escape left.

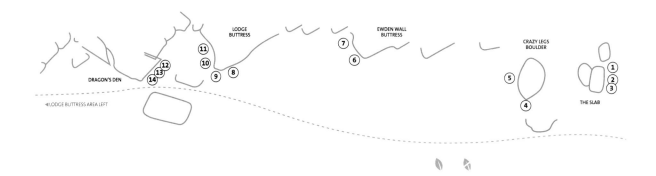

Lodge Buttress

8 *6a*
Climb the slab leftwards, starting from the boulder, to the sloping ledge.

9 **Curvaceous** *7a+* ✳
A brilliant, double arête feature – slopey hugging and a slap to a blob lead to the sloping ledge. *Jon Fullwood*

10 **Ogilvie's Direct** *6b+*
Climb the finger crack from a sitting start, with a special bonus mono move. *Terry Hirst*

11 **Ogilvie's Corner** *4+*
Traverse pockets into the direct. *Alan Clarke*

12 *3*
The right arête of the slabby wall.

13 *3*
The centre of the slabby wall.

14 **Jelly Groove** *3*
Sit-start the flakes and left arête of the slabby wall.

Dragon's Den

15 The Dragon's Den 6a+ ✳
Start on undercuts in the back, reach out to the lip and climb the wall above.
Jon Fullwood

16 Dragon Flake 4+
Climb the big flake from undercuts.

17 Dragon Slayer 7a+ ✳
An eliminate line. Start low (left of *The Dragon's Den*) and climb the flake as a prow, avoiding the right wall. *Iain Farrar*

18 A number of problems climb the centre of the wall, with varying degrees of eliminate-ness:

a) 6b
The easiest way, starting on the rib and moving right to the big hold.

b) Jorge 7b ✳
A direct finish to a) missing out the big hold and the pocket, with a frustrating slap for the top. Fantastic. *Kim Thompson*

c) Jorge Jr 6c+
A halfway house. Start as for a) but span right to the slopey pocket, not the big hold.

d) Crouching Tiger 7a+
Direct dyno start to a), jumping to the big sloper from the thin break. *Kim Thompson*

19 Blunted 7a+
From a sit-start sharing the edge, climb to the break and then up the rib above. No footblock on the right – 7a with it.

20 Sweet Release 7c+
Start up *Blunted*, traverse the thin break left, make a shoulder-busting span into the flake and finish up the *Dragon's Den*. *Jon Fullwood*

JOHN COEFIELD ON *DRAGON'S DEN* **PHOTO** JON BARTON

Lodge Buttress Left

A collection of jumbled blocks, left of the *Dragon's Den*.

21 *3*
Arête.

22 **The Bear Pit** *7b+*
Start in the pit, cross the roof on pockets and finish up the wall above. *Iain Farrar*

23. *6a+*
Arête - can be wet.

24 *5*
The groove.

25 **Jellyeyes** *7b+*
An eliminate (no undercuts) flying up the wall left of the groove.
7a without rules. *Jon Fullwood*

26 *5+*
The left arête.

27 **Fishboy** *7a*
Climb out of the cave starting from the good hold near the back. Bridging, kneebars and a bit of struggling are all required.

28 **Sushi** *6b*
Sit-start the leaning arête left of Fishboy. All manner of foot shenanigans are required to avoid dabbing the block. *Robin Mueller*

29 **Blu Wig Sheep** *5*
The slabby graffiti-covered block, without the arêtes.

LODGE BUTTRESS AREA RIGHT ▶

The Outlook Area

A compact little area with many roofs and highballs.

1 *6a+*
Traverse the lip from left to right into problem 3.

2 *6c*
Hard mantel. *Jon Fullwood*

3 **Outlook Roof** *6a* ✳
A quality problem that climbs through the roof from the low break to a rockover.

4 **Pete's Route** *5*
Climb out through the roof, via a horn. Highball. *Pete Hoy*

5 *6b*
Through the roof – needs a clean.

6 **Kim Span** *7a* ✳
From a sitting start, climb the small leaning wall and make a big span to an edge near the arête of the roof, and hence the top. An easier finish goes leftwards. *Kim Thompson*

7 **Lembas** *6c+*
The big, scary, highball wall. E4-ish. *Kim Thompson*

8 **Pixie's Arête** *4*
Good moves up the overhanging arête. *Jon Fullwood*

9 **Sneaky Little Fingers** *7a*
The wall left of *Pixie's Arete*, with a crux span to a slot in the seam. *Robin Mueller*

10 **Slab and the Beanstalk** *6a+*
A tight line left of the corner to the left.

The last problems are on blocks below, which tend to be dirty.

11 *6b*
Pockets. The sit start is 7a. *Kim Thompson*

12 *6b*
The problem just left.

13 *6b*
Slappy moves up the steepness from a low start. *Kim Thompson*

14 *7a+*
Sit-start the face and then climb it using the arête on the right. *Kim Thompson*

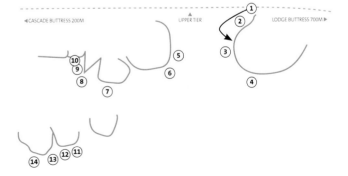

TOM RANDALL ON BUTTERFLY CRACK   PHOTO: RANDALL COLLECTION

Upper Tier Boulders

More problems have been done on the boulders around and below the Upper Tier, although they aren't great and the area doesn't really deliver on the potential it once promised.

Long John's Stride

There are several good problems here, some getting quite high. Grab a BMC guide and check out the slab on the buttress left of *Autumn Wall*, starting in a niche – 5. Three good problems are to be found on the small buttress right of the pinnacle (see topo photo opposite):

15 **Impish** *6b*
     The scary arête.

16 **Imp Wall** *6a+*
     The wall to the right.

17 **Long John's Arête** *6b*
     The sharp, hanging arête of the next buttress right, climbed on the right from a sitting start.

Belle Vue Boulders

These are a disappointing cluster of boulders below *Belle Vue Buttress* at the right-hand side of the popular end of the crag. The best bit is the large boulder just beneath the buttress, with several up problems with grades up to 6b, and a 6c+/7a traverse starting in the crack, with a section of weird climbing to move around the arête.

Popular End

Hell Gate Area
Butterfly Crack *6c+*
Down and right of the *Hell Gate* area is this 70 degree overhanging offwidth. Stand start at the back and butterfly and footjam your way out, using the block at the end. Brutal. *Tom Randall*

Tower Face Area
Face Wall *6b*
The crimpy, slabby wall below the *Tower Face/Himmelswillen* area.

Tensile Test Area

At the far left-hand end of the crag, a short, clean wall offering good highballs, including: *Tensile Test* (E1/6a), and *Elastic Limit* (E1/5+).

Bell Hagg

Bell Hagg offers suburban climbing, well within the city limits. Located in a well-to-do neighbourhood of Sheffield, it suffers only occasionally from the graffiti and cider-soaked tramps that you may have encountered at less up-market city venues. Instead we have delightful, shady, hillside bouldering with good views and the occasional admiring dog walker.

The climbing is characterised by positive holds and – *Bell Hagg* being a 'real' crag – the problems can get quite high. Some of the rock is a little dubious, but suspect holds are easily identified (they rattle). Because *Bell Hagg* is situated within walking distance of probably the highest concentration of climbers in the world, every hold has its own set of eliminates and in light of this fact we have only described a selection of the problems.

Good conditions are common. The crag is north-facing, so summer evenings can be tolerable even on the hottest days. The main climbing tends to stay dry and clean, but the top-outs can get green. You don't need to top-out everything, just make sure you spot the escape traverses before committing yourself and getting too high.

There's also *Fox Hagg* and *Wyming Brook* a little further along, for when you have *Bell Hagg* all climbed out. See individual sections for approach info.

Access and Approach

Park at the end of Moorbank Road and follow the dirt track, then path, taking the steps up on the left. Follow the path for approximately 200m. The first climbing is on Burglar Buttress, the large flat-topped buttress adjacent to the path. Access is via the path that drops down just past the buttress top.

Alternatively, park on Sandygate Road and follow the Public Footpath across the golf course (be courteous), popping out just before *Burglar Buttress*.

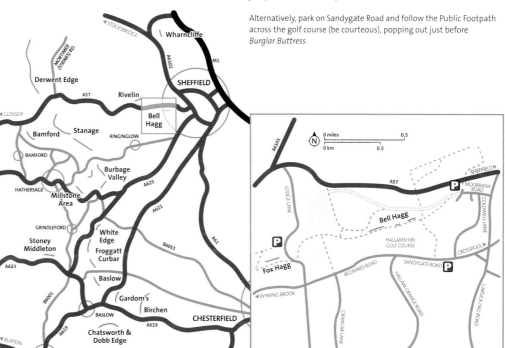

Burglar Buttress

A reassuringly steep buttress that stays dry in the rain. Littered with good holds, *Burglar Buttress* offers massive potential for imaginative eliminates and – if you're very strict – some of these will be very hard indeed. Fun and games can be had with steep dynos, feet-first ascents and improbable heel-toe jams. A good low traverse exists at a powerful 6b, while the higher rail of jugs is quite easy. By the time you have done the traverse footless you should be warmed up.

Len's Buttress

1 **Jan** *3*
   Slanting cracks.

2 **Len's Edges** *6a*
   Crimps to the break, using underclings to start.

3 **Len's Areet** *5* ✳
   A classic.

4 **Alleluia** *3*
   More good holds.

Nunn's Eliminate Buttress

Fun is to be had on the stepped roof past the green wall a little further right.

5 *3*
   The left-hand line, useful as a descent if you traverse off the other problems rather than topping out.

6 **Monk's Bulge** *4*
   Two edges and a stiff pull get the jug.

7 **Nunn's Eliminate** *5* ✳
   Sidepull action.

8 *5*
   Right of the sidepulls.

9 *4*
   Spike to a leftwards exit.

10 *5+*
   Traverse right, variations exist.

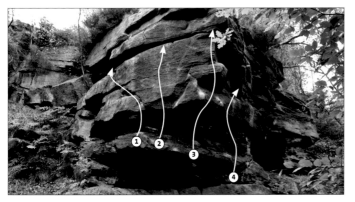

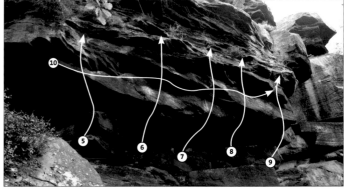

Lurcher Buttress

A compact, solid series of walls and overlaps, with several fine mid-grade problems and one nails-hard, ex-project.

11 Rodger's Arête 5
The high arête on good holds.

12 Banner's Ridge 5 ✳
Right of the arête is slightly less intimidating, but excellent.

13 The Brig 5
The crimpy wall left of the groove.

14 Brown's Unmentionable 5 ✳
The scary groove.

15 Lurcher Direct 6a ★
A classic up the blunt rib.

16 Whippet 8a+ ✳
The brutal sit-start to Lurcher was a longstanding project that fell to one of the Peak's finest. Pull on under the roof, feet wedged at the back, go for the good crimp on the lip, slap for nothing, hold the swing and slap for the *Lurcher Direct* start holds. *Mike Adams*

17 3
Slabby wall.

18 4
Sit-start the arête on its left or right.

19 6c
Scratch up the undercut slab.

20 5
Slim groove.

21 6c
Sit-start and follow the crimps.

150m further on from Lurcher Buttress, on a barrel shaped boulder just down from the edge, is:

22   The Barrel Slap Problem   6c   ✳
From the ledge and an undercut get the layaway and slap the top. Amazing.
The problem just left is 6b.

Hyde's Buttress
After crossing a small, often dry, stream, there is a short vertical wall with an obvious pocket. This is *Sputum*, 5+, and to its right on the second block over is *Hyde's Mantelshelf*, 5+.

23   Son of a Birch   6b
About 70m further along is a short, slabby outcrop. Below this is a detached block. This problem climbs the right arête from a sit-start on a flake.

The Other End
The final problems are 20m further along from *Son of a Birch*, up a short, slabby buttress, with a dodgy landing – *The Other End Buttress*. *Master's Revenge* (6b+) is the pick of the bunch, climbing the right arête of a crack on its right.

Fox Hagg
Fox Hagg is found further along the same ridgeline that is home to *Bell Hagg*. It offers up a bunch of problems in a similar vein to *Bell Hagg*, and is worth a quick hit if you're in the area.

Access and Approach
Park in the small car park at the hairpin bend on Lodge Lane. Cross the motorcycle barrier and walk for about 50m along the higher of the two paths. Fork left up the footpath and up the steps – the crag is visible up and left. Double back to it on the ridge-top path.

1   21st Century Fox   6b+
Start at the base of the groove and follow the thin break right into *Thought Fox*. Dave Parry

2   Thought Fox   6b+
Climb straight up through the bulges from the break. The low start from the pocket may be unclimbed.

3   Foxy   5
The arête from a sit-start in the break.

4   Foxy Loxley   5+
The right sidewall from the pocket.

5   Life Gets Easier   6b
Traverse the low break, starting far left and finishing up *Foxy Loxley*.

Wyming Brook

An esoteric spot, only 5 minutes from Sheffield. Although it looks mucky on first appearances, *Wyming Brook* is actually a lovely little valley, and, thanks to *Dan Varian* and friends, a few lines have been cleaned up, including a rather good 7b. There's likely to be other stuff to go at, and some of the older routes could be highballed, but they'll need a good clean first.

Access and Approach

Turn off the A57 in western Sheffield into Crosspool on Sandygate Road. Follow this for about 3 ½ miles, passing the Hallamshire Golf Club. Sandygate Road turns into Redmires Road. Just before Redmires Reservoirs the road wiggles through a dip and passes over a bridge. Turn right into the Wyming Brook free car park here.

Superbrook and *Brookside* are situated on the left of the brook (looking down) just up the bank from the wide track of Wyming Brook Drive, about 150m from the car park.

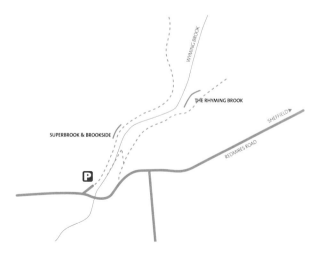

1   Superbrook   7b   ✳

The right arête of a mid-sized buttress, 150m from the car. From a juggy pocket and a pinch at the same height, launch directly up the arête. Escaping left at the top would be just that. Brilliant climbing and a striking line. The sit-start is bottom end 7b+, started on the left side of the arête. See photo on p483.

2   Brookside   7b+

10m right of *Superbrook*, just right of a crack, is a blunt arête, climbed on its right-hand side, avoiding the crack for hands and feet. Start off a low sidepull for RH and a rippled seam near the crack. A right heel allows a tiny hold for the RH to be gained and used to windmill the LH to the better bit of the arête high up. Grab a poor sloper and claw upwards for the finishing jug. Top out to the right up the groove.

The next problem is situated on the right of the brook (looking down). Cross the brook and walk the top path until you see a shed in the field on your right. Drop down and left upon seeing the shed and the lonely slab should appear. *The Rhyming Brook* takes the left side of the high arête, left of the slab.

3   The Rhyming Brook   7a

The left-hand side of the high arête from a standing start. Drop off when matched on the ledge. Highball.

DAN VARIAN ON *THE RHYMING BROOK*   **PHOTO:** NICK BROWN

Rivelin

The bouldering at *Rivelin* is very much a combination of the old and the new. Several problems are really routes, while others (the hard ones) are the work of a few dedicated modern explorers.

Generally shady and clean, the crag is often in good condition. South-facing and sheltered it can be a good alternative on cold windy days, or indeed when it's banging it down in the Peak proper.

Access and Approach

Rivelin is located just off the A57 about 2.5 miles from Sheffield. Park on the south side of the dam in the Water Authority car park, walk back across the dam and up the footpath, over the stream and head up to the crag, bearing left at the fork to emerge near the *Rivelin Needle*. Follow the vague path up and down beneath the crag to access the different areas.

Note: *Rivelin* is situated in an environmentally sensitive area: no big groups, no tree cutting, no climbing right of *Altar Crack* (the big buttress 40m right of *Chimp A*), and please use the described approach paths only.

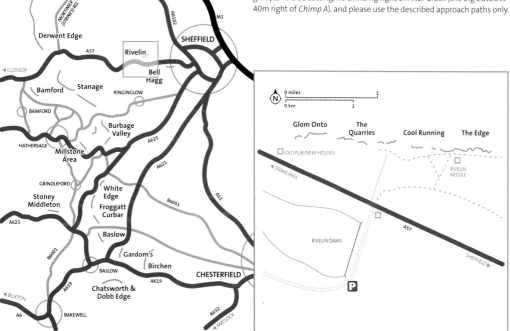

The Edge

The main 'boulder-able' highballs are included, with the problems described from right to left, starting about 70m right of the unmissable Needle.

1   Chimp A   7a+
The undercut arête just left of the large slab of *Wilkinson's Wall* (VS). Highball.

2   Boulder Club Right-Hand   6c
The right-hand side of the hanging slab, between *Chimp A* and *Sparks*, past the horizontal slot, using a small, high crimp for the right hand, before rocking back left into the slot. No arête. The original, chipped direct/left-hand line has apparently lost a hold and is harder. See photo previous page.

3   Sparks   7b
The left-hand rib is climbed with slopers on the arête and edges, staying strictly left. Straying right is 7a. *Adrian Berry*

4   Sharks   3
The fun arête immediately left from a sit-start.

5   Europe after Rain   7a   ✳
The right-hand side of the highball wall on thin, crimpy breaks. *John Allen*

6   Wobbly Wall   6a   ✳
The central, highball groove.

7   Fumf   5   ✳
The highball arête.

8   Shelf Wall   3+
Mantelshelf up past the large flake.

9   Where Bulldykes Daren't   6c
The vague rib, climbed worryingly on sidepulls, undercuts and crap footholds.

There are various micro-routes left of here – including the two *Face Climb* routes – but they're stretching the definition of 'bouldering' due to their height and landings. Next up, right next to the Needle, is:

10   Acid Reign   6c   ★
The brilliant sharp arête, with a worrying final move. *Twin Hole* leans out from the ledge on the left to twin pockets before lunging for the top – 5+.

11   Trivial Pursuits 1   6b
Set just below the edge, around to the left of the Needle and the arête of *Blizzard Ridge* (E1), is a short wall. Climb the left-hand crack.

12   Trivial Pursuits 2   6a   ✳
The right-hand crack up the wall.

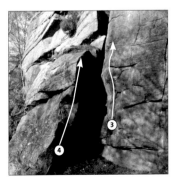

13 Moontan *7a+* ✳
A vertical wall, at the foot of a tall, undercut buttress left of the wide *Kremlin Crack*. Thin wall climbing on small crimps. Finish at the break. *John Allen*

14 Friday Club *6c*
About 30m left of *Moontan* is *President's Buttress*. This roof is up on the right-hand side. Start under the roof at a flake, reach a pocket and then the arête. Finish up this.

Cool Running Area
A fine collection of problems in between the edge and the quarries.

15 Purple Haze *7a+* ✳
From a sit-start, traverse the lip from left to right. 7b if you stay on the lip holds all the way and don't use the high edges. *Nik Jennings*

16 Master Kush *7c+* ★
The awesome, undercut right arête from the low jug. *Ryan Pasquill*

17 Galleon on Green *6c*
A poor lip traverse on a block left of *Master Kush*. From the hold on the left, traverse right to finish around the arête and up the prow.

20m to the left is the neat little buttress of *Cool Running*. See topo photo overleaf.

18 Hot Dog *4+*
The right arête on either side.

19 Cool Running *6b+* ✳
Really E1, but a good highball. Start in the centre of the wall and head left to finish. Traverse off left at the break. *John Allen*

20 Faze Action *7b* ✳
The direct finish to *Cool Running* on vague seams. Harder since the pebble snapped off. Finish at the break. *Andy Crome*

21 Cool Running Left-Hand *6b*
The left arête.

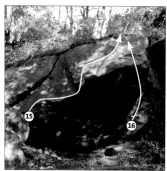

The Quarries

From *Cool Running* follow a vegetated path left below the crag, heading up almost to the top of the crag. Cross a stream, then head back down again to meet a quarried, yellow wall. This is *Nik's Wall*. The first problems are up and right of the quarry.

22 Boffwidth *6b*
Without bridging out right, layback and jam out the offwidth roof crack. 7a if exclusively jammed.

23 Mini Beak Rib *6b+*
The left arête of the small roof from a low start.

24 Mini Beak *7a*
From low on the left of the small roof, climb to the lip and traverse rightwards. Finish up the right arête, on its right.

25 Beak No Weevil *7a+*
Sit-start the small roof on the right (feet above the break). Gain the jug on the arête, then rock right to the top. Beta helps. A lot.

26 The Beak District *6c*
The thin wall right of the next problem.

27 Cheeks n Beaks *7b* ✳
The centre of the steep, undercut wall. *Jon Fullwood*

28 Happy Campus *7b* ✳
The arête right of *Nik's Wall*. The clue is in the name. *Cheeses of Nazareth* (6b) gains the arête by bridging in from the left. *Paul Houghoughi/Jon Fullwood*

29 No Class *7b+*
The low start to *Happy Campus*. *John Welford*

30 Non-Rib *7a*
The vague non-rib on the right-hand side of the wall to the left.

31 Nik's Wall *8a*
A thin crimp-fest up the centre of the yellow wall. Possibly unrepeated. *Nik Jennings*

32 Iain's Arête *7b*
Dyno arête left of *Nik's Wall*, avoiding the big holds around the side. *Iain Farrar*

In the bay around to the left are some minor problems:

33 Greenbeard *7b*
Situated in the back left corner of the bay. From a sit-start on the rock, dyno from the low flakes to the ledge. Finish on the obvious higher ledge. *Nik Jennings*

34 Spudd Webb *7a*
On the boulder to the left of the bay, dyno from the detached flake to the top. *Dave Mason*

35 The Rookie Road *6b*
Climb straight up from the detached flake.

36 Dribble *6a*
Sit-start on the arête and traverse to finish at the same place as *Spudd Webb*.

In almost the final quarried bay, 300m left of *Greenbeard*, is:

37 6a+
The arête right of the route *Ipecacuanaha Groove* (HVS).

38 Glom Onto *6c+*
Climb the centre of the wall left of *Ipecacuanaha Groove* to an obvious jug. This and the next problem are worth the walk.

39 Chimp B *7a*
Layback the arête left of *Glom Onto* to reach a hold on a ramp, and then make crux moves right onto the finishing jug of *Glom Onto*.

JON BARTON ON *PLAY HOOKAY* PHOTO: JOHN COEFIELD

Derwent Edges

A quartet of wild bouldering venues guaranteed to lift you far from the crowds at Stanage and Burbage, and high onto the moorland above Ladybower Reservoir. The walk-in is hard work, particularly with a big pad, but there are some fine problems here, including a contender for the best of its grade in the Peak – the *Perfect Porthole Problem*. Just be careful up here, it's a long crawl back to the car with a sprained ankle.

Conditions

The edges and boulders almost all face west, ensuring they catch the sun. They also catch any and all wind going, which although it ensures they stay clean, means it can be a bit much up here at times. The best times to visit are late spring, through the summer, and into early autumn – just be sure to pick a fine day when the wind is up: no wind equals midges.

Access and Approach

There are a number of possible approaches, although we've described the approach from the A57 at Cutthroat Bridge. There's also a parking area just north of the Strines Inn on the Strines road, with a path that leads you straight up to the edge between *Dovestones Tor* and *Back Tor*, however it's closed at the time of writing. Probably not a bad thing, as it's a hotspot for car break-ins.

Park in a large lay-by on the south side of the A57, about halfway between the Strines road and Ladybower Reservoir. Walk downhill for 100m to Cutthroat Bridge and cross the road. Pass through the gate and follow the wide rocky path as it contours around left, and diagonally northwest across the hillside to an intersection of paths at the col below *Whinstone Lee Tor*. Turn sharp right uphill here. Once on the ridge *The Hurkling Stones* can be seen to the right of the path. *The Wheel Stones* are a further 600m on, next to the path. *Dovestones Tor* is a further 1km again, to the left of the path, and *Back Tor* another 1km again. It's about 30 minutes from the car to *The Hurkling Stones*, and over an hour to *Back Tor*, although it doesn't feel too bad as the walk is broken up by the other areas.

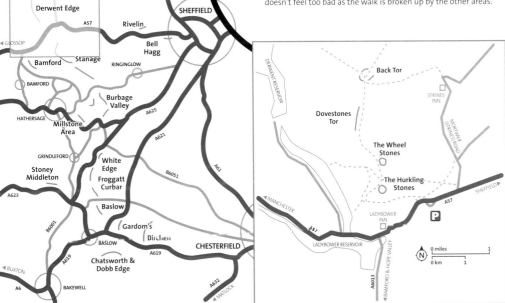

The Hurkling Stones

The first rock reached from the car, and a welcome sight for weary legs and sweaty brows. Home to a collection of sub-7a problems with predominantly sloping top-outs.

1   **Baby Bulge**   *3+*
    The block left of the main slab.

2   **Arête and Seam**   *4+*
    The left arête of the slab.

3   **Hurkling Towards Earth**   *6a+*
    The left-hand slab line, using the seam for the left hand.

4   **Pothole Slab**   *6b*   ✳
    The centre of the fine slab to the hueco.

5   **Landfall**   *6c*
    The right-hand slab line up the green streak, and above the sketchy landing. Spicy.

6   **Little Arête**   *5+*
    The right arête of the slab.

7   **Other Arête**   *6a*
    The bulging arête at floor level is climbed to a sloping top-out. The large flake line to the right is *Rock Ahoy* (5+/HVS) – the off-balance climbing making it feel more route than boulder problem.

8   **Wall Past Flake**   *6a+*
    The side wall past a flake hold at the lip to a sloping top-out.

9   **Captain Ahab**   *6c+*
    Undercut up with difficulty just right of the arête to another tough top-out.

10 **Wall Above Flake**   *6a+*
    The right-hand wall from the ramp/flake.

ANDY BANKS ON *POTHOLE SLAB*   PHOTO: JOHN COEFIELD

The Wheel Stones (Coach & Horses)

Approximately 600m further along the path is this collection of gritstone blobs, the 'Coach' being the big one and the horses the smaller ones. Many, many problems can be climbed on these blocks, most of which lack identity. We've chosen to describe the better lines below and leave you to discover the rest for yourself.

1   Shelf Wall   6a
The centre of the wall on sloping shelves to a tough top-out.

2   Low Coach   6a+
Start low hanging the shelf and climb the arête.

3   Jupiter Collision   7a+   ✳
A classic of the area. Sit-start and climb the centre of the wall on slopers with footlocks.

4   Man Calls Horse   6b+
The right arête from a low, hanging start.

5   6b
The left-hand side of the sidewall from a sit-start.

6   Sidepull Stretch   5+
The centre of the sidewall.

The next problems are around the back, to the right.

7   Nose Horn   5+   ✳
Start low and pull up to heave over the nosey horn.

8   Horn Arête   5+
The arête just right.

The final two problems are around to the left.

9   Horse Roof   6b
Sit-start under the very low roof and span out to the lip from a good flake. Finish around left on good holds. Finishing right of the nose is 6c.

10   Horse Play   6b
Traverse the low roof from right to finish around the nose on the left.

11   4+
The flake/ramp in the sidewall. Traversing the sidewall from right to left, below the shelf, is a decent 5+.

Dovestones Tor

Characterised by a number of big, significant buttresses, *Dovestones Tor* is the most northerly proper 'edge' of the Eastern Edges, and the bouldering here is found on the smaller buttresses and boulders above and below the crag. The edge starts at roughly the same point as the paving flags on the main path: zig-zag up these onto the top of the edge, pass *Ripple Roof*, the *Roof of Mantels* and other flat rocks, and drop down to the lower bouldering to the north of the main edge.

Ripple Roof

The first problems are on a north-facing roof above the largest section of the edge, to the left of the path.

1   **Ripple Roof**   *6b*
    Sit-start the roof and span for the slopey rail and the top. Can be done at 7a+ by using the crimpy ripples and going direct to the widest point of the roof.

2   **Galaxy Ripple**   *6b*
    Sit-start on the right and traverse the rail up and left.

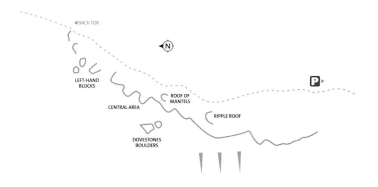

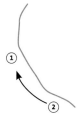

Roof of Mantels

50m further north from *Ripple Roof* is another north-facing block, just after a huge, super slabby rock left of the path.

3 Roof of Mantels 6b ✳
Sit-start on the flake, reach the lip, move right and mantel out above.

4 Mantel Man 6a
Start as for the previous problem but hand traverse the lip rightwards to finish right of the jutting nose.

5 Andy's Arête 7a ✳
Sit-start the steep arête from handjams and slap up slopers. Watch the poor rock at the start for the feet. See photo on p49. *Andy Banks*

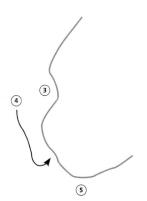

Left-Hand Blocks

The next problems are on smaller blocks and buttresses to the left of the main edge. There is other bouldering in this area, but the quality is generally poor. We'll leave you to discover it for yourself.

6 Roof Route 1 6a
Span through the left side of the roof from a square hold.

7 Roof Route 2 6a+
The centre of the roof from the square hold to the niche and nose.

8 Roof Route 3 5+
Span out right to breaks and roll onto the top.

9 5+
Sit-start the overhang left of the arête and make powerful pulls to the breaks above.

10 5+
Start as for the previous problem but swing right to the arête.

11 3+
The crack in the sidewall. The wall to the right is a 5.

Central Area

The next bouldering is on the edge, just left of the largest buttresses, and above the *Dovestones Boulders*.

12 Squawk 6b
The undercut arête, from a low start, with a big span at the top.

13 Squawk Traverse 6c
Start as for the previous problem before traversing edges left below the roof. Finish around the left-hand side of the roof.

Squawk Traverse Direct 7a
A better, direct start to the previous problem, coming in from a pinch left of the arête.

14 Stingray Arête 5+ ★
The fine arête.

15 Galaxy Dove 7a
The wall right of the arête. Sit-start at 7a+.

16 Interstellar Pigeon 7a+
The wall to the right, using a left hand sidepull just above the break and a small crimp up and right. Throw for the sloping break above.

17 The Cavendish 4+
The wall above the large hole, aiming for the upper niche. Other lines can be climbed on this wall, although they lack identity and, in some cases, holds on the top-outs. The slab to the right is also rather good for a play.

18 Boneyard Arete 6a+ ✳
The highball, curving arête on its right-hand side.

19 The Compressor 7a
The equally highball wall to the right, aiming for the sloping pod and a gripping top-out.

20 Black Crimp Problem 6a
The wall right again with a useful black crimp.

Dovestones Boulders

Below the *Central Area* is a jumble of large blocks, covered in classic lines. Sadly a few of them fall short in the landing department.

21 Perfect Porthole Problem 5 ★
The wall past the too-perfect porthole. One of the best at the grade in the Peak. A sit-start is 5+.

22 Huway-Cold 6a
Use a flat edge to gain the hole above. It would be a decent problem if it had a landing.

23 Huway-Day 5+
From the huge hole just left of the arête, gain the next one up and left. Note that the second one is often full of water.

24 Hip Hip Huway 6c+
The right side of the arête, stepping off the block. Needs a few pads and spotters.

25 Play Huway 5+ ✳
A tricky little problem from the big hole to the small hole, with a scary pull on a small edge. See photo on p40.

26 Up Up and Huway 4+
The crack.

27 Curving Arete 6b+ ✳
The fine, curving arête, climbed on its left-hand side.

The Dove From Above 7b+ ✳
The sit-start to *Curving Arete*, from a dink on the arête, features powerful slaps into the stand-up. *Andy Harris/Rich Heap*

28 6b+
The low roof on the block to the right. A right-hand variation is the same grade.

29 4
Around the back is a low problem. Sit-start at the flake and slap into the holes above. The foot blocks are in at the grade.

Back Tor

The fourth and final crag in the Derwent trilogy, and possibly the least frequented as it's furthest from the car. Bring sandwiches.

Back Tor Left-Hand

The first problems are on the far left end of the crag, past the trig point, at the upper level.

1 **Sidewall Scoop** *6a+*
   The east-facing scoop in the sidewall.

2 **Slanting Arête** *6b+* ✳
   Sit-start the slanting arête.

3 **The Blob** *6c*
   Straight up from the 'blob' hold.

4 **Sharp Rib** *5+*
   15m right of the previous problem is this narrow, hanging rib.

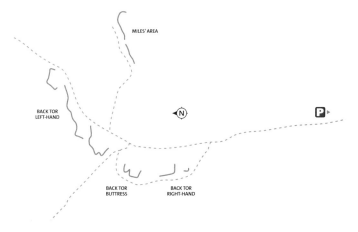

Back Tor Buttress
Down and left of the approach path is this angular, pocketed wall.

5   The Bone Cruncher   7b
Starting on the left-hand side of the main wall, traverse right on pockets and edges, past the niche, to finish up the right-hand wall. Keep feet up at the grade.

6   ET   6a+
Through the bulge from low pockets.

7   Hoplite Start   5+
Climb up to the roof from a sitting start (the full route is E3 6b)

8   Hueco Wall   6c
Start low on holes 1m right of the arête and climb the wall, trending left to finish.

9   Eyes Without a Face   7a
The wall to the right on pockets then edges.

10   Rainbow   6a+
Make a couple of big pulls below the roof crack before crimping off right to the arête below the crack. Finish up rounded breaks. The crack itself is *Spartan*, 6a (E1).

11   Codfinger   6c
From the plinth at the back, span through the left-hand side of the low roof past a painful two finger pocket and finish up the wall above. Reachy. *Adam Coefield*

Back Tor Right-Hand

A collection of naturally sculptured boulders and buttresses about 50m right of *Back Tor Buttress*.

12   Slab Mantel   *4+*
Mantel onto the slabby boulder left of the wide niche.

13   The Carving   *3+*   ✳
The wide niche.

14   Universal Squab   *6c*   ✳
Sit-start at a small flake (not the loose one), lean out to the lip wafer, reach slopers and rock left to the break. *Andy Banks*

15   Interplanetary Cushat   *7a*
Lean out from a jug to sharp edges in the roof, slap up the right arête and lock to the break. Mind the scrittley top-out. *Andy Banks*

16   Better Than a Guppy   *6c*
A one move guppy puppy. Sit-start with left hand guppying the arête and roll round for the top.

17   The Wave   *4+*
Step off the block and climb the right-hand side of the curved arête.

18   Muffin Top   *6b*
Sit-start at a ripple on the arête and haul up to the hueco.

Miles' Area

A small selection of steep problems about 100m directly behind *Back Tor* proper, to the right of the main approach path.

19   Small But Big   *6a*
From crimps, reach out right and over the roof.

20   Small But Wild   *7a+*
Dyno straight out from the starting crimps.

21   The B8   *7a*
Sit-start under the right arête, reach out to the sloping nose and do battle with the top.

22   Back to Front   *7a*   ✳
Sit-start the left arête. A fine problem.

ANDY BANKS ON *UNIVERSAL SQUAB* **PHOTO**: JOHN COEFIELD

Smallfield Roof & Hurkling Stones

An outlying area developed by Mike Adams and Tony Simpson in late 2006, *Smallfield Roof* offers a small yet surprisingly good series of roof problems on good rock. Nothing here is too hard, and if you operate at 7b, you could clear up in little over an hour.

Access and Approach

The roof is located just off the Strines road that runs between the A57 and the A616 near Stocksbridge and Langsett. If heading from the A57, approx. 6 miles after passing the Strines Inn there's a turning on the right, just after Agden Bridge. Turn down here onto a narrow lane and park up on the verge after 100m, taking care not to block the road. The roof should be visible up on the left.

There are no access issues that we're aware of, but please make sure you park considerately.

Also worth checking out is the nearby *Hurkling Stones*. Drive about a further 200m up the Strines Road towards Langsett and park in a lay-by. Walk west along the track for about 500m and the rocks are on the left. The left wall of the main block is a 7a+, the arete on its left is a 6b+, on its right a 6a+, and the front face is 6b+. All problems are sit-starts.

Smallfield Roof

1 Jive Arete 6a
Sit-start and climb the undercut arête on its right.

2 Dancing Man 7a+ ✳
Sit-start 1m left of the arête on the ledge, take the slot with your left hand, pocket with the right, and reach/jump around the lip to the decent break. Morpho.

3 Dancing Man Left-hand 7b
Start as for *Dancing Man*, but take the slotty flake with your right hand and roof pocket with your left. Reach to a decent hold with your left and tic-tac up decent edges to finish. A morpho direct start can be climbed from the pinchy ledge left of the *Dancing Man* start.

4 Larger Lout 6c+
From the crack, reach to a good flake and head up on good edges with the use of heel/toe jams. A good problem.

5 Boning Technology 6c
Start in the crack as for *Larger Lout*, but traverse holds in the roof to finish up *Jive Arete*. Finishing up *Dancing Man* is 7b.

Bamford

Bamford? In a bouldering guide? Hell yes! The bouldering at Bamford, although spread out, is actually pretty good, with strong, natural lines on good rock in a wonderful setting. It's a good choice if you're after something different and don't mind the walk between problems. *Spike* and *Ping Pong Pocket Rib* are among the best problems of their grades on grit.

Access and Approach

Important: the moor on which *Bamford* sits is private, and access to the crag is historically sensitive, so it's very important that you read, understand and adhere to these access notes.

Under the *Countryside Rights of Way Act* (CRoW) we now have access to *Bamford*, but only via the agreed access points. These are the paths we've marked on the map, adjacent to the main parking lay-by on New Road that is approximately 50m up from the area of woodland. Under *CRoW* the landowner has the right to close the land, or any part of it, for up to 28 days (with some restrictions), so, if a closure is in place, do not climb at *Bamford*. Simple. Closures will be signed at the parking area and access points, and up to date information can also be found on the BMC's *Regional Access Database*: www.thebmc.co.uk/bmccrag

No dogs allowed, regardless of whether they're on a lead. It is also very important that no damage is done to walls, fences, and all ground nesting birds and their nest sites.

From the lay-by on New Road, pass through the wooden gate and follow the sunken path northwest to the edge. If you park in the lay-by some 300m further down New Road, then walk up the road to this access point and follow the same path. **Do not** cross the fence and approach as the crow flies. As noted by the BMC in the Burbage, Millstone and Beyond guidebook (2005); "*we do have rights, thanks to CRoW, but we also have responsibilities.*"

So, once again: **No dogs**. Act responsibly. Enjoy. Here endeth the sermon.

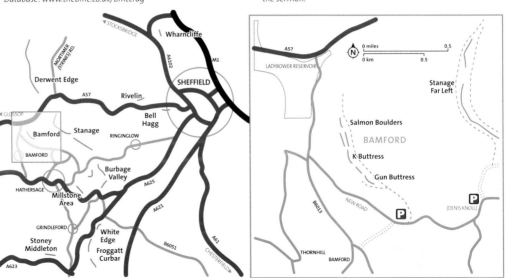

Gun Buttress Area

The first area reached is characterised by a couple of roofs, and a high gun-shaped buttress angled towards Win Hill. A good warm-up area with some steady short solos and a few steep, mid grade problems.

1   **Green Parrott**   *5+*
The undercut nose.

2   **A Minah Variation**   *6a*
Traverse in to the previous problem from a sit-start on the right.

3   **Three Real Men Dancing**   *6b+*
The overlap and thin wall above on poor, slopey breaks.

4   **Long John**   *6a*   ✳
Swing onto the undercut arête from the left. Can be jump started too. Various other little bits hereabouts.

Business Boy (6b+) **is a wall on breaks, just left of the big** *Neb Buttress*, **halfway between** *Gun Buttress* **and** *K Buttress*.

K Buttress

Home to some of the best problems at Bamford.

5   **Spike**   *7b*   ★
Pull on at the cutaway (just left of the route *Jasmine* – E6) with the help of undercuts and a kneebar, reach thin edges in the break, swing left to a sidepull and span to the break above. Finish direct. Excellent. See photo on previous page. *Jon Fullwood*

6   **Bamboozer**   *6c*
From the crack, swing right onto the face past the crescent shaped holds to a high top-out.

7   **5+**
20m below *Spike* is this leaning arete.

8   **Bookend Right**   *6c+*
The arête on its right-hand side.

9   **The Bookend**   *6b+*   ✳
The end of the fin, front on. Slightly shonky landing.

10   **K Kole Arête**   *6b+*   ✳
Sit-start the big leaning arête from the jug in the big hole and climb it on the right all the way. A low crux, followed by big pulls between good holds.

EMMA FLAHERTY ON *NOTHING MORE* PHOTO: DAVE PARRY

Salmon Boulders

Past the meat of the route climbing is a collection of fine boulders perched high on the hillside.

11 Snap *4*
The flake.

12 Wriggly Crack *4*
The crack, trending left.

13 Flaky Fluster *6b+*
Undercut flakes on the front face, with a crux stretch to the top.

14 Ping Pong Pocket Rib *7a+* ✳
The fine arête is climbed with subtle slopers, edges and pebbles, with a couple of useful pockets at the top. Brilliant.

15 Lose Hill *6b*
The pillar to the left.

16 Win Hill *5*
Trend left onto the ramp on the block left again.

On the big block left is; *Something Silly*, the front left arête, 6c; *Something Else*, the right arête moving left on the break, 5; and *Nothing More*, the back right arête, 5+.

Stanage

The most famous climbing venue in England consists of nearly 4 miles of gritstone blocks, neatly arranged into a handy line. The *Plantation* offers arguably one of the finest circuits on gritstone; you won't be queuing for problems at *Stanage Middle* or *Stanage Far Left*; and *Stanage Far Right* is the place to go for a top quality, lower-grade circuit.

Access and Approach

From Sheffield, head along Ringinglow Road past Burbage Bridge and fork right after the hairpin bend. *Stanage Far Right* is the first area reached, with parking in the large lay-by around 150m after the fork. Alternatively, drop down the hill to Hook's Car and turn right here at the large parking area for the *Popular End*. Keep going down the hill and turn right in the dip to reach the *Plantation* pay and display car park. Keep going still, below the edge, to parking for the *Buckstone*, *Middle* and *Far Left*. *Far Left* can also be accessed directly from the A57 – park in a lay-by near the county/city boundary sign and take the footpath opposite Moscar Lodge. Approx. 20mins approach this way.

From Hathersage, take a left just outside the village centre, uphill past The Scotsman's Pack. You'll reach the large *Popular End* car park at Hook's Car after about a mile.

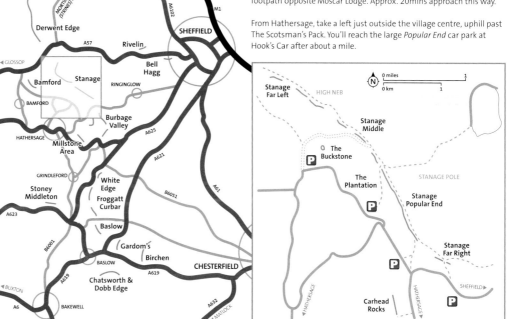

Stanage Far Left

The bouldering at the far left end of *Stanage* is in the same, broken-up manner as that at *Stanage Middle*. What problems are here though are very good, and some of them are hard to boot. Expect to do plenty of walking, but also expect a bit of solitude (maybe not at *High Neb*) and excellent views over the fabulous, desolate moorlands below.

Conditions

Exposed to most of the wind that's going, it can be very cold up here in winter. The advantage is that in summer it's cooler and less midgy than the Plantation, and because the edge curves round to face west, it's shady until later in the day.

Access and Approach

Continue north along the road past the Plantation car park. After about ¾ mile there is another car park on the right – Denis Knoll – just before a left-hand bend, and next to plantations on both sides of the road. Park here, walk up the Stanage Causeway (the track) towards the edge, take the first stile on the left and follow the paths up and left below the crag. Approx. 10 mins to the first problem.

(Limited) alternative parking is available in a small lay-by on the A57 to the north, opposite Moscar Lodge, just as the road from Sheffield starts to drop towards Derwent. Hop the stile and follow the wide footpath up to *End Slab*. Approx. 20 mins.

DAVE NORTON ON *FALLEN ARCHANGEL*. PHOTO: JOHN COEFIELD

High Neb

The first large buttresses above the point where the path stops approaching the edge and begins countouring below it are *High Neb*, home to one problem on a large fallen boulder below the large roof that is *Jeepers Creepers*.

1 Fallen Archangel *6c* ✳
The fallen arête down and 20m right of *High Neb Buttress* from a sit-start to a tricky top out. See photo opposite.

Beauty & the Beast

There are three isolated problems in the cluster of boulders down and right of the route *Seranata*, which is on the last buttress before the edge curves out of sight to the west. There's also *21 Today Sit-Start* 100m before *Beauty & the Beast* up an undercut arete – 7a.

2 Beauty *6c+* ★
The blank slab is a great exercise in gritstone smearing. See photo on p62. *Kim Thompson*

3 The Beast *7b* ✳
The grim mantel just right (no arêtes), starting from the break under the roof. There's a small scallop in the slab that you may not have noticed – doesn't help much, does it? *Jon Fullwood*

4 Dowager's Hump *6c*
A similar mantel on the next block right, but much easier as it's not undercut. *Jon Fullwood*

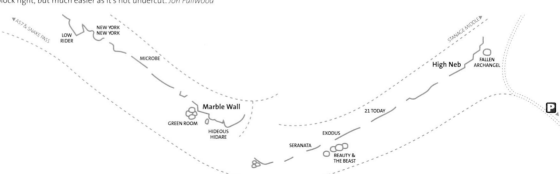

Seranata Buttress

The small buttress up and left of *Beauty & the Beast*.

5   **Cutunder Crack**   *5*
    Sit-start the jamming crack.

6   **Bottomless Crack Direct No. 1**   *6b*
    Start on the good hold in the middle of the wall and pull up leftwards to flakes and the ledge. The sit-start is a nice 6b+.

7   **Bottomless Crack Direct No. 2**   *5+*
    Rock up the wall directly, via a pocket to the ledge. Escape.

8   **Seranata Start**   *5+*
    Start with both hands in the break and slap to jug.

EMMA FLAHERTY ON *BEAUTY* **PHOTO:** JOHN COEFIELD

Marble Wall

The next problems are situated around *Marble Wall*, which is the second set of large buttresses reached once the edge re-starts after it has curved out of sight. The crag here is tall, steep and angular. Keep following the path round from the *Seranata* problems. *Hideous Hidare* is on a short buttress 10m right of *Marble Wall* itself, just over some boulders and sandwiched to the left of the buttress containing the route *Slap 'n' Spittle* (E4), left of the gully.

9   Hideous Hidare   *6c*
Smart moves off the sloping ledge to the break are followed by a shuffle right and a troubling exit onto the scrittley, sloping top. Highball. *Paul Mitchell*

Green Room Problems

The *Green Room* is an almost subterranean chamber formed by the large pile of stacked boulders at the left-hand side of *Marble Wall*. It's dry in the rain and can be cool and shady in hot weather.

10   Green Room Slap   *7a+*   ✳
At the back of the *Green Room* is this fantastic problem. Hang the sloping rail and power up to the holds above. It's about 1–5, but with your feet on, if you catch the drift. Escape left. *Kim Thompson*

11   Green Room Slap Sit-Start   *7c*
A low sit-start in the pit on the left. The last move is still the crux, but you're going to be lacking a bit of oomph by the time you get there. *Kim Thompson*

12   Soft Top Beetle   *6c+*   ✳
The rib in the sidewall of the entrance tunnel from a sit-start. A classic problem, spoilt only slightly by the landing. There is also a sit-start down and left which traverses right to top out up this problem, 7a. *Ian Barnes*

Below the Green Room, and next to the path, is a lone boulder with a prominent arête.

13   4
Sit-start and climb the arête on the left-hand side.

14   5
Sit-start under the roof on the plinth and climb through the bulge and up the arête on the right-hand side.

15   3+
The slab in the middle of the wall to the right.

Microbe

A fine collection of quarried micro-routes, which are now more regularly climbed as highball boulder problems, and some newer boulder problems.

16 Heels and Beef 7b
From a lie-down start climb the low fridge-hugging prow situated in a pit around to the left and below *Old Salt* (HVS). The supporting block at the back is 'in' for feet at the start. *Andy Banks*

17 Skimmington Ride 6b+ ✳
The lower arête of *Old Salt* (HVS) on its steep right side. *Jon Fullwood*

18 Little Oedipus 7a+
Gain a thin break by climbing the crack (of *Valediction* – HVS). Traverse it right to finish up *Monad*.

19 Monad 6c ✳
Jump to a good hold and finish above, or start by bridging in from the right. The non-jump start using the arête is slightly harder at 7a.

20 Quiver 5+
The left crack and reachy finale.

21 Arrow Crack 5 ✳
Thin layback crack. *Blinkers* – 5+ – is the thin wall just right.

22 Thin Problem Crack 4+
The thin crack just right of the descent route.

23 6b+
The wall just right. Crimpy and technical at the start.

24 Microbe 5+ ★
The classic highball up the thin crack via layaways and pockets.

25 Germ 6b+ ✳
A crimpy start leads to better holds, a ledge and a scary finish.

26 Problem Corner 5
The right corner of the quarried bay, bridging between the two walls.

27 Flags of the World 6b ✳
The wall and crimps immediately right of *Problem Corner*.

28 Love Handles 6a ★
The aesthetic rib in the sidewall makes for one of the best problems of its grade. Excellent. A crimpy line exists at 6c between *Love Handles* and *Flags of the World*.

29 Mr M'Quod and the Anti-Rock Squad 5+
The right arête.

30 7a
Start at the right arête and traverse left at a low level to join and finish up *Flags of the World*.

Stanage End

The final bits of Stanage are worth the walk as the quality remains high, particularly if you're on the hunt for one of the best 7c+ problems on grit.

31 These Vagabond Shoes 6c
Sit-start the wall, trending leftwards. *Jon Fullwood*

32 New York New York 6b ★
Classic highball arête. Bail out at the break. The sit-start is 6c.

33 Wilbur's Wall 6a
The wall left of *New York New York* from the low break, slapping to the top. *John Welford*

34 Wilbur's Rib 6a
The rib just left again, from the low break, again slapping to the top. *John Welford*

The next problems are on the final large buttress, the *End Slab*.

35 Opposition 7c
Bridge and undercut up the centre of the scooped wall right of the *Chip Shop Brawl* arête, in the crevasse, behind *Low Rider*. Traverse the break left to finish below the hanging arête. Morpho. *Kim Thompson*

36 Chip Shop Brawl 7a+ ★
The hanging arête. Another route that has been promoted to a highball with pads. Start in the break and veer left onto the face higher up. *John Allen*

37 R.I.P. O.D.B. 7c
Climb direct through the *Low Rider* traverse on slopers. *Ben Bransby*

38 Incursion Direct Start 6a ✳
Lean out from the arête and pull almost straight up on slopes. To finish, keep going (E1), jump off, or traverse left with difficulty. Variants exist at the same grade.

39 Low Rider 7c+ ★
From the arête, traverse along the lip, then power up slopers to the break. A Peak classic, and well worth the (repeated) walk. See cover photo. *Jon Fullwood*

40 Chip Shop Buddy 8a ✳
Link *Low Rider* into *Chip Shop Brawl*. Phew. *Ben Bransby*

Stanage Middle

This is the bit of *Stanage* between the ancient *Causeway* and *High Neb* that you never go to. Well, you should. You'll need to put in the man-hours trekking between the problems, but there are some classics here, and you're unlikely to be queuing up for them. We've described the main stuff, which, in some cases, is a single problem, but they come together in a sort of circuit when linked together.

Access and Approach

There's no easy approach, as the climbing is dotted along the broken-up buttresses along the edge. It's probably best to park at Denis Knoll, as for *Stanage Far Left* (see p60), and approach along the ancient causeway. Several paths break off left – don't head off too soon – and the *Causeway Slabs* are adjacent to the *Causeway* at the very top.

Causeway Slabs

A series of short, quarried walls just above the *Roman Causeway*. Generally not too high, and with grades in the lower end of the spectrum.

1   Beaky Direct   6a   ✳
Gain the good hold on the arête direct.

2   Sidepull Slab   4
The centre of the slab on sidepulls.

3   Broad Rib   4+
The rib/arête to the right.

4   Rusty   4+
The arête on its right. 5 on the left.

5   Crispy Wall   4+
Crimpy slab.

6   The Skid   5+
Rock up from slots.

7   Miss Sunshine   5+   ✳
Jug and nose. Pretty good.

8   Sunny Barger   5+
The crack.

9   Iranu   7a
The technical wall, from the low break to the high break past a mono and a gaston.
6c with the arête.

10   Uvavu   5
The right side of the wall.

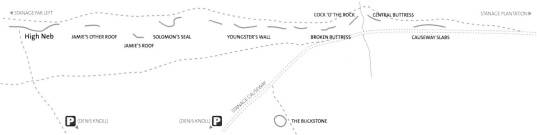

Central Buttress

200 metres or so left is *Central Buttress*.

11 Central Buttress Direct 6c ★
The roof below *Central Buttress*, on its left hand side. Get the flake and pass it with difficulty.

12 Iain's Prow 7a+ ✳
Jump start to the lip of the roof, and stay left to finish – highball. *Iain Farrar*

13 Iain's Prow Right-Hand 6c+ ✳
Jump start again, but reach right to finish. *Jon Fullwood*

Cock o' the Rock

Further left again is a drystone wall that rises up to meet the edge. At the top of this is a small arête – *Cock o' the Rock*.

14 Cock Crack 5+
The crack left of the arête.

15 Cock o' the Rock 7a
A strange little arête whose grade is anywhere from 6a-7b, depending on exactly where you pull on. The given grade is for pulling on with the big sloper. *Martin Veale*

16 Rocksucker 6b+
The wall right of the arête past the breaks.

17 Historical Arete 6b
Traverse the break leftwards to finish up the arête.

18 Cock Groove 6a+
The short groove.

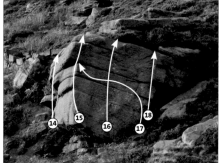

Broken Buttress

The next problems are 100m left of *Central Buttress*, past the brook.

19 Blow Out *5+*
Make a big span on the blunt arête and finish more easily above. Highball.

20 Blow Peter *6c+*
Make the first span of *Blow Out*, then traverse the thin break right to finish up the thin crack before the arête.

To the right, and higher up, is a jutting prow – *The Prowler*, HVS. The wall right of this, dynoing to a hollow death flake is *Wu Tang Span* (7a), while the sit-start wall to the right, from loose jugs is *Crimp Shrimp* (7b).

About 100m before *Solomon's Seal*, at the foot of *Anniversary Buttress*, is a lone problem worth seeking out:

21 Youngster's Wall *7a*
The thin wall yields to a fingery sequence using the seam. Harder for the short.

Solomon's Seal

A tall, vertical wall, perched perpendicular to the main edge. Home to a small handful of hard problems, the micro-routes hereabouts are also worth seeking out should you be the proud owner of a Stanage guide.

22 Solomon's Seal *8a* ✳
Crimpy wall with a big-ish reach. The arête is not used. *Kim Thompson*

Solomon Grundy *8a+* ✳
The sit-start to Solomon's Seal starting down and slightly left in the break. An excellent, sustained wall problem. *Dan Varian*

23 The Jester *7b*
A little one-mover, from two poor, slopey edges. *Iain Farrar*

24 Slabenger *7a*
The slab to the right between the cracks.

A short distance further on from *Solomon's Seal*, and about 20m right of the only tree, is:

25 Jamie's Roof *7a* ✳
Lean out to the lip and climb direct up the face on slopers. *Jamie Lilleman*

26 Jamie's Other Roof *7a*
80m further on from *Jamie's Roof*, and about 80m right of the big obvious *High Neb Buttress*, is a tall wall with a low roof. From low jugs climb out and up direct. 6c with the right arête.

The Buckstone

The Buckstone used to form part of the wall of an inn of the same name and there are still stones and bits of wall remaining in evidence. These days, however, there's less drinking but a whole lot more dyno action going on. The back of the block also has some lovely easier problems.

Conditions

The block is in an exposed position on the moor below the edge. It catches the breeze and sun, and as such it dries quickly. The huge holds of the *Buckstone Dyno* mean that it is possible when warm, but you will need better conditions for *Ron's Wall* and *Spring Voyage*.

Access and Approach

Continue north along the road from the Plantation car park and park in a lay-by on the left, opposite a wide gate, just before the road meets the trees (before the cattle grid). Pass through the gate and follow the vague path direct to the block. It's the big, obvious one dumped in the middle of the field.

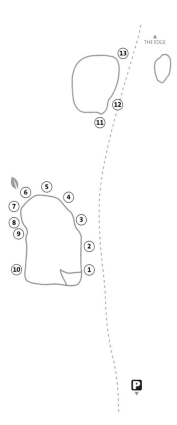

THE EDGE

1   *3+*
The short-lived arête, staying on the right to the top.

2   **Spring Voyage**   *7c*   ✳
Undercut to sloping edges and pop to the sloping top. Morpho. Don't feel bad about putting a foot in the big chip – it's not an eliminate. *Ben Moon*

3   **The Buckstone Dyno**   *7b*   ★
A big dyno using holds that were originally a structural part of the boozer. *Jason Myers*

4   **Ron's Wall**   *7c*
Sit-start on crimps right of the groove and then contrive a sequence up the rubbish slopers, using the right side of the groove as a layaway. Most use the start holds of the dyno for feet. *Ron Fawcett*

5   **Buckstone Bulge**   *6b*   ✳
The bulge just right.

6   **Buckaroo**   *6c*
Right again, mantel the nose.

7   **The Buckshelf**   *6a*
The hard, sloping shelf right again.

8   *5+*
The blunt rib left of the groove.

9   **Buckstone Groove**   *5*   ★
A lovely problem. Variations abound on the wall to the right.

10   *4*
The slabby rib/arête climbed on it's left, 3 on it's right. The wall around to the right, facing the road, has some great easy problems in the 3 to 3+ range. See photo opposite.

The block 50m nearer the edge contains a few more easy problems.

11   *6a*
The nose and crack.

12   **Sarah**   *6a*
Slopes up the wall

13   *5*
The rib facing the crag.

The Plantation

A world-class bouldering venue, the *Stanage Plantation* is home to a concentration of historic and unique problems of all grades. The only downside is the 5-minute slog up the hill to get there. Unfortunately, the inevitable popularity is having its effect. The grass is gone from below the *Face of Business*, the landing below *Deliverance* is wearing lower and lower and the paths are getting wider each season. The boulders themselves are suffering too. **Please read** our environment notes and help to preserve this superb but increasingly fragile crag.

Conditions

South-facing, the *Plantation* catches the sun throughout the day, and dries relatively fast after rain. When it's really cold the *Plantation* can catch too much wind to be bearable – if this is the case you could try *Burbage West* which is sheltered from the predominant westerlies.

Access and Approach

Park in the large pay and display car park and follow the path up to the edge. For the Right – *Pebble/Green Traverse* – area, bear right after the second gate up to the boulders or carry on up the main path for the Left – *Grand Hotel* – area. See map on p59.

The Plantation – Right

A collection of world-class boulder problems, including the legendary *Green Traverse*, *Deliverance*, and Jerry Moffatt's *The Ace*.

Blair Witch Project   *6c*
In the bottom, western corner of the woods below the *Plantation* approach path (turn left after you've passed through the first gate into the woods) is a lone boulder. The low blunt arête is climbed on its left. Worth seeking out.

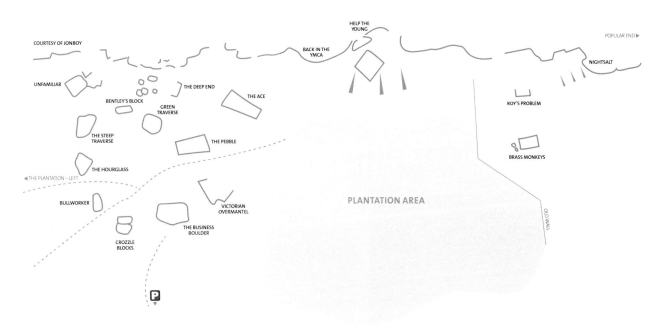

COURTESY OF JONBOY

UNFAMILIAR

BENTLEY'S BLOCK

THE DEEP END

GREEN TRAVERSE

THE ACE

THE STEEP TRAVERSE

THE PEBBLE

THE HOURGLASS

◀ THE PLANTATION – LEFT

BULLWORKER

VICTORIAN OVERMANTEL

CROZZLE BLOCKS

THE BUSINESS BOULDER

BACK IN THE YMCA

HELP THE YOUNG

POPULAR END ▶

NIGHTSALT

ROY'S PROBLEM

BRASS MONKEYS

PLANTATION AREA

OLD WALL

The Business Boulder

A large, prominent blob of gritstone, home to both pleasant easy problems and some of the hardest at the crag.

1   Nobody's Business   3+   ✳
The groove line.

2   6a+   ✳
Sit-start on the low slot and climb the slab via the flake. 5 from standing.

3   Zippy's Traverse   7b   ✳
Sit-start and traverse right from the good slot to flakes around the arête – tricky. See photo opposite. *Mark Pretty*

4   4+
Yard up the jugs on the shield. Variations abound.

5   Jerry's Finish   6c
Rock over right from slopers to the edges below the top. The final moves of *Jerry's Traverse*.

6   Danny's Problem   7c
Brutal crimping from a sit-start. Easier if you get the lower edge with your left and rock for the top hold using the higher crimp as an intermediate, although the 'proper' way uses the holds in the obvious order and is more powerful. ***H Top* is the superb stand-up version at 7a+, pulling on with the crimps. *Danny Brooks*

7   A B Top   6b
Slap up from the left end of the shelf and mantel.

8   Business Launch   6b
Slap the top from edges in the centre of the shelf. Using the intermediate is, bizarrely, harder.

9   Jerry's Traverse   7c   ★
Traverse left from the centre of the shelf, keeping low around the vague arête, and do a big finishing rock over (without the large jugs). A Peak rite of passage, slightly spoiled by an eliminate last move. *Jerry Moffatt*

10   Ben's Extension   8a   ★
A hard extension to *Jerry's*, starting from the horizontal slot above the boulder on the right side wall and featuring an infamous drop-down move onto the shelf. *Ben Moon*

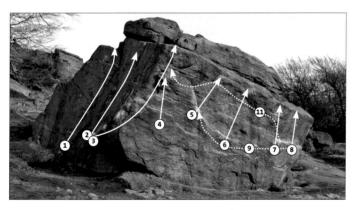

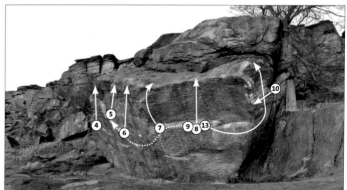

11 Rose and the Self-Employed Business Man   7a+   ✳
An easier alternative to *Jerry's Traverse*. Start in the centre of the shelf, but from the left end move up to holds beneath the top and traverse these left below the top to finish with a totally unnecessary 'rose' move to reach the jugs.

12 Malc's Traverse   8b
A hard connection: *Ben's Extension* into *Danny's Problem*. The grade is guessed and unconfirmed. *Malcolm Smith*

13 Ben's Reverse   7b   ✳
From the centre of the shelf, traverse right to the arête and then the top via the pod on the right. Essentially a reverse of the drop-down section on *Ben's Extension*, but using a different sequence.

14 Jason's Traverse   8a
Do *Zippy's Traverse*, but keep low at the end. Now reverse *Jerry's Traverse* and then dyno to the top from the middle of the shelf at the end. Not quite as hard as *Ben's Extension*. *Jason Myers*

15 Close of Business   8b
The final test of endurance. Link *Jason's Traverse* into *Ben's Reverse*. *Steve McClure*

Around the back are some good easier problems.

16 Black Arête   4+
The left arête. The wall immediately right is 3+.

17 Black Bulge   4   ✳
The middle of the overlapped wall. Sit-start 5. Variations abound.

18 3+
The vague arête next to the descent.

Over to the right is a low block.

19 Victorian Overmantel   7c
A powerful mantel. Hang the lip and start manteling. Keep manteling. Now hernia. Those with long arms may be able to rock to a crimp first. *Johnny Dawes*

20 One More Inch   7a+
Climb the low roof a few metres left of the *Victorian Overmantel*, from a sit-start on a jug. Lowball. *Andy Harris/Rich Heap*

DAVE NORTON ON *ZIPPY'S TRAVERSE*   **PHOTO:** JOHN COEFIELD

Crozzle Blocks

Left of the *Business Boulder* are two boulders leaning against each other.

21 Crozzle Slab 5 ✳
The crozzly slab on rough holds.

22 *3+*
The juggy arête. Sit-start is 5.

23 *5+*
Traverse the low lip next to the path from left to right and mantel out. Thuggy.

24 Crozzle Wall *6a+* ✳
The awkward wall just right of the groove. Eliminate the crack to boost the fun.

25 Crozzle Arête *6a+* ✳
Climb the arête on the left, with a pop for the good sloper. 6a on the right-hand side reaching in from the block.

***Bristol Stool 5* climbs the centre of the downhill face, right of problem 25, with a committing first gaston move and a scrittly top-out – 7a.** *Nic Sellars*

Bullworker

Across the path is a double arête feature.

26 Bullworker 6b ✳
Bullwork up the arêtes.

27 Bull Flakes 6b+
Just left of the *Bullworker* arêtes, the short flakey wall from a sit-start.

The Hourglass

Further up the hill is the *Hourglass* boulder.

28 Born Slappy 7a
Crouching start on slopers on the left-hand side of the block, with a really tricky slopey slap. A good one-move wonder.

29 Glass Hour Left 7a
The left side of the arête, but it doesn't climb like an arête. The wall immediately left of the arête is also 7a – *The Pendulum*.

30 Glass Hour 7a ★
The same arête, climbed on its right-hand side. Cunning and satisfying.

31 Born Snappy 7b+
The thin, snappy wall between the hourglass arêtes. *Richie Patterson*

32 The Hourglass 5+ ★
The right-hand arête starting on the right-hand side. Harder on the left-hand side all the way – 6a+.

33 Pockets Wall 5+ ✳
The lovely little wall on the right, climbed on pockets.

The Steep Traverse

The next problems are on the jumble of blocks to the right.

34 Steep Traverse 6c ★
The steep traverse from the shelf; a *Plantation* classic. Finish around the arête. *Airlie's Extension* starts on the detached block to the left and joins the original.

35 Popp's Pop 6b
A fingery pull through the middle of the traverse.

Bentley's Block

Right again is another low boulder.

36 Bentley's Gonna Sort You Out 7b+
Start low at the left end of the roof, traverse right a move and finish by rocking back left using a pebble (left hand) and a dish (right hand). Awkward. *Neil Bentley*

37 Captain Hook 7b ✶
From the start of *Bentley's* stay under the roof. Get an undercut under the roof then slap to the nose and exit. *Mike Lea*

The Green Traverse

38 The Green Traverse 7a ★
From the rounded blob on the arête traverse left displaying as little technique as possible. *Martin Veale/Mark Stokes*

39 Full Green Traverse\Dope on a Slope 7a+ ★
Extend *The Green Traverse* by doing a sit-start in the middle of the sloping shelf to the right. *The Full Works* (7b+) extends things further by reversing into the starting position from a standing start on the slab. *Martin Veale*

Ron's Reach 7a ✶
An eliminate on *The Green Traverse* that spans between the large holds missing out the finger rail.

Dope Mantle 6b
Mantel out the start of *Dope on a Slope*

Green Slap 7a ✶
Dyno from the crimp rail on *The Green Traverse* to the sloping top and mantel it out. Eliminate, but too good to miss. Locking the dyno statically (feet on smears) will earn you the respect of your peers.

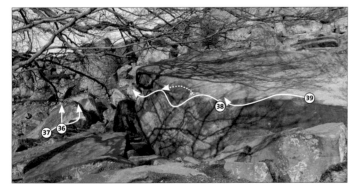

CAPTAIN HOOK **PHOTO:** PETE O'DONOVAN

The Pebble

This is the house-sized block that dominates the right-hand side of the *Plantation*.

40 Smear Test *6b+*
The left arête is a touch intimidating.

41 Pebble Face *3+* ✳
Approach the ramp line from the left. You can even do it without using your hands, the crux is retaining your dignity and ribs as you jump into the belly flop top-out (*The Design Award* – a *Dawes* special).

42 6b
Direct up the thin face above the start of *Pebble Face*.

43 Pebble Flakes *4+* ✳
The beckoning ramp line approached from flakes on the right.

44 Thin Slab *6b*
A squeezed-in problem up the slab, avoiding holds on the previous problem.

45 Ron's Slab I *7b*
The thin slab immediately left of the arête. If it feels anything but very thin you're on the wrong holds. *Ron Fawcett*

46 Pebble Arête *6a* ★
The classic arête. It has been done from a sitter at 7a, but really, have you nothing better to do? Direct on the left-hand side it's a tad harder at 6a+.

47 Pebble Face Traverse *7a+*
Traverse the front, pebble face from left to right, with a thin crux to gain *Pebble Arête*. Finish up this.

48 Andy Brown's Wall *7c+*
The direct up the wall above the crack from the start of *Deliverance*. *Andy Brown*

49 Deliverance *7b+* ★
The superstar dyno, named due to the imminent arrival of Dr Fisher's child. Start from the crack, make a tricky foot traverse to the flake and jump. Or start direct. *Quentin Fisher*

50 Deliverance Traverse *7a+* ✳
A very thin exercise in smearing from the start of *Deliverance* to the right arête.

>>

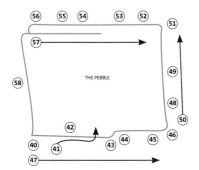

51 Delivarête *6a+* ✳

The right arête of the *Deliverance* face, climbed on its left from a sit-start on an undercut and edge, is pleasant but not straightforward. 5+ from a stand-up.

52 4+

Just right of the arête.

53 Pebble Ledges *4*

The big holds just right, often used as the way down.

54 Bogside Flakes *5*

The flakes in the centre of the wall.

55 Boston Mess *6c–7c+*

Various eliminates using tiny undercuts and smears for feet. The original method started from a very low undercut (not quite sitting), pulled on, moved left hand to the left-most undercut, moved right hand to catch the middle undercut – the crux – and then up to the ledge via a couple of other holds. Since then it has been done by pulling on and jumping straight for the ledge (7b), by pulling onto the left-hand undercuts and then up (7a+) and from a standing start (6c).

56 Twister *7b*

Sit-start in V-slot, move up to undercuts, then left to more undercuts to reach the high ledge. The low ledge on the right is out. A bit of an odd eliminate but good moves.

57 Original Sloper Traverse *6b+* ✳

From the ledge on *Twister*, traverse left on massive slopers with big slaps.

58 Pebbledash *6b* ✳

The excellent thin end wall starting up the groove.

The complete girdle traverse of the block is a worthwhile, and hard, 7b.

MIKE ADAMS ON *THE ACE*   PHOTO: ADAM LONG

The Ace

Up and right is one of the most historic problems in the Peak: *Jerry Moffatt's The Ace.*

59   Spades   *7a*
The arête from a sit-start on the block. *Andy Harris*

60   The Ace   *8b*   ✳
One of the hardest problems in the Peak. It looks really hard, but is actually harder than that. Start on a jug on the left side of the cave and then levitate past the two pathetic holds to the top. *Jerry Moffatt*

The Joker   *8a*   ✳
The original problem reached into the 'crimps' on *The Ace* from the adjacent block. *Jerry Moffatt*

61   Honorary Caley   *7a*   ✳
The slab right of the crack at the back is so named because it's pebbly and it's often green. *Richie Patterson*

In the jumble of boulders up and behind the *Green Traverse* is:

62   The Deep End   *6c*
Hop on the block at the right-hand side, shuffle left for about three moves, or until you run out of rock, then mantel out the slab and arête above. *Allen Williams*

63   Badger   *7a*
The overhanging arête from a sit-start. Rock right at the large pocket, or keep going – slightly harder. *Richie Patterson*

64   Ten Shadows to Midnight   *7b*
In the cave above the *Unfamiliar* pinnacle, sit-start the left arête and slap to the lip out right. Traverse this right and rock onto the slab to finish. *Robin Mueller*

Further up and on the crag 40m left of the *Unfamiliar* pinnacle is:

65   Courtesy of Jonboy   *7c*   ✳
The hanging arête left of the wide crack. No bridging out right. *Ryan Pasquill*

66   National Breakdown   *7b+*
The tall, technical wall to the right.

67 Back in the YMCA *7b+* ✳

Reach from undercuts to pockets in the steep wall and use these to snatch the break.
Neil Travers

68 Winner Stays On *7b*

Climb the left-hand side of the arete using the seam in the face, with a dynamic move to
a good hold high on the arete. Finish at the break. Morpho, but rather good. *Dave Norton*

69 Help the Young *7a+* ★

This modern classic arête is climbed initially on the gully side with a jump start,
before rocking back left to the shelf at the top. *Paul Mitchell*

Help the Young Sit-Start *8a* ★

Powerful leg hugs lead into the standing start. No footblock. *Adam Long*

70 Between the Two *6a* ✳

The rib/arch feature using an aesthetic pocket. Very good. Move left above.
The rib direct is *Plug*, 6c.

On the boulder just below *Help the Young* is:

71 Hippocampus *7b*

The left arête from sitting.

72 All 14 8,000m Peaks *6b+*

The centre of the downhill face, moving left to finish. *James Hogg*

73 Nightsalt *7a+* ✳

The tricky, reachy and slightly worrying arête above the drop opposite the route *Telli*.
Finish at the break (to go to the top is E3 but you have done the hard bit) and reverse
the chimney to get down. See topo on p73 and photo topo opposite.

74 Roy's Problem *7a*

In a small pit facing the crag, directly above *Brass Monkeys*, is this little problem.
From standing – LH arête and RH undercut – pop to the lip and mantel out.
Roy Moseley

Brass Monkeys

Down the hill on the far side of the trees is a large boulder.

75 Dirty Monkey *7a*

The arête left of *Brass Monkeys*, on its left throughout. Likely filthy.

76 Brass Monkeys *7c* ★

The powerful roof starting from the detached block at the back. Morpho – the initial reach is practically impossible for the short, but it may be possible to contrive something using the various slopey pods in the roof instead. *Iain Farrar*

The Plantation – Left

Things get bigger over left, and no less classic. Home to, among others, *Crescent Arête*, and Ron Fawcett's *Careless Torque*.

The Lone Boulder

On its own, stuck on the path between the *Right Plantation* and *Left Plantation* areas. Problems are described anti-clockwise.

1 **The Lone Arête** *5* ✳
   The slabby arête on its right.

2 **The Lone Slab** *5+*
   A hard step-up onto the slab just right of the arête.

3 **Lone Scoop** *5+* ✳
   The vague grooveline just right.

4 **Steep Side** *4+*
   Reach from the ledge to the top, hard for those with short arms.

5 **The Lone Ranger** *6a*
   Odd little groove in the next arête right.

6 **Tonto** *5*
   Mantel onto the nose.

7 **Silver Bullet** *4+*
   Arête. A fun sit start is 6b.

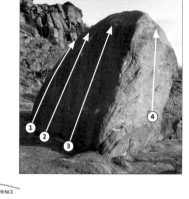

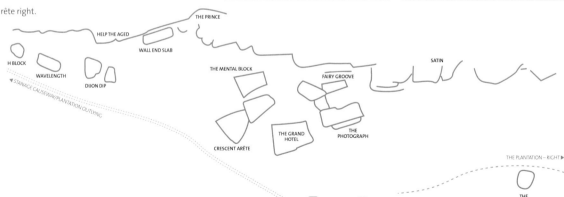

The Grand Hotel Area

The cluster of boulders 100m or so left of the first *Plantation* boulders are also often called *The Grand Hotel* area. *The Grand Hotel* is the huge block taken by *Not To Be Taken Away*, and refers to the once popular bivvy that can be found underneath the boulder.

1   **Broken**   *6c*
    The flakes on the right-hand side of the face.

2   **Not To Be Taken Away**   *6c*   ★
    The ramp line is still one of the best problems on grit. *John Allen*

3   **To Be or Not To Be**   *7a+*   ✳
    Make the first couple of moves of *NTBTA* and then dyno direct from crimps in the middle of the wall. *Mark Leach*

4   **Careless Torque**   *8a*   ★
    The stunning left arête is guarded by a blank undercut start. It has been climbed ground-up. *Scareless Torque* and *Not to be Taken Carelessly* are two self-explanatory link-ups with *NTBTA* that have been climbed by bored uber-wads. *Ron Fawcett*

5   **Careless Youth**   *7c*
    The enticing, rippled side wall, above a poor landing. Top roped prior to the first ascent, not yet climbed ground-up. *James Pearson*

The Photograph

6   **Adults Only**   *6c*   ★
    Climb out to the arête from slots and move up to a high finish.

7   **Delusions of Grandeur**   *7c*
    A low start to the *Adults Only* arête, on the right-hand side, swinging left to finish up *Adults Only*. Morpho. *Mike Adams*

8   **The Hit Man**   *7b+*
    Extend *Adults Only* around the arête, traversing the thin crease rightwards to finish up *The Negative*. *Simon Weill*

9   **The Positive**   *5*
    Rock up the slab a couple of metres left of the next problem.

10   **The Negative**   *3*   ✳
    The groove.

11   **The Crown**   *4*
    Mantel onto the block, starting from the block behind.

12   **Snatch**   *8a*
    Make a hard slap from two low opposing crimps to the top. *Paul Bennett*

13 GOO5.E *6b*
The back arête from a sit-start

14 The Aniston Slap *6c* ✳
Dyno from the sloping shelf to the top.

15 Brad Pit *7c* ★
Down in the pit is this famous and unique groove. World class. *Jason Myers*

Brad Pit Sit-Start *8b*
A massive hard span into the start of *Brad Pit*. Morpho. *Thomas Willenberg*

16 Fairy Groove *6c* ✳
The left-leaning groove in the wall above and behind the pit, below the large wall of *Fairy Steps* (VS), is an oft-ignored classic with a bad landing. See topo on p84.

17 Left Spur *7b*
Start at the low jugs. If you're wondering how to do this, you use the pebble that's now snapped off. *John Allen*

18 Right Spur *6c* ✳
Starting again from the low jugs, move up and right using the square-cut rib.

19 Spur Traverse *6c+*
Traverse the low flakes from left to right to a crux exit left of the arête.

20 Pressure Drop *7a+* ✳
The left-hand overlap and slab. *Adam Long*

21 Satin *7a* ★
The overlap and thin slab up the centre. Traverse off at the first break or press on for E3. *Johnny Dawes*

22 Pullover *5+*
Climb the overlap via the flake – HVS as a route.

The fine technical arête at the foot of the buttress 30m right of *Pullover* is *Four Star* – 6c. Traverse off at the break to finish or solo an HVS. The blank slab to the left is *Force Tart* – 7a+.

NED FEEHALLY ON *BRAD PIT* **PHOTO:** JOHN COEFIELD

Crescent Arête

To the left of the *Grand Hotel* is another iconic boulder and problem.

23 Ron's Slab II *7b+*
A hard highball slab, trending up and left from the start of *Crescent Arête*. The direct start is a project. *Ron Fawcett*

24 Crescent Arête *6a* ★
The classic, curving, highball arête on its left-hand side. *Gabe Regan*

Crescent Arete Right-Hand *6b+* ✳
The right-hand side of the arête.

25 Crescent Slab *7a* ✳
The tall, thin slab just right of the arête.

26 Mono Slab *7a+* ✳
The superb slab just right again using a small pocket.

27 Crescent Groovelet *5+* ✳
A nice short problem using the sloping ledge.

Just behind Crescent Arête is another large boulder in a cluttered gully.

28 Snapper Arête *6c+*
Sit-start the arête. Just left is a crimpy 6c+ up the brittle wall.

29 Pocket Wall *6b+*
The wall on pockets.

30 Ramp Thing *5+*
The wall just to the right, from the ramp thing to top.

31 Issue 53 *5* ✳
The steep, left side of the photogenic arête. 3 on the right.

32 *4+*
The wall right of arête, stepping in off a block. 6a without the block to start.

The Mental Block

Behind is another large block.

33 Storm *7b+* ★
The modern, classic, massive rock over. Possible even for the short – just rock further. It feels hard until you get it right. See photo on p91. *Jerry Moffatt*

34 Deadline *7b+*
From the start of *Storm* continue traversing right to the arête via a large pocket and slap up. Very high. *Richie Patterson*

35 Breadline *6c* ★
The upper arête from a standing start on top of the large block on the right. Classic highball.

36 Beneath the Breadline *7b* ✳
Start on the left off the low block and swing around right to finish up *Breadline*. Classic. *Pat King*

Baseline *7c*
Start up *Beneath the Breadline*, span left into the pocket, finish up *Storm*. *Pat King*

37 Highline *7c+* ✳
From the start of *Breadline* traverse ripples and fingertip slopers right into the pocket of *Big Air* (E6) and gain the top. *Pat King*

Bloodline *8a* ★
The *Beneath the Breadline/Highline* link creates a classic, sustained highball problem. *Pat King*

38 Scoops Groove *6a* ✳
Pleasant groove with a reach to a pocket.

39 Scoops Slab *4+*
Scooped wall, just right. Sit-start past the pocket at 6b.

40 Scoops Arête *4* ✳
Right again the arête on left-hand side.

41 Grooved Arête *5* ✳
The arête on it's right-hand side.

42 The Doorpost *4*
The angular arête next to the approach path, below the *Grand Hotel* boulder. Topo on p84.

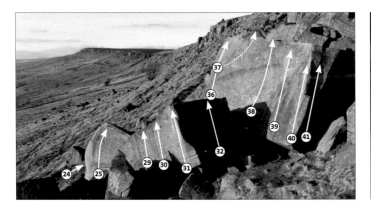

HELEN KEAN ON *SILK START* **PHOTO: ADAM LONG**

Above the Path

The final problems in the main *Plantation* area are dotted above the path as it climbs to the edge.

H Block

43 H Block *3*
The left arête.

44 The Dirty Protest *4+*
The slabby wall up the centre of the block.

Wavelength Block

A number of mantel problems exist on the path-side face of the low block.

45 Sidetrack *5+*
Mantel above jug on the left arête.

46 The Trough *5*
Mantel the lowest part of the block.

47 Wavelength *6a*
The rib, just right of centre.

48 Dijon Dip *6c*
The short arête and roof further down the hill.

Help the Aged

Set back on the edge, to the left of the large *Wall End Slab*.

49 Help the Aged *7a* ✳
Hang poor lip slopers and slap the jug; *Cortomaltese* comes to Stanage. Much easier in good conditions. There are some even poorer slopers just right which yield an identical, but harder, problem. 7b. *Johnny Dawes*

50 Polished Bump *7a+*
The bulge just right of the VS crack.

51 Silk Start *7a+* ✳
Awkward mantel onto the bulge – jump off. Smear precariously left up the rib to pockets for a very highball 7b (E6). See photo on p89. *Johnny Dawes*

Silk Sit-Start *7c*
A smattering of crimps, smears, heel hooks and the arête lead into the mantel of the stand-up problem. *John Welford*

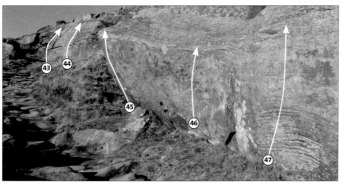

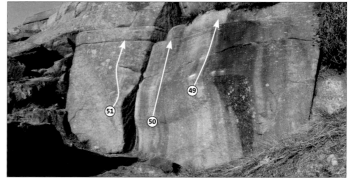

Just right is the big detached block of *Wall End Slab* with a range of easy, polished problems with grades from 4–5 at its base.

52 **Wall End Grab**   *6a*   ✳
Up and right again is a nice little wall with rounded slopey holds.

53 **The Prince**   *7a*   ✳
Behind and right of *Wall End Grab*, at the top of the edge, is a short low wall. Climb the wall left of the groove using a flake.

54 **Bunny Wailer**   *6c*   ✳
The attractive groove to the right.

55 **Mo Tucker**   *5*
The rib right of *Bunny Wailer*.

Plantation Outlying

A collection of outstanding problems and highballs located along the edge, to the left of the main, paved path. Walk up the path and break left along a vague path before the hairpin at the top.

Poundland

56 Surprise *5*
The left end of the slab.

57 Surprise Direct *6c* ✳
The undercut slab has a hard move on good holds.

58 Poundland *7b+*
Start at a shallow pocket on the lip and traverse left on slopers to a rock up before the crack. *Allen Williams*

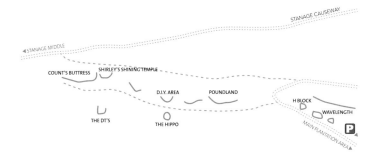

NEIL KERSHAW ON *D.I.Y.* **PHOTO:** JOHN COEFIELD

D.I.Y. Area

59 Black and Decker *6c*
Climb the left side of the wall to a ledge and then the left arête above.
The direct finish is a touch harder.

60 D.I.Y. *6b* ★
The classic highball via a vague groove and flake.

61 Torture Garden *7a* ✳
Pop to the slot – no bridging – and climb the wall left of the crack.

62 Sithee Direct *6b* ★
The centre of the wall right of the crack. 5+ by coming into the upper wall from the right.

63 Toxic *3*
The big chunky flake and wall above, 10m right of *D.I.Y.*

64 The Hippo *7a+*
A steep prow below *D.I.Y.* Sit-start (no footblock) to a worrying finish. *Iain Farrar*

Peahound *7b+*
The left-hand finish to *The Hippo*. *Ben Bransby*

Shirley's Shining Temple

Left again is another highball slab with two classics that are both often climbed as boulder problems due to their (relatively) low cruxes.

65 Shirley's Shining Temple *7c* ★
The centre of the slab, starting at a small overlap, keeping direct, left of the flake, on the upper slab. Thin and technical climbing on small breaks and pebbles, from 1984, courtesy of *The Boss*. E5 7a without pads, you still get 7c for the start. *John Allen*

66 Shock Horror Slab *7a+* ✳
Brilliant pebble pulling and smearing up the vague flake line. Starting slightly right is 6c. *Steve Bancroft*

67 The DT's *7c* ✳
A hidden R–L traverse of the sloping lip on a boulder down and left of *Shirley's*. The footblock at the start is in. *Andy Harris*

Stanage Far Right

Clustered around the southern end of Stanage, this area is often referred to as *Apparent North* – the main buttress hereabouts, so-called because it does – surprise surprise – appear to be the northern end of the edge. Expect a large circuit with some of the more classic low grade problems at Stanage, all at a good height, all on good rock.

Conditions

Slightly more sheltered than the rest of Stanage, but it still catches the breeze and can be cold on a very windy, winter day. With the exception of the *Cowper Stone*, the area is very quick drying after rain, being exposed to the wind and the sun.

Access and Approach

Park on the road between Burbage and Stanage in the large purpose-made lay-by and follow the path over to the rocks – the path meets the crag at *Apparent North* buttress by the large, fallen millstones. The *Cowper Stone* can also be approached by parking at the Burbage North car park and then walking directly over from the hairpin bend.

The Rim

A long, low block perched on top of the crag at the far left-hand end.

1   The Rim   6a+   ✳
Start on the left and follow the vague break rightwards, to a move to the top where it fades. Great shuffling. Extend into *Rimmer* at 6b+. One of many one move mantel problems exists just right of the finish, 4+.

2   Rim Flake   6a
Direct to the top from the same start.

3   Rimmer   6b
A similar straight-up problem.

Capstone

A small jumble of blocks with an obvious capstone.

4   Snout Groove   3+
The groove left of the arête.

5   The Snout   6a
The arête. Top out rightwards.

6   Snout Wall   5

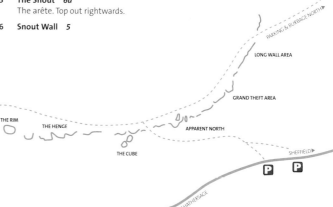

THE BACK ROOFS

THE COWPER STONE

PARKING & BURBAGE NORTH

LONG WALL AREA

GRAND THEFT AREA

THE RIM

THE HENGE

APPARENT NORTH

THE CUBE

SHEFFIELD ▶

HATHERSAGE ◀

The Henge

A larger jumble of rocks, also with a capstone.

7   Sparky Slab   *3+*
The slab left of the nose. Climb the hard crimpy wall on the left of the nose at 6b.

8   Sparky   *6c*
The nose direct. A bit of a challenge with an equally challenging landing.

9   The Henge   *6a*   ✳
The front face of the prow, beneath the balanced block. High but full of great holds.

10   The Doorstep   *6b+*
The crimpy wall above an uninviting landing.

11   The Hinge   *6a+*
The wall right again, from the second platform.

12   Staircase Flake   *5*   ✳
The flakeline, from a sit-start.

13   Al's Attic   *7a*
Climb Staircase Flake to the first thin break and traverse right to finish up *Quick Wall*.

14   Front Flake   *4+*   ✳
The crackline. Best from sitting, award yourself another point.

15   Quick Wall   *6a+*
From slots to the thin crack. Topping out is a bit of a thrutch. Traverse the slotty break leftwards to *Front Flake* at 6b.

16   Tweedle Dee   *3+*
The wall left of the ramp feature.

17   Steps   *3+*   ✳
The ramp feature.

18   Tweedle Dum   *3+*
The wall right of the ramp feature.

19   Hook Line and Sinker   *4*
The blunt arête to pock marks.

20   Slotted Arête   *4+*
The left arête of the next block right.

21   Slotted Wall   *5*
Break-to-break-ing up the wall.

Pert Block

22 Pert Block Arête *3+*
The left arête

23 Pert Wall *3*

24 Pert Bloke *5* ✳
Right arête from sitting. Rather good.

The Cube

The next problems are on the two blocks below the line of the edge. The upper one is a huge easy-angled slab.

25 Cube Arête *5+*
The left arête.

26 Cube Root *5+*
Wall to slopers.

27 The Cornflake *6c* ✳
The centre of the wall, from the break, past the small 'cornflake' hold.

28 Slots *5+*
The wall just right again.

29 Cubing *6a* ✳
Excellent high traverse from the left arête. Staying low to finish up *Slots* is a tricky 6c+.

30 The High Road *3+* ★
Mantel onto the slab and follow the undercut flake to the right arête and finish up this.

31 A Case of Mistaken Identity *7b* ✳
A classic slopey traverse along the bottom of the huge slab. Sit-start.
Rich Heap/Andy Harris

32 *7a*
Sit-start and mantel straight through the previous problem.

Gripple Buttress

33 Gripple One 5
After a tricky start, the left-hand line soon eases.

34 Gripple Two 5+
The wall left of centre. Bad landing.

35 Gripple Three 5+
The centre of the wall past big sidepulls and slopers, above a poor landing.

36 Gripple Graunch 6b
The undercut arête from an extremely low start is harder for people with legs.

37 Gripple Nipple 5 ★
The lovely wall to the right. Can be done from a sit-start. Variations abound.

38 6c
Up above the edge. Lean out from the back to a ramp and mantel it out.

20m further along, next to the path is:

39 The Hatchet 6c
Climb the arête from a low start.

Easy Jamming

The walls left of *Apparent North* are home to some great, easy, short routes/high boulder problems reminiscent of the first bits of Burbage North.

40 Sleazy Jamming 4
The left crack.

41 Easy Walling 5+ ✳
The wall between the cracks – hardest at the start. Good fun.

42 Easy Jamming 3+
The second crack.

43 Trainer Failure 5
The blunt arête.

44 The Real 20 Foot Crack 4+ ★
Lovely jamming and/or laybacking.

45 The Shiznit 7a
A double dyno eliminate. Climb the wall right of the crack, double dynoing every move. The last couple are quite high up. No double dynos, no tick.

46 The Fudgie Budgie 5
The right arête on the right-hand side.

47 Minah Variation 6c
The wall above the ledge. Great.

Apparent North
The main buttress hereabouts, with the first problems on a couple of mini-buttresses to the left.

48 Left Leg 3+
The left arête.

49 Middle Leg 3+
Pleasant climbing up the centre.

50 3+
The right arête on the left.

51 Howdy Rowdy 6b+
The slab just left of centre, moving left at the top.

52 Rawhide 7a+
Thin climbing up the centre of the wall on super-sharp pebbles. Please clean your blood off afterwards.

53 My Crazy Head 6b ✳
The right arête, climbed on the left-hand side.

››

THE REAL 20 FOOT CRACK **PHOTO:** JON BARTON

54 Gully Flake *6a*
Start on slots on the right of the gulley on the left side of the buttress and move up to a flake, and then leftwards around the arête.

55 The Shaft *6c*
Start on the left wall of the block at a rounded boss on the lip, by the crack. Gain the break above and traverse left to finish up *Gully Flake*. A fair workout.

56 Shatner's Bassoon *7a+*
From the back of the niche span to the rounded boss on *The Shaft* and finish at the break.

57 Skinless Wonder *7a+* ✳
A hard start to a route, undercutting up the wall on pebbles to the break. Jump or traverse off. Topping out via a horrendous skin-grinding mantel is very hard and E6, even with gear. A harder variation – *Ron's Reach III* – undercuts up and right.

58 Hamper's Hang *7a* ★
From the flake jug right of the niche traverse right, down the sloping undercut shelf – crux – and along the break in the right-hand wall. Extend the start across the niche at 7a+.

59 Hamper's Mantel *7a* ✳
From the ledge, climb direct through the slopey overhang to an awkward mantel.

60 5+ ✳
The higher traverse line from the corner, finishing on the boulder in the gully.

61 6b+
The lower traverse. Move up at the arête to join the higher finish.

62 6a+
The right arête to the break.

63 Purist Energy *7b*
The narrow wall to the right. *Mike Adams*

64 Mating Toads *6a* ✳
The prow feature. Highball.

65 Massacre Direct *5+*
The flake line to the right.

66 Pit Trip *6a*
Hidden in a pit about 20m right of *Apparent North*, bounded by blocks on both sides. Climb the left arête past the low ledge.

Moving around right are some more fine micro-routes that are paddable.

AIRLIE ANDERSON ON *ZIPPATROCITY*   **PHOTO: IAN PARNELL**

Grand Theft Area

67 Sloper Traverse *7a* ✳
The appealing line of slopers from left to right, finishing up crimps. Also, from the same starting hold, span up to the higher sloping ledge and shuffle right, 6c.

68 Slope John A *6b+*
Climbing direct through the traverse line is slopey and conditions-dependant.

69 Slope John B *6b*
The sit-start line of edges leading into the end of the traverse.

70 Almost a Hold *6c+* ✳
On the next buttress just right. While you can shuffle along all of the breaks on this wall, the best problem traverses the low break rightwards from the arête with a morpho crux reach. *No Cigar* adds a move by doing a sit-start from the ledge at the bottom of the arête.

71 Tea Left *5*
The wall past a triangular pod. The finish of *Almost a Hold*.

In front of *Almost a Hold* buttress is a scrappy sit-start on poor rock – 4+. 10m right is a little block:

72 Block Party *4*
The left arête.

73 Block Wall *5*
Sit-start just left of the arête. Tricky.

74 Block Arête *5+* ✳
The lovely sit-start arête. Same grade on both sides.

Long Wall Area

75 *6a+*
The left-most wall from a sit-start.

76 Flat Groove *6a* ✳
The groove, climbed from the same start.

77 Flat Wall Traverse *6a+*
A long right to left traverse, along breaks.

78 Get the Horn *5+* ✳
A fun, eliminate double dyno from the flake to the horn.

10m right is:

79 Three Tiered Cake *5+*
The small overhang and wall on the left buttress. High.

80 Cave Route *6c*
Climb through the low roof on the right buttress, on its left side, then climb the wall above. The grade is a little dependant on your sequence.

81 Cave Crack *6b*
The roof and crack on the right and the wall above.

82 Fig Roll *5+*
The wall via high pocket. The tall can eliminate the pocket, and indeed the problem.

83 Double Flake *4* ✳
The twin flakes split by the break

84 Crimpy Roof *6b+* ✳
The roof, wall and crack from a low start. Excellent.

85 The Medicine Ball *6a*
The right arête.

The Cowper Stone

86 Zippatrocity *7b+* ★
Fist jamming and sloping masochism in the form of a traverse from extreme left, round the arête and finishing at the extreme right. Can seep in winter. See photo on p100. *Mark Pretty*

87 The Bob Marley Extension *7c*
An extension start into a reverse of *Zippatrocity*, from the small cave on the right of the buttress. Enter the cave through the back, jam through the roof and join the main traverse. *Tom Randall*

88 Leroy Slips a Disc *7b* ✳
A hard wall via an undercut to a high, rounded top-out. Hard for the short. *John Allen*

89 *6c+*
Just right of Leroy, lurch between the breaks.

90 Headspin *6b* ✳
The wall right again, with a hard, scary, rounded top-out.

Chippy Buttress

91 Pudding *5*
The wall left of the arête, heading towards a crack.

92 Chips *5+*
The arête taken on the left – traverse right and escape at the break – E3 to continue.

93 Peas *6c*
The problem is the mantel, but if you top-out you will think otherwise – E4 5c.

The Back Roofs

On from the *Cowper Stone*, these roofs are located around the back of the edge.

94 Savage Me Softly *6c+* ✳
The first roof is 50m further than the *Cowper Stone*. Climb the hanging fissure on the right hand side of the roof, from a sit-start. Hard. *Tom Randall*

95 Fly Frisching *6c*
Another 50m further is a strip-like roof. Climb the left-hand start from sitting using jams, heel-toes and slopers. *Ian Murray*

96 *6c*
The right arête from sit-start.

Stanage Popular End & Carhead Rocks

A bunch of isolated problems along the cunningly-titled *Popular End*, and some bits at the *King of Grit's* scrappy neighbour – *Carhead Rocks*.

Stanage Popular End

Isn't very popular for bouldering, but a few worthwhile scattered problems exist. They are mostly direct starts to routes, so reference to the routes guide (Stanage, pb BMC, 2007) will assist in locating them.

Access and Approach

Either park in the large bay at Hook's Car and walk up to the unmissable *Popular End*, or wander right from the *Plantation*.

1   **Mounting Frustration** *6c+*
    A wall with a perplexing start.

2   **The Golden Path** *7c* ✳
    The committing, overhanging arête below *BAW's Crawl* (HVS). High, hard, superb. *John Welford*

3   **Verandah Buttress Direct** *7a+*
    Highball. The roof direct – a small crimp, a big stretch.

4   **Suzanne** *6a* ✳
    Situated on the far right of the popular end, this is the obvious low roof. Climb the centre of the roof and bail out, or solo through the easy breaks above.

5   **Finale Direct** *6a+*
    The roof and blunt arête right of *Suzanne*. Finish similarly.

Carhead Rocks

The rock at Stanage's poorer cousin isn't as good as that on the *King of Crags*, the crag is nowhere near as extensive, and the problems aren't up there with the (well worn) national classics over the road. That said, *Carhead* is worth a brief trip if you've had enough of the crowds at the *Plantation*, and you fancy doing a spot of exploring.

Access and Approach

See *Stanage* overview map on p59. From the big parking area at Hook's Car (*Stanage Popular End*), turn right on the road to Hathersage, cross the cattle grid and look for a gate on the right. Pass through this and walk dead straight up to the edge – the bouldering is all off to the right, starting with the roof at the far end.

Carhead Roof

1   Afterbirth   *7a*
Undercut out the left-hand side of the roof to a diagonal hold. Finish straight up.

2   Middle Line   *7a+*
From the obvious sloper at the back of the middle of the roof, and a less obvious undercut, pull around to the central diagonal feature and finish straight up.

3   Hueco   *6b*
Span from the jug on the right under the roof to the hueco, make a stiff pull past this and continue up good pockets.

4   You know I do!   *7a+*
Start up *Afterbirth* and traverse the lip to finish up *Hueco*.

5   Born Again   *5+*
The centre of the large wall right of the roof.

6   Casualties of War   *6a*
Swing right to reach the right arête, then finish up this.

Just Like Honey

7   Just Like Honey   *7c*
Back towards the approach path is this steep triangular face, climbed from a sit-start, using undercuts in the centre and avoiding the arête throughout. Sadly on friable rock, it lost its two best holds in 2009 and is probably unclimbed since, and likely harder than the given grade. *John Welford*

We've described the main problems here. Others do exist and are documented on **www.peakbouldering.info**

Burbage Valley

Welcome to *Bouldering Heaven*. The *Burbage Valley* – bigger and better looking than *Bas Cuvier* – has it all. A large, open valley sweeps north to south, with an ice cream van at the top, and a pub at the bottom. The valley sides are ringed with crags, isolated buttresses and random boulders, all of which contain superb bouldering. Shady, sunny, sheltered, exposed, steep, slabby, highball, bunched, weird or basic – there is something here for everyone, whatever the season or conditions. A climber who is tired of *Burbage* is a climber who is tired of climbing.

Access and Approach

The *Burbage Valley* climbing area is surrounded by car parks and is well served by buses. This broad valley, which the majority of the bouldering overlooks, is conveniently accessed on foot via a rough track – the Green Drive. See the individual crags for approach information.

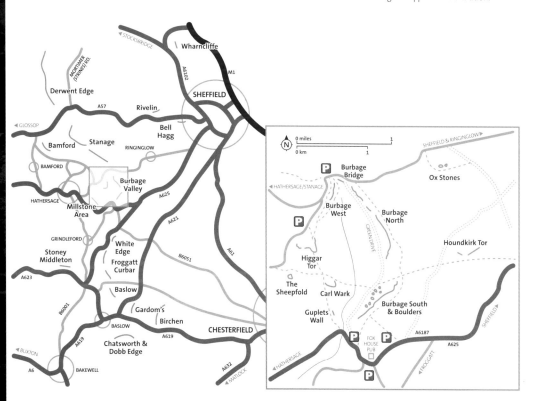

JAMES HILLIARD ON *ROCKET MAN* **PHOTO:** ADAM LONG

Burbage Bridge

With an approach to rival even the most roadside of crags, the cluster of small blocks next to the *Burbage Bridge* is ideal for the boulderer with no time to spare, and climbing to be done. Generally steep problems, which include a couple of valley classics, such as the leaning wall of *Mermaid*.

Access and Approach

The boulders are dotted halfway between the two parking areas at the top of the *Burbage Valley*: impossible to miss. No more than a 50m walk. The problems are numbered left to right, assuming you've approached from the larger car park over the first stream. See map on p107.

Conditions

Occupying a sheltered hollow, these rocks evade the wind nicely but can be sweaty and midgy in summer. The classic problem *Mermaid* often seeps in winter when conditions are at their best.

Rocket Man

The first problems are on the blocks between the two streams.

1 **6a+**
Funky, undercutty shenanigans up the rib. A bit harder from sitting.

2 **Rocket Man** **7b+** ✶
Dyno from low edges to the top. *Rob 'Rocket Man' Smith*

3 **Mermaid** **7a** ★
The twin cracks from sitting. Often wet, yet utterly classic.

4 **6c**
Arête from sitting, hands in slot. You can use the pinch on the arête at this grade, but not the holds to the right of the arête – which is annoying but a better problem (6a). Avoiding the arête completely is better still, harder (7a), but completely eliminate rather than just a bit eliminate.

Wobble Block

Hop over the eastern stream to the next bunch of blocks, directly under the main Burbage North lay-by and info board.

5 **4**
The left wall from a sit-start.

6 **5+** ✶
The arête taken on the left-hand side. Harder without the foot block.

7 **6b+** ✶
The central wall from a low start, no arête. Hard.

8 **3**
Easy little arête.

9 **Wobble Block Direct** **6c**
Hug up the left arête.

10 **Wobble Block** **6b+** ★
Direct through the roofs, past slopers. The *Wobble Block* wobbled one too many times and now resides on the floor.

11 **Beached Whale Crack** **5**
The cracks. The clue is in the name.

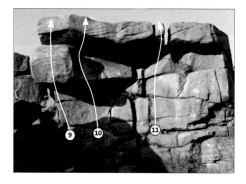

Burbage North

There's something for everyone at *Burbage North*. Home to *Ben Moon's Voyager* – the jewel in the crown of gritstone bouldering and – at 8b+ – the hardest 'up' problem on gritstone, there's also stacks to go at for the rest of us mortals. Grades range from Font 3 to 8b+, with all kinds of styles – slabs, overhangs, arêtes, walls, highballs – all on good, bullet-hard rock.

Access and Approach

Park at *Burbage Bridge*, either in the long lay-by on the Sheffield side of the bridge, or in the car park on the Stanage side. The Green Drive path leads down under the edge and gives easy access to the problems. Approach times vary from 30 seconds, to 20 minutes.

Conditions

The whole valley is generally more sheltered than exposed edges such as *Stanage*, although it can dry relatively quickly after rain if the wind is blowing and/or the sun is out. *Burbage North* is often a good cold weather venue, and *Remergence* buttress stays largely dry in the rain.

DAVE NORTON ON *SAFE BET* PHOTO: JOHN COEFIELD

20 Foot Crack Area

The first section you reach from the parking is the *20 Foot Crack* area, which provides some lovely warm-ups and a couple of classic teasers. Although they were first – and still are – climbed as routes, they are very enjoyable as boulder problems if you are confident at these grades.

1   **North Roof**   *6a*
    A small roof 10m or so left of *RT Wall*. Lean out to the lip of the roof and exit up the arête.

2   **RT Wall**   *5+*
    Undercut boldy up the left sidewall.

3   **Route 1**   *4+*   ✳
    The left arête above the cutaway.

4   **Route 1.5**   *5*
    The wall to the right.

5   **Route 2**   *3+*   ✳
    The wall via the niche.

6   **Route 2.5**   *4+*
    The wall to the right.

>>

7   Route 3   3+   ✳
The Z crack, with a fluttery move off jams at the top.

8   Route 3.5   6a+
The wall to the right with a big move near the top. The right arête is a 3.

9   Low Traverse   5+
Left to right, or vice-versa.

10   Cranberry Crack   3
The big, wide crack.

11   The Chant   5   ★
The wall left of *20 Foot Crack*, with a committing move past the slot. The wall between *Cranberry Crack* and *The Chant* is a thin 5+.

12   20 Foot Crack   4   ★
The thin hand crack splitting the buttress.

13   The Curse   5+   ★
Small crimps then big reaches.

14   Lost in France   6a
Undercut (crux) past the overlap just left of the arête.

Banana Finger Area

15   Definitive 5.12   6c+
5m left of the *Banana Finger* buttress is a cave and roof crack formed by the collision of two boulders. Ferret into the gap and jam or undercut your way out. There is a harder left-hand finish, 7a+.

16   Cinzano Roof   7b
The roof formed by the boulder cluster above and left of *Banana Finger* from an edge and pocket. Starting from the block right and reaching out to the pocket is a more amenable 6c. *Andy Harris/Rich Heap*

17   Side Wall   5
The crack just below *Cinzano Roof*, with tricky polished smears.

18   Banana Reverse   7a   ✳
Traverse into *Banana Finger Direct* from jugs on the left. Reverse *Banana Finger* to finish.

19   Banana Finger Direct   6c   ★
The direct start to *Banana Finger* is superb. Shin/knee pads are optional.

20   6c
A quick pull on slopers just right of *Banana Finger Direct*. Finish up the original.

21 Banana Finger *6a* ★
A classic traverse and up problem, listed by English Heritage as a national monument.
Follow edges and slots left to a stiff pull to the good hold in the upper break.
Knees are allowed, jeans are recommended. *Ed Drummond*

To the right is a large, overhanging buttress, split by a roof crack.

22 Little Brown Thug *7a*
Sit-start under the overlap left of the crack (tip: undercut), reach to the lip and shuffle
up and right to a big rockover to the break.

23 Wednesday Climb *5+* ✳
The big-ass roof crack.

24 Life in a Radioactive Dustbin *6c* ★
The highball overhang just right.

All Quiet Area
A small wall left of the *Remergence* buttress.

25 All Quiet on the Eastern Front *6a+* ★
Traverse right with a tough move past a pebble to a flatty on the arête, before moving up.

26 All Quiet Direct *7a* ✳
Thin wall climbing to join the original at the end of the traverse. Harder if you go direct
to the jug.

27 All Sit-Down *7b* ✳
Sit-start into the direct from the low jug.

28 The Busker *4+*
The wall left of the crack.

29 Bracken Crack *3*

30 Green Slab *4+*
The wall right of the crack.

Remergence Area

Very popular and becoming increasingly polished, this block is one of the best in the valley, especially since the puddle was stolen. It's very sheltered, which is great in the freezing wind, but bad nick can appear when the sun is out even if it's freezing cold. The first couple of problems are by the walls to the left:

31 Fallen Slab Lip *7b*
Sit-start the arête of the leaning block to slopers on the lip and head right to rockover and finish. 7a if started with left hand on the back arête.

32 Small is Beautiful *7a* ★
Climb the centre of the wall above and to the left of *Remergence Buttress*, with improbable moves between big breaks to a high top-out (hidden hold on top). *John Allen*

33 Left Arête Sitter *7b+*
The roofy left arête from a low start.

34 Arête Problem a.k.a. The Hanging Rib *6b+* ★
A Burbage classic: reach out, pinch the rib, crimp the rail, slap the ledge. Eliminates abound: eliminating the flat edge on the lip and using slopers left is 6c+, and using just one sloper and powering through to the top in a campus stylee (well you're allowed feet) is about 7b.

35 Zaff's Groove *7a+*
A squeezed-in line, climbing the open groove just right. Keep off the other problems. *Zaff Ali*

36 Submergence *7c* ★
Start on a low jug under the roof, traverse the lip left and finish up *Arête Problem*. Tallies can lank it off the sidepull at 7b+. *Jason Myers*

37 Blind Drunk *8a*
Direct to the break from the jug via a tiny dish. Unfortunately it's possible to slap from the lip to the pocket missing out the hard move if you have very long arms, grade = low to mid-7. *John Welford*

38 Remergence *6b* ★
From painful pockets below the roof, pull over to gain the crescent-shaped hold and edges above, before doing the mother of all rockovers.

39 Blind Date *7b+* ★
This Peak rite of passage starts with your right hand on the crimp on the lip and left hand on the flake under the roof. Head up past the sloper to slots in the break and over to finish. *Alan Rouse*

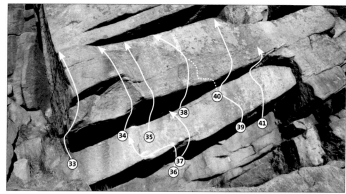

40 Blind Fig 7c ★
An eliminate on *Blind Date* (but better), matching the sloper and rocking left to a small hold on the lip of the next roof, before popping up for crimps and the *Remergence* rockover to finish. The diagonal crimp next to the sloper is eliminated. *Jason Myers*

41 Blind Fury 7c+
The featureless lip and wall right of *Blind Date* submits to a horrendous pull on a pebble. *Andy Harris*

Three traverses cross the buttress at different heights:

Blind Ali 7b+ ★
L–R traverse of the lip of the lower roof from the polished holds on the left (holds under roof are IN). Excellent. *Blind Ali's Date* links *Blind Ali* into *Blind Date* – 7c+. *Zaff Ali/Iain Farrar*

Break Traverse 7c
From the start of the *Arête Problem* traverse the line of slots and edges below the roof rightwards (eliminate the holds above). Painful.

Remergence Traverse 7a+
Lean in from the left arête and traverse the lip of the second roof rightwards.

Tiny Slab
A tiny slab on a boulder 20m or so right of *Remergence* has some lovely delicate problems that almost merge into one another.

42 4
The left-hand line.

43 4+ ✳
Just left of centre.

44 5+
Just right of centre.

45 6b
Just left of the right arête.

PAUL REEVE ON *BLIND DATE* **PHOTO:** KEITH SHARPLES

Ash Tree Wall Area

A couple of problems by the edge, and a stack of classics on blocks below. The first problem is about 50m right of *The Tiny Slab*.

46　Solitude　*6c*　✳
Sit-start from the break to the rib and shuffle up this before rocking over to finish. A variation – *Shazam* (6b+) – climbs direct via a jam. *Dave Parry/James Hogg*

47　Striker　*7c+*　✳
The line of the edge forms a small amphitheatre, with a small wall at the top right-hand side, by a dead tree. *Striker* climbs the centre of the wall just left of the arête via a very hard dyno off undercuts. Essentially a direct start to the route *Beach Tea One*. *Ben Moon*

48　Striker Left-hand　*7a+*　✳
A more amenable move, using the left arête and an undercut to pop for the break.

49　Puck　*7b*
Further right is a prominent buttress with a cleanly carved left arête – this is *Living in Oxford*, E7. Up and left of this is a highball arête above a small roof. Climb this with a dynamic move to the large pocket. *John Welford*

50　Clunge　*6c*
Jump-start the left-hand side of the wedged shield in the gully up and right of *Puck*. Pull on static at 7b.

51　Sitting in Oxford　*7a*
Sit-start the lower arête of *Living in Oxford*. A tricky one-mover. *Jon Fullwood*

52　The Terrace　*7c*　★
The powerful and technical arête from a sit-start, starting from the lowest undercling and the arête. *Paul Houghoughi*

53　Jason's Roof　*7b+*
Out via the keel from a low start under the roof. Much harder/impossible if you can't span between the keel and the face holds. 6c+ from standing. *Jason Myers*

54　*7a+*
From a low start as per *Jason's Roof* move out to and up the hanging arête. 7a from standing.

55　*7a+*　✳
Start as above, but move out and climb the narrow wall to the right of the arête. Easier if you find the knee bar. 6c from standing.

56　La Terrace　*7c+*
A link-up. Climb *The Terrace* to holds under the apex where the boulders meet, spin 180 degrees, climb down the facing wall and finish up problem 10.

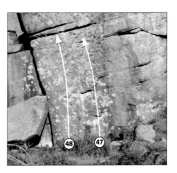

The Sphinx Area

100m further along the edge is the imposing prow of *The Sphinx*.

57 The Sphinx 7a+ ✳
The rising traverse line out to the big hanging nose. Gripping. *John Allen*

58 Giza 7b+ ✳
Straight up the wall from the start of *The Sphinx*. *Ian Fitzpatrick*

59 Voyager 8b ★
The left arête of the blank roof below *The Sphinx* has a smattering of rough, but poor, slopers and crimps on the lip. Jump-start and exit up the hanging nose. *Ben Moon*

60 Voyager Sit-Start 8b+ ★
The full line, starting at obvious holds at the back of the roof. One of the best hard lines on grit. Unrepeated to date. *Ben Moon*

61 Sputnik 7b+
The mirror line to *Voyager* taking the hanging, right-hand lip from the gully. Traverse out to a good hold, then move up via a mono, taking care not to fall into the void. *Ben Moon*

62 Cleo's Edge 5+ ★
The superb arête on its left. Slightly easier on the right.

63 Roof Goofe 6b
The small roof and mantel from the back.

64 Jetty Aretty 5+
The left arête and face of the pillar.

65 Jetty Nose 6a
The low nose.

66 6a+
Jump to the pocket and up.

67 6b
The bulge past a two-finger pebble and sloper.

68 Safe Bet 6c ★
The exquisite left-hand side of the arête. Highball. See photo on p110.

69 Long Shot 6b
The bulge right of the arête.

70 Bedrock 7a ✳
The reachy wall past a pocket.

71 Yabadabadoo! 6c
Jump to the ledge.

Stuck in no man's land along the edge, by *Hollyash Wall*, is:

Enterprise 7b+
The highball, direct start to the route *Windjammer (E1)*. Hard climbing to 6m, followed by an easier 4m. First highballed, after top-rope practice, over a very big crash mat borrowed from the Foundry. *Adrian Berry*

The Woods
In the patch of woodland beneath the edge – roughly between the routes *The Knight's Move* and *Three Blind Mice* – are a couple of hidden blocks.

72 Boyager 7b ★
At the top of the tree line is a *Voyager*-esque prow with a poor landing. Fridge-hug out from the back. *Iain Farrar*

73 Mono Bulge 7a
The filthy block beneath *Boyager*, with a crux move past a mono.

Nicotine Stain Area
Fine wall climbing on the final part of the edge, and a couple of classics on the big boulders down from the edge justifies the walk-in. *Nicotine Stain* is just beyond the trees right of the thin, jutting prow of *The Fin*.

74 6c
On a small block below the routes *Long Tall Sally* and *Three Blind Mice* is a solitary boulder. Sit-start the northwest arête. Quite good.

75 The Twenty Year Itch 6c ✳
The vague wall between *The Fin* (HVS) and the corner. Technical and committing moves above a poor landing. *Andy Barker*

76 The Enthusiast 6a+ ✳
The left arête. Tricky.

77 Nicotine Stain 6b ★
The faint crack to the right is an old-school technical classic. *Alan Rouse*

78 Spider Crack 6a
Right again. A little higher than *Nicotine Stain*, but still very pad-able.

79 Pest Control 6b
The wall between the cracks.

80 Two Pocket Sitter *5+*
Sit-start from the twin pockets and up to the arête/crack.

81 Plank Sanction *7b*
Sit-start on the right side of the arete, with a small crimp for your left hand.
Use a scalloped gaston to reach an undercut pocket on the left, and a big rock up
to the groove and an easier finish. *Andy Banks*

82 Crack Habit *5* ✳
Sit-start the low offwidth.

83 Grizzly Bear *6c+*
Sit-start the leaning wall up and right past a pocket and sloping breaks. A variant
takes the low pocket with the right hand and rolls left to the arête – same grade.

84 Pocket Dyno *7a+*
Guess the beta... A tough dyno to the pocket.

85 Capped Rib *6a*
The vague rib and capping roof.

86 Tidal Wave *3+*
The attractive wave-shaped arête.

Below *Nicotine Stain* is:

87 Velvet Crab *7a+* ★
The big left arête of the cave. The finish feels high and a bit gritty – no bridging out right.
Excellent. See photo overleaf. *John Welford*

88 *6a*
The left-hand crack in the roof apex formed by the three blocks.

89 *6a+*
The right-hand crack.

90 Zaff Skoczylas *7c* ✳
The shapely prow from a lying down start (big pocket on the left). 7b+ from sitting.
Dawid Skoczylas/Zaff Ali/John Welford/who knows

Zaff Skoczylas Right-Hand *7c*
As for the lying start, then break right at the lip slopers and layback to glory.
Andy Harris

Beyond The End Area

100m further south is an isolated block.

91   Little Cube Arête   5
The left arête.

92   Once Upon A Time   7c
Climb the centre of the block: undercut, jump. Likely a smidgeon harder as pebbles keep disappearing. *John Welford*

93   Beyond The End   3+   ★
The good right-hand arête of the small buttress. Worth the walk. *John Welford*

50m right again are The Three Bears with a good selection of easy problems:

94   Daddy Wall   3

95   Daddy Bear Arête   3+
Climbed on the left. On the right it is 4.

96   Mommy Wall   4+

97   Mommy Bear Arête   4
On the left. On the right it is 3+.

98   Baby Bear Wall   3+

99   Baby Bear Arête   3

Burbage South

Spiritual home of Hard Grit, *Burbage South* offers varied bouldering that is always of impeccable quality. The problems are spread out along the crag, with many hidden among the jumbled blocks that litter the edge. The bouldering here is outstanding, features all styles and grades, and will leave you gagging for more.

Access and Approach

There is limited parking in a small lay-by on the road at the bottom of the valley, from where the Green Drive can be followed below the edge. The quarries are hard to miss, up on the right, and provide a good point to navigate from. Alternatively, park alongside the A6187, between the A625 turn off towards *Froggatt* and the Fox House Inn, and approach across a stile and direct over the moor. You'll meet the edge just below the first quarry. Or, if you enjoy a stroll, park at *Burbage North* and follow the Green Drive down the valley. The Fox House Inn is also well served by buses from Sheffield.

Conditions

Northwest facing, the edge is shaded in the first half of the day and with a good breeze can hold good conditions well into summer. The flipside is that it can also remain damp after wet weather on the shorter, winter days. The quarries can be sheltered in a cold wind. The boulders get the sun all day – most pleasant.

The Quarries

See overview map below for the location of the first two problems, located before the first quarry.

1 *6c*
A good slab, but make sure you start from the floor at this grade – even a slight udge up reduces the difficulty a lot. Located on a small hillock in the first jumble of boulders that can be seen up and right from the Green Drive (above and right of a large, circular stone trough).

2 *6b*
The appealing rib was, unfortunately, born without a landing. Either balance your mats as best you can or do it old-school style without. It's on the right of the path, just before the entrance to the south (Cioch) quarry.

South (Cioch) Quarry

The first of two major quarries reached.

3 **The Leotard Legend** *7c* ★
On the banked, valley-facing sidewall of the huge, jutting Cioch is a series of ribs. Climb these to finish at the ledge. Quite rain and snow proof. See photo overleaf. *Andy Banks*

4 **Trellis** *7a+* ✴
A highball problem up the shield of rock opposite the vast Cioch block. Undercut, edge, edge, top. Morpho. See photo opposite. *Ben Moon*

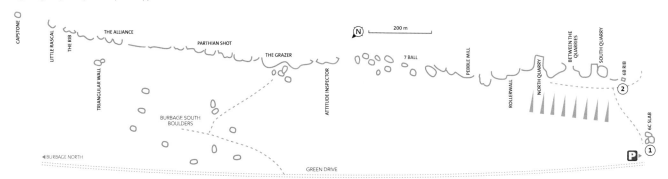

Between the Quarries

Between the quarries is a pleasing plateau with a smattering of quality problems.

5   Little Gem   *7b*   ✶
The excellent seam in the small wall. 7a+ with a jump start. *Andy Popp*

6   The Celtic Cross   *5+*   ★
The lovely arête to the left.

7   Hamburger Roof   *6a+*
The small wall and roof, climbed from break to break.

8   Sidepull Arch   *5+*   ★
The classic concave wall.

9   Rabbit Claw   *5+*
Climb the scoop from the block. Poor landing.

10   Softwidth   *3+*

11   Softwidth Wall   *4*
Squeezed in between the crack and the corner, spaced flat holds lead to glory breaks above.

North (Zeus) Quarry

The second of the two large quarries.

12 Mini Millwheel   4+
Teeter up the slabby arête to the ledge. Good problems each side are just harder.

13 Violence   7a+
Sit-start the arête on the small block in the centre of the quarry to a slopey finish.

14 Zorev   7c   ✳
The arête/prow on the edge of the quarry. Avoid the ledges out left. The sit-start is 7c+.
Jerry Moffatt/Mike Adams

15   7a+
The isolated hanging prow facing back into the quarry. Start squatting with hands on the low block and feet on the back wall. 6b from standing.

The big slab inside the quarry gives some unremarkable low grade problems.

Burbage South Edge: Central Section

The quarries now give way to a mostly natural edge. It's a superb circuit with generally good landings, some shade and isolated problems appearing every twenty feet or so. The first problem is on the big slab just north of the North Quarry.

Pebble Mill

1   Rollerwall   *7c*
The highball slab, direct. *Ron Fawcett*

2   David Traverse   *7a*
Climb (walk) along the shelf, drop round the corner and traverse the edges rightwards to reach flakes at the right-hand side of the wall. Finish at a finger jug.

3   Dork Child   *5*
The arête on its left-hand side.

4   Pebble Mill Traverse   *7a+*   ★
Traverse from the undercut on the front face, around the arête, and through the scoop to finish on the right arête. It's also possible to do it in reverse at the same grade. Rather good. See photo opposite.

5   Pepper Mill   *6c+*   ★
The tall arête on the right-hand side, finishing at the ledge.

6   Pepper Mill Traverse   *7b+*   ✳
Climb *Pebble Mill Traverse* right to left and finish up *Pepper Mill*.

7   Pebble Mill Stem   *7a*
Traverse at a higher level from the right arête, feet on the *Pebble Mill Traverse* handholds, to finish up *Pepper Mill*.

8   Trapped in Crows' Craws   *7a+*
Sit-start the twin arêtes and swing left to finish up the next problem. It's possible to finish right at 7a too. *Neil Kershaw*

9   Broddle's Baby   *6c+*   ✳
The frustrating leaning arête.

10   Little Limmock   *6b*   ✳
The slabby rib is a good problem.

>>

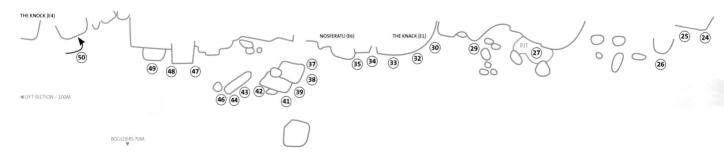

ADAM COEFIELD ON *PEBBLE MILL TRAVERSE* **PHOTO:** JOHN COEFIELD

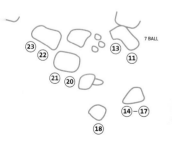

7 BALL

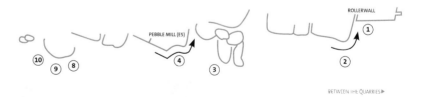

PEBBLE MILL (E5)

ROLLERWALL

BETWEEN THE QUARRIES ▶

7 Ball

A little further along is the popular *7 Ball*, plus a fine collection of mid-grade problems.

11 Corner Pocket *6a+*
The slightly awkward arête. 6b+ from sitting.

12 Middle Wall *4+* ✳
The centre of the fine wall. Slightly harder from sitting.

13 7 Ball *6c* ★
Like an easier version of *8 Ball*. Sit-start right of the groove and move left and up the groove and rib. Brilliant.

14 Matterhorn Right *3+*
The right arête and groove.

15 *5+*
Direct up the shallow groove.

16 *6a*
A thin, tight line between the previous problem and the left arête.

17 Matterhorn Left *4*
The left arête.

18 *4* ✳
The short arête from a sit-start is a good problem.

19 *4*
Layback up the fallen block just behind. Fun.

20 *6c*
The mantel just right of centre is much easier than...

21 Jason's Mantel *7a* ✳
Mantel onto the low, slopey slab from a hanging start, just left of centre.
Jason Myers

22 Oak Tree Arête *6b*
Climb the tricky arête from a low start to a tricky top-out.

23 Curving Crimps *6b*
From a sit-start left of the arête, crimp up and left.

A short distance further on is:

24 Birch Tree Arête *6a* ★
The fine, tall arête.

25 Little Artless *6a+*
Edge, edge, top.

26 6b+
Down and left is a hanging, undercut slab. Tackle the front of the small block face-on from a sit-start. Avoiding the footblock out right.

Attitude Inspector

27 Electrical Storm *7b* ★
Sit-start the lightning bolt rib in the pit and top-out right along the sloping ramp.

28 Grease Lightning *7b+*
Sit-start as for *Electrical Storm*, but at the top of the groove break left to finish.
Ned Feehally

29 Gib's Rib *7a* ✳
The fine open rib that forms the right arête of the buttress. See photo on p131. *Adrian Jebb*

30 Nick Knack Paddywack Sit-Start *7a*
Sit-start on undercuts, reach to a sidepull and pop to the break. That's it.

31 Bright Eyes *7a+*
The direct finish to *Nick Knack Paddywack*. The same grade from standing and sitting.

32 The Knack Sit-Start *6b*
Sit-start to good holds below the crack of *The Knack*.

33 The Neck *7b*
The thin, crimpy wall just right of – and without – the wide crack. Finish on a good hold in the break. Needs a few pads. *Neil Travers*

34 Attitude Inspector *7a* ★
A fantastic, flying dyno up the arête. The tall will miss out on all the fun by doing it statically. Sit-start 7a+. *Mark Wilford/Derek Bolger*

35 Bad Attitude *6c* ✳
Crimpy flakes in the wall just left.

36 Bad Attitude Sit-Start *7b*
Hard climbing into the stand up, with poor footholds. *Neil Travers*

The Grazer

The next problems are on a collection of blocks just down from the edge.

37   Sitting Duck   6b   ★
Sit-start on the pedestal, out to the hold on the lip, swing right to the arête and finish up this. Brilliant.

38   The Grazer   6c+   ✳
Sit-start on the pedestal, out to the lip and roooccckk for the pocket.

39   Definitive 5.11   6c+
Tunnel into the gap between the boulders and work your way back out along the crack. Chimneying out the other side of the cave is *Definitive 5.10* – 6b+.

40   Definitive Burlesque   7b
From the depths of *Definitive 5.11*, link into *The Grazer*. Tiring.

41   6b
Rock onto the hanging slab.

42   More Cheese Gromit   7a   ✳
Start low without the footblocks and climb the roof, with use of the arête higher up. 6c with the footblocks. *Iain Farrar*

43   Pockets 'n' stuff   5+
Step off the boulder and climb the wall.

44   Life of Pie   7c
The direct on *Pockets 'n' Stuff*, starting from the floor, RH on good hold, LH on pocket. *Iain Farrar*

45   Pigs Make Nests   7c   ✳
The scrittley rib, started LH pinch and RH crimp, and climbed past a two finger pocket to a tricky top-out. 7c+ from a sit-start. *Iain Farrar*

46   High Arête   5+
The high arête.

Back on the edge.

47   *5*   ✳
The right arête on the left-hand side. 6a+ on the right.

48   *5*
The left arête on the right-hand side. 5+ on the left.

49   *6b*   ✳
The wall past the shelf.

50   **Lip Barmy**   *7b+*   ✳
Traverse the block just right of *The Knock* from the arête to finish up slopes just right of centre. Hard.

Burbage South Edge: Left Section

Past the historic *Parthian Shot* (E9) the edge starts to shrink, and comes into its own for the boulderer. If you hear someone refer to *'Burbage Earl'*, this is it. So called due to the similarity in rock quality and problem style with *Earl Crag* in Yorkshire.

The Alliance

1 Classic Arête Problem *7a* ✳
Start on the front face and move up and left onto the left-hand side of the arête early on to finish. Started up on the left it's a 5.

2 Friar's Wall *4*
The back wall.

3 The Alliance *7a* ★
Great double arête. Highball. 7b from a sit-start. *Pete Oxley*

4 Fried Chicken *6b*
On the small block in front of *The Alliance*, sit-start on the right and swing left to finish.

5 The Wrestle *6b*
The centre of the narrow buttress. Poor.

6 Sweet Arête *6a*
The arête.

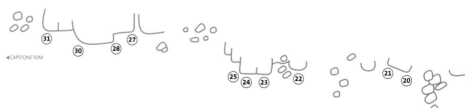

◄CAPSTONE 50M

7   Eating Out   *6c*   ✳
Climb the slab side of the arête, avoiding the jammed block (tricky).

8   Home Cooking   *7a*   ✳
Just left, the double arêtes give more fridge-hugging above a poor landing. Rock right onto the slab high up to finish. Highball. *Johnny Dawes*

9   Sublime Indifference   *5+*
The centre of the wall.

10   Clark's Route   *5*
The left arête.

>>

CENTRAL SECTION▶

KIM LEYLAND ON *ELECTRICAL STORM*   **PHOTO:** JOHN COEFIELD

Triangular Wall

On an attractive boulder just below the edge is:

11 Triangle Rib *6a* ★
The rib is a fine climb.

12 Triplet *6a+*
Sit-start right, and swing left to climb the arête on its left.

13 Triangular Wall *7a*
The lovely, rippled triangular wall is a gem from a sit-start.

14 Trident *6a*
The left arête.

The Rib

Back on the edge:

15 Desparête *7b* ★
The immaculate double arête feature formed by the right arête of the groove and the arête right again. Highball. The groove to the left is a famous project – *The Impossible Groove*.

16 Brap Scallion *6b+*
The left arête. The first move is the crux so no jump starts. *Jon Fullwood*

17 The Rib *7b+* ★
Tenuous climbing up the fine quarried rib, with a final slap to a jug. *John Welford*

18 A Moveable Feast *7b*
Sit-start the steep side of the leaning blunt arête 7m left of *The Rib*. Easier for the tall. The left arête on the front of the block is 6a. *Andy Banks*

19 Intense *8a*
Jump-start to a high right-hand sidepull and snatch to the top. Stacking mats to reach the high holds is much easier. Awaits the obvious sit-start from the slot. *Jerry Moffatt*

20 I'm Tense *7b*
From the low pocket, head up and left via an undercut and sidepull. *Mo Overfield*

21 Flat Wall Dyno *6c*
Big pulls between flat holds. The rib to the right is 5+ with the same finish.

22 Pocket Wall   6b
Pocket to sloping break. 7b+ from sitting at an undercut. A left hand sit-start is 7a.

23 5+
Dyno from the rail.

24 Fuji Heavy Industries   7a+
An awkward sit-start to the right-hand side of the arête. 6b from standing. *John Welford*

25 Kodak Lightweight Service Sector   6c
The same arête on its left-hand side from a sit-start.

26 Ronnie's Rib   7a
Sit-start the rib right of Little Rascal. *Jamie Lilleman*

27 Little Rascal   7a   ★
The groove is tremendous. Escape right from the sloping ledge. *Johnny Dawes*

28 Little Rascal Sit-Start   8a   ✳
Sit-start the crack to gain the stand-up. The thinnest of mats to start at this grade. Every udge up you get reduces the difficulty. *Neil Travers*

29 Dirty Rascal   7a
The left arete of the block to the break. Bad Landing. *Jamie Lilleman*

30 Dizzie Rascal   5+
The undercut slabby arête to the left. Bad Landing.

31 What a Way to Spend Easter   6c   ✳
The centre of the hemmed in slab, halfway between *Little Rascal* and *The Capstone*.

The Capstone
50m past *Little Rascal* is a capstone. Two problems, for those who have done everything else. See overview topo on p123.

32 The Whippet   6c+
Span from the break to the lip, and lock 'n' grovel to the top – no arête. *John Welford*

33 The Flat Cap   7a+
On the opposite, north-facing side, starting from the lowest part of the capstone. Traverse the lip left with a variety of heel hooks, shuffle moves and bunch-ups, to a top-out on the highest part of the block. *John Welford*

Burbage South Boulders

The Burbage South Boulders provide one of the friendliest circuits in the Peak –
and all on 'proper' boulders. There are stacks of easy problems, all with good
landings, and the occasional harder problem tucked in between them.
The boulders are in a beautiful setting at the bottom of the
Burbage Valley, sheltered from the worst of the winds.

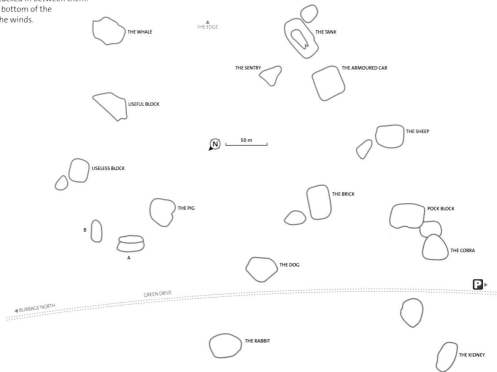

THE WHALE

THE EDGE

THE TANK

THE SENTRY

THE ARMOURED CAR

USEFUL BLOCK

THE SHEEP

N   50 m

USELESS BLOCK

THE BRICK

POCK BLOCK

THE PIG

B

THE COBRA

A

THE DOG

GREEN DRIVE

P

◄ BURBAGE NORTH

THE RABBIT

THE KIDNEY

The Kidney (see photo overleaf)

1 4+
The slab and hanging crack.

2 5
The right-hand crack.

3 5+
A delicate traverse. Start on the extreme left and traverse rightwards, walking your feet along the bottom of the slab, to finish up the right-hand crack. The traverse can be continued rightwards, but quickly gets much trickier.

The Cobra

4 The Cobra 5 ✳
A lovely traverse, starting on the right, and heading left under the nose.

5 5+ ✳
Mantel over the nose – watch your back on the boulder behind.

6 3
Around the other side of this block are some more nice 3s.

Pock Block

7 Puck 5+ ✳
The blunt arête is climbed on shallow dishes. A tasty sit-start is 7a+.

8 Pock 5 ★
A classic wall climb up bullet hole 'pocks'. A good 6c from sitting.

9 Pick 3+
The blunt arête on big sandy scallops, starting from the rock platform.

10 Pock Man 5+ ★
The precarious slab.

11 7a ✳
Tricksome slab – work up the left side of the scoop.

12 4
Mantel onto the slot.

The Sheep

13 The Shearing 5 ✳
Climb the arête on its left.

14 The Sheep 6c+ ★
The curving crack and slopey pocket. Superb.

15 The Sheep Assis 7b+
It's much harder from sitting.

16 Sickle Crack 6c
The Sheep left-hand. Layback the crack on the left with help from slopers on the arête. 7a from sitting.

17 Talk to Me Martin 7b+
A painful pull using the small edge. The rumoured problem to the left is just that, as is the sit-start. *Johnny Dawes*

The Armoured Car

18 4+
The wall right of the arête.

19 3+
The arête and flakes.

20 5 ✳
The short wall just right of centre has one of the nicest pebble holds on grit.

21 5
The wall left again.

22 5+ ✳
Traverse the face leftwards from the right arête.

The Sentry

23 Sentry Arête 6b ✳
The big arête on the right side.

24 Sentry Left 4
The same arête on the left.

The Tank

25 Chieftain 5 ★
The delightful rib.

26 6a+ ✳
Jump to the hold and top it out.

27 Panzer 6b+
Traverse the top of the block from left to right, shedding skin as you go.

28 5 ✳
The big flake. From sitting.

29 Tiger 6b ★
Classic slap from sidepulls to incut hold above. Barely discernible variants exist to the left and right at slightly harder grades.

30 5
Sit-start the small steep block to the right.

The Brick

31 Crash 'n' Gurn 7a
From a sit-start, pull on with a large undercut and a mono, and dyno to the often puddle-filled scoop. *Dave Norton*

32 6c
The slotted arête all the way on the right from a sit-start.

33 4+ ✳
The slotted arête on its left. 6a and a tricky classic from a sit-start.

34 4
The centre of the pock-marked wall.

35 4+ ✳
The arête. Climbed on the right. 4 on the left.

36 4+
The slab just left of the arête.

37 5
The slab just right of centre.

38 4+
The central slab. Those without a bit of reach may find it harder.

39 4+
The wall just right of the arête.

40 3+
The arête. Also a popular descent off the boulder, so watch out!

41 4+
The back wall of the block.

42 5+ ✳
The steep arête on the boulder just next to *The Brick*. 6b from a sit-start.

43 3+
Any which way up the slab.

The Dog

44 Dog Pound 7a
Sit-start and make a rising traverse leftwards past the slopping break and into the good pocket on *Dog Sit* and up. No footblock. *Andy Banks*

45 Dog Sit 7a ✳
Sit-start. Snatch up edges and dishes. The footblock is in at this grade.

46 Dog Jump 6a ✳
Jump to the edge and top-out.

47 Doggystyle 6a+
Traverse the rising edge of the boulder from a sit-start.

48 Dog's Arse 4+ ✳
The elephant's arse/bum feature. Sit-start and climb the crack on either the right at 7b or the left at 7a.

The Rabbit

49   Bugs   5
The short blunt arête, climbed on the right. An eliminate taking the arête straight on is 6a – *Bunny*.

50   5
The bulge to the left, via the edge.

51   5
A reachy arête.

The Pig

52   Little Pig   7c   ✳
From a sit-start on thin pockets, slap up the rounded arête to finish via a mono. Lovely moves. *John Welford*

53   Bacon Foot   6a+
The bulge right of the scoop.

54   The Trough   3+
Pull into the scoop and occasional puddle from low.

55   The Basin   5
Pull over into the bowl just left.

56   5+
The small slab, hidden in plain sight on a low boulder near the *Pig Block*.

A

57   5+
The back arête on the next boulder along, climbed on the left. 6a+ on the right.

B

58   6a
Left side of the arête.

59   3+
Scallops and rib.

The Useless Block

60   5+
An inelegant mantel onto the top.

61   4+
The blunt arête is easiest on its left.

62   5
Wall and pebbles.

63   4+
The slab and arête on the other side of the gap between the boulders.

The Useful Block

64   4+
The small rib. The short crack just left with the arête is 4+.

65   Peasy Flake   3+   ✳
The crack.

66   Easy Flake   3
The next crack right. An eliminate line climbs the wall between the two cracks – 5+.

67   Useful Slab   5+   ★
The slab and right-hand flake. Very good. An eliminate up the scoop without cracks is 6a.

68   Careful Arête   6a
The sharp quarried arête on the left side.

69   Useful Arête   5+   ✳
The sharp arête on the right side. Classic.

70   It Hurts   6b
The wall on crimpy edges.

The Whale

71   5
Rising rightwards line along the arête/top of the block.

72   5
The wall past a pocket.

73   5
The wall past a break.

Burbage West

The hard climber's grit crag of choice. This series of shady buttresses of perfect gritstone, quietly facing out across to the crowds at *Burbage North*, keeps calling the dedicated boulderer back time and time again.

Approach

From the main car park at *Burbage Bridge* cross over the stile. Either walk along the top of the edge, dropping down left after about 200m, or drop down left straight away, then head slightly up right past some boggy ground – either way brings you to some world-class problems.

Conditions

A super-useful crag. There is often a wind from the west, which, in the depths of winter, can make climbing at Stanage or other areas at *Burbage* unbearable. In these conditions you can battle from the car in a freezing gale and climb in shelter at *Burbage West* with the wind rattling overhead. The wind can sometimes blow rain over, rather than onto, the crag, which is a bonus.

Westworld

The first compact buttress reached from the car park. Below *Westworld*, on an isolated block just above the stream, is a worthwhile problem:

Countdown *7b*
The vague rib on the downhill side of the boulder from sitting. *Tim Marsh*

1 **Ledge Wall** *4+*

2 **Right Arête** *6a+*
The arête, although it often has a wet streak. Now try it on the left (6a)

3 **Not Westworld** *6b+* ✳
The wall just left of the arête, undercutting to the break. Harder if you can't reach.

4 **Westworld** *8a* ★
The wall just left again, undercutting to the break – desperate. Possibly 7c+ for tall people. The sit-start is 8a+. *Jason Myers*

5 **Blazing 48s** *8a* ✳
Bullet hole crimping on the edge of skin strength left of *Westworld*. No jump starts. *Jerry Moffatt*

6 **Scooter** *6b*
The left arête from standing.

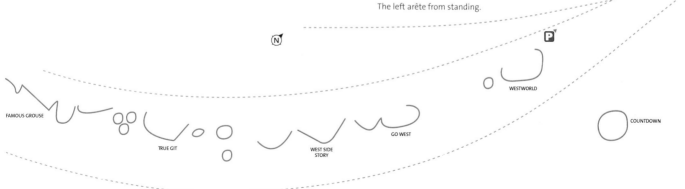

Go West Area

7 The Nose   7a   ★
The undercut nose on the right-hand side of the buttress, from low. Slightly harder for the short, and slightly easier for the tall. *Martin Veale*

8 The Nostril   7a+
Start as for *The Nose* before moving left to climb the hanging arête using a sadly chipped hold.

9 Go West   6a+   ✳
Easy when you know how – the groove up the right-hand side of the buttress.

10 4+

11 Left Arête   5

12 The Traverse   7b
From right to left along the vague low break. Worth being short.

13 6b
The middle traverse line.

14 Western Eyes   7c+   ★
The blunt overhung arête, from a low start at the back. Highball hugging. *Zaff Ali*

15 Long's Lock   7a+
A stiff pull up the hanging wall. Jump off from the break. A low start from a jug right of the crack, to the left, is 7b+. *Adam Long*

DAVE NORTON ON *COUNTDOWN*   PHOTO: ADAM LONG

West Side Story

16 Rumblefish *4+* ✳
The high arête. Start on the left, finish on the right.

17 West Side Story *7b+* ★
Classic technical wall, with a highball finish. Lots of methods, which incidentally all top-out. Traversing off half way up the problem is just that. Top of the grade since the demise of a useful pebble. *John Allen*

18 Ron-side Force-it *7b*
This variation on *West Side Story* has grown a name. Reach out right from the start of *West Side Story* then back left taking the flake as a press.

6b+
Traverse under *West Side Story* from left to right.

19 Crow Man Groove *3+* ✳
Pleasant climbing up the groove.

20 El Regallo del Mocho *7a+*
The thin wall between *Crow Man* and the groove. *Ben Bransby*

21 Crow Man *5* ✳
The lovely arête, on it's right. Nice, but sometimes green. Harder and freakier on the left. *Mark Stokes*

22 Jason's Mono Problem *7a*
The wall left of the arête, via a mono. A similar line just right is 7a+. *Jason Myers*

75m along the edge is an isolated nose on a low block.

23 True Git *7b* ✳
From the low break reach up to the vague pinch on the nose and slap to the top (hard) – or use some guile and casually reach the top. Much better than it looks. *John Welford*

24 Vague Nose *6b+*
The bulge to the left.

Famous Grouse Area

Another 75m along the edge is the excellent *Famous Grouse* area.

25 Square Arête *5*
The short arête.

26 Famous Grouse *7b+* ★
The small, hanging slab and arête. 7c from a sit-start. *John Welford*

27 West End Girls *5+* ✳
The groove line.

28 Spartacus *7c*
A big span, a dyno or levitation lands you on the jug high on the wall left of *Famous Grouse*. From here you declare loudly to the hopefully deserted valley: *I'm Spartacus!* Otherwise no tick. *John Welford*

29 Brian *7a*
A right-hand start to *Spartacus*.

30 Breakfast *7a* ★
Sit-start the right-hand side of the hanging arête. Classic. 7b without the foot block. *Martin Veale*

31 *4+*
The chipped wall left of the arête.

32 *4*
The slabby left arête.

Down the hill is a big fat lump of grit which promises much, but sadly delivers very little.

IAN THOMAS ON *BREAKFAST* **PHOTO:** TIM RUSSON

JOE LE SAGE ON *RON-SIDE FORCE-IT* · PHOTO: ADAM LONG

Higgar Tor

Higgar Tor is yet another of the superb venues to be enjoyed in the *Burbage Valley*. The bouldering here is a mix of the gentle and hardcore sides of Peak grit, with virtually all problems demanding clean technique in return for success. The majority of the bouldering exists on the east-facing ridge below the tourist path that runs over the top of the Tor.

Approach

Park in the lay-bys just beyond Fiddler's Elbow and walk through the small gate opposite. Approaching up the steps from the car, the first climbing is just over the edge on the left as you reach the summit.

Conditions

Facing mainly east, the bouldering here provides shelter from the sun on warmer evenings, particularly if there's a northerly or easterly blowing. It also provides shelter from westerlies. The stuff on the southern edge is a little more exposed.

Excreta Buttress

1 Dirty Higgar 6c
The low prow, 20m right of *Piss*, from a lying-down start.

2 Piss 7b ★
Start hanging the nose and head up using the sloper on the right. No heels on the ledge out left. *Ben Moon*

3 Shit 7b+ ✳
Not shit. Climb out from the back of the cave to finish up *Piss*. *Richie Patterson*

Hemline 7a+ ✳
Start up *Shit*, finish via *Sick*. Traversing the ledges is cheating! *Rich Heap*

4 Sick 6a ✳
Dyno or mantel the ledge.

5 Quintessential Higgarisms 7a
The blunt arete.

The next problems are 5m left.

6 7c
Right of *Pooh*. Sit-start with both hands in the break and gain the top via a tiny edge. Much easier for the tall. No arête, 7a with a heel in the break at the arête. *Mike Adams*

7 Pooh 7b ✳
Dyno from the low break to the top, without using the arête.

8 Winnie The... 6a
The left side of the arête from sitting.

>>

Left again is:

9   **5**
The side wall past the diagonal break.

10   **The Arête**   *7a+*   ★
The obvious arête to a slopey finish, climbed on its right. The lower rock, despite stabilisation work, is unfortunately very crumbly – be gentle.

11   **The Arête Left-Hand**   *6b*
The same arête, this time on the left.

12   **Krush Regime**   *7a+*   ✳
Climb the centre of the big wall on the buttress immediately left of *The Arête*. It has tiny holds and a hard start. *Greg Griffith*

13   **Harry's Hole**   *6c+*
Dynamic moves up the steep wall left of *Krush Regime*. The arête to the left is a highball 3+. *Harry Pennells*

DAVE NORTON ON *TALL ARÊTE*   **PHOTO:** JOHN COEFIELD

Short Walls

Around the corner the angle eases off and the edge hosts a selection of great low-mid grade problems on good rock. Many blur the line between problems, highballs and routes, so we've left some for you to discover for yourself.

14 Triple Cracks *4*

15 Rounded Arête *4*
The wall and arête from standing.

16 Rounded Wall *6b*
Sit-start the wall at a flake, and climb it without the arête.

17 Triple Cracks Arête *6a+* ✳
The big arête from a sit-start, with the difficulties low down.

18 Scratchy Bun Right *6a*
The front face of the small arête.

19 Scratchy Bun Left *6c* ★
Sit-start the left side. Classic.

20 Tall Arête *5* ✳
The big arête on its right with a fingery first move. A technical sit-start is 6b.

21 Ledge Wall *5+*
The side wall. A fingery sit-start is 6b+.

22 *6a+*
The tall, thin pillar is tricky. Sit-start.

The taller buttress to the left gives some good, cracky micro-routes. Just left of the tallest section is a leaning slab above a diagonal landing – 4. 50m further on is:

23 Bum Flake *6a*
Sit-start the flake crack.

24 Green Fingers *6b+*
The fingery, green wall.

Up and behind the last two problems, almost on the plateau is a small, very sharp arête.

25 Seventy Degrees *6b+* ✳
The sharp arête from a sit-start at the break.

26 Stinky Piss Wall *6a*
Over to the right is an attractive arch in a narrow gully, that sadly stinks of piss. From a low start in the break trend right to the arch and the better break above. Top-out direct. Decent moves. An obvious left-hand version is 6a+.

Higgar Tor South

Continue around the Tor and you'll reach the point at which the path drops down towards *Carl Wark* – the fortress-come-buttress due south (see p107 and p154). There are various jumbled blocks here and we've chosen not to describe every single problem in graphic detail. The main problems are:

27   *6a+*
The jutting, perched prow at the right-hand side of the small wall.

28   *4+*
The centre of the wall.

29   **Like Pommel**   *6b*   ✳
The hanging nose direct. A bit like *Pommel* at *Brimham Rocks*.

20m right is a big slab.

30   **The Big Slab**   *5*   ★
Big, freaky and impossible to miss. An essential and scary Higgar tick. See photo opposite.

The Leaning Block

The final problems are on the famous Leaning Block itself.

31   **Witness the Gritness**   *7a*   ✳
The wall right of *The Rasp*. Gain an undercut and reach through to a sloper and better finishing holds. *Morpho*

32   **Block & Tackle Direct**   *7b+*
The left arête of the buttress with a big finishing move to a jug.

33   **Higgar Traverse**   *7b+*
Traverse the face in either direction.

Burbage Area
Bits & Bobs

As well as the main *Burbage* venues, there's a number of outlying boulders and buttresses scattered across the moorland that are worth a visit. *Carl Wark*, *The Sheepfold* and *Guplets Wall* are in the Burbage Valley itself, situated down the hill from *Higgar Tor*. *Ox Stones* and *Houndkirk Tor* are up on Houndkirk Moor, back over towards Sheffield.

Access and Approach

Guplets Wall, *Carl Wark* and *The Sheepfold* don't have direct, easy access. *The Sheepfold* almost does, unless someone has parked in the sole parking spot. The easiest approach to *Guplets Wall* is to park in the small parking area at the bottom of the Green Drive, walk down the road (A6187) and cross the stile on the bend at the jutting *Toad's Mouth* boulder. Follow the path north along the hillside facing Burbage South for about 300m. For *Carl Wark*, either continue towards the fort from *Guplets Wall* and loop around the western, non-valley, side to the northeastern side where the problems are located, or approach down the path from the southern side of *Higgar Tor*. For *The Sheepfold*, there is very limited (one car) parking at the bend under the *Leaning Block* on the back road for *Higgar Tor*, about 600m further down the road from the main Higgar parking. Follow the good track up and right, heading across to the buttress when it comes into view. Alternatively, if someone has already bagged the parking spot, there are lay-bys back up the road, followed by a hop over a stile and a wander back along paths parallel to the road to the track.

Guplets Wall, Carl Wark & The Sheepfold

Three venues, 11 problems, from 6b+ to 7c+. These esoteric little gems, tucked away on the western side of the *Burbage Valley*, pack in the quality and the difficulty. They don't get a lot of traffic so be prepared to do a little lichen cleaning.

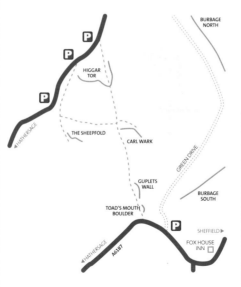

Guplets Wall

On the opposite side of *Burbage Brook*, at the bottom of the valley, around 150m above the brook is an isolated little wall.

1   **Guplets on Toast Sit-Start**   *7b+*   ★
    A sit-start to the bulging left-hand wall, on dishes. Watch that top-out and don't drift right to the arête.
    John Welford

2   **Darkstar**   *7c+*
    The very highball wall right of *Guplets*. E6 6c ish. The crux is the lower section, but the top-out was checked on a shunt before the first ascent. An overlooked problem with good climbing.
    John Welford

Back towards the main road is a small prow, about 30m north from the toad's mouth shaped block on the bend – 6c.

Carl Wark

Opposite Burbage South and across the saddle-shaped piece of land lies the Iron Age fort that is *Carl Wark*. In the jumble of blocks around the base are four more documented problems, the first three of which are on the main buttress which contains the route *Lost World* (E6).

1 Not Green Flag *7a* ✳
The wall just right of the left-hand arête on the *Lost World* buttress. From the break, head up to lush slopers and the top.

2 Green Flag *7b+*
The wall right again from a break and sidepulls, to undercuts and the top. *Richie Patterson*

3 Rugosity Dinks *6c*
The wall just left of the crack on good edges, with a pop for the top.

4 J-Warkin' Sit Start *6c* ✳
Around 30m right of the *Lost World* buttress is a small wall with a rib up its left side, situated on a terrace. Sit-start at the break and climb the rib with the help of some face holds on the right. *Dave Parry*

The Sheepfold

This isolated little buttress, next to the large dry stone walled enclosure, sits neatly between *Higgar Tor* and *Millstone Edge*.

1 Jean Marie *7a+*
The left side of the buttress. Scrittly and very close to the neighbouring block. *John Welford*

2 Just Walkin' *7a* ✳
A great little wall climb. The left side of the front of the buttress to a shallow scoop on the top. *Jon Barton*

3 Sean *7a*
Another good one. Straight up the middle of the buttress. Similar but slightly harder than the previous problem. *John Welford*

4 Here Be Dragons *6b+* ✳
Span out to the huge hueco on the lip, from the large flake on the right. Jumping to the hueco rather than using a heel/toe adds a few grades. *Mark Hundleby*

5 Roofless People *7a*
Behind and to the left of the main wall is a small roof. Sit-start and follow creaky flakes to a rightwards exit. *Robin Mueller*

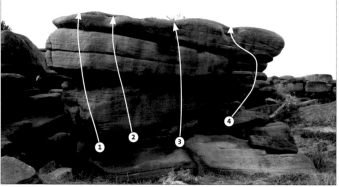

Houndkirk Tor

Hidden away over the back of the Burbage Valley, the moorland of Houndkirk is a far cry from the crowds at Burbage. It's a decent circuit, and definitely worth a trip if you're operating in the Font 6's. Most of the problems were developed by *Keith Turton* and *Neil Barden* in the 1990s. None of the problems are particularly high, and it's one of those crags where the top-outs tend to have a conveniently-placed good hold, just where you want one. No grovelling here. The rock is generally of good quality and stays relatively clean, even though it faces north and sees little action (at time of writing). It would be worth carrying a brush just in case. The crag can take a day or two to dry after wet weather.

Access and Approach

Parking is available for about two cars in a small lay-by on the approach to *Parson House Outdoor Pursuits Centre* on the A6187 Hathersage Road, approx. 500m back towards Sheffield from the Fox House Inn. The lay-by is just off the main road, and no further parking is available further up the lane (private). (Alternative parking can be found at the side of the A6187, just up from the Fox House Inn, as for Burbage South.) Walk up the lane towards the centre, but turn right through a gate signed Public Byway. Follow this wide, rocky track uphill for about 500m and, as it drops right, look for a path on the right. Take this. The *Boomerang Boulder* is up to the right of the path after 100m, and the main edge is directly ahead. Approach both through the heather.

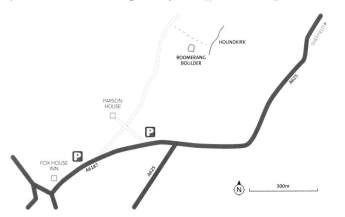

Boomerang Boulder

The overhanging prow, projecting out of the ground in front of a very small edge to the right of the path.

1   *3*   ✳
Around the back of the block, mantel the ledge with the aid of the left arête. 4+ from a sit-start.

2   **Kanga**   *4*
The slabby right sidewall of the prow, using both arêtes.

3   **Roo**   *5+*   ✳
The steep right arête, on its left-hand side. Rock right to finish. A good problem.

4   **Tigger Too**   *6a+*
Climb the prow front on, using both arêtes to an ungainly, direct top-out.

5   *5+*
The left arête, eliminating the back edge.

The Edge

The next problems are situated on the small edge to the left.

6   Not the North Pole   6b+
Sit-start the blunt arête and make awkward moves over the bulge. There's a good hold around the arête, but it doesn't really help as it's nigh on impossible not to dab the blocks to the right.

7   An Expotition   6b+   ✳
A good problem that sit-starts at the left-hand side of the shelf (left-hand sidepull, right-hand sloper), makes a big pull to an edge above and then grabs the top.

8   3
The short, dirty arête.

9   4+
The crack, climbed mainly on big holds either side of it. *Piglet's Too Short* (5) is an eliminate span on jugs up the wall immediately left.

10   4
The all-too-brief leaning crack right of the arête. Add value from a sit-start by logically eliminating hand and foot holds right of the crack – 6a+.

11   Friends and Relations   6b+   ✳
Sit-start the arête. The tick of the crag.

12   4+
The wall left of the arête. Effectively a mantel problem.

>>

13 *6a*
Sit-start the undercut arête, avoiding the larger foot ramp out right. 4 from standing.

14 An Uncoloured-In Problem *6b*
Sit-start under the overlaps left of the arête and pull direct up sloping edges without the juggy ramp.

15 3
The juggy ramp. 5+ from a sit-start in the previous problem.

16 Green Slab *4+*
Just left is a tall green slab, with pock marks up the centre.

17 4
The wall past a slotty pocket.

18 4+
The crack in the niche isn't as bad as it looks thanks to holds either side.

19 The H.O.P. *5+*
The flake/crack in the blunt arête on the right-hand side of the slab.

20 Way of the Spaniel *6c* ✳
Direct up the centre of the slab, without the right or left cracks.

21 Eeyore *6a+*
The flake/crack line on the left-hand side of the slab.

22 A Stoutness Exercise *6b*
The left-hand side of the leaning arête from a sit-start.

Houndkirk Tor proper is the rocky outcrop over to the northeast. It promises much but delivers little. The only thing of note is *Made in Sheffield*, a leaning roof in a pit, midway along the edge. Start both hands at the back and climb direct to mantel out the front – 7a+. See photo opposite. *Jamie Lilleman*

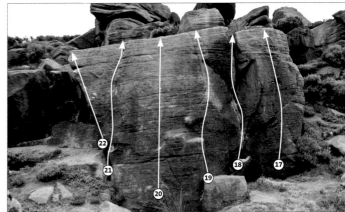

The Ox Stones

It might be *Ox Stones*, plural, but the climbing of note here is found on the largest of several blobs of grit, dumped unceremoniously on the moor behind the *Burbage Valley*. There's only a handful of problems to go at, yet the *Ox Stones* offer a little bit of welcome solitude on a spring or summer evening. The views back over Sheffield and South Yorkshire aren't bad either.

Access and Approach

If approaching from Sheffield along the Ringinglow Road, drive through the village of Ringinglow and continue towards *Burbage* with the plantation to your left. As the plantation ends there's a lay-by on your right – don't park here but in the next one on the right at a bend, just before the cattle grid. Cross the road and the stile opposite. Follow a thin path over the moor, and continue as it bears back towards Sheffield. The rocks soon come into view. See *Burbage Valley* overview map on p107.

1   5
Left of the largest blob is a hanging lip. Monkey along this in either direction.

2   4+
On the main block, start at a cutaway and pull directly up and over to an awkward, gritty top-out.

3   5+
Sit-start at the left-hand side of the flake/shield and pull through the roof, passing a sloping boss.

4   5+ ✳
Sit-start at the right-hand side of the flake and pull through the roof on big holds, with a crux section passing the sloping shelf above. A good problem.

5   4+
Sit-start at a pair of attractive 'cup' holds and climb the wall/slab above. Don't veer too far right. An easier problem climbs the wall to the right but it's not very good.

6   5
Start as for problem 5 and traverse the lip left to finish up problem 2. Variations abound.

The smaller blocks visible 70m or so back towards the plantation promise and offer little. The northwest arête is worthwhile:

7   4+
The short, ledgy arête just about warrants the jog over from the main blocks.

JAMIE LILLEMAN ON *MADE IN SHEFFIELD* · PHOTO: LILLEMAN COLLECTION

Millstone Area

An extensive area comprising big and small crags and bouldering spots with many classic problems. The varied nature of the rock – quarried or natural, edges or boulders – makes for equally varied climbing: Millstone deals in angular, manmade testpieces such as the arête of *Technical Master*, or the corner of *Green Death Super Direct*; the *Secret Garden* and *Mother's Pet Rock* are quite the opposite, with powerful sloper problems that will test your grit feel to the limit; *Mother Cap* gives tall, natural walls on a wonderfully isolated block; and *Owler Tor* is a heavenly collection of fine, low – grades and proportions – problems, perfect for a spring or autumn evening.

Access and Approach

All the areas are accessed from the large Surprise View car park (pay and display), which is off the A6187 between Hathersage and the Fox House Inn, on the *Burbage* side of the apex of the hill. See individual areas for approaches.

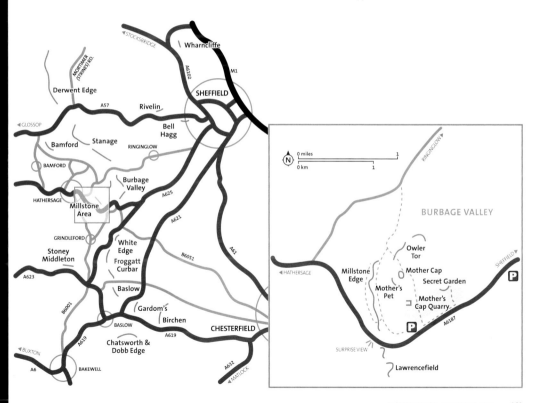

Millstone Edge

Tall angular walls, edges and corners, all thanks to the quarrymen, make up this big, impressive crag. Of course it's the domain of the route climber, but there's enough here to justify a trip by the dedicated boulderer, particularly if you're after ticking a couple of the Peak's technical classics: *Technical Master*, and *Green Death Super Direct*.

Access and Approach

Pass through the gate out of the northwestern end of the car park and follow the path diagonally across the moor, away from the road. As the path meets another path, cross the stile ahead and drop down to join the wide track which runs under the crag. Head right, uphill, to the bouldering. The first problem is in the back of the bay that you pass through before joining the wide track.

Keep an eye out for and adhere to any restrictions that might be in place due to nesting birds.

The first problem is on the highball slab, just before the first bay, passed on the approach described opposite.

1   **Helping Hands**   *6a*
    The slab on the left of the wall, left of the cracks. The slab just right, left of the cracks, is *Annabella Superstella* – 6b.

2   **The Keyhole Traverse**   *7b+*
    A stamina exercise for those confused about their place in life; start on the left of the huge wall and traverse as far right and duck under as many ropes as your embarrassment allows.

3   **Pot Leg Wall**   *5+*
    Peg scars up the wall right of *Keyhole Cave*.

100m further on is the *Embankment*.

4   **Seventies Style Wall**   *6b+*
    Crimp up the wall, old skool style.

5   **Little Lotto Arête**   *5*   ✳
    The sharp arête with the slot.

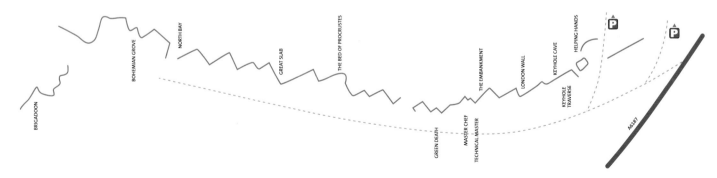

6 **Tip Top** *7c*
The thin left-hand crack, finishing on a good rail at 4m. *Ryan Pasquill*

7 **Technical Master** *6b* ★
Climbed on the front face, the arête is a classic Peak testpiece. It's quite a bit harder on its left-hand side, without the crack, but 6c with it. See photo on p167. *John Allen*

8 **Technical Baiter** *5c* ✳
The flake and groove just left. The way up is also the way down, which is a consideration. (You can walk off the ledge too, but it takes ages.)

9 **Master Chef** *7b* ✳
The rib/arête just left of *Technical Baiter*. The sit-start is a tricky 7c. Escape from the ledge as per the previous problem. *Johnny Dawes/Mo Overfield*

10 **Green Death Start** *6c* ★
Edges in the wall left of the corner lead right to good sloping holds. See topo overleaf.

>>

11 Green Death Super Direct *7b* ★
Unique, smearing, stemming, weirdness up the corner to a good edge on the left wall.
Or keep going a bit to a good hold higher in the groove −7b+.

12 Cherry Bank Road *7c+*
The square-cut arête around and left of *Green Death* is climbed predominantly on
its left-hand side avoiding the shothole around right. Steady moves at the start
are followed by hard, tenuous arête work to finish at a good edge at 5m. 7a with
the shothole. *Iain Farrar*

13 The Bed of Procrustes *8a+* ★
The stunning, tall leaning wall below the classic route *Twikker*. Pull on direct (no bridging
in from the right) and climb the wall past a diabolical undercut and the attractive ramp
feature. Easier with a jump start. Impressive stuff. *Iain Farrar*

At the far north bay of the quarry is the tall back wall.

14 Bohemian Grove *8a*
Start just right of the chimney groove and climb on small crimps, eliminating the arête,
to good holds at 4m. *Mo Overfield*

Over to the left are some shorter walls and arêtes. At the left-hand side is:

15 Brigadoon *7b* ✳
The fingery wall, climbed on crimps and undercuts to a high-ish finish. *John Welford*

Mother Cap

Mother Cap is the squat, square tor of rock that can be seen from miles around on the hill above *Millstone*. Most of the problems were originally climbed as routes that finished over the capstone on the top. Climbed as boulder problems they finish on the ledge below, so shuffle/jump off as best you can.

Access and Approach

Follow the walkers up the path that exits north from the centre of the Surprise View car park, straight up the hill, after which *Mother Cap* will be unmissable.

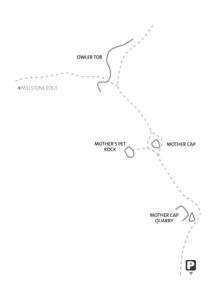

1 **Ink Cap** *4* ✳
The juggy arête. Traversing the juggy break rightwards is 4+.

2 **Milk Cap** *4+*
The wide crack right of centre on the south face.

3 *6a*
The wall left of the crack.

4 **Conan the Librarian** *6b+* ★
A classic; climb the centre of the south face on small, sloping breaks. Walk off right at the ledge. *Johnny Dawes*

5 **David** *7b* ✳
The wall left of *Conan* from the crack on tiny holds. Shuffle right at the break. *Richie Patterson*

6 **Oyster Cap** *6a+* ✳
The left arête of the south face.

7 **Elf Cap** *6b+*
The centre of the west face. Harrowing.

8 **Blue Cap** *5*
The left arête of the west face.

Mother's Pet Rock

A low-slung slug of perfect gritstone with a range of great problems all characterised by the mother of sloping top-outs. It's hidden about 50m to the left of *Mother Cap* as you approach from the Surprise View car park.

1 6b
The right-hand side of the left-hand arête.

2 6c ✳
Climb the front face using sloping pockets, finding these with your feet proves to be the crux.

3 Orca 7c
A tight line between the previous problem and *Mother's Pride*. Reachy. *Mike Adams*

4 Mother's Pride 7b+ ✳
Climb the centre of the wall to the sloping top. Harder for the short. *John Welford*

5 Pet Cemetery 7a+ ★
Don't let the big starting holds make you complacent. *Jon Fullwood*

6 6a+
Move onto the ledge from the left. Starting from *Pet Cemetery* is a classic 7a.

7 Top Shelf Mantel 7a
Mantel through the shelf right of centre. *Pots Win Prizes* is a mantel left of centre – 6b+.
Simon Wilson

8 6b
Move onto the right-hand side of the shelf from the low break. Direct from flakes under the roof is harder, 7a. *Simon Weill (Direct)*

9 Proper Grit 6c+
Attain the 'proper grit' finish from a low edge and small pocket. *Jon Fullwood*

10 Pets Win Prizes 7b ✳
Sit-start. Clever footwork may assist in climbing the right-most wall. Very good.
Jon Fullwood

11 Pet Whale 6c
The mid-height traverse, from left to right, finishing up problem 6. Curious moves with your legs stuck deep into the break.

PETS WIN PRIZES **PHOTO:** JON FULLWOOD

Mother Cap Quarry

Not as good as any of the other bouldering spots in the area. The tiny quarry is down to the left of the approach path before *Mother Cap* is reached. The quarry has a prominent natural boulder balanced on the edge and the first problems are on this.

1   *6b*
The wall left of the arête.

2   *6c*
The bulging arête just right.

3   *6c*
The right wall.

Down in the quarry itself, the wall starting just left of the arête and trending left is *Flat Cap*, 6a. Starting on the arête and drifting rightwards up the ramp features is *Dog Brush*, 6a. The centre of the wall right of the cracks is *Night Cap*, 6b+.

Owler Tor

Keep walking up the main track past *Mother Cap* and drop down just before the pinnacle of the edge. Welcome to *Owler Tor*. The bouldering is in an open, west-facing bay just south of the main pinnacle. From right to left as you look at the crag, the obvious clean arête and crack of problem number 4 is a good basecamp. Great problems from 3 – 7a+.

1 *3*
The fin-like arête just right of problem 2.

2 *5* ★
An excellent problem up the arête – a bit bouncy. Sit-start.

3 *5* ✳
A classy right-hand variant on the previous problem, swinging right for the big pocket.

4 **Golden Arête** *6b+* ★
A superb problem up the arête and crack to finish on the arête.

5 **Spider Crack** *7a+* ✳
Sit-start the crack, eliminating the arête, which bizarrely doesn't help much anyway. A good problem.

6 *4+*
A good one move wonder, up the wall, left of the arête.

7 **Sisyphus** *7a*
Sit-start the left-hand side of the arête and somehow gain the slot in the face.

8 *3*
On the back of the block is a short slabby wall. Climb the lovely right arête. A similar line just left past a flake is also 3. For a bit more fun, double dyno from the slabby wall to the jug on the wall opposite.

9 *4+*
The short arête is good if you just use holds on the arête. Has a good sit-start. The side wall is a good 4+.

10 *4*
The crack using everything.

11 *4*
The left arête.

12 *5+*
The right hand of two low roofs.

13 *6b* ✳
Start at the back of the low roof, reach out to the slopes and mantel to glory. A great little problem.

14 *6b*
Traverse under the roof from the right round the corner to the obvious top-out – ugly for all but the very short.

15 *3+*
The arête and undercut flake feature.

16 *5*
Good climbing up the left side of the arête, which turns into a route after the break.

17 *6a* ✳
The little crimpy wall is surprisingly technical.

18 *3+*
Good holds on the arête to the left.

19 *6b* ✳
A good problem up the crozzly wall of the block to the left, with a gritty top-out. Another problem climbs through the cutaway to the left, at a sketchy 6c.

20 *7a* ✳
50m around to the left, under the main crag, is a leaning, square-cut block with an overhanging, valley-facing face. Sit-start at a mean sidepull and two finger pocket, pull to another edge and get the top. Rough, painful rock.

There are other minor bits and bobs on the broken edge behind.

Secret Garden

Not much of a secret any more, the *Secret Garden* is home to some modern classic Peak problems. Developed relatively recently, most gaps are now plugged and there's great climbing here from Font 4 to 7c+. The climbing is brutal: the starts characterised by steep roofs, and followed by sloper-slapping above. Tenacity and good skin are pre-requisites for a good visit.

Access and Approach

Walk east out of the Surprise View car park, on the path parallel to the A6187 towards *Burbage*. As you reach the end of the wooded area on the left, the path breaks left and up into the trees, just opposite a metal milepost. The main area should be visible up and left of the path after 150m or so.

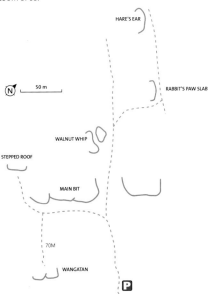

Main Bit

The first area of rock reached, on the left of the path.

1   *6b*
Sit-start, and move left, or direct slightly easier.

2   *6c* ✶
A great little problem. Sit-start the bulging arête. Straight up the wall, eliminating the arête is 7b.

3   *6a* ✶
Pockets and edges up the side wall.

4   *5+*
Pockets and crack up the wall. Also good as a sit-start and with eliminates – crack only, just pockets and so on.

5   *6b+*
Pull up and leftwards after starting with one hand under the roof and one on the lip.

6   *7a*
From the back of the roof use assorted slopes to gain the sloping top-out.

7   Zaff's Problem   *7b* ✶
From the back of the roof move out to the lip and try and match the poor sloper above before taking the small divot/pocket over the bulge to top-out. *Zaff Ali*

8   *7a+*
From the back of the roof, bail out to the lip and move left to take the rounded pocket with your left hand. A further left-hand variation takes the pocket/rib with the right hand – 7a+.

9   Beach Ball   *7a* ★
A thuggy classic, just right of the previous problem. Start as for that problem, and slap direct up slopers to finish.

10   *6b*
Just right of *Beach Ball*, with a big move from the holds on the lip to a hidden pocket over the bulge.

11   *5+* ✶
The right-facing crack.

12 *6c+*
Traverse the lip break/sloper leftwards from the crack to finish up problem 5, with your feet on the back wall. Completing this traverse footless is the almost mythical *Zippatricks*: grade – Very Hard.

13 *6c*
The faint groove from a sit-start. Better as a stand up, as the top-out is the best bit.

14 Nigel's Problem *7a+* ✳
Sit-start left of the arête, reach up and right for a pair of poor slopers and slap into the flake.

15 Left-Hand Man *7b+* ★
A brilliant sit-start problem. From the shelf, use holds on the arête to reach the top pocket with your right hand. *Ian Fitzpatrick*

Left-Hand Man Direct *7c+* ✳
Climb the wall left of centre direct to the pocket from a sit-start on the shelf, with no arête holds. *Rupert Davies*

16 Middle Man *7c*
A diagonal line starting at *Dick Williams* and crossing the face leftwards to join *Left-Hand Man* at the top pocket. *Ian Fitzpatrick*

17 Dick Williams *7b+* ★
One of the best problems of its grade on grit. From a sit-start on the shelf, climb the rounded bulging arête to a scary, sloping exit. *Zaff Ali*

18 5
The left-hand pocket line on the side wall.

19 4+ ✳
The right-hand pocket line.

The block over and right has a few lines: the bottom arête facing the road is 6c; the wall left is 6b+; the top arête is 6a; and the back wall is 5+.

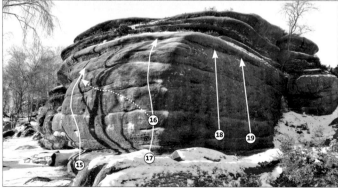

Walnut Whip

20m up and right of the main area is another block containing some good sit-start problems.

20 Hulley Pulley 7b+
Just left of the gap in the boulder is a short wall with some tiny pockets. Climb this from a sit-start. The grade depends on where you allow yourself to put your feet. Obviously bridging behind yourself will make the problem about 3+, but cunningly letting your feet drift around to the right will also reduce the grade. Being very strict makes it harder. *Tim Hulley*

21 Fireball 7b+
The slanting, rounded arête from a sit start. *Mick Adams*

22 Walnut Whip 6c ✳
The undercut, rounded arête from a sit start on ripples. Nice moves, but not many of them. Top-out over the funny egg thing.

Stepped Roof

Up and left of the main area is a great stepped roof with body-tension dependant problems on good and interesting holds. To some extent the problems described are a little arbitrary as the roof is covered in close-together holds, so all the problems mix and match a little.

23 6c ✳
The left-hand line. From jams move out to match the great sloping edge of the block, pop to a good hold in the break and top-out. *Richie Patterson*

24 6b+
The middle line. From a sidepull (right hand) and undercut or jam (left hand) move out to good slots in the break using a big span or other holds in the roof – top-out. *Richie Patterson*

25 7a+
The right-hand line. Start as problem 24, out to a slopey rib in roof (right hand), small holds in the roof (left hand) then again (left hand) to holds in the break right of the good slot. Control the swing and top-out.

26 7b+
Traverse below the lip on edges, pocket and slopers to top-out around the right-hand arête. *Zaff Ali*

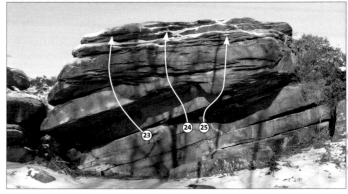

Rabbit's Paw Slab

Walk from the *Secret Garden* to the *Walnut Whip/Fireball* block, and bear diagonally right down towards the trees and jumbled blocks. This is the first block reached.

27   Rabbit's Paw   6b
The centre of the slab.

28   The Fur Side   4
The right arête.

Hare's Ear

Approach as for *Rabbit's Paw Slab*, but continue for a further 50m along the vague edge formed by the jumbled blocks.

29   Hare's Ear Left   6c   ✳
Rock from the starting jug out left, with heel on a cleaned foothold, to the top via an intermediate sloper if you need it.

30   Hare's Ear   7a
From the jug rail, get a good left hand edge and right hand up to a sloper out right. Top out with whatever you can reach.

Wangatan

70m below the left-hand end of *Secret Garden* is this lone block.

31   Wangatan   7b+
Sit-start the right arete to a slopey top-out. *Jamie Lilleman*

32   7a
Mantel through the sloping top to the left. Tough. *Kim Thompson*

Also of interest: *The Talented Mr Kiping* (7a) is up and right of *Hare's Ear*, facing the Burbage Valley, the left arête of a big block on pock marks. Crumbly rock so take care.

White Edge, Yarncliffe Quarry & Padley Gorge

White Edge is home to some decent roof problems and a few other bits and bobs. The potential for more problems is marred somewhat by the quality of the rock, some of which has a structural integrity that is only slightly better than cake.

Despite the fact that *Yarncliffe Quarry* has been padded out by including the start of an E6, this is really only a one-problem venue. In the trees and sheltered.

Padley Gorge is home to one excellent problem and a café – the 'fall back tick' if you like.

Access and Approach

For *White Edge* park in the lay-by just below The Grouse Inn on the A625, and take the signposted bridleway on the other side of the road across a field, through a gate, and up a bit more path. Where the path forks, there's a handy sign – turn right (or left for *Lodge Block*). The edge is surprisingly small and soon appears on your right. The easiest way to access the problems is from the path that runs above the edge.

For *Yarncliffe Quarry* park in a lay-by on the B6521, halfway between the Fox House Inn to the north and Grindleford to the south. Cross to the gate and follow the track to a clearing. The problems are on the striking sharp arête through the trees on the left.

For *Padley Gorge* turn off the B6521 road at the northern end of Grindleford, signposted for the railway station. Park in the car park at the bottom of the lane. Walk past the café, over the bridge and take the footpath on the right before the brook. *Mossatrocity* is about 100m up the path on the right.

Yarncliffe Quarry

There's a warm-up area in the main part of the quarry through the trees and down the slope to the left. A steep, stepped wall on which some very easy juggy problems can be found to get the blood flowing.

1   **Crème de la Crème**   *7a+*
The left-hand side of the arête, above a poor landing, is the problem start to the E6 route. *Ron Fawcett*

2   **THEM!**   *7c*
The right-hand side of the arête has a hard jump-start that favours the tall and lucky. This is followed by powerful pulls to the ledge above. It has been done without the ancient bolt head used on the first ascent. We're not sure this warrants a new name but anyway it's called *US!* – 7c+. *Mo Overfield*

Padley Gorge

Mossatrocity   *7c*   ★
Discovered and put up by *Ben Thompson* in 2008, *Mossatrocity* is now one of the most sought after ticks at its grade on grit, the very definition of 'classic'. Sit-start back left and fridge-hug out and up the jutting prow. 7a from a standing start. A modern classic. See photo on p479. *Ben Thompson*

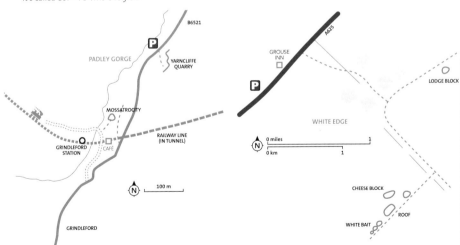

White Edge

Diamond White

The roof and prow feature yields a surprisingly good problem, the mixed quality of the rock being the only thing preventing it being a classic. Other low-quality easy problems here too.

1   Diamond White Left-Hand   7a   ★
From the back of the roof, move left via a flake and various scoops and edges to a reach out to a bullet-hole pocket on the hanging left arête with your right hand. Graded for avoiding the ledge on the left with your feet. *Jon Barton*

2   Diamond White   7b
The original line on the roof takes a slightly more convoluted path to the same finish, that is to say it takes on the roof at its full length. Start at the back of the roof and move out to the flake. From here, make a bid for the mono pocket on the lip of the lower prow and use this to move back left for the holds on the left side of the prow – finish as for *DWLH*. *John Welford*

3   Cream   7b
Another variation, which would be a worthless eliminate in anyone else's guide. Climb *DWLH* until the edges on the left side of the prow are reached, then slap for ripples on the headwall. Use these to reach left to the bullet hole on the arête, as used on the previous problem. *Rupert Davies*

4   Whitebait   7b   ✳
The undercut wall 5m right, eliminating the right arête. A tricky span from an undercut to a sloping feature and a tentative/powerful step up. *John Welford*

The block down below has some lower grade problems on poor rock.

Lodge Block

From the junction of the path at the finger post, head left along the bottom of the vague edge through a gate. After 200m the block can be seen on the right, just before the spooky house.

5   Snow White   7a+
Pull on the steep side of the block with an undercut, throw for a left hand hold, then right hand to the lip. Rockover to finish. A new version of an old problem – *White Rose*, 7c – which lost holds and is no longer climbable.

6   Lodge Arête   5   ✳
From the lowest point, traverse up left and rock over to finish. A good sit-down start to this exists, starting from the lowest point at about 7a.

7   Mantel   6a
A straightforward mantel onto the block.

8   Back Lip   7a
Head up and right. *John Welford*

Froggatt

Since our last guide was published the amount of bouldering at *Froggatt* has expanded dramatically, to include problems on isolated boulders in the woods below the edge and on buttresses and boulders that stretch back to the *Hairpin Boulder*, as well as those scattered among the routes on the main edge.

The problems range through the full gamut of styles: traverses, dynos, technical walls, starts to routes, hard highballs, roofs, arêtes and slabs. And the quality is outstanding throughout – a fine circuit that can easily be linked with the problems in the *Moon Buttress* area of *Curbar*.

The edge is not as sheltered as might be expected, but the more esoteric boulders beneath the edge are well protected by the trees. Some of the less frequented problems in the trees – *Computer Say No, The Barrel, Downes' Buttress, Brook Side Area, Sunset Boulders* – can get a bit dirty so bring a (non-wire) stiff brush and an open mind. Things should improve with more traffic, indeed the very reason many of these problems are included.

Access and Approach

There are two main approaches, and of course Froggatt can also be reached along the top of *Curbar*. (The approaches to the *Computer Say No* buttress and the *Sunset Boulders* are described separately.)

Park in the large lay-by on the A625 about 400m downhill from The Grouse Inn. Take the gate on the left, and follow the path along the top of the edge. The *Hairpin* boulder is almost immediately on the right. Continue along the track for the other areas.

Alternatively, limited parking is available in a small bay adjacent to the Chequers Inn car park on the A625 – **Do not** park in the pub car park unless you're having a pint – and in a small lay-by on the bend about 100m further down. A steep path breaks up the hill just downhill from the pub. This passes through a gate and soon arrives at the base of the crag near *Joe's Slab*.

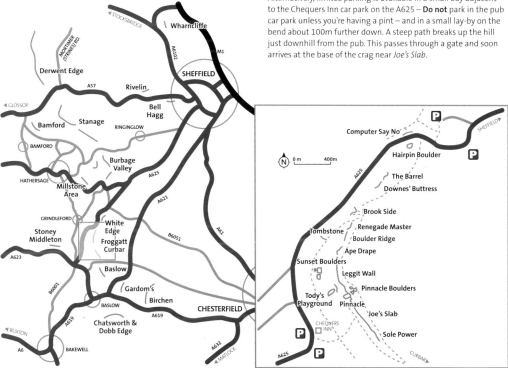

Computer Say No Buttress

The first problems are on a tall, often dirty buttress, under the A625. From the lay-by on the A625, cross the road, go through the gate and drop down the path. At the stream break left and follow it for 150m. Bear left when it joins another path, and keep a look out for the buttress, right under the road, after another 50m.

1   **Tall Arête**   *5*
The highball left arête.

2   **Sideways Says Sigmund**   *6b*
Start bridged between the slab and the right-hand block (that is *Computer Say No Left-Hand*). Swing left to finish on the arête.

3   **Ants On The Moon**   *5+*
Layback up the big, cracky flake.

4   **Computer Say No Left-Hand**   *6a+*
The left arête, gained from undercuts below and the seam out right. A good problem.

5   **Computer Say No**   *7a+*
Mantel the slopey ledge right of the arête and make hard moves with the thin seam direct to jugs at the tree. No arête. Highball. *Paul Mitchell*

Hairpin Boulder

An excellent, if over-used, boulder, with not a hold or sit-down start left unclimbed. A few easy warm-ups and good beginners' problems can be found left and right of the steps.

1   **Hairpin Arête**   *5*
Climb the arête on the right using the large horizontal slot. 4 on the left. The top-out is a lot harder if you don't find/use the chipped hold.

2   **Hairpin Scoop**   *4*   ✳
Up the wall via a mantel on the low shelf.

3   **Crash Test**   *6a+*   ★
The excellent arête from a sit-start from the two low cracks. A variation starts on flat holds to the left and climbs the arête on the left – 6b.

4   **Jump Before You Look**   *6b+*
Sit-start under the left side of the arête and finish up the crack.

Vanishing Point   *6c+*
Traverse from right to left, starting on the shelf, around the arête to finish up the crack, and then awkwardly into the rounded groove.

5   *6c*
From the bullet hole chip at head height on the wall left of the arête bounce up to the base of the groove and then the top.

Bullitt   *6c+*
Direct to the top, from the bullet hole chip.

Jelly Bomb   *7c+*   ✳
Fierce sit-start to *Bullitt* on an obvious edge. *Iain Farrar*

ASHLEY LEWIS ON *CRASH TEST*. PHOTO: RUPERT DAVIES

Froggatt Woods

Continuing along the edge, the next bouldering reached is buried deep in the woods, and of interest almost exclusively to the esoterica enthusiast. If you have a preference for easy access, paths, clean rock and good landings, then this won't be 'your bag', baby. We've listed the better problems here.

The Barrel

Approximately 600m from the *Hairpin* boulder a small path breaks off right towards some rocks on the edge, about 30m away: visible in winter, not in summer. The main rock is *The Boat*, and has some green highballs in the 4–5 grade range, the ledgy wall on the left wall of the gully being the best. 20m below the right-hand rock, looking out, is a barrel-shaped boulder. Either approach by following a path left downhill and then swinging back right beneath a tall slab on a ledge, or break right from the right-hand boat and quest through the undergrowth – more direct.

1   Barrel Organist   7a
Jump to the break on the left side of the wall and follow the vague rib. *Iain Farrar*

2   Glorious Gritstone Mantelshelf   7a+
Jump for the sloper in the centre of the wall and mantel it out with the aid of poor undercuts. *Iain Farrar*

Downes' Buttress

A short distance further along – about 50m along the main track – another path breaks off to another collection of buttresses. The upper tier contains several problems in the 6s and low 7s, although the landings are poor, and some will require tied-down spotters. Full details in the BMC's *Froggatt* guidebook. Around on the lower tier is:

3   Matchbox Arête   6a+
Sit-start the right arête of the block right of the gully. *Iain Farrar*

4   Glass Slipper   7a   ✳
Climb the fine angular arête on its right to a rounded jug. 7a+ from a sit-start. Add a grade to both if you keep going on the right-hand side to the break. See photo on p178. *Iain Farrar*

5   Downes' Crimps   6b
Follow crimps on the right-hand side of the back wall to meet the arête. Finish at the ledge and either top-out or reverse the arête and jump off. *Iain Farrar*

6   Chin Mania   7a+
The highball nose down and right. Climb the flake to a slot, rock left into the groove and then finish back right.

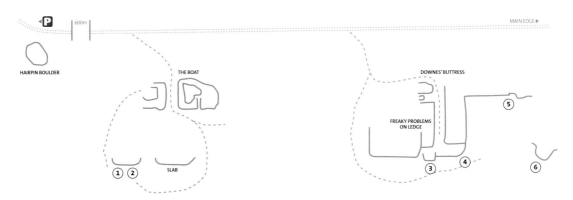

Brook Side Area

A cluster of problems on various buttresses on either side of the small brook which runs down just before the kissing gate. The first problem is on the right side of the brook (looking out into the valley). For the *Ladies Wall* problems pass through the gate and approach down the other side of the brook. At the time of writing the problems are quite dirty, although things should improve as the area sees more traffic.

7   Old King Cascade   7b+   ✳
An unusual feature in an interesting spot, just next to the little waterfall. From right at the back climb out to and up the hanging arête. No sidewalls, obviously. See photo on p176. *Robin Mueller/Dawid Skoczylas*

Ol' Man River   7c
The sidewall of *Old King Cascade* from the jug. No back wall. *Paul Bennett*

8   Ladies Wall   7c   ✳
Sit-start at small edges on the right and climb the overhanging wall on yet more small edges with a lunge at the top. Spotter useful. *Iain Farrar*

9   Burnt Sienna   6b
A good highball up the wall with the blunt flake. Spotters recommended.

10   Kimb's Limbs   7a+
Around to the right, on a higher level is another set of walls. This problem climbs the left-leaning rib. *Iain Farrar*

11   Carry on Screaming   6b+
Layback the crack to a tricky top-out.

12   Les Grand Doigts   7c   ✳
The rounded arête is a strong line. *Jamie Lilleman*

13   Bad Landing Crack   6a+
The thin crack around to the right.

14   Flipworker   6a
Sit-start at the plinth and hug your way up the upside-down, triangular shield.

15   Rowan   6a+
The small wall over to the right. Mantel into the scoop and climb the wall above.

RICH SHARPE ON *RENEGADE MASTER*   **PHOTO:** NICK BROWN

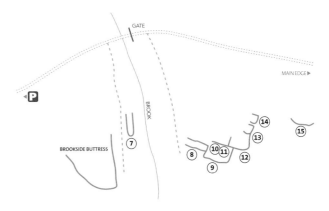

Boulder Ridge

The edge starts to open up now and the next problems are dotted along a ridge between the woods and *Froggatt Edge* proper.

Renegade Master

Shortly after the gate and stream, a grassy track leads diagonally downhill between blocks towards the impressive *Renegade Master*.

16   Renegade Bulge   *6c*   ✳
Sit-start the small bulge in the middle of the front face and climb direct. No right arête.

17   Bulge Right-Hand   *6c+*
Sit-start the bulge with one hand on the flake and finish with use of the right arête.

The block left of the bulge gives a poor 6c problem, and the arête and sidewall of the tall slab to the right give highball 4s.

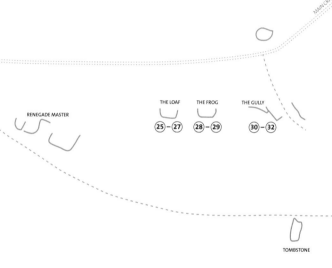

18   Renegade Master   *7c+*   ★
The awesome, highball overhanging face. Start under the roof on the left, work rightwards across the lip and wall on campus board edges to top out on the right side of the arete. A more commonly bouldered, and less terrifying finish, rocks right onto the shelf and jumps off from there – *Renegade Padster*, also 7c+. Jerry's original finish went direct up the crack left of the arete using a pre-placed wire for protection – E9 7a. See photo on p181. *Jerry Moffatt*

19   Dave's Dyno   *7c*
Start left hand on undercut, right on arête, dyno to the break. *Dawid Skoczylas*

Thuggy Bear   *7a+*
The arête on its right from sitting, without the low ledge around the arête. Finish by traversing the ledge off right. *Robin Mueller/Dawid Skoczylas*

The Tombstone

Continue down the path past *Renegade Master*. After a few hundred metres the *Tombstone* boulder becomes obvious in front of you. The problems are on the side facing away from you.

20   Tombstone Groove   *4+*
The left-hand groove can be quite green.

21   Shallow Groove   *6a*   ✳
Just right of the left-hand groove via a blind flake.

22   Shallow Grave   *7a+*
Slightly eliminate so it may be easier with a more liberal sequence. Anyway, climb the more central line. *Ben Heason*

23   Tombstone   *7a*   ✳
Right of centre past an obvious pocket to the top. Can be dynoed.

24   Right Arête   *5+*
Steady climbing up the right arête.

The back of the boulder gives low quality problems in the 3–4 range.

Boulder Ridge

Back on the main edge, the next problems are found on a buttress about 100m further along and up from *Renegade Master*. See topo on p182.

The Loaf

25 Toasted *6b*
From the break climb the ramp into the crack.

26 Hot Butter Knives *7a*
Sit-start at the right arête and swing left along the thin break to finish up *Toasted*.

27 Stottie *7b* ✳
Sit-start the arête direct. *Andy Banks*

The Frog

A short distance further along is a boulder with a rising L–R break line.

28 Froggit *5*
Traverse the break from L–R and finish up before the arête.

29 Kermit's Finger *6a*
The centre of the wall to a sloping top-out.

The Gully

50m or so further along is a broad, rocky gully, roughly opposite a couple of small blocks on the left of the path. On the right side of the Gully is a north-facing wall.

30 3
The juggy arête on the slabby boulder to the left.

31 Gully Dyno *6c* ✳
Dyno the wall from a good hold to a sloping top.

32 Fiddler's Arete *6c*
The arête.

JOE BROWN ON *RAMBEAU* PHOTO: JOHN COEFIELD

Froggatt Main Circuit

We're now into the standard Froggatt circuit, starting with the classic *Ape Drape*.
The boulder is just below the edge, around 50m before the route *Strapadictomy* (E5).

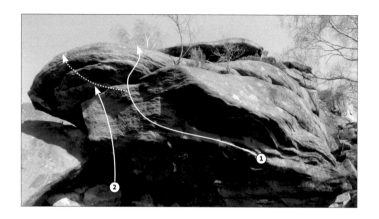

1   Ape Drape   *6c+*   ★
Start low on the right and traverse leftwards on flakes to finish on the right side
of the capstone. *Martin Veale*

Ape Drape Direct Finish   *7a+*   ✳
Finish left of the original via a heinous mantel onto the capstone. *Mark Stokes*

2   Monkey Man   *7b+*
The left lip of the roof starting from the jammed block at the back and finishing up
Ape Drape Direct Finish. Tallies can unfortunately span to the lip with feet still on
the back (7a), but it's much better and harder without. *Kim Thompson*

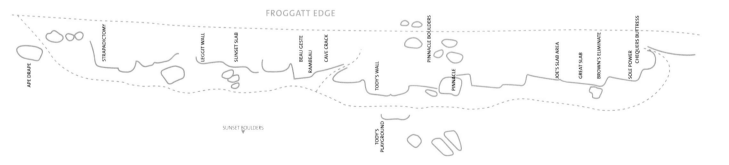

Leggit Wall

Between *Strapadictomy* and *Sunset Slab* is a neglected short crack in a little bay, above some boulders.

3   Pig Heart Boy 7b ★
The left-hand line, starting in the pit behind the boulder jumble. Reach up to the very slopey break and do a big rockover from here for the top break. A great problem. *Adam Long*

4   Leggit 6a+ ★
The crack. Escape via a tricky descent, or jump. Really quite good.

Beyond Beau Geste is a large cave, taken by the route Cave Crack.

5   Rambeau 7b ✳
Jump-start into superb burly moves up the overhanging arête to reach a break. Once here, traverse right into *Cave Crack* or jump off. See photo on p184. *Mark Leach*

Tody's Playground

A wonderful spot, located underneath the path that runs below the crag. The finishes are high, but are all juggy.

6   Tree Wall 5
Climb the wall behind the tree.

7   The Eyes 6a ✳
Gain the upper flakes from poor holds in the blank wall below. 6a+ from sit-start.

8   Tody's Pocket 4+ ✳
Climb directly to the pocket, finishing on jugs.

9   Thin Wall 6a ✳
Use poor edges in the centre of the wall to reach good edges and eventually jugs above.

10   Tody Boy 5+ ✳
Use small flakes to gain the upper rail.

11   Tody Bear 5
Gain the big flake from directly below.

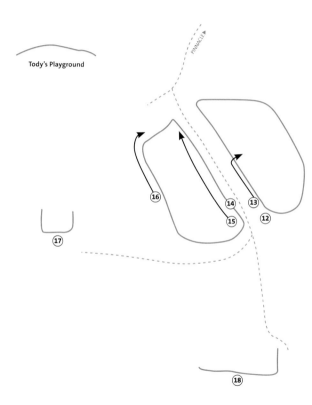

Tody's Playground

PINNACLE

Down and left as you look out into the valley are some large, ominous-looking boulders.

12   **The Sound of One Foot Slipping**   *7a+*
Climb the right arête from the low break on its left until a flake and a sloper allows a precarious roll onto the slab. *Ben Bransby*

13   **My Orange**   *7c+*   ✳
Start up *The Sound of...* and traverse the sloping lip leftwards to a highball top-out. E6-ish as a route. *Iain Farrar*

14   **Jetpack**   *7b*
Big, weird, steep dyno, starting off two obvious sidepulls at the left-hand side of the long slopey boulder. 7a if intermediates (which have appeared since the first ascent) are used. *Jon Fullwood*

15   **Pea Crab Shuffle**   *7c*
A 45-move traverse along the lip of the boulder. Sit-start on the left and traverse all the way right. *Iain Farrar*

16   **Scandalous**   *7b*
On the back of the block, traverse the break right to left, starting in the middle, and finishing around the left side of the arête. Poor landing. *Tom Randall*

17   **Gibsonitus**   *7b*
On a block 10m left of *Scandalous*. Climb the arête from sitting – start by hugging the steep rib. The arête is higher than it looks, but it gets easier with height. *Percy Bishton*

About 25m directly below Jetpack is an overhanging boulder topped by a green slab, facing away from the crag.

18   **The Green 45**   *7a*
From the short arête left of centre, stretch to the broken hold below the lip and use this to gain good holds on the green slab above.

Froggatt Pinnacle

The problems here are good, clean and fingery. Not everyone's cup of tea, and lacking in classic status as none of them really finish anywhere. Of course if you top them out as highballs, they're all totally classic.

19 Pinnacle Traverse *7b* ✳
Start low on the left wall, swing round the arête, finish along *Oedipus Traverse* in reverse.

20 Neon Dust Direct *7c+*
The thin wall between the crack and arête (*Narcissus* – E6). The grade depends on which starting holds are used. Finish at the thin breaks. *Ron Fawcett*

21 Oedipus Direct *6b+*
Direct to the flake at the end of the traverse. More like 7a for the short. Good.

Glamourpuss *6c+*
A tight, crimpy line up the very blunt rib left of *Oedipus Direct*.

22 Oedipus Traverse *6b* ✳
From the cave on the right, traverse the break left to finish on the flake. Now buy the route guide and finish up *Oedipus* (E4). Otherwise hang around for a bit and wait for someone to move your mat over so that you can jump off.

23 Mint 400 Direct Start *7b+*
Crimp direct to the centre of the *Oedipus Traverse*.

Pinnacle Boulders

A cluster of boulders on top of the crag, behind the *Pinnacle*. A good spot for low-grade climbers and beginners due to the flat landings and well-featured rock, the climbing here is good and less generic than you might think. The first problem is just left of the track on a low boulder, when approached from the A625 parking.

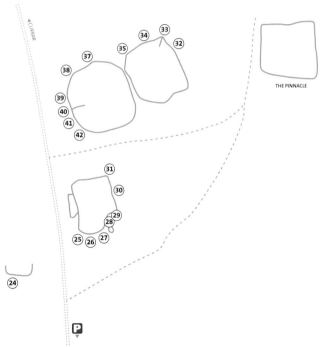

24 4
Sit-start the low overhang.

25 Areet 4 ✳
The arête. Best started right and finished left. Slightly harder finished right.

26 Starter Motor 5
The wall right of the arête.

27 Pick Pocket 4+
Sit-start at the flake and climb the pocketed bulge.

28 The Northerner 5+
The centre of the bulge direct.

29 3+
The right trending groove. Sit-start is a 4.

30 3
The ledgy wall around to the right is easy and quite enjoyable, climbed pretty much anywhere.

31 3
The back arête is quite good too.

32 Flatulence 4+
Fine holds on the sidewall lead to a slopier top.

33 Air Bear 4+ ✳
The crack.

34 Mini Mantel 3+
Mantel through the centre of the front face.

35 Mantelicious 6b
Mantel the nose.

36 Care Bear 4+
Traverse from *Mini Mantel* to finish up *Air Bear*.

37 Naughty 4+
Use the seam to gain a couple of small chips and mantel out.

38 Groovy 4+
The chunky groove. A line just left, avoiding the groove holds is a tricky 5.

39 Rib Tickler 4+ ✳
Layback the fine rib on its left.

40 Come Together 3+ ✳
The crack has hidden jugs.

41 Nasal Passage 4+
The nose, avoiding the biggest jugs around right.

42 5
Sit-start at the right-hand end of the lower shelf and pull over the bulge.

43 Ledgeway 5+
A low traverse, starting under the crack and finishing up the previous problem.

Joe's Slab Area

This perfect little slab is getting nicely polished. The slab has been climbed in every way possible but the classics still stand the test of time.

44 Downhill Racer Direct *7a+* ✳
The thin slab directly below the classic E4. You're going to have to use your common sense to know when to back off this one as it quickly stops being a boulder problem. *Johnny Dawes*

45 The Arête *6b* ★
The technical arête is harder than it looks, and very, very good.

46 Thin Slab *7a+*
A hard, thin line up the slab right of the arête.

47 Mono Seam *6c+* ✳
Climbs the slab left of *Joe's Original* direct to the crescent hold at the top, via edges and two small divots. Do not use the holds on *Joe's Original*.

48 Joe's Original *5+* ★
The classic of the wall. Link the flat edges to the slot to the crescent. Superb. *Joe Brown*

49 Slab Pop *6c*
The slab right of *Joe's Original*, without the crack.

50 Joe's Slab Traverse *7a*
R–L traverse with feet at head height and hands below the top, finishing up the left arête.

Low Traverse *7b+*
Traverse from R–L using the small edges at the change of angle, finishing up the arête.

Just beyond *The Great Slab* is a collection of problems on a detached block.

51 Spinal Crack *5+*
Climb the crack, if you can jam.

52 Spinal Tap *6c+* ✳
From the back of the cave, pull out to the lip then grapple up the slanting crack to jugs. Excellent.

53 Lankaster Bomber *7c*
Reach out from the edge of the niche to a small crimp and soon after the top. Graded for normal-sized people; easier for the tall. *Kim Thompson*

Right again, and around the arête is:

54 Slingshot 7c+ ✳
The steep, highball wall right of the corner to the ledge, involves dynoing to a thin finger edge above an awkward landing. The crux first move is easier for the tall. Top-roped originally by *Jerry Moffatt* in 1988 then soloed much later by *Mo Overfield* above mats. Flashed by *Ryan Pasquill* in 2009.

55 Chequers Groove 8a ✳
The groove right of *Slingshot* is again very highball and dynamic. It was soloed above a very, very large mat borrowed from The Foundry Climbing Wall. *Jerry Moffatt*

56 Business Lunch 7c
The highball wall, left of *Sole Power* and right of the crack. *John Allen*

57 Sole Power 7c ★
The hanging arête below *Chequers Buttress* was named in honour of *Jerry's new Firés*, which gives you an idea of how old it is. No? Ok then, it was first climbed in 1983. *Jerry Moffatt*

Our Soles 7c
The same arête on its right. *John Welford*

58 Jankers Groove Sit Start 6c
A sit-down start to *Whillans'* direct on this route. Evil fist jamming. *Jon Barton*

Sunset Boulders

A collection of biggish blocks dumped unceremoniously on the hillside below the edge. Undoubtedly climbed on before, but only recently developed and documented properly by *Robin Mueller, Dan Arkle* and *Dawid Skoczylas*. Often dirty, they scrub up to provide a decent circuit and we've included them here in the hope they'll stay cleaner with regular traffic. Fairly sheltered, they'll still be damp after a wet spell. Approach by either continuing down the path past *The Tombstone* for a few minutes and keeping an eye out to the left or, if approaching from the Chequers Inn, pass through the gate, up the steps, and follow the path left for a few hundred metres, keeping an eye out on the right – they're just after the big house on the left. See map on p177.

The first problems are on the two smaller boulders, to the left.

1   Bottoms Up   *4*
Sit-start the back arête on its right, from the protruding boss.

2   Scurry   *5+*
Sit-start the front left arête, on its left.

3   Daylight Grubbery   *6b*
The left arête of the offwidth from a sit-start.

4   Goodnight Tiger   *5*
The right arête of the offwidth from a sit-start.

5   Holy Green   *7a*
A tight line up the centre of the wall without either arête. Start left hand sidepull and right hand gaston, then up past pockets.

6   Morning Wood   *6b*
The right arête of the downhill face on its left side. Easy and fun on the right.

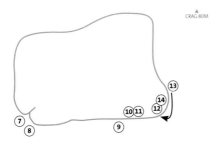

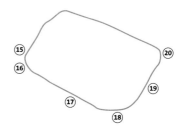

The next problems are on the biggest boulder.

7   Splattacake   *6a+*   ✳
Climb the cracky groove from a sit-start. Highball.

8   Rampage   *6a*
Start as for *Splattacake* and traverse the upper break right to finish up the crack.

9   Dreamboat   *7a*   ✳
The excellent steep slab, started from the slopey pocket, and finishing in the high niche.

10   Breeze   *6a+*
Climb leftwards-leaning slopers direct to the ledge.

11   Cheese   *5+*
The vague rib, just right of *Breeze*.

12   Ease   *4*
The slab and arête. *Squeeze* – 5+ – climbs the wall left of the arete, eliminating holds on adjacent problems.

13   Teddybear's Picnic   *6c*   ✳
Sit-start on a good rail right of the arête and traverse left around the undercut arête, pulling up to finish up *Ease*.

14   Big Surprise   *5*
The right side of the arête, rocking onto the slabby side higher up.

Big Surprise Sit-Start   *7a*
From the good rail, layback the arête on its right, with a dynamic move to the break. Finish as for the stand up.

About 30m right is another big boulder.

15   Eat Your Greens   *6a+*
Sit-start the undercut left arête, on its left.

16   Nobody Nose   *6c*
Sit-start the same arête, this time on its right.

17   Emerald Aisle   *7a*   ✳
Sit-start the mossy wall at a good sidepull, reach up and right for another sidepull then slap for the top. No footblock.

18   Wolfenstein   *5+*
The right arête.

19   White Lycan   *6a+*
The right-hand face of the boulder, using holds on the stepped arête to the right.

White Lycan Sit-Start   *7b*
Power into the stand-up.

20   The Other Half Has Hairy Legs   *6c*
The stepped arête right of *White Lycan*, from a sit-start.

ROBIN MUELLER ON *WHITE LYCAN*   **PHOTO:** DAWID SKOCZYLAS

Curbar

A great area, with problems from 3–8a+. You'll find authentic 'bouldering' at *Curbar*, with perfectly-sized blocks dotted down the hillside, and the place is littered with classics – *Trackside*, *Strawberries* and *Gorilla Warfare* to name a famous few. As if that wasn't enough, the bouldering along the edge has exploded in popularity in recent years, and lends itself to a good, spread out circuit of walls and arêtes, with more than a few of them highball.

Curbar dries quickly and is close to the car, so it's a good choice of venue in 'variable' weather. Even if it does rain, you may be able to get some in on the *Gorilla Warfare* block. It can be a bit sticky/midgy on still summer days, mind.

Access and Approach

Park in the lay-bys by the side of the road just below *Curbar Gap*. Walk down the road towards Warren Lodge and take the path right to and through the gate. *Trackside* is the first boulder encountered, with the rest scattered above. *Ben's Wall* is about 150m further on, set among the trees, and the *Ultimate Gritstone Experience* is miles further on! Most of the edge bouldering is best approached along the top from *Curbar Gap*, or even from *Froggatt* in the case of *The Art of White Hat Wearing*.

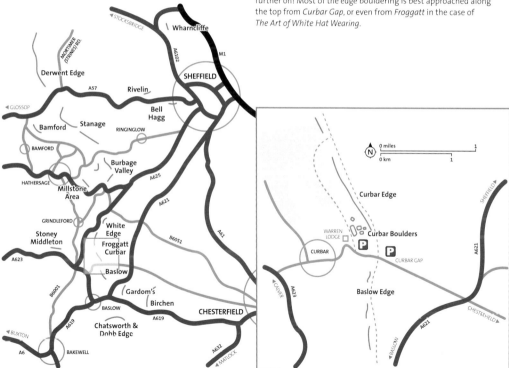

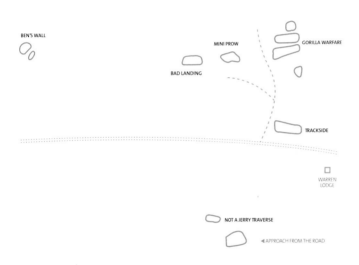

BEN'S WALL

MINI PROW

GORILLA WARFARE

BAD LANDING

TRACKSIDE

WARREN LODGE

NOT A JERRY TRAVERSE

◀ APPROACH FROM THE ROAD

Trackside Boulder

Complete with in-situ wood-chip landings, this is perhaps the ultimate convenience boulder. A good spread of problems that should last most people a lifetime. It's the unmissable, big flat block, passed on the right as you approach along the track.

1   *3+*
The right-hand side of the short arête.

2   *3*
The crack.

3   *4+*   ✳
Link the lower flake into the smaller, upper flake.

4   *5*   ✳
Mantel up past the slot. With the arête it's a 4.

5   *5*
The short crack from the low break.

6   *5+*   ✳
The left-hand side of the front face using the obvious pockets.
Plus: massively fun double dyno from the lower pocket to the top.

7   *4+*
The wall right of the pockets. Harder if you start on the low break – 6b.

8   **Strawberries**   *6b*   ★
Can feel strangely hard, or indeed trivial, depending on how you do it.
Sprag/layoff the thin cracks/seams to a direct finish.

9   *4*
The crack.

10   **Play Hard**   *7c*   ✳
Eliminate – no crack. Right of the crack is a two-handed sloper. Head to the top from this, via a poor hold just right of the crack and more poorness next to the top. *Jason Myers*

11   **Work Hard**   *8a+*   ✳
Direct up the hanging slab from the sloper. A total reach problem. Morpho. *Jason Myers*

12 *6b+*
The crack and various pockets and slopes land one with satisfaction on the summit. Various worthwhile eliminates, including; use the sloper and seam to pop to the pocket – 7a.

13 **Trackside** *7a* ★
A true Peak District classic. Reach up from the crack to grab a handful of arête, then casually reach the top with a scary toe or heel in the bottom of the crack.

14 **Sidetrack** *7a* ✳
The arête on its right-hand side is a tad trickier and more conditions dependant.

15 **Tracking** *7b+* ✳
Traverse right from problem 1 along the low slopey break, past a tricky move to exit up *Strawberries* (no crack), or continue to finish up *Trackside* at 7c+.

16 *4+*
Traverse the back of the boulder from right to left from the shelf, avoiding the top.

The next two problems are located on a large low boulder in the field below the *Trackside Boulder*. Please approach from the road, and not by climbing over the drystone wall.

17 **Not A Jerry Traverse** *7a+*
Traverse from right to left. Almost worthwhile and easier with a few toe bars.

18 **Not a Problem for Jerry** *6c*
Up the wall on slopes from the good hold just after the crux of the traverse (towards the right of the main face). The main difficulties are due to the amount of grittiness rather than the actual climbing. There is also another very similar problem next to it at about the same grade. *Mark Pretty*

TRACKSIDE **PHOTO:** TIM RUSSON

Gorilla Warfare Slab

A slabby, south-facing boulder just below the main cluster of *Gorilla Warfare* boulders. Numerous fun variations on these problems.

19   The Arête   *4+*   ✳
Climb the arête on either side.

Dan's Wall   *7a*
Sit-start the right-hand side of the arête, without the foot block. *Dan Warren*

20   The Slab   *5*   ✳
The pleasant slab.

21   The Groove   *3*
The left-leaning groove.

Gorilla Warfare

A hardcore group of problems on a superb, overhanging, partially-quarried face. The big block behind also has a few problems/routes.

22   5
The left arête from sitting.

23   Offwidth   *4+*   ✳
The awkward crack from a low start.

24   Hurricane   *7c*   ★
A big move to the top from the slopers right of the crack. Hitting the top is reasonable – holding it is very hard. *Jerry Moffatt*

25   Jihad   *7b*
Swing right from the crack to the sloper on *Hurricane*, and then again into the sloper of *Early Doors*. Finish up this. Eliminate, but good moves.

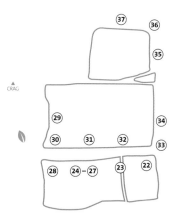

26 Gorilla Warfare *7a* ★
From a sit-start on a big flake right of *Offwidth*, traverse right on slots, edges and slopers, then rock over the top on good small hidden edges, just left of the arête. A thuggy classic.

Extended Warfare (7a) continues around – and finishes up – the arête from the final sloper.

Original Warfare (7a+) starts on the left-hand side of the boulder, traverses the top, reverses *Offwidth*, follows *Extended Warfare* around the arête and then finishes across the tricky sidewall. The original classic. *Martin Veale*

Reverse Warfare/De-extended Gorilla Doors (7b) sit-starts on good holds at the right arête and swings left along the line of slopers to finish up *Early Doors*.

27 Early Doors *7a+* ★
Start as for *Gorilla Warfare* but make a break for the top from the twin edges and past the large sloper.

28 Humpin' *7b*
Sit-start the right arête, eliminating the crack to the right, and with LH undercutting the polished foothold above the big block. Be strict, or it will feel easy. 5 from standing.

On the tall boulder behind:

29 Groovy Wall *5+* ★
An excellent problem up the vague groove.

30 Veale Thing *6a* ✳
The high arête on its left is f-f-freaky. Solid E1 5b.

31 Gusty *7a+*
Opposite *Hurricane*, pull on with LH poor sidepull, RH poor edge and bowl over for a good flatty. That's it.

32 The Scratcher *7b*
Scratch up nano-edges just right, to finish on a slightly larger edge. That's it.
Baby Belle steps off the boulder and traverses right to and up *Fab Arête* – 7b+.

33 Fab Arête *5+* ★
Climb the highball arête opposite *Gorilla Warfare*, starting on the left, finishing right.

34 Jordan's Wall *6c*
The wall just right.

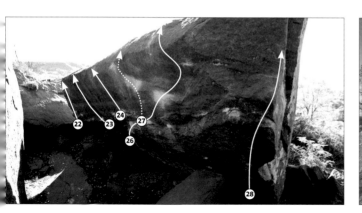

On the boulder behind:

35 **Back Slab** *6a*
The slabby sidewall.

36 **Back Arête** *5*
The back arête. Obviously.

37 **Dark Wall** *5+*
The steep wall, facing the crag.

Mini Prow Boulder

25m left of Gorilla Warfare is the aptly-named *Mini Prow*.

38 **Mini Arête** *3*

39 **Mini Crack** *4+* ✳

40 **Mini Prow** *5* ✳
A good problem.

41 **Mini Traverse** *6a+*
Traverse the back of the boulder, around the front and up the prow.

Bad Landing Boulder

Also aptly-named is the next boulder along.

42 **5+**
The left arête.

43 **6b+**
The right-hand side of the grooved arête, not using high right sidepull to start.

44 **Bad Lip** *7a* ✳
Hang the lip of the roof and yard straight up.

45 **Huffy's Roof** *7c+*
Start RH pocket on ramp and LH further up and power into *Bad Lip*. *Paul Houghoughi*

46 **Super Size Me** *8a+* ✳
Sit-start matched on the undercut at the back and *really* power into *Bad Lip*.
Curbar's hardest. *Simon Newstead*

47 **Le Musée Imaginaire** *7b+* ✳
Start hanging the lip as for *Bad Lip* and traverse left to finish up problem 43. Tough.
An extension starts as for *Huffy's Roof* at 7c+/8a. *Robin Mueller/Dawid Skoczylas*

48 **Late Junction** *7b*
Sit-start from hands on the block under problem 42 and lip traverse right to finish up *Bad Lip*.

Ben's Wall

Some 100m further left and through the trees is the impressive *Ben's Wall*.

49 Pebble Wall 6a
The left arête is good.

50 Ben's Wall 7c ★
Bounce to the large pocket. Finish round and left. Has been done static, not by a giant, but by a very talented midget. *Ben Moon*

51 Great White 7c ★
The wall to the right, with hard moves to the thin sidepull and past it to the large finishing pocket. Jump off. *John Welford*

52 6c
Traverse left to right under *Ben's Wall* to finish up the ramp on the right.

53 6b
Facing *Ben's Wall* is a tiny overhang. Sit-start from the low edge.

A small quarried face about 20m back towards *Trackside* from *Ben's Wall* has a couple of scratchy low-mid grade problems on it for the keen. A dyno off small crimps up the middle is 6c.

The Ultimate Gritstone Experience

Follow the *Trackside* path for several hundred metres to where it forks, take the right fork uphill, through the trees. Almost at the end of the crag and still on the main path is an obvious block, next to the path. Rumoured to be slightly unstable, so take care.

54 The Green Mile 6c
The left arête from a sit-start. *Dan Ogden*

55 The Ultimate Gritstone Experience 6c ★
Climb the face of the same boulder from a sit-start, using both arêtes, and exit straight up. A classic. *Dan Ogden*

56 Touch Winky 7b
The right arête and faint crack from sitting has a desperate first move followed by more amenable climbing above. *Percy Bishton*

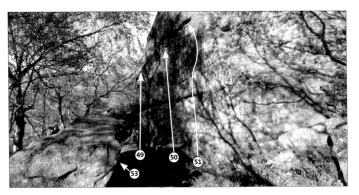

PETE ROBINS ON *TOUCH WINKY* PHOTO: ADAM LONG

Curbar Edge

As if the boulders themselves weren't enough, the edge at *Curbar* has developed into something of a classic circuit itself. Sure, stuff is spread out, but we're talking about destination problems here. Problems such as *The Art of Japan*, *Rise of the Robots* and *The Art of White Hat Wearing* are worth a trip in their own right. Note that we've used the names of famous routes to help with navigation.

Mini Walls Area

This is the first section of broken, natural and quarried buttresses happened upon from the *Curbar Gap* car park. They yield a decent, low-grade bouldering circuit, and one that sees none of the traffic of the main boulders. The first two problems are on the first set of tall pinnacles, and face *Baslow*.

1   Thomas the Tanked Up Engine   *6a+*   ✳
The right arête of the buttress on its right hand side, finishing up the centre of the wall. A good highball.

2   The Phat Controller   *6b+*
Straight up the centre of the wall.

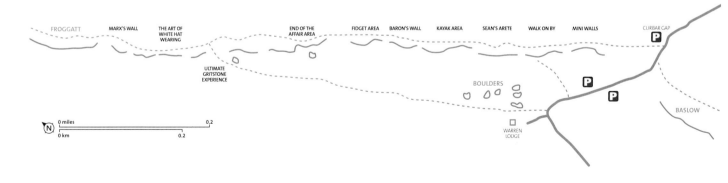

20m further on is a small, north facing quarry.

3   Curved Rib   *3*
The short rib left of the crack.

4   One Inch Crack   *3*
A one-move wonder up the little crack.

5   The Letter L   *5*
Reach into the slot and upper crack without bridging the corner.

6   Dressed Arête   *6a*
The arête taken on its left is somewhat tricky. 4+ on the right.

7   Seams Simple Enough   *7a*   ✳
The thin seam up the steep slab has handholds, but few footholds. Tricky.

8   Chimney Crack   *4*
The crack to a jug, just left of the blocky chimney.

9   Ledge Wall   *4*   ✳
Yard off the big, blocky ear to the top.

10   Thin Flake   *4+*   ✳
The gently curving, blocky flake is a good problem.

11   The Sketch   *4+*
The left arête of the tall buttress, avoiding the ledges to the left.

12   Front Crack   *3*
The recessed crack is fairly 'trad'.

13   Front On   *3+*
The projecting front face/arêtes of the buttress, climbed end on.

14   Fishy   *4+*
Around the corner, the right arête of the wall on its right.

15   Hob Nob Wall   *5+*
The centre of the wall on little, biscuit edges. For an additional pat on the back go straight to the top rather than to the cutaway to the left – 6a.

Walk on By

A little further along, and above the main *Curbar* boulders, is a large, quarried bay.

16 Walk on By *7c+* ✳
The big, blank, utterly featureless wall to the break. Now climbed with a right-hand sequence after the demise of a key edge. *Rob Gawthorpe (in 1980!)*

17 Buy Buy *6c*
Sit-start the angular arête on its left.

Sean's Arête

100m further along, down and left of the classic route L'Horla (E1) is:

18 Sean's Arête *7b* ✳
Climb the arête straight on to an improbable finishing move to the break. A classic. Keep going to the next break for 7b+. *Sean Myles*

19 Spray Mane *7b+*
A big dyno up the wall left of Sean's Arête, starting at a pair of pockets. A pad and spotter are mandatory to avoid the arse-splitting boulder in the landing zone. *Mike Gardner*

20 Ramboid *7b*
Mantel onto the sloping, triangular shelf down and right of the route *Profit of Doom* (E4), about 60m left of the previous problem. Desperate.

Kayak Area

Just right of the big slabs home to *Kayak* (E1) and *Canoe* (E2) is an attractive corner.

21 Little Stiffer *5+*
The arête right of the corner, on its left-hand side.

Jamie and His Magic Torch *7b*
The same arête on its right-hand side. *Jamie Lilleman*

22 Curbar Corner *5* ★
The corner.

23 Neat *5+*
The arête left of the corner.

Baron's Wall

About 200m further on from *Kayak Area* is this wall, with problems at its left-hand side.

24 Smoke ont' Watter Start *6a+* ✳
The wall past a pocket and sidepull. Finish at the good holds. A variation just right is 6a+.

25 Talon Man *6b* ✳
The wall starting at the big sidepull. Dyno from the sidepull to the ledge at 6c+. *Andy Crome/Jon Fullwood*

26 Baron's Direct *6a*
The right-hand side of the wall to the ledge.

Fidget Area

Mid-way along the edge is a clutch of fine highballs. 60m before these is a small cave with a sit-start up a groove, finishing up the left crack – *The Sheep Pit*, 6b+

27   Rise of the Robots   *6a+*   ★
The highball wall and flake. Brilliant.

28   Fidget   *6b+*   ✳
From the short arête a deep lock gains the upper crack. Highball.

29   Six Syllables or Less   *6c*
Start as for *Rise of the Robots* and trend left into *Fidget*.

30   Lifeseeker   *6c*   ✳
Around the other side of the jutting nose hides this fine problem. Strenuously lock up to gain the square-cut, hanging groove.

End of the Affair Area

Problems of generally good quality, at the highpoint of the *Curbar* and *Froggatt* edges. *The End of the Affair* problems, and the problems further north towards *Froggatt* can be conveniently linked with, and approached from, *Froggatt*. The first problems are below the edge, approx 60m down and right of the route *Slackers* (E6).

31   Bruno Mindhorn   *7b*
From a jug in the roof swing out to and up the arête. *Jon Fullwood*

32   Break out the Trumpets   *6c+*
The arête below Bruno Mindhorn from a sit-start.

Back up on the edge, the wall to the right of Ulysses or Bust (E5) features some nifty problems/highballs:

33   The Dog's Hole   *6b*
The thin crack up from the hole.

34   Dogleg Crack   *4*   ✳
Learn to jam, right here, right now.

35   The Unreachable Star   *6b+*
The tenuous crack has a sketchy move to the break. Very highball (E2 6a).

36 The Art of Japan *6c* ★
A couple of gullies back towards *Baslow* is this brilliant problem. Climb the wall using a layaway for your right hand and undercuts for your left hand. *The Arse of Japan* (7a+) is a variation slap just left off undercuts and smears to the edge. See photo on p205.
John Allen

Between *Ulysses or Bust* and the legendary *End of the Affair* (E8) runs a shallow gully. The west-facing wall of this has a bunch of mid-grade problems, and a tricksome 7. From left to right, starting at the top of the gully:

37 *4*
The left arête.

38 Trench Wall *6a+*
The wall just right of the arête.

39 Trench Flakes *6b+* ✳
The centre of the wall past attractive flakes to a tricky exit. A good problem.

40 The Ring *5+*
The slab above the footledge, keeping left.

41 Trench Hole *4+*
The right-hand slab above the hole.

42 Pigeon Arête *6a+*
The left arête, from the rounded boss.

43 Cloud Cuckoo Land *7a+* ✳
Sit-start to good holds and then make a hard sequence up and right to the ramp.
Allen Williams

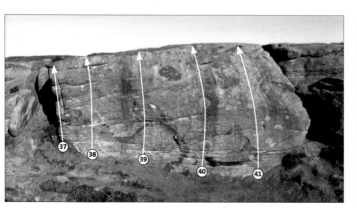

Directly below the ledge that *End of the Affair* starts from is a wall with some cracky problems.

44 Wee-Wob 5
Sit-start in the groove and trend left to top out.

45 Left Eliminette 6b ✳
The wall and thin cracks.

46 The Start of the Affair 6a
Up to the crack in the centre of the buttress.

47 Right Eliminette 6a
The roof crack. A couple of extra problems can be climbed just right.

Up and left is:

48 Downhill Gardener 7a+
Sit-start the awkward arête on its left. *Paul Smitton*

49 Button Moon 6a
Pull on with a sloper and pockets and reach edges above.

50 Last Light 6c ✳
Opposite *Button Moon* is this fingery wall, with a tough move to the break.

About 100m further on towards Froggatt is the *Cioch Buttress*. On a big, blank-ish wall down and right of the main Cioch pinnacle is:

Big Friday 7c
The centre of the big wall is fingery and highball. *Pete Robins*

The Art of White Hat Wearing

The final problems at *Curbar* are found in the rarely-visited quarried walls en route to *Froggatt*.

51 Be Somebody or be Somebody's Fool *7a+*
The bulbous wall on undercuts and edges. Tough. *Simon Wilson*

52 Jimmy Hat *7c*
Big locks on crimps, between the corner crack and the next problem. *Andy Earl*

53 The Art of White Hat Wearing *7b* ✳
The attractive groove in the centre of the sidewall is the quarryman's *West Side Story*. Superb climbing, with a little flutter at the top. One of the best at the grade on grit. *Andy Crome*

Around to the left is a series of short, slabby walls.

54 Happy House *6b* ✳
The shallow rib and rubbish pockets.

55 Happy Slapper *5*
The rib and pockets to the left.

56 Curbar Your Enthusiasm *6b*
The centre of the narrow wall, about 10m left of the descent gully.

57 Marx's Wall *6c+*
At the far left-hand end of *Curbar*, facing *Froggatt* is a sidewall around from a big, undercut slab (*Don't Slip Now* – E5). Sit-start the sidewall, left of the crack.

Baslow

In the few years since our first bouldering guide was published the bouldering at *Baslow* has matured from a disconnected circuit of a half dozen or so boulders into a disconnected circuit of a half dozen or so boulders and a bunch of great problems on the edge itself.

A trip to *Baslow* is essential: The *Eagle Stone* is one of the best single boulders on grit, with a spread of technical and powerful problems that all take strong lines; the *Walnut Whip* block offers great traversing from the straightforward but pumpy to the devious, intricate and technical; *Flatworld* – flanked by other fine arêtes and slabs – is a modern testpiece; and the edge offers some fine climbing, such as *Hot Ziggerty*, *The Ripper* and *Flying Crag Groove*. In reality, many of the micro-routes can be climbed above a pad, but we've selected the most aesthetic, pleasant and 'boulder-able' here. Grades at *Baslow* range from 3 – 7c+.

Access and Approach

Park at the car park at the top of Curbar Gap (pay and display, we're afraid – alternative parking is available in lay-bys down the road towards *Curbar*) and walk back down the road until a track on the left leads through a gate and onto the moor. Take the right-hand path to get to the *Square Stone* and the left-hand path to get to the *Eagle Stone*. For access to the other blocks see the descriptions under their individual headings. There are no access issues although keeping your dog on a lead around the moody highland cattle is not a bad idea.

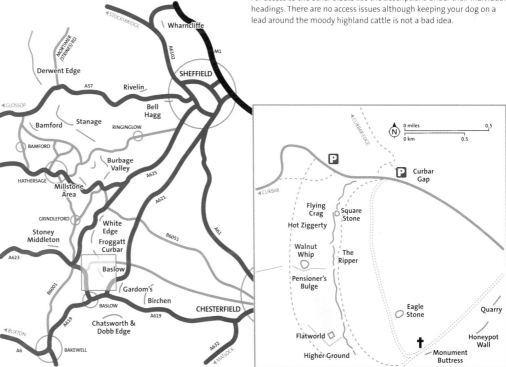

Square Stone

The square block above the edge in the clearing. The first problem is on a narrow buttress below.

1 Has Shaun Got False Teeth? *6b*
Ascend the concave wall on the front face of the buttress, avoiding the advances of the right arête. *Neil Travers*

2 4+
The left hand wall is short-lived.

3 6a ✳
Sit start on a flat edge below the lip and follow reasonable holds to the top.

4 5+ ✳
Again from a sit start, follow larger holds with larger moves.

5 5+
The right arête on either side.

6 4+ ✳
The front face can be climbed in a number of places at this grade.

7 6b+
Traverse the boulder from the left arête using the line of edges at around half height to finish up the right arête.

Flying Crag

The huge quarried wall of *Flying Crag* 50m south of the *Square Stone* gives up a handful of good lines.

8 John Wilson *6b* ✳
Climb the arête/prow on its left above a worrying landing to finish directly. Can also be started direct at the same grade. *Dave Norton*

9 Flying Crag Groove *5+* ★
The groove is a superb problem. A narrow line up the wall just right is 5+.

10 4
The blocky groove to the right is far better if the ledges to the right are avoided.

Hot Ziggerty

This quarried bay gives one of the best mid-grade highballs on the Eastern Edges.

11 Cold Diggerty *6c+*
Step off blocks in the corner at some small, but good, crimps at the top of the flake, and then follow your nose diagonally right, using crimps to a point where the arête meets the flat top. *Ben Heason*

12 Hot Ziggerty *6c* ★
Excellent. Spring off the boulder to a good edge and crimp directly upwards. Pulling on from the floor warrants 6c+ and the title *Tony Gubba's World of Rubber*. *Dominic Lee*

13 Arise Sir Freddie! *6b*
A good problem up the left-hand side of the arête. From a good hold on the arête make a hard move up and left for a small edge, before moving back right to climb the arête with the use of a blunt flake around to the right. *Dave Norton*

14 Whatisit *5+* ★
The narrow front face and right arête of the buttress.

Renaissance

Dry-humping the boundary between micro-routes and bouldering, this area 30m south of the *Hot Ziggerty* is unquestionably pleasant.

15 Route 1 *Fun* ✳
The slabby wall.

16 Route 2 *3*
A comparable line to the right. Repeat ad infinitum. See photo on p221.

17 Renaissance *5+* ★
One of Baslow's great micro-routes, giving delightful technical climbing up the centre of the pocketed wall. *Resurgence* is a traditional left-hand variant at a similar grade.

18 Grounded Bees *4+*
A worthwhile line up the right arête.

The Ripper

A good little area with a super-thin wall climb.

19 Pinch n Push *6b*
A reachy problem left of the crack. *Undercutting* is a tighter line even closer to – and without use of – the crack (7a+).

20 The Balls Test *6b+*
The left arête of the crack.

21 Green Crack *3+*
The flared crack. A bit 'trad'.

22 The Ripper *7a+* ✳
The narrow wall right of the crack with undercuts and micro crimps. A good problem and top of the grade. *Neil Travers*

23 Black Crack *3*
The flake crack. Fun.

24 Ribless *4*
The slabby wall without the arête. Fluttery.

The Walnut

We're not going to lie to you; this is not an easy boulder to access, particularly if the bracken is up and you intend to climb anywhere else in the same session. Home mainly to hard traverses, it does also feature the more amenable *Walnut* – one of the best shuffles in the Peak. Located directly below the edge, it can be approached as the crow flies or more easily via sheep tracks from the wide gully by the *Square Stone*.

25 The Walnut *6c* ★
From a sit-start at the extreme left on a flat edge, shuffle rightwards *below* the lip to top out just before – and without the help of – the small boulder leant against the large boulder. Can be started on good holds around to the left at 6c+. *Allen Williams*

26 Nutjob *6a* ✳
From the same start climb directly up and over.

27 Complete Nutter *5+*
Sit-start below the prominent fin.

28 Whip Me Whip Me *6c+*
One for those who like to lay down. Around 2/3rds along *The Walnut* traverse, slide really quite far underneath – no, keep going... – and climb out via edges and slopers.
Tip: ditch the pad. *Mark Pretty*

29 Nuts to Brazil   *3+*
The featured arête.

30 Nut Cracker   *5*
Climb to jugs from as low as you care to start.

31 Little Richard   *7a*   ✳
From a low, juggy pinch and an edge scratch up further edges and slopers to a prominent jug. A good problem and hard for the grade. *Richard Hughes*

32 Walnut Whip   *7b*   ✳
From a sit-start on the right maintain a line across the centre of boulder on slopers, edges and pinches to join and finish up the left arête. If you find yourself on the higher jugs you're on the wrong problem. *Allen Williams*

33 The Choker   *7c+*   ✳
As before but drop down low after the large sloper and traverse across the start of *Little Richard*, keeping low around the arete and up the slab. Eliminate but hard. *Percy Bishton*

34 Chunky Nut   *6b+*   ✳
From the same start rock up from the large sloper and head left to the jug rail.

On the back of this boulder in a pit is:

35 Nutrocker   *5*
Rock over onto the boulder.

Around the back of the main boulder:

36 Percy Feels Sick   *7a+*
Sit-start up the prow to an horrific grovelling mantel. *Percy Bishton*

37 Hazelnut Whirl   *6a+*   ✳
Mantel into the attractive scoop right of the small tree.

38 Dry Roasted   *5+*
The high wall from a standing start. A sitter is possible at 6a.

39 Praline   *6a*
Another highball line taking a slight right to left rising line on occasionally dubious rock. A more obvious direct line goes straight up then right at 4+.

The Matterhorn Boulder

This is the large boulder about 50m above *The Walnut*.

40 Bone At It Direct   *7a+*   ✳
With feet on the slab at the back, undercut out to the lip and make a fierce pull over onto the slab. *Andy Banks*

41 Smutt Ridge   *7a*
From the same start, gain the lip and traverse right and finish up the arête. *Andy Banks*

42 Lion   *5*
The south-west arête, pulling left onto the slab at 4m using hidden holds.

Pensioner's Bulge

A fine selection of micro-routes, on the edge up and right of *The Walnut*.

43 Rough Wall Climb   *5*
Follow the line of the crack up the centre of the wall. Variants right and left.

44 Jolly Green Dwarf   *5*   ✳
Follow the bold slabby rib leftwards to a junction with the arête.

45 Mad Bilberries   *6b*   ✳
Superb gritstone padding directly up the centre of the slab.

46 Jolly Green Elephant   *6b*
The left arête of the buttress taken on its right-hand side.

47 Pensioner's Bulge   *4+*   ✳
More of a route really. Follow thin cracks over the bulge behind the oak tree.

48 Hair Conditioned Nightmare   *5*   ✳
The centre of the narrow projecting block. Trying to avoid either arête only serves to spoil the experience.

49   *5+*
The right arête, climbed on the right.

Cave Buttress

Poppers Start   *7a+*
Further along the edge, just into the trees is the steep *Cave Buttress*. This is the short hanging arête just right of centre. Make hard moves to get established using the left-hand side of the arête and dyno for the break. *Grand Potato* – E6/7a+ – is the arête just right. *Richie Patterson*

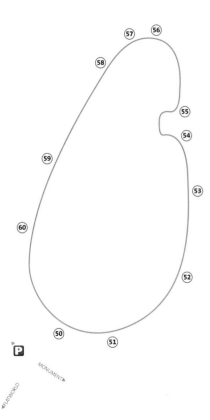

The Eagle Stone

Why you came to Baslow in the first place. Virtually all of the problems are highball, with good landings and highland cattle keeping watch. Approach along the main track.

50 Men Only *4*
The line of ancient chipped holds up the path-side face. **Note**: This is also the descent.

51 A Fist Full of Beagles *7a+* ✳
Not for the weak. Gain the mantelshelf from holds at the back of the roof. *Jason Myers*

52 Beagles About *5* ✳
Up to and through the drainage hole.

53 For a Few Beagles More *7b* ★
The first of four highball classics on the block. The bulging wall above the small corner is climbed on ever-worsening breaks. See photo on p210. *Jason Myers*

54 The Good, the Bad and the Beagle *7a* ★
Classic no.2. It is possible to climb the streak left of the bulge at this grade, it just might take you a while to figure out how. *Jason Myers*

55 A Beagle Too Far *6b* ★
The superb groove.

56 The Bright Concept *7b+*
The left-hand line on the nose reaches from a small undercut/pocket. *David Kettle*

57 Dreaming the Eagle *7a+* ✳
The right-hand line uses the break as a left hand undercut. Harder and better for the short. *John Welford*

58 The Beagle Has Landed *7a* ★
No.3. Attain, and then launch from little eggshell crimps to the break. *Jason Myers*

59 Where Beagles Dare *7a+* ★
No.4. Use a small pocket with your right hand to double dyno for the top. Using it with the left and reaching right to an edge is far easier, and the usual means of success. Not one for angry people. *Jason Myers*

60 Like a Beagle over Troubled Water *6b+*
The often-green wall on rounded breaks.

61 Roundabout *6a+*
Traverse the whole block.

Flatworld

This excellent block is situated directly under the edge, across the moor from the *Eagle Stone*. Approach from the top of the crag.

62 Heroes *7b*
30m up and left of *Flatworld* is a jutting nose, just as the edge ends. Climb it from a sit start. *John Welford*

63 *5+*
The dirty slab just below *Heroes*.

64 Lilliput *7a+*
The bulge on the left-hand end of the boulder around the back of the *Flatworld* block. From the two lowest edges, chase further edges over the bulge, making judicious use of the foot ramp. *Robin Mueller*

65 Flatworld *7b+* ✳
The hard classic of the crag, both technical and powerful. Climb the arête using seams on the right wall. The sit start is 7c+, and sadly on slightly snappy rock. *Allen Williams/John Welford*

66 Flatworld Left-Hand *7b* ✳
A worthwhile variant that begins with a big lock to a pocket on the left wall before returning to the original to finish. *Adam Long*

67 Hurry on Sundown *7a* ✳
The arête right of Flatworld from a sit start. Easier, and arguably better, from standing at 6b+. *John Welford*

68 *3*
The easy left arête of the block leaning against the former problem, on its right side.

69 Lichen Slab *5+*
The centre of the slab to the right. Climbable virtually anywhere at this grade.

70 Elmer Fudd *7a* ✳
The frustrating slab, started on the right at an obvious foothold. A left-hand variant is 6c+.

71 Fat World *6a* ✳
The brief arête to the right requires faith in friction. *Mark Pretty*

50m to the right on the final buttress of the edge is:

72 Higher Ground *7c* ✳
The centre of the big concave wall has a hard final move. *John Welford*
The arête to the left is a scary 6b+.

Monument Buttress

At the end of the track is the *Wellington Monument* with this buttress directly below. The monument is also visible from the *Eagle Stone* unless you're facing the wrong way.

73   Fact Hunt   *7a+*   ✳
The rib from a sit start is the line of the buttress. *Percy Bishton*

74   That Which Does Not Kill Me Makes Me Stronger   *7c*
Hard: follow poor crimps right of *Fact Hunt*. *Neil Travers*

75   Dirty Bitch   *7a*   ✳
A good problem that starts sitting as for *Fact Hunt*. Trend right before rocking onto the slab. No arête. *Lucy Atkinson*

A big natural boulder just left of the track, 100m back towards the edge from the monument.

76   4+
Sit-start up the steep side of the snappy flakes to top out on big jugs.

77   4
Layback up the huge flakes on the left hand side of the slabby front face.

78   Railtrack   *7a*   ✳
Awkwardly mantel the rail at the bottom of the blunt left rib.

79   Halfway Slab   *5+*   ✳
Pleasant padding up the slab.

Honeypot Wall

The rock continues in small, broken sections hidden along the southern bank that faces *Gardom's* and *Chatsworth*. There are a couple of areas of note for the sufficiently motivated. From the monument, head away from the crag along the wide track. Pass one tree on the left of the track, pass another after 150m and after a further 30-40m quest right straight into the woods. Good luck (!) – you're looking for the very well-hidden *Honeypot Wall*, a big buttress of good rock with quality climbing.

80　**Cheekbone**　*6a*
　　The left arête.

81　**Glovelove**　*7a*
　　A hard sequence up the left side of the wall using the overlap and cracks.

82　**The Genie**　*6b*　✳
　　The logical line of the wall using holds on both adjacent problems.

83　**Honeypot Wall**　*6b+*　✳
　　The thin crack taken direct.

84　**Rubbish**　*5+*
　　The right arête of the wall (the left arête of the crack).

85　**Judge Phillip Banks**　*6c*
　　50m up and right, and just below the rise, is a short undercut wall taken from a sit start. Currently being reclaimed by moss.

The Quarry

The final rock at Baslow appears to be unclimbed, and is certainly undocumented. It contains several problems, a few rotting sheep carcasses and some abandoned barbed wire. Nice. *The Quarry* can be found just before a shallow valley, if approaching from the crag

　　Registered Rhymenecologist　*6c*　✳
　　The plum line is an attractive steep groove in one of the first bays. *Dave Norton*
　　The two arêtes to the left are both 5.

DAVE NORTON ON *REGISTERED RHYMENECOLOGIST*　**PHOTO**: JOHN COEFIELD

EMILY BRAZENALL ON ROUTE Z · PHOTO: JOHN COEFIELD

Gardom's Edge

The *Gardom's* circuit has matured quite a bit since our last guidebook, thanks in the main to the development of further problems below the edge which have helped link the north and south areas together with more cohesion. Both the north and south areas are well established, with styles all of their own. *Gardom's North* is a great area with some classic hard lines characterised by powerful roofs and sloper tussles. *Gardom's South* is smaller, but features a number of standout lines, in particular the highball arête of *Suavito* and the groove of *G-Thang*. The crag circuit features all sorts, with crimpy walls, technical arêtes, dynos and highballs. *Moorside Rocks* lie just south of *Gardom's South*, offering a couple of lines worth seeking out.

Access and Approach

Gardom's Edge lies above the A621 to the east of *Baslow*. Although it's possible to walk along the top of the edge between the north and south areas, it's better to park differently for each. The problems below the edge can be approached from either parking area. See individual areas for approach information.

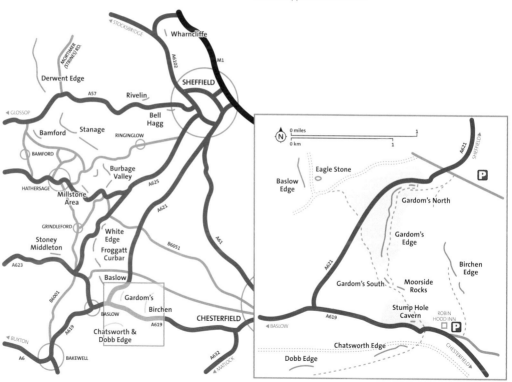

SIMON WILSON ON *NIGEL'S ROOF*. **PHOTO:** JOHN COEFIELD

Gardom's North

This is where most people likely think of when talk turns to bouldering at *Gardom's*. It's probably still the most popular of the circuits at the crag – just, although it's facing increasingly stiff competition from the crag circuit and the fine problems at the southern end. Home to the classic *Mark's Roof*, and its myriad variants, the rock here is good quality, the landings are flat and grassy, and the problems are satisfyingly powerful.

Conditions

The crag is north-facing, but most of the problems are popular enough for chalk to stop the growth of lichen. The crag can take a day or two to dry after rain.

Access and Approach

Park on the extension of the Curbar Gap road, just off the A621: it's the first right at a crossroads after passing the crag if approaching from Baslow (the village, not the crag), or the third left, just before the crag if coming from Sheffield. Cross the stile just up from the main road and walk parallel to the main road across the often boggy moor before crossing another stile to reach the first boulders perched above the road. Alternatively, walk down the road and pick up a path below the crag – better for keeping your feet dry.

1   Leaf Climb   5
A pleasant traverse, just above the descent path back to the road. Traverse from R–L with feet on the lower block, to finish up the flake. Eliminating the foot block is 6b+.

Percy's Roof   7a
The roof to the right, with a tricky top-out.

2   A Tasty Graunch   7a+
A daft, no-heels-allowed, eliminate traverse along the lip of a roof. Traverse the low roof from R–L, using edges below the top, to gain the hanging crack, at which point you're allowed to use the top. Top-out using a scoop for your left hand. Don't worry, not all the problems are like this.

3   Joint Care   7a+   ✷
The roof up and behind *A Tasty Graunch*. A classic Gardom's roof featuring a mix of heel/toes, crimps, slopers and mantle finish. Take care with the landing, which will require spotters and a few pads in order to be safe. See photo on p227. *Andy Harris*

4   Wishbone   7b
Good, but lowball roof. Start in the back and exit out of the right side of the roof, trying hard not to dab. *Rich Heap*

5   First Roof Middle   6c   ✷
A low roof. From a sit-start climb directly out of the centre of the roof and mantel out the lip, exfoliating your chin as you go.

6   First Roof Left   6b+
As above but using bigger holds on the left side of the roof.

>>

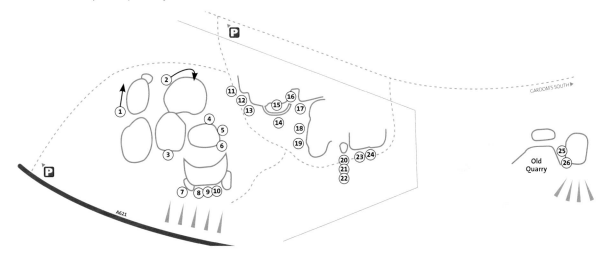

7   Mark's Roof Left-Hand   6c+   ★
Now we're talking. Take the left-hand side of the large roof from a sit-start, along the crimpy edges, to finish up the flake on the front face. Brilliant. See photo on p222.

Rock End Roll   7a+
Alternative exit to *Mark's Roof Left-Hand* up the crack on the left wall. *Graham Hoey*

8   Nigel's Roof   7b+
A tight line with good climbing, just right of *MRLH*. From the right side of the sloping shelf, reach small crimps in the roof, and then holds below the lip before swinging right to finish up *Mark's Roof*. Holds on *MRLH* are avoided. See photo on p224. *Neil 'Nigel' Kershaw*

9   Mark's Roof   7b   ★
From the shelf at the back of the roof, take the centre of the roof with a spectacular cut-loose on the lip, traverse left to the crux top-out, slapping, matching and trying to use the sloping pod above. Traversing even further left to finish up the flake is *Mark's Roof Original*, 7a. Reversing *Mark's Roof Left-Hand* to make a complete loop is 7b.

10   Mark's Roof Direct   7c   ✳
Start as for *Mark's Roof*, but from the square-cut hold on the lip take on the short blank wall above, trying to hold onto the most marginal of gritstone ripples. *Dylan's Roof* crosses the right-hand side of the roof using a sidepull – finish up *MRD*, 7c, or with arête, 7b.

11   Little Arête   6a   ✳
From a low start climb the nose using a flake.

12   Seamstress   5
Seams in the wall.

13   Prowstress   6a+
Scariness up the prow feature.

14   Ledge Roof   6a
Sit-start the roof under the ledge.

15   Ledge Wall   5+
The wall right of the crack. A right hand variant is 4+. The crack just left is 4+.

16   West Wall   5+   ✳
The sidewall, balancing onto the big footholds.

17   Alcove Nose   6b+   ✳
Thin flakes and the hanging arête – pull on and launch or balance up by laybacking the flake. Nice. A sit-start from a sidepull with feet in the back is 7b+.

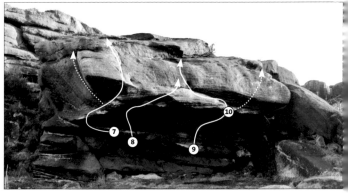

18 Ben's Bulge *7a+* ✳

The big sidewall. Undercut out to the sloper using as much of the foot or leg jam as you dare. *Ben Moon*

19 The Grasper *6c+* ✳

The big arête.

20 Soft on the G *7b* ★

The rounded undercut arête can feel easy with a bit of technique. Without it, the slopey slaps are very frustrating. Another classic. *Allen Williams*

21 Full Power *8a* ★

A sit-start to *Soft on the G*, starting with your right hand in the pocket on the lip and your left on the lowest crimp/seam on the left side of the roof. Hard slapping up ripples and slopers follows. Bottom of the grade. *Jerry Moffatt*

22 8 Ball *8a+* ★

No longer thought to be 8b but tough at the grade. Sit-start at the right side of the low roof and traverse left into *Full Power*. *Ben Moon*

23 Rock Hard Bishop *6b+*

The wall between *Soft on the G* and the groove to the right using holds on both those problems. Pull on, hit the top, that's it. *Johnny Dawes*

24 Soft Groove *6c* ✳

The lovely little groove from a sit-start. 6a+ from standing.

The next problems are on a small block visible through the trees, perched just above a tiny quarried pit.

25 Kidneystone *7b* ★

Sit-start on a large hold under the roof and slap up the left side of the bulge to a finger rail above. No footblock. Very good. *Kristian Clemmow*

26 Heartland *7c* ✳

Start on the same big hold under the roof, but exit at 90° to the last problem. Reach a high flared finger jam and use it to gain the slopers above. *Kristian Clemmow*

ANDY HARRIS ON *JOINT CARE* **PHOTO:** JON FULLWOOD

NEIL KERSHAW ON *BUSINESS AS USUAL* **PHOTO:** JOHN COEFIELD

Gardom's Crag Circuit

Much development has taken place along and below *Gardom's Edge* itself, resulting in a good, varied circuit. The problems are hard to find as negotiating the bottom of the crag is difficult, and knowing when to drop down from the top of the crag is confusing, even for locals. We have used routes as waymarks, and the problems are described north to south. Approach from either the north or the south end.

Scattered along the base of the edge proper, these problems are mainly in the trees. They take longer to dry and can become green. They are, however, sheltered on bitterly cold days.

Bloc Steno

Bloc Steno *6c* ✳

A lone problem situated on the buttress to the right of the large roof taken by the route *Spanish Fly*. Climb the rib without using the arête. 6a with the arête. *Simon Wilson*

Moyer's Buttress Area

The Gritstone Treaty *7b* ★

70m on from *Spanish Fly Buttress* immediately to the left of *Moyer's Buttress* is a wedged, leaning block, the left arête of which forms this great problem above a slightly dodgy landing. Pull on direct from the floor. *Pat King*

Mo's Problem *7a+*

The right arête is not quite as good and a lot scarier. Watch that landing – originally done with a ladder across the landing to create a flat pad platform. *Mo Overfield*

Perfect Day Direct Start *7a+* ★

This problem is on the tall sidewall right of *Moyer's Buttress*, 10m right of the *Gritstone Treaty*. The superb direct start to the route right of *Moyer's Buttress* is powerful and sports dynamic moves between edges. Jump start. 7b without the jump to the first flatty. *Ben Moon*

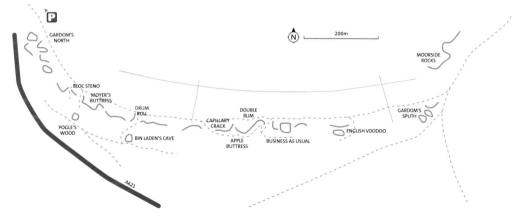

5   Pogle's Wood   6c   ★
Below *Moyer's Buttress* is a great boulder. *Pogle's Wood* follows the right arête of the downhill side of the block to a sloping finish. *Allen Williams*

Pogle's Wood Sit-Start   7b   ★
The sit-start is mean, frustrating and brilliant. From the low break slap up into the pinch on the right arête and make a decidedly tricky move to gain the sloping top. Not much change from 7b+. *Rich Heap*

6   Pogle's Wood Left-Hand   6b
Approach the same top-out from the left arête. Not as good. The sit-start is 6c.

To reach the next problems, walk downhill through the trees below *Pogle's Wood* to reach a vague path. Turn left along this, walking parallel with the edge, through the trees until a problem can be seen on an isolated block on the left after about 100m. This is *Bin Laden's Cave*.

7   Bin Laden's Cave   6c+   ★
The high, steep wall above the slab, with an awkward landing and a sloping top-out. Well worth finding. *Mo Overfield*

8   Bin Lillemule   7a+
The left arête of *Bin Laden's Cave*. *Jamie Lilleman*

The edge directly above *Bin Laden's Cave* has now petered out into a slope scattered with boulders. The next problem is on a quarried wall on the line of the edge in this boulder field, above and slightly to the right of *Bin Laden's Cave*.

9   Drum Roll   7a   ✳
The middle of the, undercut, quarried wall. Pull on with a sidepull and slap to a sloper. Tricky. *Paul Mitchell*

Another Green World   7b
The sit-start to Drum Roll. *Adam Long*

The next problems are situated on and around *Capillary Crack Buttress*. Approaching from *Gardom's North*, descend down a wide rocky slope 100m after a stone wall. 50m before *Apple Buttress*.

10   Chav's Head   6a+
The nose-shaped arête, complete with chav features, on the left-hand side of the buttress from a sit-start.

11   A Fearful Orange   6c+   ★
The high crack, starting matched on the triangular sloper in the groove. Move left at the top. A great problem. *Jon Fullwood*

12   Fearful Head   6c+
Link the start of *A Fearful Orange* into the top of *Chav's Head*. *Jon Fullwood*

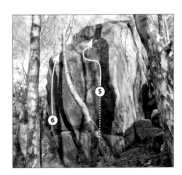

3   **Neutral Milk Hotel**   *6a*
Climb the arête behind the oak on its left-hand side. Good, high.

4   **Two Headed Boy**   *6c*
Climb the arête on the right-hand side to reach and traverse the shelf rightwards to its end, then top-out. Tiring.

5   **Ladder Coins**   *6b*
Situated up the hill to the right of the previous problems, right of a small birch tree. Climb the wall to the left of a groove, direct.

Apple Buttress

A tall slabby arête characterises this area – *Apple Arête* (VS). Approaching from the north it is about 150m after the stone wall.

16   **Double Bum**   *6b+*
Up and right of *Apple buttress* is a recessed quarried bay. Climb this wall to a sloping shelf and exit right. The problem is better and harder (7a) climbed as a dyno to the pinch (eliminating the undercut flake). Awaits a direct finish.

Business as Usual

A square-cut, overhanging block situated in a bay 100m right of *Double Bum*, above a quarry road. The finishes are highball.

17   **Dirty Business**   *6b+*
The left arête, climbed on its right from a sit-start to a highball finish. *Rob Smith*

18   **Plan D Sit-Start**   *7c*   ✳
A eliminate on *Dirty Business*, avoiding the big holds in the centre of the face. Tenuous and dynamic. Also 7c from standing, but as not as good. *Jon Fullwood*

19   **Business As Usual**   *6c+*   ✳
Jump-start to the hold in the centre of the face and finish with a flutter above. Excellent and powerful if started from standing, pulling on with the small undercut and a crimp before slapping to the jug – 7b+.

20   **The Forward Thinking Sound Engineer**   *7a+*
The right arête of the block, finishing up the right-hand sidewall. No crack.

The final problem along the edge is situated below the last main buttress on the edge, which contains the *Dawes'* route *Charlotte Rampling*. It is halfway between the wooded area and the next dry stone wall.

21   **English Voodoo**   *7a*   ✳
Below *Charlotte Rampling* is a block with an overhanging arête. Climb this via some nice moves on a pocket and pinch, avoiding the crack on the right. Sit-start is 7b. *Jon Fullwood*

Gardom's South & Moorside Rocks

A compact circuit hidden in the trees at the southern end of *Gardom's Edge*. The rock is very good quality, nicely featured and the landings are generally good with only the odd exception. Being in the trees it's sheltered in windy and cold weather, however the problems can become green in prolonged damp spells. *Moorside Rocks* is the attractive outcrop passed on the approach.

Access and Approach

Park in the free car park next to the Robin Hood Inn on the B6050, just off the A619 Chesterfield road. Walk back down the road towards Baslow, and cross a stile over the wall on the right after about 200m. Follow the path up the hill until some rocks are visible on the right – *Moorside Rocks*. Continue until a gate-sized gap in a wall is reached. Pass through this and hang a right – the boulders are tucked away under the trees over to the left.

1 *6b*
Climb the arête from the low hole on the left side. Harder than it looks.

2 *6a*
Hit the top from holds in the middle of the wall.

3 **G-Thang** *6b+* ★
The immaculate groove. *Allen Williams*

4 **G-Thang Sit-Start** *6c+* ★
Sit-start the groove using the small undercut. Graded without the arête.

5 **Barry Sheene** *7c* ★
Reach and match the crimpy rail in the centre of the wall by undercutting the break. Morpho, but hard even if you can reach. *John Welford*

6 **China In Your Hands** *7b+*
The indirect – original – start to *Barry Sheene*, starting up the groove between the two boulders, was easier before someone ignored the clue in the name and pulled too hard on the pebble. *Adam Long*

7 *6a+*
The arête just left is a bit reachy. It's also high and green.

8 *5* ★
The wall left of the arête.

9 *5*
The left arête.

10 *5+*
Arête and slab.

>>

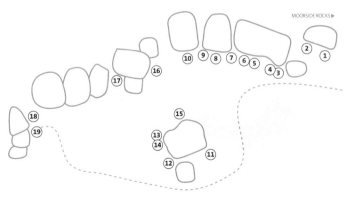

11 Suavito   7b   ★
The steep highball arête, climbed on its left side, gives great slappy climbing at an uncomfortable height, with a committing move to gain the top. Take some spotters and a few pads. See photo on p232. *Tom de Gay*

Escondido   7c
The right side of the arête, fridge hugging against opposing holds. Poor landing. *Jamie Lilleman*

12 6b+   ✳
The pocketed wall just left of the overhanging left arête. Move left to the ramp to finish.

13 6b
From a sit-start do a hard slap to catch the ledge and mantel it out.

14 Captain Cabinets   6b+
Start up problem 13 and trend right up the sloping arête to a pocket and flake.

15 6a+
Delicate arête over poor landing.

16 John Player Special   7a
The low cave and slopers, finishing up the left side of the arête. The block on the right is out. *Tom Allsop*

17 The Sausage King of Meersbrook   7c+   ✳
The hanging arête starting in the back of the roof, with a crux cut-loose. *Iain Farrar*

18 5+
The short arête and wall.

19 6a
The arête on the left-hand side – barely independent.

Moorside Rocks

Moorside Rocks is really a southern continuation of *Gardom's Edge*. The climbing is included owing to the ease of combining a visit here with the *Gardom's South* circuit. The rocks face southwest and are good, clean, exposed and out of the trees. Approach as for *Gardom's South*.

1   **Short Arête**   *6b*

2   **Right Arête**   *6c*

3   **Charlotte Dumpling Right-Hand**   *7b*
The arête of the crack (eliminating the far side) into the upper wall. 6b using everything.

4   **Superboc**   *8a+*   ★
The stunning rounded arête was climbed as a route, not a boulder problem. A stunning line that has since been bouldered ground-up with pads and spotters. *Miles Gibson*

5   **Little Latino**   *6c*

6   **The Jackalope**   *7a*   ★
The bottomless hanging crack up the centre of the wall succumbs to jamming or tenuous laybacking. Nicer with a spotter or two. *John Allen*

Birchen Edge

Better known as a low-grade route crag than a bouldering venue, *Birchen Edge* now has a number of very good boulder problems. In addition, many of the shorter routes have been re-evaluated while wearing bouldering goggles, resulting in a great circuit with problems from very easy to 7c+. The better problems along the edge are in the 6b–7c+ range while the *Three Ships* boulders provide good easier problems in a lovely setting.

Access and Approach

Park in the public car park next to the Robin Hood Inn, on the B6050, just off the A619, or in the over-flow in the field. Only use the pub car park if using the pub. Walk a short distance up the B6050 and take an obvious path on the left. This leads up to the crag after a 10–15 minute walk. The crag is visible on the right of the path. The *Three Ships* boulders are situated on top of the crag, behind the monument.

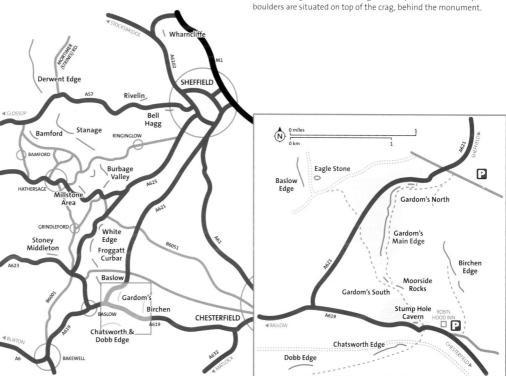

The Three Ships

Three excellent boulders with easy problems up to 6b and perfect, flat grassy landings. Endless variations can be climbed. The main lines are described. Mind the ledge above the *Defiance* and *Royal Soverin* boulders.

Victory

1　**Orion**　*5+*
　　The scoop. Awkward.

2　**Neptune**　*4*
　　Sidepulls right of the scoop.

3　**Euryalus**　*4*
　　The left side of the front face, finishing at the bowl. Sit-start at 4+.

4　**V for Victory**　*3+*　✳
　　Straight up past the chipped 'Victory'. A line just right of the 'Y' in Victory is 4.

5　**Prow Left**　*4*　✳
　　The left side of the prow, finishing with the crack.

6　**Prow Right**　*4+*　✳
　　The prow, staying right, from a sit-start. Dyno from a sit-start to the top at 5+. Double dyno at 6a.

7　**Victor's Ledge**　*3*
　　Make a move to the top and mantel out.

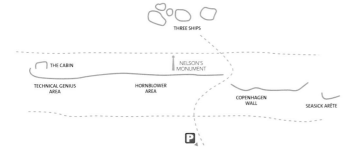

THREE SHIPS

THE CABIN

NELSON'S MONUMENT

TECHNICAL GENIUS AREA

HORNBLOWER AREA

COPENHAGEN WALL

SEASICK ARÊTE

Defiance

8   Finisterre   *3+*
The wall past the chipped *'Defiance'*.

9   St Vincent   *4+*   ✳
Sit-start into the crack.

10   Calvi   *4+*
The scoop.

11   Aboukir   *4*
The wall to a sloping dish finish.

12   Tenerife   *4+*   ★
Sit-start the prow/bulge on the right. A rare thing: a good, steep easy problem.

Royal Soverin

13   Royal   *4+*
Sit-start the wall.

14   Bilge   *4*
Sit-start the arête. Starting up *Royal* and traversing right to finish up *Bilge* is 5.

15   Buccaneer   *4*
Sit-start the arête right again.

16   Orlop   *5*
Sit-start the overhang at the left side of the big roof and pull up to more big holds.

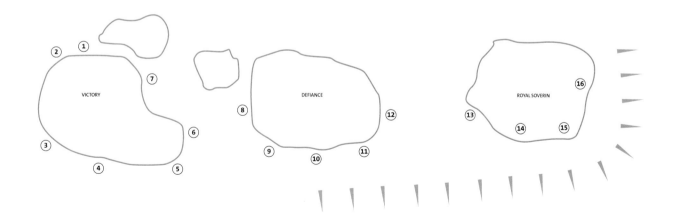

CRAG 30M
▼

The Edge

The problems on the edge itself start at the left-hand end, behind a pinnacle.
See topo on p238.

The Cabin

Situated on the rear of the pinnacle next to the scramble to the top of the edge.
Two or more pads are useful.

1   **Disabled Seaman**   *6a+*
    The left arête.

2   **Cabin Boy**   *7a*   ✳
    Dyno from crimps to top. 6c with the sidepull.

3   **Log**   *5*
    The right arête.

4   **Dan's Arête**   *6c+*
    Situated on a block down and left (when looking at the edge) from the
    Cabin Boy pinnacle. Climb the left face and arête from a sit-start.

Technical Genius Area

On the edge in front of, and to the right of, *The Cabin*.

5   **Kiss Me Arsee**   *7a*   ✳
    Sit-start the left arête of the block. Very good.

6   **Kiss Me Softly**   *6a+*
    Sit-start the right arête.

7   **Roger the Cabin Boy**   *6c*
    The left arête from a sit-start, using anything in reach on the block.

8   **Technical Genius**   *7a*   ✳
    Start matched on the rounded flake and pull to slopers. 7a+ from a sit-start. *Mark Katz*

Hornblower Area

9   Gritstone Megamix   *7a*   ★
Cross the roof on the left and climb the wall above. Highball. See photo on p236.
John Allen

10   Gritstone Mashup Mix   *7a+*
As for *Gritstone Megamix* to the lip, then traverse the lip left to finish up the arête.
Highball. *Ben Bransby*

11   HMS Daring   *7b+*   ★
The excellent highball arête, climbed on the left. *Bob Smith*

12   Splendide Audax   *7c*   ✳
The arête on the right-hand side. Deadpoint to a pocket. *Ben Bransby*

13   Thing on a Spring   *6c+*   ✳
The wall immediately left of the gulley. Sit-start on undercuts, up to slopey crimps and pop for the break.

14   Oarsman Arête   *6b+*
The left arête and crack. 6c from sitting.

15   Oarsman   *6b+*   ✳
Layback the crack on its right. Sit-start is 7a+ (no footblock left of the crack). *Mark Stokes*

16   'Oar 'Ouse/Hornblower Left-hand   *7a*
The wall between *Hornblower* and *Oarsman*. Start with right hand in the crack of *Hornblower*. Escape left at the break or finish above.

17   Hornblower   *6c*   ★
The wall left of the prow, starting left hand in the low crack/seam. Finish up the easy but high slabs above.

18   Obstructive Pensioner   *7a+*   ✳
The roof and hanging prow, starting on the break under the roof. A right-hand variation climbs up slopers on the right arête of the prow at the same grade. *Nik Jennings*

19   Jumpers for Trousers   *7c+*   ✳
The wall right of the prow, starting under the roof. The problem does not use the holds on the arête to the left, nor the big flake to the right. *Ben Bransby*

Copenhagen Wall

20 Copenhagen Corner *4* ✳
The flakey sidewall.

21 Scandiarête *6a*
The left arête of Copenhagen Wall, starting on the right-hand side.

22 Dane's Delight *5*
Span between two breaks and up. Dane's Disgust (5) climbs the wall to the right, past the flake, while Carlsberg Export (6b+) climbs the wall right again, without any of the good flakes or pockets.

23 MP3 *7b* ✳
Start under the roof, span to polished slopers then left to a larger polished hold. Rock/span to the break and finish up the wall above.

24 Mermaid *7c*
Start as for *MP3* to the big polished hold, but continue to traverse left via a poor pinch and slopers to finish up the wall 2m right of the arête. *Mark Evans*

25 Chasing the Dragon *7c*
Something of an enigma. The problem is found on the slabby, undercut boulder right of, and below, *Copenhagen wall* (while facing Baslow). Sit-start on the left side of the long pod under the lip, traverse right, dyno for a flake and finish up the right arête. *Mark Evans*

26 Lowside *6c+* ✳
A low start to the arête, reaching out to crimps on the lip and then around left to the flake.

27 The Buccaneer *7a*
Lean across to the sloping pocket at 10ft (and the crack if you can reach) from the block on the right. Pull boldly up to better holds in the hanging crack. Not a great landing, sadly.

The Brigand *7c+*
A direct start to *The Buccaneer*, from really poor holds below. *Mark Katz*

28 Sodomy *6c* ✳
Around to the right is an undercut, slabby buttress. Traverse the lip from right to left on pockets, finishing up before the crack/arête.

29 Men United *6a*
15m below and to the right of *The Brigand* is a lone obelisk. Climb the left arête on the right-hand side.

Seasick Arete

30 Seasick Arête *4+* ★
The polished arête bears the scars of its classic status. *Ernie Marshall*

31 Seasick Slab *4* ✳
The wall to the right.

Stump Hole Cavern, Chatsworth Edge & Dobb Edge

Three little esoteric areas, a stone's throw from Gardom's and Birchen, each with a destination problem worthy of a visit in its own right.

Access and Approach

All three areas are reached from the car park next to the Robin Hood Inn below Birchen, on the B6050, just off the A619. See the map on page 237.

Stump Hole Cavern

One for seekers of isolated, steep and powerful 7b+ walls, with optional 7c+ dyno finishes. The first bit does tend to stay dry in the rain.

Access and Approach

From the car park, walk down past the pub and follow the pavement alongside the main road for about 300m, passing the stile and footpath up to Gardom's and Moorside Rocks on the right. About 100m after the stile, at a kink in the road, the Cavern can be found set 10m back in a small quarried bay.

1   **Stump Hole Cavern**   *7c+*
    Blast up the steep wall from a sit-start to the ledge. Only a massive five-foot dyno now separates you from the finishing jugs and glory. *Brian Chase*

2   **Stump Hole Cavern (first bit)**   *7b+*   ✳
    Needless to say, most people bail out at the ledge. Sit-start as for the main event and follow the crimps and slopes to the mid-height ledge. 7b from standing. *Percy Bishton*

3   **Stump Cream**   *5*
    The easy warm-up on the wall to the left, off a layaway.

Chatsworth Edge

Chatsworth is really of very limited interest to the boulderer, although it is worth stopping off en route to *Dobb Edge*, and the two together will get you away from the crowds at the more popular eastern crags. If you're operating at 7a, then *Desperot* alone is worth a visit.

Access and Approach

From the car park walk down the road past the pub, looking out for a stile and path on the opposite side of the road after about 100m, just before the 'Reduce Speed Now' signs. Take this, drop down to cross the bridge over the stream, and follow the path to join a wide track. Turn right onto this and walk below the crag breaking uphill after the first big buttress. Desperot is on *Emperor Buttress*, which is about 300m along the crag.

Desperot   *7a*   ★
The direct start to the route *Despot* was a mythical English 7a problem, before someone actually went and tried it and the myth was smashed to reveal a classic Font 7a. Edges and sidepulls lead to slopey sidepulls and a committing launch to the break. Traverse or jump off. See photo on p2. *Ben Moon*

Dobb Edge

Another small handful of problems, which make the trek along *Chatsworth* worthwhile. Five main problems are described, although more fun can be had.

Access and Approach

Approach as for *Chatsworth*, but at the wide path, cross it, hop a stile and pick up the clifftop path. Follow this for about 500m, dropping briefly down and along through the bracken at a gap in the wall. After a gap in the edge in a field, *Dobb Edge* is the next crag along. The first problem is on a leaning block, detached from the main edge, next to a lovely little oak tree.

1   Dobb Egg   *6a+*   ✳
Sit-start and fridge-hug up the steep double arêtes.

The pinnacle behind has a bunch of routes, with the E1 5b up the Chatsworth-facing side – *Stevie Ray Has Passed Away* – being just about highball, with a brief crux pull at the crack and positive holds above: 4+.

2   Dobbin's Log   *6a+*
Behind and to the right of the pinnacle is an undercut bay with a steep, leaning rib up the middle, left of a holly tree. From a low start, reach out and crimp up edges on the rib to good holds in the grass. Belly-flopping onto the top isn't half as bad as it looks! A similar, slightly easier line exists to the left.

20m further along is a square-cut quarried bay.

3   Excavator's Arête   *4+*   ★
The excellent highball left arête. 5+ from sitting.

4   Dobbin's Blog   *7a*   ✳
The centre of the highball wall, from the finger rail, succumbs to either a big slap, or a thin pull on a nano-crimp out right. At the time of writing the top out is a death cornice made up of grass, heather and loose rock, so heroes can top out direct while their mates call 999, or alternatively shuffle left to the arête to top out. Sit-starts, below or down and right, are 7a+.

5   Cummerbund   *6b*   ✳
A great sideways problem that makes the most of the fine finger rail across the wall. Sit-start at the left arête and traverse the rail right to an unlikely crux pulling onto the shelves at the end.

ANDY BANKS ON *CUMMERBUND*   PHOTO: JOHN COEFIELD

Access and Approach

All the areas are reached from the B5056, just off the A6 sou___
of Bakewell. Roadside parking is available on the road for *Cratc_____*
and *Robin Hood's Stride*, while *Rowtor Rocks* and *Stanton Moor* are
accessed from the village of Birchover. *Clifftop Boulders* are found on
a back road, near the village of Elton. See individual crags for detailed
approach information.

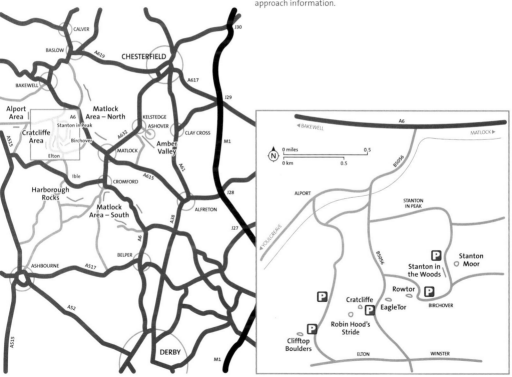

NEIL KERSHAW ON RAZOR ARÊTE · PHOTO: ADAM LONG

Cratcliffe

Often combined in circuit with *Robin Hood's Stride*, *Cratcliffe* is a fantastic bouldering venue. Grades extend from 3 through to the high 7s, and the crag offers a superb combination of technical offerings that smear up rounded scoops and blobs, to steep, powerful climbing on incuts, slopers and some gratton-type crimps that are peculiar to the local gritstone. *Cratcliffe* also harbours more than its fair share of must-do Peak classics.

The grattony crimps and incuts mean that there's a lot to do in warm weather when you just can't hold the slopes, especially in the shade given by the trees. The circuit below the crag can be dirty and damp after wet weather, but the exposed top boulders dry extremely fast. There is some soft rock in places, and the area has been subject to chipping in times long since past. We know that you'll treat these natural sculptures with the respect that they deserve.

Access and Approach

From the A6 follow the B5056, and turn left after 1km, before Alport. After 3km, park in the lay-bys at the side of the B5056 **(don't block the farm track)** and take the track up the hill. Ignore the track right to a farm and continue uphill. *Robin Hood's Stride* is to the left of the track. For *Cratcliffe*, take a small path into the wooded area on the right next to a bench. *Cratcliffe Middle* is up on the left. For the main area, pick up the path that contours east along the hillside. Hop over a stile and *The Egg Boulder* is on your left. Fork right here for the *Crag Boulders*, or break left up and out of the trees for the *Top Boulders*. A path links *The Stride* and *Cratcliffe* directly over the large field. See overview map on previous spread.

Alternative parking is available on the back road between Alport and Elton, with space for about 6 cars. After making the left turn before Alport, turn right up a minor road after 200m and follow this to a T-junction. Turn left and drive for 2km until the crags are visible on the left. Park considerately on the verge near a gate and follow the path to *The Stride*. Bear left to *Cratcliffe*.

Cratcliffe Middle

The first area is between *Cratcliffe* and *Robin Hood's Stride*. The best feature is the roof, which has some very good lines on it. Just to the left of the roof are two boulders stacked against each other and forming a roof crack.

1   Middle Slab   4   ✳
Climb the left side of the slab on the left face of the left block.

2   Middle Right   5+
The right side of the same slab.

3   Look at Me!   7a
Chimney/jam through the roof crack/cave. *Adam Long*

4   Look Right   4+   ✳
The double arêtes on the right-hand boulder. 6a+ from sitting. Left arête only is 7a.

5   Razor Arête   6c+   ✳
The left arête of *Razor Roof* using cunning but slightly worrying footwork. Nice.

6   Razor Roof   6c   ✳
The central line of the roof. Pull out from the jugs on the left side of the cave and use razor-sharp crimps to slap the top. *Martin Veale*

7   Cave Wall   6a
Start low on jams and use small, protruding crimps to reach the break up and right.

8   RZA Roof   7a+   ✳
Starting up 7 and traversing the lip to finish up *Razor Roof* is the classic link-up. A harder finish to the right of *Razor Roof* is 7b. Or start up *Razor Roof* and finish up *Cave Wall* – 7a.

Some problems have been climbed further right and on a slab below, but these have got dirty through lack of use and are slowly returning to nature.

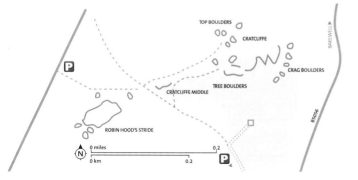

Top Boulders

A nice selection of low, easier problems: a great place to learn the grit art of smearing and a nice spot for a picnic in the sun. Virtually every inch of these blocks is climbable, so defining individual problems is somewhat arbitrary. We have pointed out some of the best features, but the most fun to be had is just messing about with mates and seeing what you can find.

1   **The Scoop** *3* ✳

2   **Scoop Arête** *4*
Arête on the left-hand side.

3   **The Squirm** *5* ✳
Into the runnel thing.

4   **Flake Problem** *4*
Short flake.

5   *5* ✳
Arête on left-hand side. 6a without the sidepulls.

6   **Top Rib** *6a* ★
The rib using the lovely pinch, eliminating the arête on the left. 4+ with the arête.

7   **The Ramp** *4*
Pad up the left-trending rampline.

8   **Blind Pocket Arête** *5+*
Right arête and pocket. Highball.

9   **Blind Pocket Wall** *5+* ★
Pockets up the wall. Reachy and highball.

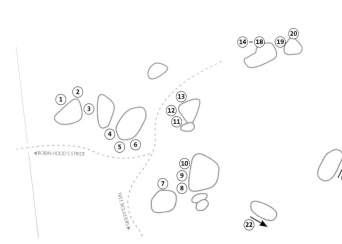

10 Blind Pocket Rib   5+
The left-hand side of the slab and rib. Highball.

11 Pink Slab Right   4   ✳
The slab is straightforward using the chip. Without, it is a good exercise in smearing that will improve footwork confidence (if you can do it).

12 Pink Arête   4   ✳
The chipped arête is elementary.

13 Pink Slab   3+
Another chipped slab that's better without the chips. A similar line is to the left.

14 Right Slab   4+   ✳
The slab without the arête or chips. *Foot Tickler* (5) foot traverses the lip up and left.

15 Johnny's Groove   6b+   ✳
You'll either walk up this groove or struggle like hell. 7b from sitting. *Johnny Dawes*

16 Lip Slap   6c+
Traverse the lip from *Johnny's Groove* to the arête.

17 Through Mantel   6b+
Mantel it out between the arête and groove.

18 Last Arête   6b
Sit-start the chipped arête. Easier these days due to the worn foothold.

19 Junior Arete   4+   ✳
The slabby arête on the block left.

20 Junior Flake   3+   ★
The flake and arête left again.

21 Hidden Arete   5
Hidden in the bracken is a rarely found boulder. Start the obvious steep arête from the low shelf via slopes. *Suicide Bummer* (6b) gets stuck into the inexplicable bum feature to the left.

22 Low Slung   7a   ✳
Sit-start at the left end of the low block, make crux moves up and right, keep traversing and exit up the scoop.

Lower Slung   7c
A lower eliminate that starts as for *Low Slung* but drops onto poor crimps below the top. Head right with a hard move to gain the top at the right-hand end. *Richard Ames*

23 Tit Traverse   7a
More sloper shuffling. Left to right traverse using the pair of intimate features.

Tree Boulders

Down in the trees the problems get harder and steeper. *Jerry's Traverse* and *T Crack* are two of the Peak's must-do 7b problems.

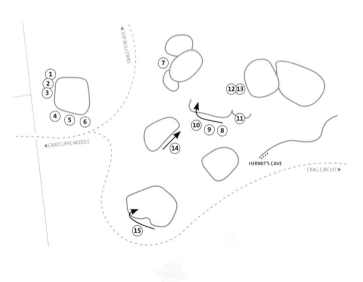

The Egg Boulder

The big green grit blob is covered in big green grit slopers.

1 **Left Egg** *4*
   The left arête, climbed on the right-hand side.

2 **5+** ✳
   The left-hand slab line, starting with an undercut for your left hand. A lovely problem.

3 **Eggy Scoops** *5*
   The central slab line above the scoops.

4 **Egg Arête** *6a+* ★
   The blunt arête is a classic grit thing. Pull on the slopes? Press off your palms?

5 **Eggs is Eggs** *7b+*
   Suction onto the slopiest of slopers using all of your gritstone 'feel'.

6 **Egged on** *5+*
   The right arête using the high flake.

7 **T Crack** *7b* ★
   A powerful grit classic. From the detached block under the roof, gain the sloping break via hard pulls on rippling undercuts and the pod-like crack. Then use strength or cunning to turn the final bulge. The foot-block on the right is out, and using the chip in the break is similarly not cricket. See photo on p257.

Mr. T *7b*

Start as for *T-Crack* but swing right to the arête from the base of the 'T' and finish up this, eliminating the break on *T-Crack*.

8 Jerry's Traverse *7b* ★

Classic a-technical traverse with powerful, sideways campus moves. Sit-start and traverse the slots from right to left, to a final lunge for the slanting shelf at the extreme left. The strong can do a there and back, finishing up the next problem – 7c. Ironically, Jerry remembers doing it first left to right – back around everyone! *Jerry Moffatt*

9 The Lark Ascending *6c+* ★

The wall above the start of *Jerry's Traverse*. Sit-start from low slots and head up the steep wall on good edges. A variant swings left to edges and rolls onto the slab – 7a. *Martin Veale*

10 Little Robin *5*

Dyno from the jugs near the end of Jerry's to the top.

11 Converted *7b+*

The big bulbous roof up and right of *Jerry's Traverse*. Scoopy undercuts, a sloper and a big reach lead to a sloping ramp and a high top out with the arête of the crack. The terrible landing can be sorted out with lots of pads and a big spotting team. *Neil Mawson*

Up above is a low roof.

12 Serpico *6c+* ✳

Span out from the back via a pocket on the lip.

13 Shunting Biscuits *7a+*

Start up *Serpico*, then traverse left up the obvious ramp to a nasty mantel.

Below *Jerry's Traverse* is a jumble of boulders.

14 Green Slopey Traverse *6c*

Traverse the top of the block down and left of *Jerry's Traverse*, from L-R. Sloper shuffling at its most boring.

15 Slopey Green Traverse *6c+*

R-L traverse. Another exercise in sloper shuffling, but crossing the wide crack/gap using knees and whatever provides some interest. Fun.

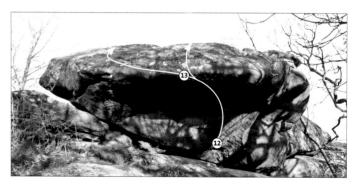

Crag Boulders

A mini-circuit below the crag. Many of the boulders around have only recently been opened up and will need more attention before they clean off properly. The first feature is the wall right of the metal bars of *The Hermit's Cave*.

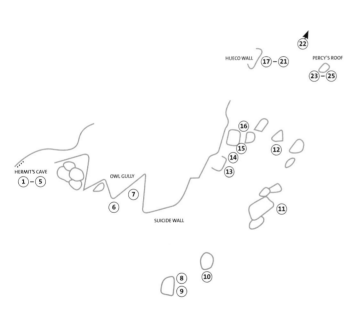

The Hermit's Cave

A hermit lived here until at least 1549 when local records show payments being made to him. Inside, on the wall, is a 4ft high carved crucifix that is thought to be contemporary with a 14th century rule requesting that all hermits have an image of the crucified Saviour.

1   **Hermitage Traverse**   *6b*
  Traverse right from the bars, along an assortment of natural and hermit-made features.

2   **The Fence**   *4+*
  The thin crack. Escape off.

3   **The Bishop**   *6b*
  Crimp up from the left-hand chip to the higher one.

4   **Chip and Thin**   *4+*
  The wall left of the groove using the diagonal runnel. *Hermitage Rib* (6a) climbs the slanting feature just right.

5   **Hermitage Hand Jam**   *4+*
  A direct start to the crack. The grade assumes you can jam.

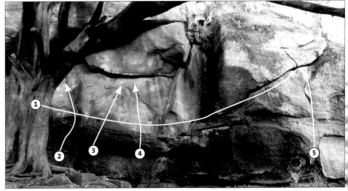

Owl Gully

Contour below the crag until the huge v-notch gully containing the classic route *Fern Hill* is reached.

6   Three Hundred Pounds Of Musclin' Man   *7c+*   ✳
The long awaited solution to the arête. *Ben Bransby*

7   Percy's Cornflake   *7a+*
Sit-start on a jug on the right-hand side of the low roof and climb the wall above to the break. *Percy Bishton*

Below this, in front of *Suicide Wall*, is a dirty detached block with an arch feature:

8   *6a*
The arête from a sit-start.

9   The Arch   *6c+*
Sit start, and climb the arch. *Percy Bishton*

Right of this block, looking towards the crag, is a smaller block with *private* written on it.

10   Brian's Private Arête   *7b*   ✳
A dynamic problem with prescribed rules. Sit-start the right-hand arête – left hand undercut, right hand arête – pull on and launch for the top. *Brian Chase*

11   Brain Dead   *6c*   ★
The big, square-cut, sharp, highball arête. Easier on the left, better on the right. 7b from a low start on the left. *Martin Veale*

12   *6a+*
A lost arête up behind *Brain Dead*, with a good hold halfway up.

13   Babu Yagu   *7b*
The nice rampline feature situated to the left of the arête situated at the top of the slope above the *Brain Dead* boulder, in the trees beneath the crag. Climb the rampline to the end and reach right to the arête to finish. Try cunning instead of strength. *Jon Fulwood*

14   Chess Boxer   *7a+*
Climb the arête on its left-hand side. High. *Dan Honeyman*

Over to the right is a big boulder with a steep, downhill face and a big prow.

15   Sparrow/My Best Friend the Watermelon   7c
The left arête/prow is highball!, and there's no real landing to speak of. The crux is leaving the floor, and the high top-out is much easier. The problem wasn't named twice, it was named once, but with two names. *Ben Bransby*

16   Sparrow Right-Wing   7b
Traverse slopers in from the right to the finish of the last problem. *Ben Bransby*

Hueco Wall
Approximately 50m further than the right-hand end of the crag is an attractive wall with some obvious large huecos. It seems to stay dry even in the most foul of weather.

17   Moss Ridge   5+
The often-dirty left arête.

18   Chapel of Rest   7a+   ✳
Gain the left hueco and undercut it to reach the sloping top. *John Allen*

19   Wish   7a+   ★
Gain the right-hand hueco and leave it via undercuts and edges to reach a hidden hold over the top. *John Allen*

20   6c
Traverse the deceptive break-line from right to left.

21   Percy's Start   6c+
Start low at the left-hand side of the wall and use edges to gain the higher traverse, which is followed rightwards. Finishing up *Wish* or *Chapel of Rest* is 7b. *Percy Bishton*

About 50m further on from *Hueco Wall* is a very mossy block.

22   Brother Lee Love   7b
Hang the sloping lip and pinch, pull into the scoop and exit left. Filthy at the time of writing.

Percy's Roof
A good set of problems (when clean) down the hill and facing away from *Hueco Wall*.

23   72   7a
Climb leftwards through the roof from a sit-start with both hands in the big hole to gain the boss on the lip. Traverse left along the slopey rail and mantel. *Percy Bishton*

24   72 Direct   7a+
Start as for *72* but continue straight up the hanging arête from the boss on the lip. *Percy Bishton*

25   P Crack   7b   ✳
The central line through the middle of the roof. Sit-start in the pocket at the back of the roof then head out via the pockets to a sloper under the lip. Gain the hanging crack in the headwall using toe hooks in the big hueco under the roof and climb this to the top. *Percy Bishton*

BEN BRANSBY ON *MY PRUNE*. PHOTO: ADAM LONG

Robin Hood's Stride

A lovely spot to visit even if you do not intend to climb; *The Stride* is a place of ancient mystic beauty. The bouldering ranges from technical arêtes to thuggy roofs with grades from 4–8a+, but the best climbing is to be found below 7b, and that alone makes it one of the best bouldering areas in the Peak.

Hundreds of problems and variations have been climbed here over the years in the spirit of exploration and experimentation – the problems detailed here take the strongest lines with the least amount of eliminates possible and avoid those boulders that have been covered with a cloak of lichen and moss after years of neglect.

Open in aspect, with bouldering on 360° of the tor, *The Stride* gets any weather coming at it. Having said that, the ancient gods have ensured a very special microclimate for this gathering of stones and the weather is often better here when things are closing in on the Eastern Edges.

Access and Approach

Park in the lay-bys on the side of the B5056 (don't block the farm track) and take the obvious track up the hill. Ignore the track right to a farm and continue up the hill. *The Stride* is the twin monoliths and boulders to the left of the track: look out for a low stile and one higher up to access the climbing.

Alternative parking is available on the back road between Alport and Elton, with space for half a dozen cars. From the A6 follow the B5056, turning left after 1km. Turn right onto a minor road after 200m and follow this to a T-junction. Turn left and drive for approx. 2km until the crags are visible on the left. Park on the verge near a gate and follow the path directly to *The Stride*. See overview map on p247.

Robin Hood's Stride is unfortunately covered in carved graffiti, and some of the easier problems use chipped holds. This has, in the recent past, encouraged inexperienced climbers to chip further holds, a practice that is wholly inappropriate. Please refer to the notes at the front of this book. However, there is one large (50cm) circular carving on a horizontal ledge, behind the Eastern chimney, that, although of uncertain age, is allegedly very old indeed and may relate to druidical practices in the area. It was uncovered in the 1970s and may have been preserved by the vegetation that covered it.

RICH DRAISEY ON *DRY WIT IN A WET COUNTRY*   **PHOTO:** ADAM LONG

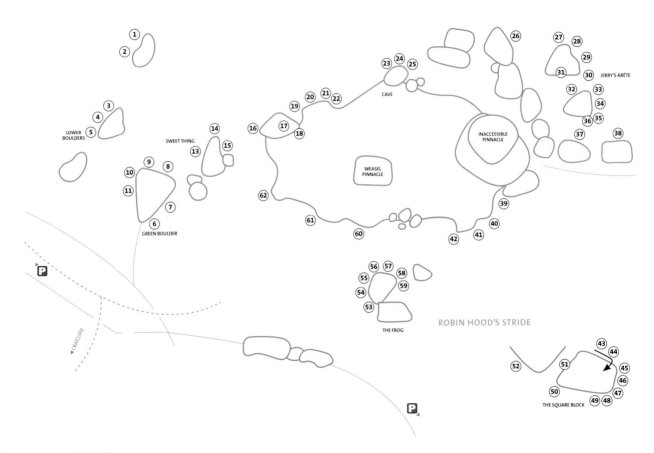

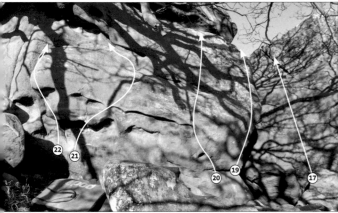

Lower Boulders

The first problems are on two slabby boulders down the hill.

1   **5+**
Flake and slab.

2   **3+**   ✳
Climb the centre of the nice slab via a slopey ledge. 5 if climbed trending up and left. Other variations possible.

3   **The Arch**   **4**
Slab and bulgette. Eliminating the holds on the left arête makes for a nice padding problem too, 5.

4   **T Slab**   **4+**   ✳

5   **T Slab Arête**   **4+**   ✳

Green Boulder

Up the hill is a boulder beside a tree.

6   **Short Arête**   **6b**   ✳
The rounded arête just right of the remains of a wall is great.

7   **Short Wall**   **7a+**
Hard smearing up the wall to the right. If it feels easy, you're too far right.

8   **Boysen's Crack**   **6c**   ✳
A tussle up the awkward, hanging hand-sized crack.

9   **King of Fools**   **7b+**
The arête, staying on its left side all the way. The problem moves leftwards and uses the right edge of the crack. Morpho. *Mike Adams*

10   **Slap Bass Odyssey**   **7b**   ✳
The blunt rib on the left side of the sloping shelf. Gain the rib direct via seams, and stretch to the sloping top. *Joe Le Sage*

11   **Zaff's Mantel**   **7a**   ✳
Start as for *SBO*, hand traverse 1m right along the sloping shelf and mantel.

12   **6c**   ✳
Start as for *SBO* but hand traverse the sloping shelf to the right arête and finish up this, or by rocking back left via the shelf (less scary).

Sweet Thing

13 The Staircase *Fun* ✳
The chipped slab.

14 Sweet Arête *6a+* ✳
The left side of the arête from a sit-start.

15 Sweet Thing *8a+*
Sit-start on undercuts (bit cramped) and use a poor two-finger dish and a chipped edge to slap the sloping top. The edge is now much bigger than it was on the first ascent. *Ben Moon*

16 My Prune *7c* ✳
Climb the arête to the break and finish leftwards. Hard climbing to the break and easier but scritty and worrying above. Highball (E5-ish). *Ben Bransby*

17 Dry Wit in a Wet Country *7a* ★
The wall up to the hanging crack direct is barely highball with a good pad and some spotters. See photo on p259. *Johnny Dawes*

18 Dry Whit *6c+*
The left arête. *Kim Leyland*

19 Grizzly Arête *7a+* ★
The tricky arête past a thin guppy and a wide pinch. *John Allen*

20 The Growler *7c* ✳
Sit-start under the right side of the sloping pod, climb up to it using edges and exit with a big span from the undercut. The top moves were originally climbed on *Martin Veale's Mock Beggars Wall* (E4). *Percy Bishton*

No Regrets *7b+*
Start as for *The Growler* but traverse the pod left, to exit stepping onto the blocks on the left, or finish as for the next problem. *Percy Bishton*

21 The Kid *7a+* ✳
Sit-start underneath flowing undercuts on the left side of the face. Pull into the undercuts and span to the flake on the right. Finish on the break above and escape left. Reachy. *Martin Veale*

22 Hugo First *6a*
Up the flaky arête, starting as for *The Kid*.

The Cave

A steep, all weather spot at the back of *The Stride*.

23 The Cave Problem *7a* ★
The right edge of the cave from a low start. *Martin Veale*

24 The Blobs Eliminate *7a+* ✳
Start in the back and work back right to the lip pinching the roof blobs. Avoiding the lip on the right and climbing to a crimp on the top edge of the block before gaining finishing jugs is also 7a+.

25 *6a+*
Lock from the pocket on the left hand wall to the top. No arête. A poor problem climbs the wall to the right from a hanging start. *Martin Veale*

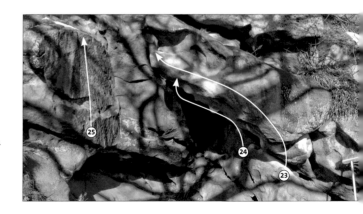

Jerry's Arete Area

eep contouring around and more shapely boulders come into view.

6 4+
The chipped slab set back.

7 Roscoe 6b ∗
Arête on right-hand side. *Daisy* is the groove to the side – 4.

8 Bossa Nova 6c
Mantel the nose. *Martin Veale*

9 Boss Hogg 5
Use the flake to swing onto the nose and up the slabby side of the arête.
Starting down on the nose is 6a+.

0 Jerry's Arête 7a ∗
The classic arête on the left-hand side using a finger jam to start. An extended start,
traversing in from the right arête and avoiding the juggy flake is 7b+. *Jerry Moffatt*

1 Hoppin' Mud 7b
Jump-start the wall left of *Jerry's Arête. Jerry Moffatt*

32 5
A rising line on the side of the slabby block to the left.

33 Diamond Slab Right 6b ∗
Enter the scoop and use the right arête with a little trepidation.

34 Diamond Slab 6c+ ∗
Enter the scoop again and head straight on up the slabby wall with more
than a little trepidation. Can be spotted high on left. *Martin Veale*

35 Diamond Slab Left 5+ ∗
Enter the scoop for the final time and trend left up the arête with less
trepidation than the other two.

36 Ben and Jerry's Love Child 7a
Sit-start the left arête on its steep left side. *Joe Barrell*

37 Concave Crimper 6a ∗
Grattonny-type crimps up the slab.

38 Jams O'Mantel 6c
Grovelling mantel onto the block.

The Pinnacles

Up and left is a collection of problems below the main pinnacles.

39 Picalli's Pickle *7a+* ✳
The roof crack, hear it growl. Start on jugs at the south end and head north. *Jimbo Kimber*

40 Muscle Slab *5*
Slab and flake.

41 Nobody Knows *6b* ✳
Into the scoop using a bit of route mentality. Finish dramatically over the steep, juggy nose.

42 Big Al Qaeda *7b* ★
The left arête was a last great problem at *The Stride* for quite a while – it's now a technical, modern classic. See photo on p246. *Michael Duffy*

The Square Block

The big, square lump over in the field.

43 Scoop Slab Traverse *5+*
Hop on the slab on the right and smear leftwards to top-out up the arête – only use the top to finish.

44 Scoop Slab *4*
The brief slab. Variations possible.

45 Angle Arête *5*
Short arête on the left. 3+ on the right.

46 Spinal Slab *7a* ✳
The thin, tenuous slab between the arêtes.

47 Stepped Arête Right-Hand *5* ✳
Classic stepped arête on the right-hand side.

48 Stepped Arête *6b* ★
The arête on its left. Classic.

49 Ben's Wall *7c* ✳
The wall left of the arête – undercut to the high sidepull and use it to exit direct or rock over leftwards into the scoop – it's hard either way. No arête. *Ben Moon*

50 The Nose *6b+*
The nose approached from the hole, wriggling onto the top.

51 Flake Crack *4*
Large flake/crack in sidewall.

52 Shadow Slab *Fun*
The very easy-angled slab to the left.

The Frog
Back towards the main blocks is this free standing pillar.

53 Potty Time *4*
The scoop facing away from the crag.

54 Vandals *5+*
More eroding chips, best finished left. It is easier – 5 – if you jump for the top chip, rather than pulling on first, and top out right.

55 Jaws *7a+*
The right arête without any chips.

56 Flipper *6c* ✳
The hanging crack used to be approached from the chip that has now worn away – undercut the left wall and reach to the crack, share and up. 6a if you use the left arête as well.

57 JT Crack *3+*
The crack.

58 JT *3*
The wall.

59 Dorsal Arête *3*
The wall and arête.

The final few problems are back on the crag.

60 Grovel *6b+*
The high scoop requires more survival instinct than skill – reach into it and start swimming. *Mark Stokes*

61 Burley's Bridge *6b*
The little arête.

62 Boomerang-erang *5+* ✳
The sharp arête on the left-hand side. 6a from a sit-start. The wall left is a 5.

Clifftop Boulders

A couple of nice blocks in a nice place with some nice problems, plus an esoteric quarry passed en route with some trashtastic esoteric arêtes. The climbing varies from straightforward pulling between mostly positive holds, to some tricky, technical arêtes at the quarry. The climbing faces west and is relatively quick drying after rain, although some problems at *Clifftop* can suffer run-off after heavy rain. The quarry is often dry when it's still raining. Grades range from 4+ to 7c+.

Access and Approach

Leaving the village of Elton going west, take the first road on the right. Follow it round a few bends and park sensibly just after a corner with a bench, gate and water trough. Follow the path after the gate – *Harthill Quarry* is on your right after a short distance. For *Clifftop Boulders*, keep to the left-hand path, take a stile into a field and follow the path rightwards towards the obvious blocks on the hillside, to the left of a large wooded area. Vault the wall beneath them with care.

Please note that it's best to keep a low profile in the quarry, and avoid it when the monthly motorcycle meets are on.

Harthill Quarry

A big, fairly unattractive gritstone quarry passed en route to the *Clifftop Boulders*. Included for the esoterica enthusiast.

1   **Chinka Choo**   *6a*
    The leftmost arête of the quarry on its right side.
    Jon Fullwood

2   **Kata**   *6a+*
    Around the middle of the quarry is a heap of junk. Left of the junk pile where the crag is set forward is a vague rib and hanging flake, climbed to a juggy ledge. Reverse and jump off.

3   **Kappix**   *7a*   ✳
    The curvy arête right of *Kata*, climbed on its left side with tricky moves to get over the angle change and a gripping stretch left to finish. Escape down *Kata*. A low start is 7a+ from matched on the obvious rail.
    Paul Worsdale/Jon Fullwood

4   **Scrap Heap Challenge**   *7a*   ✳
    The steep, leaning prow 6m right of *Kappix*.
    Dry in the rain. *Jon Fullwood*

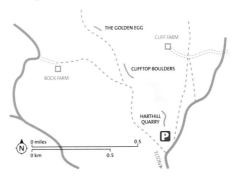

Clifftop Boulders

The main block has a number of good up problems and two good traverses. The first problems are on the block on the left.

5   **Nose on Left**   *4+*
    Climb the nose on the left, padding up the slab.

6   **Nose Direct**   *5*   ✳
    The nose direct.

7   **Right Nose**   *5*
    The nose approached from the right via the diagonal hold.

8   **Emergency Room**   *7a*
    Dyno from the break to the top with your feet smearing on the triangular bit of wall below.

9   **Clifftop Arête Left**   *7a+*   ✳
    The left-hand arête from a sit-start down and right is very good and offers up some crispy pinches at the top. No pushover. *Ben Groom*

10 **Middle Wall**   *6b*   ✳
    The central line up the face from sitting has a stretch for the top. A good, basic problem.

11 **Original**   *6a+*   ★
    From low in the scoop, climb up and right using the protruding crimp, then out to the arête and up using the thin flake.

12 **Boing Boy**   *7a*   ★
    A direct start up the arête from sitting – jugs, edge, pinch on the arête, jump to jugs, finish up the arête above. Classic. *Andy Crome*

13 Cracker Block   6b
Sit-start on the jug under the slab and then up the wall using the grippy sloper.
Left and right variants possible.

14 Steep Arête   6c
Sit-start the steep arête to the right, on its right, making use of holds in the crack.

15 Rib Arête   6a
Just right is a ribby arête. Climb this from the low jug. 6c without the big hold up and left. An extension start – *Appetite for Distraction* – shuffles in from the left, avoiding the shelf for feet: 6c with the big hold at the finish, 7a+ without. *Jon Fullwood*

16 Brad's Block Traverse   7b   ✳
Start on the juggy break on the extreme left of the block (the start of *Emergency Room*), drop down immediately onto crimps and traverse the low line rightwards, into and out of the scoop, to finish up *Cracker Block*. An extension shuffles right from the mid-height break on *Cracker Block* to finish up problem 14 – 7b+. *John Bradbury*

Brad's Block High   6c
The higher level traverse – start as above but continue along the upper break and finish up *Cracker Block*.

50m left is a small cave, just before the field corner.

17 Sheep Dip   6c
The hanging groove feature left of the wide crack.

18 The Golden Egg   7c+   ✳
The stunning prow. Climb out from the low left arête and an undercut, avoiding the blocks on the left. Harder for the short at the start. *Jon Fullwood*

19 The Furry Egg   7c+   ✳
Start as for *The Golden Egg*, but after a couple of moves swing onto and up the centre of the front face on slopers, with the help of toe hooks on the back arête. Reach left to finish. Next generation stuff. *Ned Feehally*

There are some more blocks visible on the hillside over to the left, although they promise much they aren't really worth the walk over.

JON FULLWOOD ON *THE GOLDEN EGG* – PHOTO: JAMIE LILLEMAN

Eagle Tor

You are not allowed to climb here. Rather than trying to pretend that the crag does not exist, we have instead chosen to include it for the avoidance of doubt with regards the current access situation. The landowners, once tolerant of climbers visiting what essentially amounted to their back garden, have understandably had enough. Too much noise, litter and poor behaviour.

Access and Approach

You are not allowed to climb here. The information opposite was collated at a time when climbing was allowed and it is included here for historical reasons only, and in the hope that access will once again be permitted in the future. For up to date information, visit the BMC's *Regional Access Database*: www.bmc.co.uk/bmccrag

Eagle Tor can be approached either from the roadside parking below *Cratcliffe* or from the village of Birchover. From below *Cratcliffe*, walk back up the road in the direction of Bakewell and cross a stile on the right after a few metres into a muddy field. A path rises up the hill and through a gate. Double back and follow the path round to the right of the *Tor* until the remains of a stone building are reached. The blocks of the *Tor* lie up the hill on the left. From Birchover, follow a track past the side of the Druid Inn to a gate marked *Rockingstone Farm*. Turn left up the path to reach another gravelly track. Then turn right and head down this track for 40 metres until a small path (below a wall) runs up the hill to a gate leading onto the *Tor*. See overview map on p247.

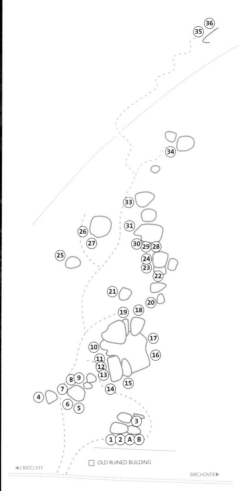

◀ CRATCLIFFE   ☐ OLD RUINED BUILDING   BIRCHOVER ▶

1   **Knuckle Duster**   *6a*
    The left side of the wall.

2   **Invisible Touch**   *6a+*
    The wall to the right. A) *Dave's Arete* is right again – 5+.
    B) *Sloper Wall* is right again on very grim undercuts
    and ledges – 7a+. *John Bradbury*

3   **Tourettes Arête**   *6c*
    On a terrace above a drop is this steep little arête/prow,
    started from the shelf. *Tourette's Rockover* (6c) rocks onto
    the slab from the RH start. *Percy Bishton/Jon Fullwood*

4   **Diamond Slab**   *5*
    The slopey shelf.

5   **Undercut**   *6a+*
    Up from undercuts.

6   **Boeing**   *6b*
    Sit-start. Up the arête from the massive undercut.

7   **Jumbo**   *6b*
    The rib arête and slopes up the front face.

8   **Brush**   *5*
    The short crack line.

9   **Pocket Problem**   *6c+*
    Pockets and small features up the wall from a sit-start.

10 **Ribbed for Her Pleasure**   *7a*
    The rib. No jump-starts. 7b from sit-start.

11 **No Mercy**   *7c*
    The left arête was originally climbed by jumping right
    to the crimps on *Autumn*. It has since been repeated
    straight up the arête. Morpho. *Thomas Willenberg*

12 **Autumn**   *7b+*
    Jump left to razor crimps from the start of *Feel Good*.
    Harder if you pull on first before jumping (7c). A direct
    start – *Fall* – jumps straight to the better crimps and is
    allegedly easier. *Jerry Moffatt*

13 Feel Good *7c+*
Tiny crimps to a sloping top. Use pads or a stone to reach the crimps, and the coldest weather possible to hang them. *Jerry Moffatt*

14 Heart Arête *6b*
The blunt arête. The slab right is 5+.

15 Smears Fears *6c*
The rounded arête on the block left.

16 McThud *7a*
Sit-start the offwidth. *Justin Critchlow*

17 Pocket Mantel *6a*
The low roof with a rounded pocket over the lip.

18 Rollin' Pat *7a*
Sit-start, make fingery moves out to and up the arête left and back right to the arête.

My Lemon *7c+*
The arête, climbed on the right, from a sit-start. Very morpho. 7b+ from standing *(The Eagle has Landed)*. *Primal Light* (7b+) swings right from the start of *My Lemon* past a poor undercut to the groove. *Kim Thompson/Andy Harris/Pat King*

19 Free Flight *7c+*
Spring up the tall rib. *Ben Moon*

20 Shamon *6c*
A little sit-start up the pinches and crack. *Percy Bishton*

21 Scaramanga *7a+*
The slab used to climb via three nipples, hence the name, now it climbs the two remaining ones. *Percy Bishton*

22 Curvaceous *7a+*
Sit-start onto the curving hold, match and reach left to slopers and up. The original straight up is unclimbed since the starting jug snapped off.

23 Bulb Sit-Start *6c*
The unusual gritstone tufa feature from the sidepull down and right. A sit-start directly beneath the tufa is easier but much less satisfying as you can just miss out the tufa altogether. A direct finish from the sidepull via a big dyno is much harder – 7a+ ish.

24 Shroom *7a+*
The roof on the left via a poor pocket and sloper.

25 I'm With Stupid *7b*
The small rib. Start sitting and launch for the top as your spotters sympathise with the name. *Percy Bishton*

26 Brad's Arête *7a+*
A technical classic. The sit-start is 7b, but the hard bit is still on the original. *John Bradbury/Thomas Willenberg*

27 Angel Falls *6c*
Smear up the centre of the slab – no arête.

28 Winter *6a+*
Smearing and palming up the right-hand side of the slab.

29 Spring *4+*
The centre of the slab.

30 Crack and Arête *4*
The crack and arête on the left side of the slab.

31 5+
More friction work up the slab.

32 6b
Sit-start the leftwards trending arête. *John Bradbury*

33 Parachute *6a*
The ramp feature is started by a tenuous rock onto an obvious foothold.

34 Face Arête *7b*
Sit-start the hanging arête from low jams, eliminating blocks on the left. 6c if you use the left block for your feet. *Percy Bishton*

The final problems are on a hidden wall on the other side of the plateau. Cross the fence via the barbed wire gate and jungle bash rightwards until you find it.

35 Mona *7c*
The wall is climbed using the small sidepull, a jump and some finger strength. Scary and high in the grade. *Dawid Skoczylas*

36 7c
From low edges campus up the wall to the left.

ANDY HARRIS ON *CHIMPANZEE*. PHOTO: JOHN COEFIELD

Rowtor Rocks

Rowtor is another local curiosity with many strange rooms and shapes carved into the rocks, maybe by druids. *Rowtor* takes its name from the two huge rocking boulders found at the east end of the top terrace. From these came the name Rootor, from the localism 'roos' which means anything that moves to and fro. At least one of them doesn't rock anymore after someone tried to push it over. The climbing is mostly steep and powerful with plenty of roofs and hideous sloping mantels. The majority of the un-attributed problems were probably first cleaned and climbed by John Bradbury in '96–'97.

Rowtor is covered in trees, slow to dry, and can get green. Once dry though, it's pretty sheltered and some of the steep problems stay dry in the rain.

Access and Approach

Park sensibly in Birchover village and take the track past the Druid Inn. Just after the Druid, turn right along a path that goes behind the pub and wanders up and left to the rocks. The first problem is just off the path up from the pub, down and left of the big roof and tunnel. See overview map on p247.

Note: although you have every right to be there, it is worth keeping numbers on the *Short Sean's* area to single parties to avoid upsetting local residents.

1 Catch 7c+
Stand start from a bad pocket (right-hand) & sidepull or undercut (left-hand) and make a hard dynamic move to the runnel, hold the swing (crux), match and pop to the crozzly jug. *Andy Harris*

2 Chip Shop Mantel 6b+ ★
Hand-traverse the rain gutter around the corner then mantel up. *Gutter Snipe* continues all the way to the finish of *Pink Lady* and is the easiest way up the block but pumpy – 6b+.

3 The Brazilian 7c ★
From the gutter climb directly up the side wall to a big dish via a hard heel rock-over using a small crimp. *Andy Harris*

4 The Yoghurt Hypnotist 7b ★
The overhanging arête/rib below the rain gutter is climbed from a sit-start, without the use of the gutter on the left wall, to top-out up the arête above or up the *Chip Shop Mantel* if dirty. *Percy Bishton*

Continuing under the canopy, a door is reached on the left that provides access via a tunnel to the terrace above.

5 Abyss 6c ✳
The horrendous looking, but brilliant, off-width above the tunnel door. Overhead knee bars and undercutting, or get in and squirm. Originally climbed at HVS.

6 Pink Lady 8a ✳
The left arête of the *Abyss* from a sit-start is a fierce problem. 7c+ from standing, 7a+ with a jump start. *Dave Mason*

On the top terrace:

7 Humpty Dumpty 6c+
One for the keen. Sit start with feet in the recess under the roof and move up on slopers. *James Pearson*

8 Blood Falls 7a+ ✳
The prow and pockets from a low start on slots under the roof. There is some crumbly rock, so please treat it with care. Easier now the first pockets have improved. See photo on p275.

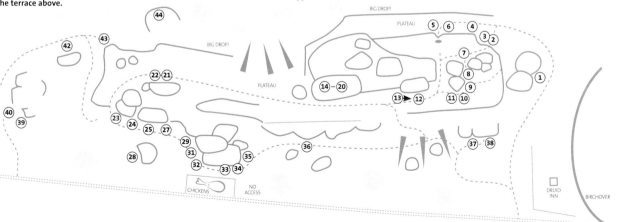

9   The Nose   6a+
The little nose on the left, from the break.

10   7a
Sit-start the wall to the left. No jugs out right.

11   Men in Small Cars   7b
Just left again dyno from undercuts to the sloping top. *Robin Mueller*

Continuing along the top terrace, a carved seat is reached with a sloping canopy above. Have a nice sit down or attempt:

12   The Bus Stop Mantel   7b   ✳
Mantel out the canopy roof. This problem has seen failure by some of the best boulderers on the planet and has been flashed by others, so the grade could be anything really.

13   Ron's Traverse   7a
Traverse the lip, left to right and mantel at the end – no 'seat' for feet. *Ron Fawcett*

14   6c
The right arête from sitting.

15   Kermit's Arête   7b+   ✳
The same arête without the back arête. *Andy Harris*

16   Dissolution   7c
Start on edges left of the right arête, move up and left on edges and slopers.

17   The Line   7c
A once-great problem before the small crimps snapped off. Sit-start on the flaky crack and proceed upwards using whatever you can reach to mantel out the scoop. A good 7a from standing.

18   Raw Power   7b   ✳
Jump to, and mantel out, the highest point of the block

19   Raw Deal   7c+   ✳
The hanging slab, using a shallow pocket for your right hand and a rib. *Mike Lea*

20   4+
The left arête, 6c from a sit-start. A traverse of the whole block starting up this problem would be a great project.

MARK KATZ ON *QUINE*   PHOTO: JOHN COEFIELD

Further on, and down some steps with sculpted chairs on the left (*history bit*: believed to be more modern than the rooms) is a low boulder with a very steep wall/roof. Neither of these two problems use the rock underneath the boulder for your feet.

21 Quine *7c* ✳
Power out to the lip from a sit-start on the sidepull/pinch. There are two different methods: the original undercuts the pod, but most subsequent repeats dyno for the lip. *Rupert Davies*

22 *6c*
The little arête just right from sitting, using a sidepull. Nice move. The path now goes down and left, to some boulders beneath the terrace.

23 Jam and Blast It *6c*
Start in the small cave and climb out via a crack to a hard leftwards finish.

24 *6b*
The crimpy flake in the wall.

25 Crimp Monkey *6b+*
Sharp crimps up the wall, to a sloping top.

26 Crimpanzee *7b+* ✳
The sit-start to *Crimp Monkey*. See photo on p270. *Andy Harris*

27 *6a*
Just left of the arête, using a flatty.

28 *6a*
The slab above a funny landing.

29 Domes *7a+* ★
The hanging prow above the cave formed by the stacked boulders.

30 Domes Sit-Start *7c* ★
Starting on the ledge on the right-hand wall, move out to join *Domes* using some fancy footwork. *Percy Bishton*

31 *6b*
A high line climbing the left arête of the main boulder on its left-hand side. *Percy Bishton*

32 Pat's Roof *7a* ★
A big line through the left side of the roof, starting in the break and reaching out to the lip from big undercuts, before moving left to finish up the previous problem. The landing is poor, and a long way away. *Pat King*

A traverse starts at the same point, moving right under the roof to finish up problem 34 – 6b+. Finishing up *Short Sean's* is 7a+.

33 Another Roof *7a*
The roof between *Pat's Roof* and the next problem finishing up the left-most gutter.

34 6b ✳
Start on the right arête under the roof and then pull out and up the nice rounded runnel.

35 Short Sean's Reachy Roof *7a* ★
The right side of the roof. From the break in the back undercut out to the break on the lip, move right and lock or slap for the top. The block to the right for feet is in at this grade, 7a+ without. The direct finish without the large holds in the break is 7b. *Andy Harris*

36 The Mantellist *7a*
Mount the protruding blob feature. *Adam Long*

37 Kim's Problem *7b+*
A hard pull on crimps to the top. *Kim Thompson*

38 6a+
The right arête on the left. An eliminate dyno from the flake to the top is 7a.

My Apple
A high roof situated around the back of the crag, just above the lane and facing *Eagle Tor*. Follow the lane past the Druid Inn: the block is on the right, in the trees, just before the track breaks right.

39 Dass Crab *6b*
The highball right arête of the buttress.

40 My Apple *7b* ★
Start on the arête below the right corner crack, traverse the chipped holds left to gain and climb the hanging groove. A great climbing experience. *Jon Fullwood*

41 My Buddy the Apple *7c* ★
Gain the groove from the block under the roof using 'freestyle lip-work'. *Ben Bransby*

The next problems are below the crag, around to the left of the *My Apple* area. Check out the topo and get to them as best you can.

42 Hang 'em High *7a*
Right to left lip traverse of the block.

43 I am the God of Hellfire *6c+*
Sit-start the double arête up and left of *Hang em High* at the bottom of a large face. The right arête on its right is the same grade. *Mike Lea*

44 The Ornithologist *7c*
The stacked boulder from the back via slopes. **Not** holding the swing is out of the question. *Mike Adams*

SEB GRIEVE ON *MY APPLE* **PHOTO:** JON FULLWOOD

JON FULLWOOD ON *BLOOD FALLS* PHOTO: ADAM LONG

LAURIE SMITH ON *BRAD'S ARÊTE* PHOTO: JOHN COEFIELD

Stanton Moor

You could easily go for a stroll over *Stanton Moor* without seeing a single problem. They are there though, hidden behind trees, down slopes and behind bushes. The problems range from 4–8a+, with one of the Peak's most sought-after 7's – *Brutal Arête (Spare Rib)* – hidden on the hillside overlooking Matlock. Don't panic if you're not quite operating in the 7's as, courtesy of John Bradbury from 2009, Stanton is also home to one of the Peak's best high 6's, the snappily-titled *Brad's Arete The Presence of Absence*. John was responsible for much of the early development of Stanton and returned in 2009 with a clutch of great, new problems.

Access and Approach

To access the moor, turn off the B5056 signed *Birchover* and drive up through the village, passing the Druid Inn and *Rowtor Rocks* on your right. Keep going through the village. At the top of the hill the road veers left, and a smaller road appears on the right. To access the *Andle Stone* and the *Cork Stone*, follow the road left and then back right to park in lay-bys by the road after a few hundred metres. The best parking for the other areas is to be found by taking the small right-hand road to Stanton Lees, soon reaching some small lay-bys on the left (limited parking). See overview map on p247.

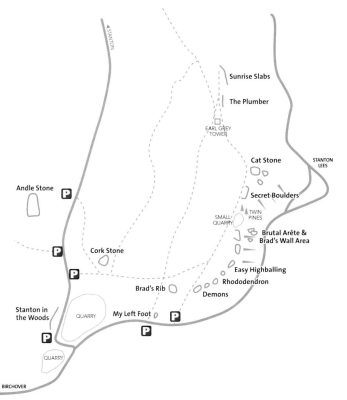

The Andle Stone

The Andle Stone is situated on the left-hand (northern) side of the road, just after the main parking for *Stanton Moor*, in a copse of rhododendrons in the middle of a cow field. The problems are described clockwise, starting just right of the handy rungs.

1   Mug   *6b*
Traverse the entire block, clockwise from the shelf right of the rungs. Everything is 'in'. *Simon Holmes.*

2   Ron's Problem   *7c*
Climb the wall just left of the rungs and right of the next problem. It's a bit squeezed in and the grade depends on which holds you allow yourself. Reachy. *Ron Fawcett*

3   Andle Stone Wall   *7b* ★
The steep slab right of the arête is a real classic in the same mould as *L'Impossible* at *Roche aux Sabots, Fontainebleau*. Technical moves gain good crimps in the middle of the wall, after which poor holds trend up and right to the top. Don't veer left to the arête. *John Bradbury*

4   Witches' Sabbath   *6b*
The arête climbed on the right.

5   No Bull   *6c* ✳
The arête climbed on the left is very good.

6   Spook   *7a*
The reachy wall left of the arete. Those under 6' will find this much harder. *Pat King*

7   4+
Crack and wall.

8   Nettle Tea   4
The arête.

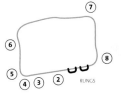

The Cork Stone

Park on the road just before the *Andle Stone* (as approached from Birchover) and cross the stile on the right. A path leads out onto the moor from here, and after 100m or so the *Cork Stone* becomes obvious on the left – an isolated pinnacle with yet more carved steps and rungs. The problems are described clockwise, starting just left of the rungs.

1   **The Mammoth Book of UFOs**   *7b*
    Sit-start the arête left of the rungs on its left side. (On poor rock – please **take care** and **do not brush**.) *Percy Bishton*

2   *7a*
    The left arête on the right-hand side.

3   *6a*
    The left arête on the left-hand side is very good. 7a+ from sitting. *John Bradbury*

4   *5*
    Climb the arête right of the rungs on its right-hand side using anything within reach, including the other arête.

My Left Foot

An isolated but convenient problem, just next to the first path to be found on the left if you take the right-hand turn at the top of the hill after leaving Birchover. About 100m southwest of *Brad's Rib*, in the trees by the road.

5   **Overlook Arete**   *7a+*
    The left arête from a sit-start. *John Bradbury*

6   **My Left Foot**   *6a*   ✳
    The vague arête and hanging scoop/crack. 6a+ from a sit-start. *Lucy Atkinson*

NAT EVANS ON *LITTLE BROTHER*   **PHOTO**: PAUL BENNETT

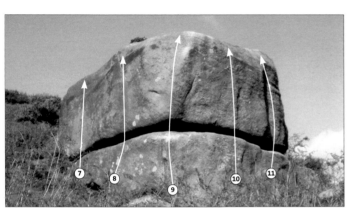

Brad's Rib

Obvious when approached from the low parking on the road to Stanton Lees, but hidden from view when approached from the *Cork Stone*.

7   **6b**
Sit-start the wall with the crack.

8   **Mike Tyson**   *7b+*
Climb the wall from double fist jams in the cheese-grater break, up to and past the seam. Much more painful than having the top of your ear bitten off. *Justin Critchlow*

9   **Brad's Rib**   *7a+*   ★
The arête is technical, but the main difficulty is in topping out. It is the same grade from sitting. *John Bradbury*

10   **Tom Thumb**   *7b+*
Exit the wide break and cross the leaning wall right of Brad's rib with the help of pebbles. *Jamie Lilleman*

11   **Pulling Teeth**   *6b*
The wall and flakes.

Demons Area

An obvious, blocky tower of rock is situated on the plateau, about 100m east of *Brad's Rib*, on the other side of the main path and fence. *Demons* is in a gulley behind this, facing into the valley, while *A Rural Object* is closer to the path, just north of the main pinnacle.

12   **A Rural Object**   *6c*
From the break, move out to the arête and a slopey finishing mantel. *John Bradbury*

13   **Demons**   *7b*   ✳
A good find. Start in the break under the arête and concoct a sequence using the undercut arête and the mono. Awkward landing. *Jamie Lilleman*

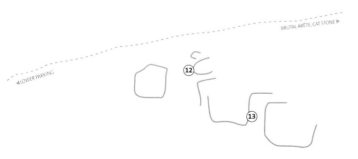

Rhododendron

The blocks along the eastern rim of the plateau now form a discontinuous edge. *Rhododendron* is between *Demons* and *Easy Highballing*.

14 Rhododendron *6b* ✳
The arête and flakes, climbed on the right-hand side, in the gulley facing away from the path. Start matched in the break. Worth seeking out. Eliminating the arête is 6c.
Rupert Davies

Easy Highballing

The large buttress 100m or so north of *Rhododendron*. Excellent rock providing some lovely high problems that feel like short solos.

15 Undone Rib *4+*
The mini prow/arête.

16 *3+*
Jamming crack and bridging.

17 Make it Stick *6c*
The roof on the right hand end of the buttress. Start matched on the vague dish/seam on the lip, with feet on the back wall. Aim for the break and then top-out. Tricky.
John Bradbury

Brad's Wall Area

A pair of small, clean buttresses 30m right of *Brutal Arête* (looking into the valley) give some more good problems.

18   **Chick Factor**   *6b*
Climb the short wall on undercuts, to a hard top-out. Reachy.

19   **Drizzle**   *5*   ✳
Climb the wall from the low break – nice.

20   **Brad's Wall**   *7c*   ★
The wall left of the arête, climbed from a sitting start, is a mini classic. *John Bradbury*

21   **Rex Rgis of Rusticus Res**   *7a+*
Mantel the nose right of Brad's Wall. *John Bradbury*

The slabby boulder below has two very good problems:

22   **Chicken Ninja**   *5+*   ✳
Very smeary padding up centre of the slab. *Yan Thompson*

23   **Chicken Ginger**   *7a*
The steep right arête, climbed on the right hand side, from a sit-start. *Jon Fullwood*

Brutal Arête Area

Continue along the path until two pine trees are reached on the right. In front of these is a small hidden quarry. With the quarry on your left, walk to the edge of the moor and start dropping down the slope – hidden in the hillside is the stunning *Brutal Arête*.

24   Brutal Arête (aka Spare Rib)   *7b*   ★
A beautiful piece of rock, an elegant arrangement of ribs that fade out into a rainbow of shockwaves. A technical sequence on sidepulls up the ribs is made more tenuous by poor footholds until all holds disappear and only the final pop to the top remains – with the floor way below. Highball. *Brutal Arête* was the original name, *Spare Rib* is the more popular one. *Jason Myers*

25   Stanton Deliver   *8a+*   ★
The stunning highball groove and arete right of *Brutal Arête* was a longstanding project. Start standing at the foot of the arete with LH on a fairly obvious slopey crimp and RH on a pinch on the arete. Climb the groove into the thin crack above; high and hard until the end. *Dan Varian*

26   Stanton Warriors   *7b+*   ✶
The right arête of the front of the buttress, without the crack. At the time of writing it moves right to the crack at the top to top-out. The direct is possible, and bold. *Dan Varian*

27   The Stanton Shuffle   *7c+/8a*
Sit-start on the grassy block beneath *Stanton Warriors* at the right-hand side of the roof and traverse left to finish stood, in control, one move in at the start of *Brutal Arête*. An obvious finish awaits. *Andy Crome*

28   *6b*
Around the corner to the right, on the next block along, is a mini prow. Climb the front face using both arêtes.

29   *7a*
Climb the arête on the left from a sitting start.

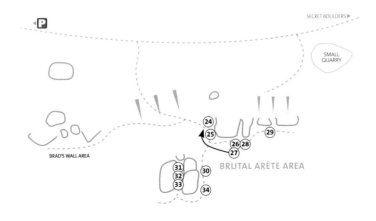

Directly down the slope below *Spare Rib* is a cluster of boulders containing some good problems.

30 **Wonder Bra** *6c*
Climb the left arête from a sit-start and rock onto the wall. *Lucy Atkinson*

31 **Big Brother** *7a+* ✳
The highball arête – get a good spot. Sit-start. *Percy Bishton*

32 **The Cresta Run** *7b*
Lowball. Sit-start under the arête and cross the wall on slopers and a tiny undercut to finish up *Little Brother*. *Percy Bishton*

33 **Little Brother** *6b+* ✳
Climb the arête from a sit-start. See photo on p278.

34 **The Toboggan Run** *5+*
Climb the middle of the wall from a sit-start. *Percy Bishton*

Secret Boulders

A collection of fine blocks, developed by John Bradbury in 2009, hidden away down the hillside between *Brutal Arête* and *The Cat Stone*. Drop down through a clearing about 60m before *The Cat Stone*, when approaching north on the main path.

35 Secret Places *7a* ✳
Squeeze up the hanging double arête/prow from the bottom of the seam.
John Bradbury

36 Safe House *6a*
Undercut up the wall right of *Secret Places*. Reachy.

37 Brad's Arete – The Presence of Absence *6c+* ★
A modern classic. The large, square-cut arête, just right of the tree. See photo on p276.
John Bradbury

38 Sworn to Secrecy *5+* ✳
The right arête on its left, finishing up the flake/groove.

39 Secret Sidewall *5+*
The right arête on its right, using the blocky flake.

40 Classified *4+* ✳
Lean out the steep side of the projecting prow to a seam, and haul over on jugs.

41 To Have It All *6c+*
Sit-start hanging the lush, sloping edge in the steep face, pop to the good blob and mantel out. *John Bradbury*

42 The 1980s Were The Days! *7a*
Sit-start below the hanging, bottom arête and traverse left on slopers to finish up around the easier upper arête. An extension, *Pump Action* (7a+), starts at the top arête and circumnavigates the block clockwise by dropping (walking) down the slabby, north side of the block into the start of *The 1980s Were The Days! John Bradbury*

The Cat Stone

Continue along the path across the top of the moor above *Brutal Arête*, and *The Cat Stone* soon becomes obvious in the trees on the right at a point where the main path angles left. Easily identifiable by a plaque carved into the boulder.

43   The Plaque   *6b+*   ✳
Climb the arête starting from undercuts in the roof. 7a if the cracks on the left are eliminated. *Al Williams*

44   The Green Man   *7c*   ✳
Jump out right from the plaque itself to a sloper, then up. *John Welford*

45   Aces High   *6c+*
Classic break-to-top dyno on a wall 10m behind and to the right, as you look at *The Cat Stone*. Some good easy problems are to be found round the back of this block.

Sunrise Slabs

Keep following the path north from *The Cat Stone* and you'll pass the unmissable *Earl Grey Tower* on your left. The first two problems are over the edge, just north of the point at which the path from the tower joins the edge top path. *Grande Ramp* and *Rollercoaster* are a further 100m or so – look for the top of some walls just right of the path.

46   The Plumber   *6c+*
The right side of the biggish arête on the left. *Jamie Lilleman*

47   Rue d'Awakening   *6b*
Another left pointing arête about 4m right. Nice climbing above a spicily-narrow landing. *Jon Fullwood*

48   Grande Ramp   *5+*   ✳
The large rampline up the face leads to a fluttery final stretch at the top. *John Bradbury*

49   Rollercoaster   *6a+*
Crimp up the wall, up and right. *John Bradbury*

50   Sunrise   *6b*
The short sidewall right of the corner can be climbed many different ways eliminating the arête.

Stanton in the Woods

Hidden away in the woods, just a few metres from the Birchover-Stanton road and within spitting distance of *Stanton Moor*, this collection of blocks has remained in relative obscurity for years due to a combination of access issues and the fact they are often hideously filthy for much of the year. Both these problems should now be solved: the BMC secured access here in 2008 and this right of access and the fact it's in both our guide and the BMC's *Froggatt* guide should mean increased numbers of visitors and therefore cleaner boulders.

These blocks have been discovered and rediscovered time and again, with the earliest known activity by Martin Boysen and friends in the 1970s or 1980s. In between the periods of rediscovery nature takes over, leading many to believe they are the first to climb here. Even the Herculean cleaning binges only appear to have a short-term effect. What this crag needs is a bit of traffic, which it should now get. So, be prepared for some esoteric classics likely under a moss and pine needle carpet. Take a stiff brush (not wire – please) and an open mind.

The following is an attempt to document the climbing here, but it should in no way be taken as definitive.

Access and Approach

Access was secured to this enigmatic venue by the BMC in 2008, although a low-key approach is still advised. Park in the small car park opposite the quarry. Walk down the footpath away from the road for a few metres before questing off right on a vague path past a block. This joins a wall – follow this for a few metres to an obvious crossing point and continue into the woods on vague paths. Avoid losing height as most blocks hug the upper reaches of the hillside, just down from a drystone wall. See overview map on p247.

The Leaning Block

The furthest right boulder is a smallish leaning block behind a short sharp arête, close to the wall line.

1   **The Knife**   *7b+*   ✶
    The sharp arête is more difficult than it looks.
    Kim Thompson

2   **Lean-to**   *6c*   ✶
    Sit-start the right arête of the leaning block

3   **Bumlog Millionaire**   *7a*   ✶
    Sit-start the leaning wall, gain the rail and slap the top.

4   **Arête and Mantel**   *6b*
    The undercut arête and mantel finish.
    6c from a sit start.

5   *5+*
    The centre of the wall without the arête.
    6a+ from a sit start.

6   *4+*
    The left arête from sitting.

The Big Slab

About 30m left of the previous problems is a big slab, sadly with iffy landings under the main face.

7   *4+*
    The right-hand side of the fine looking arête sadly uses little of the actual arête.

The Little Slab

Directly below the big slab is a much friendlier block with a clutch of slabby problems above decent landings.

8   *4+*   ✶
    The attractive groove and arête next to the tree.

9   *5+*
    Press off the groove and straight up without the arête.

10   *6a*
    The slab right of centre to the seam.

11   *6b*
    The slab left of centre.

12   *6a*
    Sit-start the prow at the end of the block.

Up and left is a large green buttress with a fine line beside a fallen tree, Jon Fullwood's *Elgar's Belljars* (E4 6b) – could be highballed at about 7a. The left scoop is home to *Okie Noodling* – an E4 6a route by *Percy Bishton*. Both routes use the tree as a runner. The back arête of this block gives a rambling 6a+.

Hangman

Back up the slope and just back a touch is a narrow vertical wall and below it a hanging block.

13   **Clandestiny's Child**   *7a*   ✶
    The fine right arête of the block. A dynamic problem also climbs to the wall to the left at 7a.

14   **The Noose**   *3+*
    The flake line.

15   **Hangman**   *6b+*   ★
    The hanging block is one of the classics of the crag. From a start on the lower block hug up the bulging prow. A possible right-hand finish looks great.

The Big Block

Next up is a line of three big blocks positioned one above the next on the slope. The lowest block is an impressive, often mossy monolith with a pair of fine highball arêtes/prows.

16 Appliance Friction *6b* ★
The slab right of *Green Chapel* is a smeary number. Great, when clean.

17 Green Chapel *7a* ✳
The right prow climbed on its worryingly-high left-hand side. 6b+ on its gentler right-hand side.

18 The Church *6c+* ✳
The left prow is another beauty climbed from a sit-start on the right-hand side. 6b+ on its left-hand side.

Eyes to the Skies

Above *The Big Block* is a big slab. Behind this is a steep high wall, home to the crag classic *Eyes to the Skies*.

19 Eyes to the Skies *6c* ★
The classic of the crag with a testing final stretch to a juggy mono. Highball.

20 5
The right-hand arête of the crack down and right.

Heading further left the boulders become gradually more jumbled and broken up. A few titbits are available for the keen, including a mega-looking sit-start dyno project with absolutely no footholds. There's also a dodgy-looking cave and some filthy, yet good-looking, arêtes and slabs – all undoubtedly climbed in years gone by.

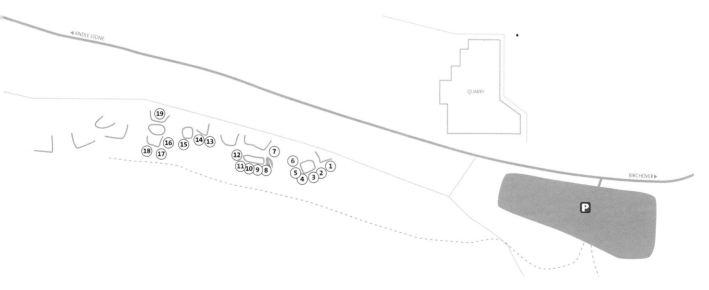

Amber Valley

Where's the *Amber Valley* we hear you cry! Well, there's a good chance you'll have heard of *Eastwood Rocks*, and a slimmer chance you'll have heard of *Turning Stone Edge*. These crags bound the east and west sides of the valley, respectively, just a short distance from the town of Matlock in the southern Peak. Thanks to the development of bouldering at crags other than *Eastwood*, the *Amber Valley* now warrants its own section. *Eastwood* offers a good, steep and hard circuit on sound rock; *Cocking Tor* is a newly-developed circuit worth a quick hit, or as a warm-up for the limited, yet brilliant, bouldering at *Turning Stone*. Finally, *Bradley Edge* is a mixed bag; there's some good stuff, but plenty not so good – we've included pretty much all of it to allow you to make your own mind up.

It's worth noting that bits of *Eastwood*, *Turning Stone Edge* and *Bradley Edge* can stay dry in the rain and snow.

Access and Approach

The *Amber Valley* is about 3 miles north-east of Matlock, and about 5 miles south of Chesterfield, accessed from the A632. For *Eastwood Rocks* and *Mervyn Stutter Crag*, turn off at Kelstedge and head for the village of Ashover. *Cocking Tor*, *Turning Stone Edge* and *Bradley Edge* are approached from Holestone Gate Road at the top of the steep Slack Hill. See individual crags for detailed access information.

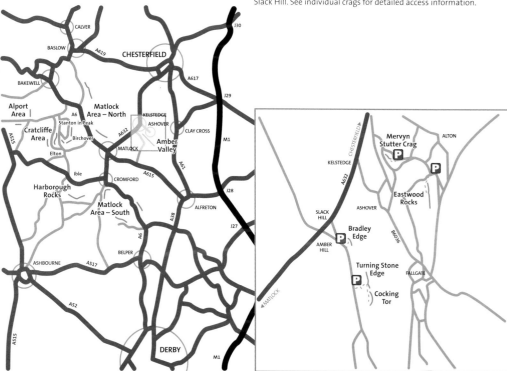

VICKIE BARRETT ON THE EASTWOOD TRAVERSE PHOTO: KEITH SHARPLES

Eastwood Rocks

The most salient feature of *Eastwood Rocks* is that **you are not allowed to climb here**. The inclusion of this crag in the guide does not imply that you have a right to climb here. The problems are of great quality and mostly in the harder grades. *Eastwood* also features one of the best traverses on grit. *Cave Buttress*, around which most of the problems are centred, is steep and can stay dry in wet weather. Since the last guide was published a number of excellent problems have been added. This doesn't mean that you are now allowed to climb here which, for the avoidance of doubt, you are not.

Access and Approach

In case you skipped the introduction, **you are not allowed to climb here**, so obviously the approach details are only included for completeness – and in case the farmer at Eastwood Hall ever changes his mind and decides to allow access in the future.

Approaching the village of Ashover from Kelstedge (on the A632 Matlock to Chesterfield road) take the first left turn, past a school, and turn right at the top. Take the second left past the pub and the next left again up a steep road. The road rises over a hill, at the top of which is a rough lay-by on the right. Continue past this until a T-junction is reached shortly afterwards – turn left and park. Access the crag from the lay-by – cross the wall and fence and follow a vague path, around a wall, until *Cave Buttress* is reached.

Cave Buttress
The first problems are centred around the first buttress reached from the road.

1   Bristol Dreaming   *6c*   ✳
The highball left arête of the buttress, using the crack for your right hand. Escape boldly right at the ledge. *Simon Lee*

2   Hats for Clowns   *7b*   ★
Just right of the left arête. Gain a layaway at the base of the steep finger crack from the flake/crack on the right via a jump-start. A hard move gains jugs on the arête. A quality Kyloe in the Woods-esque problem. 7c from a standing start. *Jon Fullwood*

3   Hats for Percys   *7a+*
A left-hand start to *Hats for Clowns*, which avoids the jump-start, but is unfortunately a bit eliminate due to the proximity of the arête. Gain the layaway as a gaston from edges on the left (avoiding holds on the arête), and then work back leftwards to the high jugs on the arête. *Percy Bishton*

Hats for Weasels   *7b+*
A sit-start to *HFP's* starting from the juggy break underneath the roof. *Ian Vickers*

Hats for Weasels low-start   *7c*
Start from the very back of the roof. Soft for the grade. *Rupert Davies*

4   Westwood   *8a*   ★
The sit-start to *Hats for Clowns*. *James Pearson*

5   Hats for Youths   *8a*   ★
Start as for Westwood and climb the finger crack above, eliminating the arête. Hard. *James Pearson*

6   The Eastwood Traverse   *7b+*   ★
The *Powerband* of grit, done from right to left, starting sitting at *Corpse Crack* and traversing left to finish in the big break of the green slab right round the corner. It's also been done the other way, to finish on the ledge beneath *Corpse Crack*, at the same grade. Top of the grade. *Rich Heap*

7   The Pessimist   *8a*   ✳
Sit-start at the good jugs 2m into *The Eastwood Traverse* and traverse left to finish up *Hats for Youths*. *Den Caffsquill*

8   Corpse Crack   *5*
The crack is a great feature, and as a boulder problem is climbed from hanging the ledge to finish at the vegetated break. Traverse off right. See photo on p288.

9   Jon's Traverse   *7a+*
Traverse right from *Corpse Crack* to finish up the groove problem. Still awaits a link with the *Eastwood Traverse*. *Jon Fullwood*

10   Ten Inch Zombies   *7a+*   ✳
The wall on chicken-heads right of the crack, finishing at the break. *Jon Fullwood*

11   Spooky   *6a*
Sit-start and climb the wall immediately left of the groove without the arête.

12   *4+*
The slabby groove right again. The slab itself is 4+.

>>

13 Tony's Problem *6c+*
Gain the hanging prow above the tree and climb it rightwards. *Tony Simpson*

14 The Grimper *7a*
Right of the easy slab (on the far side of the tree) is a brushed wall climbed on crimps past an overlap. A left-hand variant is 6a. *Mike Lea*

15 Worm in a Teacup *6b+*
Traverse the sloping shelf left from the crack to finish in the corner crack. Gaining the end of the traverse from the tree is 6a. *Jon Fullwood*

16 Percy's Highball *7b+*
Further right still is another buttress with a 45° prow and an arête above. Climb this. Highball. *Percy Bishton*

Nod's Buttress

Past the massive bolted roof of *Eastwood Neb*, is another big buttress consisting of a slabby wall with big roofs above and below it. This is located after *Cave Buttress* but before *Sublux Roof*.

17 Slanty Man *5* ✳
Finger traverse the thin crack right to the arête.

18 Seismic Start *6b* ★
Sit-start the steep arête. Very good.

19 Culpeper's Practice *7c* ✳
About 2m right of the arête. Start by reaching the flake at the lower left end of the rail, and work up and left on crimps then slopers, making for a large, shallow, open scoop in the middle of the slab. Once there, finish more easily up the slab above to the large break. *Andy Banks*

20 *5+*
Traverse the juggy rail rightwards to pull up and finish up the easy slab.

Sublux Roof

After the last route-height buttress is a small steep wall up in the bushes. To find it, after *Nod's Buttress* follow the path down around and back up. The problems at *Sublux Roof* and *Pen Six Roof* were developed by *Dan Warren*.

21 The Flakes *6c+*
The flake line on the left side of the roof, from a sit-start. Top out direct.

22 Sublux *7b+*
The centre of the roof, starting on a sidepull and an undercut. From the jug on the lip rock over right to finish. The foot ledge is in.

23 IDB *7a*
Sit-start and climb the vague arête on slopey crimps.

24 Holly Dab *6b*
Sit-start as for *IDB*, but reach right to a large layaway.

25 Lip Traverse *6b+*
Traverse the lip from right to left, finishing up the arête.

26 Farmers Pride *5+*
Behind *Sublux Roof* is a high, juggy arête. Topping out is the crux.

Pen Six Roof

30m past the *Sublux Roof*, at the far right end of the edge is another low, steep wall.

27 Pen Six *7c*
Sit-start on twin sidepulls (a sidepull and a gaston) at the left side of the roof. Reach a horizontal crimpy 'ear', then the ramp and juggy fin above. Top out leftwards. No foot ledges.

28 Juggy Wall *6a*
The left hand of two sit-starts at the right side of the roof.

29 The Other One *6c*
The right hand of two sit-starts at the right side of the roof.

30 The Hard Way *7a+*
A R-L lip traverse behind *Pen Six*.

Mervyn Stutter

An isolated venue with a warm-up boulder, a 7a+ and a hard project. Located approx. 1km further north along the edge from Eastwood, near Hill Top Farm. Follow the path past the warm-up boulder in the horse field. After a further 60m, in the small, wooded quarry to the right, is:

Skooter Ram *7a+*
The hanging arête/groove feature. The arête to the left is a hard project.

Cocking Tor & Turning Stone Edge

A series of east-facing buttresses, a short distance apart, with a collection of varied problems scattered along their length. Some of the problems are excellent: destination problems worth a trip in their own right – *River of Life* in particular, is one of the rare hard roof problems on Peak District grit that isn't just a span to the lip. Both crags are good for a short session, but would need to be combined for a full day out. Being east-facing, both venues provide shelter from westerly winds, but can be slow drying after wet weather.

Access and Approach

Turn off the A632 near the top of Slack Hill at Amber Hill, and drive south along Holestone Gate Road for about 1km. Look for a gate with a track leading along a field edge to a circular copse of trees on the left. Park sensibly here (limited parking), well off the road. Follow the track to, and around the right side of, the copse and continue towards the woods. For *Cocking Tor*, turn right before the woods along the field edge, and left at the field corner to drop down to the crag top path: *Salad Fingers* is directly below, while the main Tor is 150m down to the right. For *Turning Stone*, head straight into the woods from the copse, past a big old tree: this brings you to the descent gully for *River of Life*. See the individual problems for approach information.

Cocking Tor

A fine group of problems, off the beaten track. They were developed mainly by on Fullwood with a couple of additions from *Lee Anderson*.

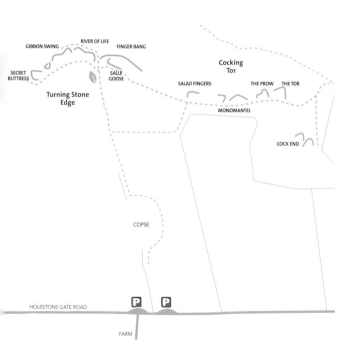

Cock End

Two boulders about 80m south of the main *Cocking Tor* crag.

1   **Cock Jockey**   *5*
    The left arête.

2   **Cock End**   *6c*
    The right arête bears left at the top. An eliminate without the pocket and arête is 7a.

3   **Split Tip**   *6a*
    Sit-start the wall right of the corner.

The Tor

A couple of problems under the Tor itself.

4   **Jelly Tot**   *6a+*   ✶
    The arête at the base of the crag. A 6b eliminate climbs the wall to the left, while *Stridesque*, also 6b, sit-starts the slabby flake into the arête on the boulder just below *Jelly Tot*.

The Prow

An unmissable prow, about 20m right of the Tor. Look for the Pagan Cross, carved into a small block beneath the prow.

5   Crack 'n' Slope   5
The crack left of the prow.

6   Sun Worship   6a
Span out from undercuts and up the left side of the prow.

7   Pagan Cross   6b+   ★
From a low start, climb the prow just right of centre. *Jon Fullwood*

8   Wicker Man   7a   ✳
The tricky groove and rib up and right.

Monomantel

A large wall of good rock with some fine problems, about 20m right again.

9   Rockabilly Rehab   6b+
The ledges and edges left of the ramp. *Lee Anderson*

10   Monomantel   7a+   ✳
Mantel onto the thin ledge direct, using a mono. *Jon Fullwood*

11   Gravy Boatsmen   6b
The ramp. The direct start is 6c.

12   The Radjy Man   6c
The fallen block 10m to the right, with shot hole marks on the left-hand side. Sit-start under the right arête and swing left to finish around the left rib.

Salad Fingers

About 70m right of *Monomantel*, directly below the point at which the public footpath meets the crag top path.

13   Salad Fingers   7b
The right side of the wall left of the arête via a quintessential sloper. *Jon Fullwood*

14   Hubert Cumberdale   6a+
The arête on the left-hand side.

15   Jeremy Fisher   6b
The same arête on the right.

Turning Stone Edge

The edge continues, now largely engulfed by rhododendrons, although an epic trimming mission at the time of writing has cleared things up dramatically. Prepare to get a bit frustrated when it comes to finding things – we've done our best to make the approaches as simple as possible!

The first problem is perched high on the crag at the southern end. To find it, walk right for about 20m from the top of the main descent gully and look out for a rooty descent to a suspended platform (up above the *Happy Landings* buttress). The problem is here.

1   Salle Goose   *7c*   ★
A slopey masterpiece. Lean out from good holds and a heel-toe cam to gain a pocket on the face and a magical pinch on the rib. Slap the top. *Jon Fullwood*

For the next problem, drop awkwardly down the descent gully and hang a right. The large roof of the *Happy Landings* buttress is unmissable.

2   Finger Bang   *7a+*
The hanging prow looks very high but falls can be protected by placing pads on the springy rhododendrons, although they've been trimmed a bit at the time of writing. Lean out through the roof and follow the lip to the ledge on the route *Happy Landings*. Traverse or jump (!) off. *James Pearson*

Hang a left at the bottom of the descent gully for the next three problems. *River of Life* is the obvious chalked roof after about 10m. *Gibbon Swing* and *Overton Arête SS* are about 40m further along.

3   **River of Life**   *7c+*   ★
One of the best roof problems on grit, slapping up sidepulls, with funky footwork. An alternative right-hand sequence takes the good two finger hold in the centre of the roof as a left hand gaston and crosses straight into the slot – more basic but less pleasing. See photo on p294. *James Pearson*

4   **Gibbon Swing**   *7a*   ✳
Dyno up the undercut, overhanging arête. A brilliant, knacky move. *James Marsh*

5   **Overton Arête Sit-Start**   *6c+*
Sit-start the double arêtes below the big HVS arête. Finish at the break.

Secret Buttress

From the top of the central descent gully, head left (looking out) through rhododendron tunnels for about 70m until a block very reminiscent of those at Brimham is reached – *The Turning Stone*. The next problems are on the buttress below. Good rock, which can take a day or two to dry.

6   *6a+*
The left arête of the slab.

7   **The Cherub's Bit**   *7a*   ✳
Gain the slab as for previous problem, then pad right and delicately climb its centre. *Jon Fullwood*

8   **Velveteen Whisper**   *6b+*
Continue the rising traverse of *The Cherub's* Lot to finish via the right arête. *Jon Fullwood*

9   **Nice Pinch, Shame about the Ledge**   *7a*
A tricky move off undercuts to the break. Use the perfect pinch to reach the prow/arête, and climb this avoiding the ledge.

10   **Riding the Stang**   *7a+*   ✳
The line of the wall. Climb to the break as for the previous problem, then shuffle right for 1m and climb the wall above. *Jon Fullwood*

11   *6b*
The arête of the lower boulder has a big move to a slopey topout.

12   **Secret Dyno**   *7b+*   ✳
Known for ages as the *Secret Dyno Project*, it was eventually climbed static. Imagine the disappointment. Climb the scooped wall from the crescent-shaped ramp hold using undercuts to stretch to the sloping top. *Neil Mawson*

13   **The Seeker**   *7c*   ✳
Stand-start from an undercut and the crescent-shaped ramp hold and climb the impressive rib with a final stretch for the top. *Dan Varian*

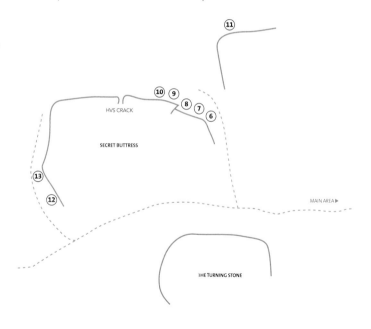

Bradley Edge

The western rim of the Amber Valley continues north, and eventually swings to face north-east, just before the main road. *Bradley Edge* sits here in a clearing, surrounded by plantation. The problems are found on the edge and on the boulders scattered below, on rock that varies from good to average to poor. Note that the undergrowth springs right up in summer, making it a pain to get around.

Access and Approach

Turn off the A632 near the top of Slack Hill at Amber Hill, and drive south along Holestone Gate Road for about 600m. Park on the left off the road at the bend by the phone masts, but not on the track next to the phone masts, taking care not to block either gate or the road. Parking is limited to a maximum of 2 vehicles, although we would recommend only single parties climb here and visits are kept low key as the current access situation is unclear. Pass through the gate ahead, and turn left at the edge of the woodland, next to the wall. **Do not** cross the farmer's field to get to the crag, and **do not** head through the woodland towards the masts – the owner of the woodland in which the masts sit does not allow climbing. The first problems reached are on the edge.

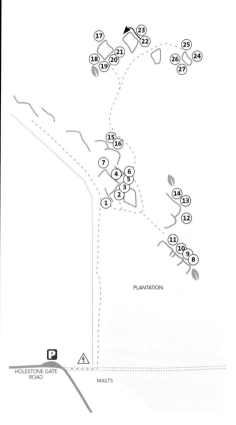

1   **Vegetarian Cannibal**   *7a*
The offwidth crack, from the back of the cave, finishing on the face as for *Top Dog*.

2   **Top Dog**   *7a*
Jump-start the middle of the wall past the niche.

3   **The Gap**   *5*
Step off the boulder onto the right arête above the drop.

The next problems are on the steep wall below. The slab behind has some easy lines.

4   **Growl Tiger**   *6a*
Sit-start the left-hand side of the wall, past the big sidepull. Finish at the break.

5   **C'mon Tiger**   *6a* ✳
Sit-start the right-hand side of the wall and crimp up to the capping roof.

6   **Easy Tiger**   *5*
The steep side of the right arête. 4+ on the right.

Dogma   *7b+*
Start up *Growl Tiger* and finish up *The Gap*. Mike Adams

Back at a higher level is:

7   **Walking the Dog**   *5*
The arête above the ledge. Poor landing. *Ma Wall* (6a) sit-starts the wall to the left, *Valentina* (6c) the wall to the right.

The following problems are just in the woods: a broken up series of roofs, and a decent rippled slab below.

8   **Il Pleut**   *7a*
Sit-start the left-hand side of the overlap using a small crimp and a pinch on the lip. Tom Allsop

9   **Mug of Beans**   *6b*
Sit-start the slabby wall on the next block right and climb direct without the arête.

10 Heads Up *6b*
Sit-start slightly right of *Mug of Beans* and traverse the roof right, pulling up just before the crack formed by the next block. Hard not to dab the block.

11 Wet Toes *6c*
Sit-start the roof right of the suspended block, lean out to a sloper and up. Top out right.

Andy's Traverse *7a*
Start up *Heads Up* and traverse the low lip to finish up *Wet Toes*. *Andy Banks*

12 Secret Lemonade Drinker *6b+*
Sit-start under the left arête and climb it on its left side.

13 Wee Wall *5* ✳
The slab just left of centre, past the rippled holds.

14 Tree Wall *6b*
The thin slab right of centre, rocking onto an obvious lip foothold.

A vague path drops down from the *Top Dog* area towards the boulders below. Directly under the main crag is an impressive roof.

15 Swingers Party *7b+* ★
A modern classic. Span out from blocks back right to the lip and work leftwards along this, making use of the unlikely rib in the roof, to finish up the centre of the nose via good crimps. See photo on p298. *Andy Banks*

16 Morris Dancing *7a*
Reach out from the left sidewall and crack to good crimps on the nose. Finish direct.

The next problems are on the biggest boulder which isn't as good as it looks.

17 Western Front *6c*
The highball arête on the back of the boulder has a poor landing.

18 Spiderman *4+*
Step across onto, and climb, the right-hand side of the undercut, green slab. A similar line just left is 3+.

19 Eat Less Bread *6b+*
The undercut arête, starting matched on the lip. A 7b sit-starts on poor rock.

20 Three and Four Pence *6c*
The large sidewall, climbed just left of centre, past the niche.

21 Probably *3+* ✳
The downhill arête on its steep side.

Just below is a low boulder with some interesting runnel features.

22 Trench Foot *6b+*
A left to right lip traverse on slopers, finishing around the right arête.

23 Gone for a Burton *4+*
Hang the edge just right of the left arête and mantel it out. *Mantel 2* is a similar, slightly harder, line to the right – 6a.

The final problems are on the tall boulder back towards the plantation, which carries the inscription *'Sept 25 1915 FT'* – a WW1 reference.

24 Crimp Master Nasty *7b*
The downhill face, started low, moving diagonally up and right to finish. A direct finish is slightly harder. Sadly some of the holds, including the key handhold for the crux last move, are sandy and quite fragile. *Tony Simpson*

25 The Big Push *6b* ✳
The razor sharp arête, climbed on its left. 6c from sit-start.

26 Uphill Arête Right-Hand *5*
Climb the arête on its right. Quite good. Climbed on its left it's 6a.

27 *4+*
The centre of the slabby wall.

Matlock Area – North

A number of small crags can be found north of Matlock, which give decent low-grade bouldering on a mix of quarried and natural rock. *Beeley Hilltop* comprises a number of small, wild craglets situated high above the Chatsworth Estate, although only two are worth a visit by the boulderer – and they aren't Stanage: you have been warned. *Harland Edge* and *Rabbit Warren* do offer keen, open-minded, lower grade boulderers something to go at though, with generally good landings and largely positive holds. While almost in Matlock itself, *Bank Quarry* and *Jackson Tor* mix quarried and natural rock to give a good low-grade circuit with some highballs which are good fun. There's also a brilliant 7a at *Bank Quarry*.

Access and Approach

Approaching *Beeley Hilltop* from Matlock, turn right off the A6 onto the B6012 in the direction of Chatsworth. After 1 mile, turn right into the village of Beeley and follow the narrow road through the village and up the hillside. After 1½ miles, there's a parking area on a right-hand bend – park here for *Rabbit Warren*: walk along the track for about 500m and cross a stile onto the moor as the track bends left – the crag is on the left after a further 1km.

»

For *Harland Edge*, keep driving along the road, fork left, and then turn left. Park in a small lay-by on the right before a right-hand bend. Walk up the road and hop the wall before a stone finger post. Follow a vague path past the finger post, and bear left towards a trig point. Skirt around the back of the hill and back left towards the crag on very vague paths. Both *Beeley Hilltop* crags are on CRoW land, but please keep dogs on leads and don't damage walls and fences.

For *Bank Quarry* and *Jackson Tor*, head out of Matlock on the A632 Chesterfield road, and turn left into Wellington Street at the Duke of Wellington pub. After about 200m, bear right onto Cavendish Road and park up near a playground. *Jackson Tor* is directly below the playground – follow the path around and down at the far end of the playground. For *Bank Quarry*, walk up the road and turn left onto the lane next to the tennis courts and football fields. Bear left behind the pavilion and turn left onto a minor path into the woods, just after the fence corner. Follow the fence down to the quarry, almost directly above *The Boulder*. Do not traverse the hillside between the two crags: this is private land. The area is also residential, so keeping the noise down and acting responsibly is a good idea.

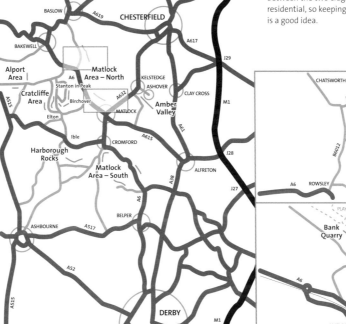

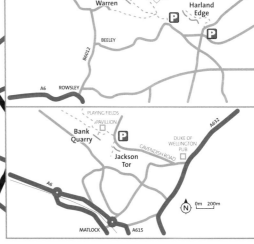

Beeley Hilltop

Wild climbing, high above the Chatsworth Estate.

Harland Edge

A collection of rough, wild buttresses, with problems mainly in the 5's and 6's. The best climbing is on the furthest wall, which is about 150m on from the first buttresses. The problems are described right to left, as approached.

1   **Fascism**   *3+*
    The right arête.

2   **Harland Globetrotter**   *6a*   ✳
    The finger crack above the overlap. A good problem. *Jon Gilthorpe*

3   **Come Harland High Water**   *6b+*
    The left arête, eliminating the crack and rock left of it.

4   **Meat Balls**   *5*
    Sit-start the crack.

5   **Spangle**   *5+*
    The right-hand side using the thin crack and arête. 6a+ eliminating the arête. The left-hand line on the wall is also 6a+.

6   **Papa Hobo**   *5+*
    Sit-start the groove.

7   **Happy Feet**   *5+*
    The left-hand side of the wall.

8   **Bread and Water**   *4+*   ✳
    The centre of the wall. The wall to the right past the slot is 5. The rib is 3.

9   **5**
    Lean around the overlap and mantel it out.

10   **To Harland Back**   *6b*
    Traverse the lower break R–L and back. One way, R–L, is 6a+. The top break, R–L, is 5.

11   **Harland Shuffle**   *6a*
    The right-hand side of the wall. *Jon Gilthorpe*

12   **Me-oh My-oh**   *6a+*
    A tight line up the blank centre of the wall.

13   **Miss Ohio**   *5+*   ✳
    The good flakes near the arête.

14   **Swollen Tongue**   *5+*
    The arête. 6a+ from a sit-start.

15   **Between the Bars**   *6a+*   ✳
    Sit-start the scooped wall. A good problem.

Harland West

The western end of Harland, detached from the main buttresses thanks to 500m of wild moorland terrain, has a decent boulder that can be easily combined with a trip to *Rabbit Warren*. Low-grade problems on good, rough rock. Approach as for *Rabbit Warren*, but bear right alongside a wall when over the stile. Keep right on a good path alongside the next wall at the woodland. Bear back south-east at the next path junction along the ridge line. Don't cross the SSSI direct. See map on previous spread.

Rabbit Warren

A series of small, broken buttresses, with some good low-grade problems, and some not so good. The rock is a little suspect in places, and the top-outs do have some loose rock: so be careful. We've described what we think is of interest to the boulderer; there's a bit more here which we've left out due to height/rock stability/rock quality issues.

1 Bugs' Arête 5+
The furthest left arête, on its right, without the crack.

2 Bunny Wall 4+ ✳
The good flake/crack up the wall, with a tricky final move.

The next bay along is rather tall and features some higher lines with biscuit-esque top-outs. A big span to start the hairline seam on the left wall, followed by big pulls is *Killer Bunnies* – 6a. Midgets could contrive a much harder start.

3 Cwningen 5
The left side of the wall, past an awkward mantel start, finishing near the arête.

4 Cwningod 4+
The right arête, with big pulls on good holds. The centre of the wall is a freaky 6a.

5 Choux-Fleur 5
The left arête, starting from the higher break. Mind the dirty top-out.

6 The Seeker 4+ ✳
The groove up the centre on lush holds.

7 The Bunny Run 3+ ✳
The wall left of the arête, starting by a crack. A good problem.

8 The Tomb 6b
Sit-start from the very back and hug up and out the hanging prow/arête. 4+ from standing.

9 Teal'c 5+
Sit-start the offwidth crack.

10 Bummer 5
Sit-start the small arête, with a crux first move past the nose.

11 5
The same arête on its right-hand side from a standing start.

12 Ace in the Hole 5+ ✳
About 200m further along is a slab, just left of a holly tree. The centre of the scooped slab, with a tricky mantel to finish.

Bank Quarry and Jackson Tor

They might not be extensive, but these angular, urban dens offer enjoyable low-mid grade problems and highballs. They're also accessible too, lying just to the north of Matlock with easy walk-ins.

Bank Quarry

The main problems are on a tall boulder, almost directly below the approach path.

1   **Jimmy**   *6b+*
The left arête, started on its left.

2   **The Chiseller**   *6b*
The narrow front face has a tricky start, followed by stretches between hidden chiselled slots. 5+ if the arêtes are used at the start.

3   **Boulder Arête Left-Hand**   *5*   ✳
The right arête, climbed on its left side. See photo on p302.

4   **Boulder Arete**   *4*   ✳
The right arête, on its right, is a good low-grade problem.

5   **Chisel On**   *5+*
Yard through the overlaps on chiselled finger jugs.

6   **Glory Days**   *6a+*   ✳
The left side of the concave wall, with a tricky move from the flat hold past a two finger dink. 6b from a sit-start at the flake.

10m to the right is *Yew Buttress*. In the centre of the buttress is an angular arete to its right.

7   **Back Street Abortionist**   *7a*   ✳
Climb the arete direct past the slot and chickenhead – a great sequence. Escape off right at the break.

There are also a couple of low-grade problems on a small wall at the far left end of the quarry. An arete 50m or so right of *Yew Buttress* is worthwhile: *Red Rum*, 5+.

JOHN COFFIELD ON *THE ARETE*, JACKSON TOR   PHOTO: ANDY BANKS

Jackson Tor

The first problems are towards the left-hand end of the quarry.

1   Moai   6a   ✳
A good highball up the tall arete. Start direct – powerful – or from the right – delicate.

2   Thinrib   3+
Layback up the left side of the narrow rib before rocking on to finish.

3   Jackson Bollock   6c
The blunt, right-hand rib next to the tree.

To the right, below the edge, are two boulders.

4   Spitting Cobra   6a
Sit-start the front of the block. 6b without the foot ramp at the start. *Paul Hayward*

5   Cottonmouth   6a   ✳
The wall right of the crack, using a lovely pinch on the rib. Avoid the chossy blocks for feet.

6   Boomslang   5+
The right arête on its left, without the footledges.

15m to the right is an angular bay.

7   The Arête   6a   ★
Positive edges and a good landing make for a good, not-too-high, highball up the arête. A left-hand finish from the pinch is a touch harder.

8   Sickle   5   ✳
Layback the high, juggy corner crack. Great fun.

9   Po   6c+
An awkward sequence up the sort-of arête right of the corner to a good hold at about 3m. *Malcolm Taylor*

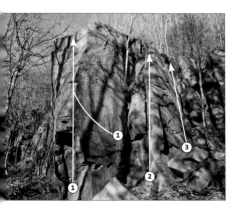

Matlock Area – South

Three esoteric bouldering areas south of Matlock that each have their merits. *Black Rocks* is unusual to say the least, and the problems here aren't your bog standard fare. It's also home to some state-of-the-art highballs. Of course, by 'highballs' we mean 'routes'! *Chasecliffe* and *Shining Cliff*, although limited, offer some good problems; *High Speed Train*, *Chaste*, *Goosecreature* and *Peaches & Crust* are worth a visit. What's more, *Shining Cliff* can be a good bet when the rest of the Peak is wet.

Access and Approach

Black Rocks is located just out of Cromford, south of Matlock. Turn off the A6 in Cromford onto the A5012 and drive up the hill as it becomes the B5036. The crag is signposted on the left after about 1km. Pull into either the upper or lower car park.

For *Chasecliffe*, drive south from Matlock on the A6 and turn left onto the B5035 at Whatstandwell, at the Derwent Hotel. After about a mile, turn right onto a minor road – Chadwick Nick Lane – and look for limited parking on a bend after a couple of hundred metres. Follow the footpath down towards the edge. Walk right along the edge for 80m and the boulder is below.

For *Shining Cliff* turn off the A6 in Ambergate onto Holly Lane, between the church and the cricket ground, signed *Shining Cliff*. Follow this for about 1.5 miles to a gated track on the right at the third farm, Netherpark Farm (signposted *Shining Cliff*). Follow this rough track to a parking area. Walk in along the right-hand – chained – track, with the Goose Roof up on the left after about 150m.

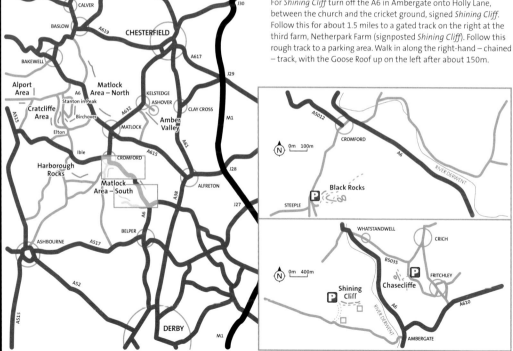

Black Rocks

The routes at *Black Rocks* were made famous in the film *Hard Grit*, and include numerous hard classics. However, the bouldering at *Black Rocks* is still esoteric and 'varied' to say the least!

Railway Slabs

The first problems are on two unmissable big slabs 50m along the *High Peak Trail*.

1 Percy *6a*
The left arête on its left side.

2 Trevor *5+*
The centre of the chipped slab.

3 Thomas *6b*
The central rib.

4 Gordon *4*
The tall slab on big chips.

5 The Fat Controller *6b*
Traverse the slab right from *Percy* to finish up *Gordon*.

6 Edward *4+*
The slab on the sidewall. Often mossy.

7 Route 2 *4+*
The left arête of the slab on its right side. 5 on the left. Highball.

8 Route 1 *4+* ✳
The chips just right of centre. Highball. The eliminate slab just left is 6a+.

9 Mallard *Fun*
The easy angled crack.

10 Harold *6b+* ✳
Sit-start the arête on its right side and follow it all the way.

11 The Buffer *5+*
From good holds on the sidewall, throw for the arête and top-out.

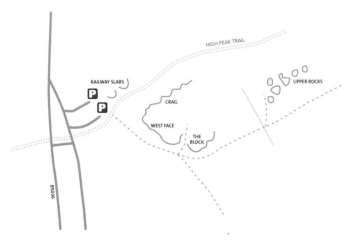

West Face

A varied collection of weird problems on the crag's western face.

12   Goya   *7c*
The steep arête on its steep side, with a gripping throw for a hueco on the lip. *Tom de Gay*

13   Curve Ball   *6b*
From the dogleg crack climb direct to the next break using the pocket. *Jon Fullwood*

14   Taxi to the Crag   *7b*   ✷
The arête directly below *Gaia*, climbed front on, starting on the ledge. See photo on p313.

15   Desert Island Disco   *6c*
Pockets and chips up the wall. Technical.

16   Route 66   *7c*
Sit-start under the overlap at a rectangular slot and climb up and right to a chip/pock on the lip, then traverse the lip leftwards on slopers before rocking onto the slab to finish. Don't use the good crack at the back. *Mark Evans*

17   Hat Trick   *7a*   ✷
Sit-start the rib to the pocket. Frustrating/satisfying. Can be dynoed. *Mark Evans*

18   Non Stick Vicar   *7b+*
The next rib right, without the arête, to a gripping pull onto the slab. Escape down the chimney. *Johnny Dawes*

19   Runnel Rib   *6b+*   ✷
The bulging arête. Escape off right from the ledge. Very cool.

20   The Runnel   *6c*   ✷
Tip-toe up the runnel, with no shortage of trepidation, to a rounded finish.

The Block

Around to the right is one of the most iconic pieces of gritstone in the Peak. The routes/ problems are included to demonstrate the state-of-the-art highball bouldering in the Peak, as much for their own individual aesthetics and they really do blur the line between routes and bouldering. As such, we've included trad grades too. The first problems are on the west-facing sidewall.

21   Shredded Feet   *7a (E3 6b)*
Traverse the sloping shelf rightwards to finish up *Golden Days*. *John Allen*

>>

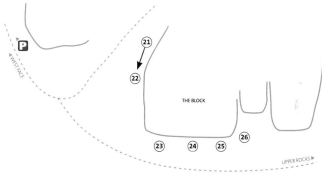

22   Golden Days   *6b+ (E2 6b)*   ★
The lovely flake to the break, with a fluttery stretch to good holds to finish.
John Allen/Steve Bancroft

Three classics climb the slabby face to the right, all starting with a depressing mantelshelf move onto the chipped gutter.

23   Jumpin' on a Beetle   *7b (E6 6c)*   ★
Step left from the gutter and smear across to the left arête, where difficulties soon ease.
Johnny Dawes

24   The Angel's Share   *7c (E8 7a)*   ★
From the right-hand side of the gutter smear directly up the big blank slab to a very slopey, rather high top-out. Concept. See photo on p308. *Johnny Dawes*

25   Velvet Silence   *7a+ (E6 6c)*   ★
A breathtakingly beautiful piece of climbing. This time, step right from the gutter to the right arête and layback tentatively up this. *Gabe Regan*

26   Make it Slappy   *7b+ (E6 6c)*   ✳
The steep side of the same arête is gained via a lurch onto chipped pockets.
Above, roll back left around the arête to finish up Velvet Silence. *Simon Hunter*

Upper Rocks
On top of the crag, set back a bit, is a collection of green boulders. Some good 'uns here.

27   AP   *5*
Trend right up the slab to the pocket and arête.

28   Maybelle   *6b*
Smear up the slab to the twin pockets.

29   Ledge Climb   *5+*
The wall from the ledge.

30   Dolly   *6b*   ✳
The tall arête on its right side. Tricky to start, tricky to finish. A peach.

31   Easy Slab   *3+*

32   Flaked Slab   *3*
The flakey slab above a poor landing.

33   The Clam   *5+*
Span through the roof from the break and pull over direct.

34   King Edward   *7b+*
From twin opposing sidepulls slap into the slopey pod and finish direct. *Mark Evans*

35   Ruby   *5*
The groove.

36   Valerie Ann I'm Desperate Dan   *4+*
Layback the arête to the ledge, walk across it, and finish up the far arête.
Or finish direct up the first arête.

37   Crack and Face   *5*

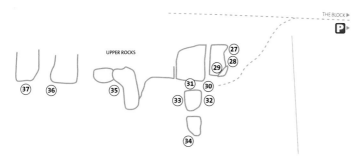

BEN BRAMSBY ON TAXI TO THE CRAG. PHOTO: ADAM LONG.

Black Garden

There's also the *Black Garden*, which can be found around 400m past the *Railway Slabs* along the *High Peak Trail*, over the fence and down the hill, pretty much in the garden of the houses: the main reason it doesn't get a full write up. Be discreet if you try to find it. It's also been reclaimed by nature at the time of writing. When clean, the left arête of the main east-facing block from a sit-start is *Chinese Cadbury Wolf* (6c); the central line on the wall, also from sitting, is the very good *T-Bone Wilson* (7a); the ramp just right from sitting is *Tasty Yellow Beef* (6b); the wall to the right is *Camden Leisure Pirate* (6b); and the steep arête is *Forest Casual* (7b, or 7a+ with a jump start).

Angel Boulder

An isolated block of minor interest. Follow the path that runs east parallel to the *High Peak Trail*, around a hairpin, and up the hill. At the clearing, break left on a minor path next to a broken wall. The boulder is just over the edge, about 30m past a green waymarker. *Neanderthal* (6b) stretches up the arête from an undercut; *Megalythic Man* (7a) climbs the wall to the left; *Angel Delight* (7a+) traverses into *Megalythic Man* along the obvious break.

Chasecliffe

A good boulder under the edge and a handful of problems above it. There's more rock dotted north and south of what we've described, but it's not worth exploring.

The Boulder

1   Nasal Arête   6a+
The left arête on its right side. The wall just left is 5.

2   High Speed Train   7a   ✳
Pull onto the slab using a small pocket on the lip and edges.

3   Chaste   6b+
Sit-start the rib to finger jugs at the lip and then make a hard roll onto the slab.

4   The Droop   6a
The right arête from a crouching start.

5   Chase Me   6c
Start up *The Droop* and traverse the lip left to finish up *Nasal Arête*. *Chase Me, Chase Me* (6c+) circumnavigates the entire block.

6   Hanging Scoop   5+
The scoop just right of the arête.

7   The Bulge   5+
The awkward bulge just right.

8   Chastity   5+
Sit-start steep left side of back arête.

9   Back Slab   Fun
The easy-angled slab round the back. Great fun – try it with no hands.

Mistral Wall

A small handful of problems on a steep wall above the boulder.

10   Geek Passion   6a
The left arête.

11   Mistral   6b
The centre of the wall. An eliminate variant using only the small crimps just right in the central break is 6c.

12   Warm Up   5+
The right arête.

Shining Cliff

A small crag but a surprisingly good bet when the rest of the (upper) Peak is soaked. Best appreciated in the winter months when the foliage is less rampant. Some good problems here.

Goose Roof

The first rock reached is an obvious big double roof up to the left of the path, 150m from the car park.

1 Foie Gras *5+* ✳
The groove at the left-hand side of the buttress, and the juggy roof above.

2 Goose Cannon *7b+*
Link *Foie Gras* into *Goosecreature* by aping along the lip. *Jon Fullwood*

3 Goosecreature *7b+* ★
Reach out and climb the widest part of the roof and the rib above. Avoid the ledge on *Goosegg Groove* at this grade. A modern classic. *Jon Fullwood*

4 Goosegg Groove *6a*
The groove from the ledge. *Jon Fullwood*

80m further along is a small vertical wall with a crack up its right-hand side.

5 Peaches & Crust *7a* ✳
The left-hand line, on cracks and layaways to the sloping ledge. *Jon Fullwood*

6 Got Milk *6a+*
The right-hand crack and headwall, trending right.

Much further on, on the buttress up behind the old youth hostel, is an attractive scooped wall with an overlap at half height, the upper part of which is taken by the route *Gecko Blaster* (E7).

7 Moo Cow *7a*
A technical, direct start to *Gecko Blaster* up the scoop. Good moves. At the time of writing, it hasn't been linked into the upper route. *Jon Fullwood*

WESTERN
CRAGS

The Churnet Valley

The *Churnet* gets less esoteric with every new guidebook, and should really be a prime venue on any Peak boulderer's map. Lovely crags on two sides of a river, easy walking from the car park on good tracks and pockets of sound where the quiet is punctuated every 10 seconds by screams from the nearby Alton Towers. The climbing is brilliant – a number of classic long traverses and classic boulder problems that range from the very easy to 7c+. The rock in the *Churnet* is a sandstone conglomerate – some of which is fantastic, with solid pebbles, nice flakes and deep pockets in good, fine-grained sandstone – but in other parts it's like flapjack. Happily, almost all of the bouldering takes place on the former.

The bouldering described is in *Ousal Dale* and *Dimmings Dale* – the most popular *Churnet* areas. New craglets of varying quality are being discovered and cleaned regularly in the area and we have included as many buttresses as space allows.

Access and Approach

The bouldering in the *Churnet* is found in the lower *Churnet Valley*, near the village of Alton, southwest of Ashbourne. From Alton take the Red Road (to be found behind the pub if you take the first right after the bridge, after passing the entrance to Alton Towers) and park at the Rambler's Retreat café on the left. Follow the track behind the café into the dale – then see approaches for the individual crags.

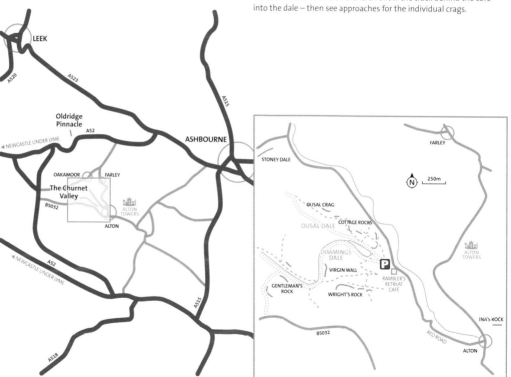

Ousal Dale

The crags on the right-hand side of the valley, when approached from *Rambler's Retreat*.

Cottage Rocks

Follow the right-hand path from the *Rambler's Retreat Cafe*, branching off right up a track about halfway along the pond. Follow this track uphill – the crag is up on the right just before the zigzag bends. A lovely spot with a range of good, predominantly lower-grade, problems on interesting features. The trees offer some shade from the sun and the right-hand side of the wall is steep enough to stay dry in showers.

1 **Adam's Arete** *7b*
The crimpy arête from sitting.

2 **Billy Bunter** *5*
Use the big pebble. A variant shares the same finish from a start just left.

3 **Crusty** *3+*
The cracks.

4 **Sid the Sexist** *5* ✳
Slab and pockets.

5 **Cottage Slab** *5* ✳
The wall just left to a hole.

6 **Green Wall** *6b* ✳
The wall using the finger ramp for your right hand.

7 **Sapling Bulge** *6b+*
Climb just left of the arête, using the finger ramp feature for your left hand.

8 **Tufa** *6a* ✳
Use the pinchy feature on the arête.

9 **Orange Crush** *5+*
Pull up pockets right of the arête.

10 **Pocket Wall** *5* ✳
The central line up pockets, with a final move to the break using the big square pebble. A sit start is 6b+.

11 **The Wafer** *5+*
The initially fingery wall using the wafer feature. 6a+ from a sit start.

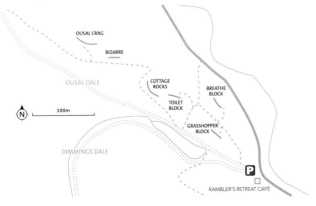

2   Strenuosity   4+
The wide crack at the right-hand side of the buttress.

3   Cottaging   6c   ✳
A right to left traverse. Start sitting and use holds immediately left of the crack to traverse the break and finish around the corner up *Billy Bunter* (finishing up *Tufa* is 6b+).

Glory Hole   6b
A mid-height traverse starting in the crack and finishing up *Tufa*.

The next problems are situated on a small buttress 10m right – *Pine Buttress*. All the problems start low to make the most of the good rock and then stop about 4 moves higher in flapjack land.

4   Left Pine   6c   ✳
Sit-start on the obvious crimp/undercut hold, with feet on pebbles on the vertical wall at the back (no ramp), and climb up through the bulge.

5   Pine Wall   6a+
The central groove feature from sitting.

16   Right Pine   6b+   ✳
Move right from the same start as *Pine Wall*. The foliage has been well trampled since the first edition of this guide. Can be started direct at a similar grade.

17   Lonesome Pine   6c+
Start on the far right and traverse left at a low level to finish up *Left Pine*.
Eddie Stephenson

18   Push   6b
Approximately 30m above and right of *Pine Buttess* is a lone arête in a bay. Climb this from sitting. Worth finding.

Bizarre
19   Bizarre   7b
On the main path from *Cottage Rocks* to *Ousal Crag*, this is the obvious path-side steep wall. Sit-start on the flake, lurch up for the crimp in the break and then slap for the top. Unfortunately the holds snap and erode regularly and the problem doesn't respond well when damp. Take care. *Stuart Brooks*

AL WILLIAMS ON *BIZARRE*   PHOTO: IAN PARNELL

Ousal Crag

A crag covered in pebbles with two classic Churnet-style traverses and a few up problems. Continue up the main path from *Cottage Rocks*, passing *Bizarre* on the right – *Ousal Crag* is up in the trees on the right after a further 100m.

20   Ousal Low   7a+   ★
The low traverse, starting on the blunt arête on the right then traversing left and finishing by pulling up to the jugs above the bulge at the left end.

21   Ousal High   6b   ✳
The higher traverse line is good too.

22   Ooze   5
Reach the end of the high traverse line through the bulge from a low start.

23   Sneezy   6a+
Sit-start, hit the big sloper and pull left into the high traverse line.

24   Booze   6a   ✳
Sit-start on twin crimps and pull into jugs. Finish on the high traverse line. 4 from standing.

25   Little Rib   4+
Sit-start the vague arête.

26   Uzi Lover   5   ✳
Sit-start the blunt arête at the start of the traverse. 4+ from standing.

Green Boulders

A series of blocks and buttresses on the ridgeline above and right of *Cottage Rocks*. To find them, pick up the footpath that doubles back up the hill, just before the gate on the right-hand fork up to *Cottage Rocks* and *Ousal Crag*. At the top of the hill the path meets a wall corner. Walk left here along the line of the wall on a vague path to the *Toilet Block* – approx 70m. For *Breathe Block*, walk right along the ridgetop path, ignore the first main path off left and take a vague path left about 30m later. The path meets the edge and *Breathe* is the furthest left wall (looking out). For *Grasshopper Block*, keep going along the ridgetop path and pick up a vague path on the right about 20m before the ridge starts to descend – *Grasshopper Block* is hidden, facing south.

Toilet Block

A decent chunk of rock with some nice big holds.

27   Double Trouble   6a+
Situated on the boulder to the left of the main block, climb the vein from a sit-start.

28   Bog Trot   6a
On the main block, climb the left arête on its left from a start on the right. *Stuart Brooks*

29   Touching Cloth   6b
From a sit-start climb via good holds to a tricky mantel. *Dave Mawer*

STUART BROOKS ON *THE TOMAHAWK TRAVERSE*   **PHOTO:** BROOKS COLLECTION

0 Follow Through *5+*
More good holds up the wall left of the vein. *Kyya Morroll*

1 Toilet Duck *6b+*
From jugs on the right climb the hanging nose to a rounded top-out. *Matthew Isles*

2 Toilet Traverse *5+*
Traverse left to right, or vice versa.

Breathe Block

A good block, with a fine sloper on the namesake problem.

3 Footprints *6b* ✳
Sit-start the rightwards-slanting arête under the bulge. Starting standing on holds just to its right it's called *Fingerprint* – 5+. *Stuart Brooks*

4 Breathe *7a* ★
Gain the sloper from sharp crimps below, and move left to finish. A sit-start (left hand mono, right hand crimp) bumps the grade to 7b. *Stuart Brooks*

5 Suffocation *6a+*
Jump to the break, then make a big move to the top. The sit-start on monos is 6b. *Dave Mawer/Dave Kettle*

Grasshopper Block

Steep climbing on positive holds. Slow drying.

36 Down Under *6a+*
Sit-start using holds either side of the small niche, gain a crimp in the roof and throw for the lip. *Stuart Brooks*

37 The Grasshopper *6a+* ✳
Climb the middle of the steepness from a sit-start. *Stuart Brooks*

38 The Duck Billed Platypus *7a* ✳
Sit-start on the left of the arête. Use a hold in the roof to pull through to the break and finish directly above. *Stuart Brooks*

39 The Kookaburra *5+*
Sit-start on the right of the arête, gain the break and move left to finish as for the previous problem. *Stuart Brooks*

40 The Tomahawk Traverse *7a+*
A bit contrived, but quite good fun. From the sit-start of *The Kookaburra* traverse left along the lowest break line. Move up and follow the next line of holds where you pass the start of *The Grasshopper*. Use the crimp in roof to hit the slopey jug on the next level of holds. Catch your breath then head left all the way along this break to the end of this block, there you can throw one on for the final break and traverse right to victory. *Stuart Brooks*

Dimmings Dale

The left-hand valley when approached from the *Rambler's Retreat* is home to yet more classic traverses and the Churnet's harder 'up' problems.

Virgin/Long Wall

From the left-hand track behind the café, continue until opposite a small bridge on the second leftwards bend. Scout up the hill as best you can and make for the rock.

Virgin/Long Wall Traverse   *6a+–7b*   ★

An awesome traverse – at least 25m long. The full thing – starting from the extreme right via technical pebble pulling, dropping into the juggy central section, and regaining the higher pebble line to a redpoint crux continuing left to finish on the ledge is 7b. The central section alone is 6a+ and the central section plus the excellent puzzling sequence along the higher pebble line at the left-hand end is 7a.

Gentleman's Rock

Continue on the left-hand track, around a series of bends until opposite the first small waterfall *Gentleman's Rock* can be seen in the trees on the left. Yet more traversing, intersecting with modern 'up' problems.

1   **Jill the Traverse**   *6b+*
  The low-level traverse line to the central crack. It's not as good as the other long traverse in *Dimmings Dale* as it's just a line of crimps with big footholds on often damp rock. Finishing up *The Nose* via the *Low Traverse* is better and harder – *The Mega Traverse*, 7a+.

2   **Moon Jumper**   *6b+*   ✳
  From the juggy ledge, climb the vague arête using a high pocket. Cross the roof and finish in the pod on the lip. A better 6b finished at the first jug. *Dave Parkin*

3   **Lunar Direct**   *7c*
  Use two poor pockets to reach a sidepull and use it to join the *Electrofly* finish. *Mike Adams*

4   **Electrofly**   *6c+*
  Reach from the traverse line to the two-finger pocket in the middle of the green crud, and lock to jugs (6c to here). Traverse left and rock up to finish on the rail. *Rob Mirfin*

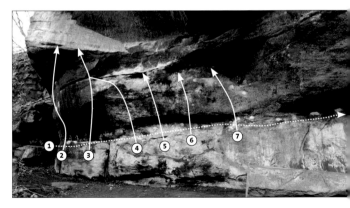

Martin's Mono *7a+*
Start under the small roof, undercut to mono and jump to the big pocket.
Martin Dearden

Fifty Pence Problem *7b*
Reach the pebble shaped like a 50p piece and use it to gain a pocket above and to its left.
Dave Kettle

Humpty Dumpty *7a+*
Climb pebbles up the wide groove.

Gentleman John *6b+*
Steep finger crack nastiness. Finish at the high jugs.

High Speed Imp Act *7a* ★
From low edges attack the leaning wall with final committing lobs between good pockets. Finish on the high jugs. See photo on p326. *Martin Veale*

0 Crash Damage *7b+*
Start as for *High Speed Imp Act*. From the big pocket, cross over leftwards with your right hand to a first joint mono and make a big move to better holds. *Mike Adams*

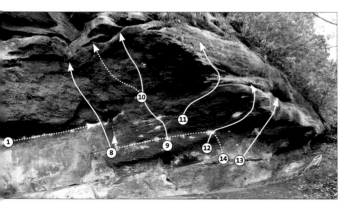

11 Clover Field *6c*
Slot to ledge, then climb the dirty wall above. Rarely clean. *Rob Mirfin*

12 The Nose *6c* ★
Sit-start and climb the good edges/slots through the steepness.
Pegasus – 7b – dynos straight to the ledge/break from the first good hold.

13 Slow Worm *7b*
Sit-start on low shelf, use a crimp to throw for the letterbox (this bit is *Lockit to the Pockit* – 6a+). From the letterbox use a slopey crimp on the lip to hit the break (this bit is *Limp Lizard* – 7a+). If you have the reach you can go directly from the letterbox to the break at 7a. *Dave Parkin*

14 Low Traverse *6b+*
From the shelf at the start of the previous problem traverse up and left to the jug on *Gentleman John*. Reversed into *Lockit to the Pockit* it is 7a.

15 Mindbenderjelly *7a*
R–L traverse, starting right of *Slow Worm* and finishing on the *Gentleman John* jug.

Spookyland and Square Pusher
Follow the track that breaks left uphill off the main track after *Gentleman's Rock*. *Spookyland* is over on the left after 150m.

16 Spooky Wall *6b+*
Starting in the break on the left wall, pull on and slap to the next sloping, break.
Stuart Brooks

17 Spooky Arete *6a+*
From sitting at the triangular hold in the niche, head left and up the arete. *Stuart Brooks*

18 Flowtation *6c*
Up and right from the same start. *Stuart Brooks*

The *Square Pusher* wall is 20m to the left, in the trees – a 3m vertical wall under a tree.

19 Square Pusher *6b+* ✳
Pull on with a high right hand hold (stack mats if necessary) and a low left hand hold. Reach another small hold to the left and pop to the top. Usually damp Oct–Apr. *Rob Mirfin*

20 Skint *6b+*
Climb the right side of the wall from a sit-start. *Rob Mirfin*

The Chained Block

Hidden 50m up the slope, on the other side of the river and directly opposite *Gentleman's Rock*. The best approach is direct, or over the bridge further down the Dale. Dries out Apr–Sept.

21 The Chained Block Traverse   *6b+*
Start on the left side of the block, left of the crack. Follow the break and take a rising traverse line past the obvious pocket to finish up the nose. *Stuart Brooks*

22 Superstring   *6b*
Sit-start on the central blunt arete, move left to the top via the same obvious pocket. Finish matched on a sloper. *Stuart Brooks*

23 The Revival   *7a+*
Sit-start on the central blunt arête, reach lovely crimps up and right and move left via a pocket to the top. *Stuart Brooks*

24 The Awakening   *7b*   ✳
Sit-start. From the crimps on *The Revival* reach a sloper right of the arête and a hard top-out. *Stuart Brooks*

25 Lean, Green, Bean Machine   *6b*   ✳
Sit-start right of the arête, bounce to slopers, rock right to finish. *Dave Mawer*

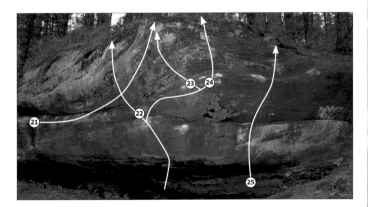

Wright's Rock Area

Whereas the other crags are enclosed in the trees, *Wright's Rock* overlooks an open meadow above the valley. There's a good long traverse and lots of powerful problems that cross steep bulges. Grades from 4–7c+.

North-facing, the crag gets almost no sun. It stays dry in the rain and is great in hot weather, but the lower section of rock can become green after damp periods – such conditions will also bring out the midges. Recently a fence has been erected and although there are no access issues at present, be on your best behaviour.

Take the left branch of the track behind the café, then take a smaller track that scouts up and left into the trees after about 50m. The track comes out into a meadow, from where *Wright's Rock* can be seen up on the right. Cross the stile and pass through the gate to the left, picking up the path up the hill. The first blocks described are left of the main crag, at the top of the approach path.

Instant Funk Block

The left-most steep block, at the top of the approach path.

26   Out There and Back   7b   ✳
Crouch start on a small pocket and crimp, use a pocket to reach the break and finish on the rail above. An easier exit links into the finish of *Instant Funk – Instantly Out There*, 7a+. *Stuart Brooks*

27   Been Caught Stealing   7a
Sit-start, reach the break and use a sloper to reach the rail on the left. *Martin Dearden*

28   Instant Funk   7b   ✳
Left to right traverse starting on the low break, reaching the higher continuation break and using a big pocket to reach the top rail. *Rob Mirfin*

STUART BROOKS ON *THE AWAKENING*   **PHOTO:** BROOKS COLLECTION

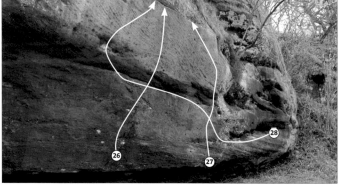

Sharp Holds Block

The more vertical wall a few metres to the right.

29 **Fatherhood** *7a+*
Sit-start the arête.

30 **Motherhood** *6c*
Trend left from a sit-start in the low hole.

31 **Navuku** *6b+*
The pebbly wall.

32 **Wright's Giza** *7a+* ✳
Pebbles to break to crimp to top. *Rob Mirfin*

33 **Keith Sharp Holds** *7b* ✳
Climb the wall using sharp holds. *Rob Mirfin*

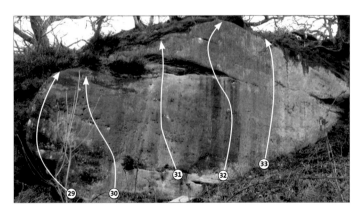

The Niche

The left side of the main crag is home to a number of good, technical problems.

34 Wright's Unconquerable 7a+ ★
Start on a thread and span through the steepness above. Burly. Morpho. *Rob Mirfin*

35 Crumble Roof 6b
Climb the steep wall from a crouched start.

36 Dave's Traverse 6b
Start up *Crumble Roof* and traverse the break left into *Wright's Unconquerable*.

37 Jug Wall 6b
Climb the left side of the bulge on big holds.

38 Threapwood Bulge 6a+
Climb the bulging wall from a low start

39 Threapwood Arete 6b+
The arête left of the recessed wall, climbed on pockets and pebbles.

40 Niche Traverse 6b+ ★
Traverse the wall at the back of the niche, left to right. Extend to the *Sauroff* jug at 6c+.

41 Rocket Ride 6c+ ★
Climb the middle of the recessed wall, left hand on quartz pebble, right hand on crimp, and lock/press to the break. Very good. *Stuart Brook*

Several variations have been done:

a) Davros 6c ✳
A right-hand version gains the crimp with your left hand before cartwheeling leftwards to the same break. A sit-start from a pocket to the right is 6c+. *Rob Mirfin*

b) Albatross 6c+
Sit-start on the pocket and continue as for *Davros*, but use the left hand crimp to span to a large pocket out right. *Rob Mirfin*

c) Albatross Direct 7b+
A further eliminate on *Albatross* avoids the left hand crimp.

42 Sauron 5
The corner, finishing at the pocket on the left.

43 Sauroff Sit Start 6b ✳
Sit-start the arête to the break. *Iron Pebble* – 6b+ – rocks right using the shiny pebble.

The Main Crag

44 Wright's Traverse *7b* ★
From *Thorns*, traverse right to finish up *Last Wrights*. Jugs, pockets and plenty of steep, positive pulling.

45 Thorns *4+*
Climb jugs up the left side of the niche.

46 Blazes *6a+* ★
Direct up the wall of the niche and through the roof on sidepull flakes. Very good. A right finish is 6b. *Fireman Indirect* – 6c – continues traversing right to gain the curving ramp.

47 Quill *7c+* ✳
The thin grooveline, started with a right thumb on the high gaston. *Ryan Pasquill*

48 Sam Tan *7b* ✳
Gain the jug on the lip as for *Simple Simon* then climb leftwards to the ramp. *Mike Adams*

49 Simple Simon *7b* ★
Gain the jug on the lip (jump, or climb from the back – 6b in its own right, but no increase in overall grade) and continue with steep pulls on reasonable crimps and flatties to gain the good break. *Andy Brown*

50 Simple Simon Indirect *7a* ✳
Sit-start down and right on small flakes, reach good holds under the roof and span into the starting jug of *Simple Simon*. Linked with *Simple Simon* it's 7b+.

51 Thumbs *7b+*
From big pockets under the roof span to the lip and traverse left on edges into *Simple Simon* and finish up this. The sit-start is 7c.

52 Pie Hard *7a+*
The wall to the left of *Fingers* to the break. 7b+ if continued up the highball wall above. *Rob Mirfin*

53 Fingers *7a* ★
The nose/arête/prow just right. Gain good holds over the lip and continue on slopes and edges to the break. Sit-start 7a+. See photo on p328. *Simon Nadin*

54 Wrong's Traverse *7b*
Sit-start on a flake below *Simple Simon* and traverse right below *Wright's Traverse* on pockets and crimps, avoiding all holds on that problem, to finish up *Last Wrights*. An eliminate, but good. *Rob Mirfin*

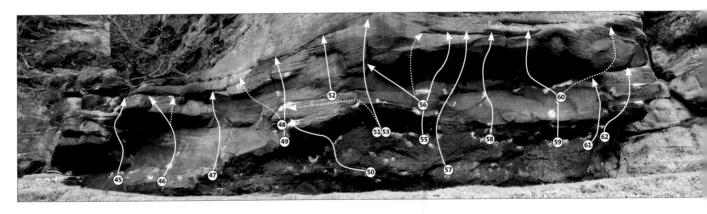

55 Alternative Three *6b* ★
Good, steep, juggy pulling through the bulges just right, then cross the roof using the flake underneath it to finish at the break. 6c from a sit-start.

56 Johnny Utah *7a+*
Link *Alternative Three* into *Fingers* via an undercut in the roof. A direct finish, just right of the *Fingers* crack, is 7a+.

57 Tyler *7a+*
A good eliminate. Sit-start the groove right of *Alternative Three* and don't use any holds on that problem until the flake in the roof for your left, together with an undercut with your right, to cross the roof. *Mike Adams*

58 Point Break *7b+* ✳
Good pockets and a powerful pull gets you established on the blocky pinch below the roof. Then undercut through the roof to the break to finish. Climbed to the blocky pinch gives the classic problem *The Undercut* – 6c+. *Mike Adams*

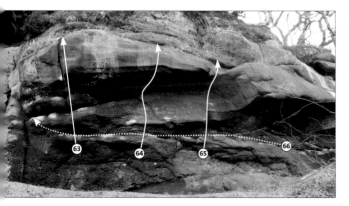

59 Warchild *7c+* ✳
Cross the bulge on awkward diagonal crimps to reach the sloping break, traverse left for a move or so, then cross the roof on undercuts. Finishing matched on the sloping shelf is 7a. *Mike Adams*

60 Bhodi *7a+* ✳
Start as for *Warchild* but traverse the sloping shelf right and join last *Last Wrights* at the higher break. See photo on p318. *Mike Adams*

61 Little Groove *6a+*
The little groove just right. Link into *Bhodi* at 6c+.

62 Last Wrights *6a* ✳
Pull through the square bulge to the break. 6c if finished at the high break past the roof.

Right's Rock
The final rock is just to the right.

63 The Crack *7a* ✳
Gain the crack from a sit-start using slopers and climb it to a dirty top-out. The grade may drop with a cleaner top. An eliminate – *No Crack*, 7b+ – climbs the same line without the crack.

64 Calyx *7b*
Sit-start. Tackle the central roof. *Rob Mirfin*

65 The Hob *3+* ✳
The scoop. An eliminate climbing the arête to the right is *Hob Nob* – 6b+

66 The Hob Traverse *5*
Traverse the break from right to left. Or the other way. Your call. A good warm-up.

Churnet Outlying (see map on p319 for locations)
There's also *Ina's Rock*, famous for two 8m high routes/extreme highball problems; *Cornelius* (7c/E8) takes the roof and prow, *Thumbelina* (7a/E6) climbs the centre of the wall. *Stoney Dale* and the Quarries gives decent, but in some places slow drying, bouldering from about 4–mid 7's. Further afield, *Oldridge Pinnacle* gives more high routes up an isolated pinnacle that can be padded.

The Roaches

The Roaches has some of the best routes and bouldering in the world. The climbing is spread out over a vast area and caters for all grades and all styles. With blank slabs on perfect grit, fine arêtes, proud flakes, beautiful fingertip ripple features, scallops, steep walls, roofs and the best traverse-line on grit, the Roaches has it all.

The moorland surrounding the Roaches is environmentally very important. Please keep to paths, and your dog under control, particularly on the *Skyline* and the *Five Clouds*.

Access and Approach

The Roaches lie behind Upper Hulme, just off the A53 between Leek and Buxton. Turn off the A53 towards Upper Hulme and bear down through the village passing a ford and the factory. The road now winds uphill passing the *Roaches Tea Rooms* on the left and the imposing bulk of *Hen Cloud* on the right. There is a lot of designated parking in lay-bys beneath the crag, but this fills up fast, so please park considerately. Be sure to park well within the marked lay-bys too, so as to avoid getting a ticket.

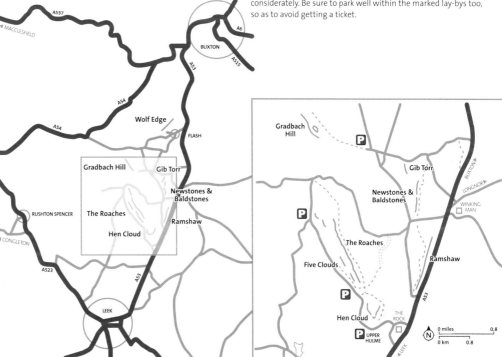

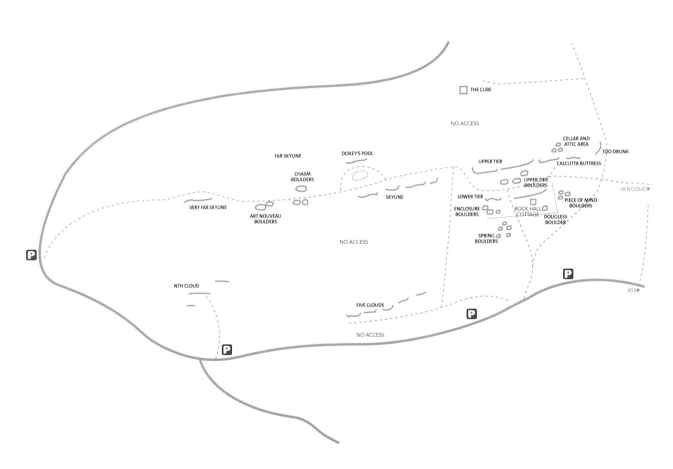

THE CUBE

NO ACCESS

CELLAR AND
ATTIC AREA

TOO DRUNK

FAR SKYLINE

DOXEY'S POOL

UPPER TIER

CALCUTTA BUTTRESS

CHASM
BOULDERS

UPPER TIER
BOULDERS

SKYLINE

HEN CLOUD ▶

VERY FAR SKYLINE

LOWER TIER

PIECE OF MIND
BOULDERS

ART NOUVEAU
BOULDERS

ENCLOSURE
BOULDERS

ROCK HALL
COTTAGE

DOUGLESS
BOULDER

NO ACCESS

SPRING
BOULDERS

NTH CLOUD

P

FIVE CLOUDS

A53 ▶

P

NO ACCESS

P

P

Spring Boulders

The *Spring Boulders* offer a great selection of 'easy angled' problems that climb scoops, slabs and arêtes on rough, pebbly rock. They are open of aspect, quick to dry, close to the car and are surrounded by semi-permanent bog. The first problems are on the very small boulder just next to the path. See topo overleaf.

Boulder A

1. **Gentle Slab** *3+*
The small slab next to the path with the shallow scoop. Similar problems to the left.

2. **Nose Seam** *5*
The arête with the seam.

3. **Noseam** *5*
Climb slopers from low, left of the seam.

Boulder B

4. **Spring Roll** *4+*
The arête on the right-hand side. 5+ on the left.

5. **Slabby Seam** *3+*

6. **Blunt Arête** *4*

Boulder C(3PO)

The next boulder is probably the best in this circuit. It not only has a fantastic array of smearing slab test-pieces that get gradually harder, but you can also walk up to it without sinking.

7. **Bobarête** *6c+* ✳
The big, bald arête is directly above an ankle-snapping hole. 6c and nicer with a jump start.

8. **Boba Fett** *7b+* ★
Ultra tenuous moves climb the slab left of – and without – the bald arête.

9. **C3PO** *7a+* ★
A classic. The central line on the slab gives more faith-in-friction climbing.

10. **Spring Slab** *7a* ✳
The left line on the slab is now harder since the demise of some pebbles.
Boba's Traverse starts here and follows a rising L–R line to finish at *Bobarête* – 7a.

11. **4+**
Climb the arête on the left-hand side.

12. **Sprung** *6a* ✳
From a sit start, climb the flake on its left. *Sprat* heads up and right – 5.

13. **Easy Wall** *3*

NEIL KERSHAW ON *BOBA FETT* **PHOTO:** ADAM LONG

Boulder D

14 Blind Flake *5*

15 Scoops *5+* ✳
The scoops to the top. Graded for climbing using rock shoes and not wellies, but we know which we'd wear.

16 Pebbles and Seam *6a*

17 Pebbly Wall *6c*
Hard pebble-pulling above the quagmire.

18 *6b*
Climb the arête on the right.

19 *Fun*
The left side of the arête and the scoops.

20 *4+*
The wall from undercuts.

21 *3*
Big holds left of the arête.

22 Poxy *3+* ✳
Climb the scooped slab. Nice climbing above an often-dry landing. The slabs to the left are also 3+.

Boulder E

23 Slab to Summit *4+*

24 *3+*
The arête on its right.

25 Mantel *3+*
Mantel. There's a similar line to the left too.

Boulder F

26 Melt *5+* ✳
The appealing scoop.

27 *6a*
Gain the hole and then the top.

28 Flakes *3+*

29 *5+*
Up through the left end of the pod.

30 *5*
Up through the centre of the pod.

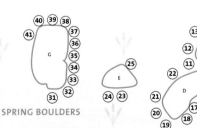

SPRING BOULDERS

Boulder G

31 Violence 6a ★
The scoop is harder than it looks, but it is very good.

32 Impotence 6a
The blunt arête to the right.

33 Lout 5
Up from the ledge to a slopey top-out.

34 Seconds Out 5+ ✳
Climb the offwidth crack. The left arête of the crack is 6a.

35 The Grind 7a ✳
Undercut the holes to reach the sloping top.

36 Skinned Rabbit 6b
An almost identical problem to *The Grind*, situated a few holes to the right. 7a from a sit-start (on your raft).

37 6c+
Climb the arête on the left-hand side.

38 6c ✳
Climb the arête on the right-hand side.

39 Mr Nice 6b+
The blank wall is climbed using the chipped foothold.

40 6c
From the right arête enter the scoop on the left and climb it to the top. Climbing the arête all the way on the left is 6b.

41 Ledgy Arete 3+

Boulder H

42 6a
Traverse the break to the left arête.

Boulder I

43 Easy Slab 3 ✳

44 Heave Ho 6a
Ledges.

45 The Lurch 6b+
Jump to the scoop and top-out.

46 The Fly 7a+
Climb the steep prow from a low start on the flake. The landing under this problem is so waterlogged that it actually flows. Quite fast.

Lower Tier Boulders/The Enclosure

The *Lower Tier* offers a great circuit of easy slabs and arêtes on *Velcro*® rock, a few classic 7's and two stunning 'big numbers'. The trees can give shade in summer, but they also keep the boulders damp after rain. The *Inertia Reel* wall and *Mushin* can both take seepage so finding them in condition can prove to be frustrating.

Slabotomy

The first problems are on a clean slab 200m or so left of the main bouldering, under *Maud's Garden*. 6m left is another square cut block with a crack up the centre.

1   Boobage   *5+*
The left arête of the left block.

2   Malted Milk   *6b+*
Climb the crack in the centre of the face, without using either arête.

3   *4*
The left arête of the slab.

4   Slabotomy   *7b*   ✳
The slab starting on the right-hand side and climbing directly up the face. A good find. A left-hand start is slightly easier – 7a+. See photo on p341. *Rob Mirfin*

Lower Tier Boulders

Back at the main area, on the boulders below the crag.

5   Slab   *4+*

6   Crack   *3*   ✳

7   *4+*   ✳
The slab right of the crack offers good smearing practice to help you get your gritstone head on. Great fun with no hands.

8   *3+*
The chips.

9   The Flake   *4+*   ✳
'Nuff said.

10   The Greener Traverse   *6b*   ✳
Traverse down the ramp and slap back up to the rounded top. The crimpy sit start is 6b+ and the final slap up, on its own, is 6a.

11   *6c*
Manteling onto the rounded top left of the left-hand arête is hard work.

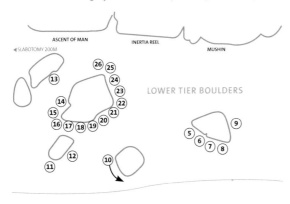

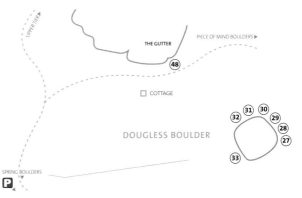

12   A number of nice problems based around the rising cracks:

The Grasper *4+* ✳
The obvious, independent problem up the front and using anything.
5+ from a sit-start on the jug left of centre.

The Undercutter *6a* ✳
Sit-start on the jug left of centre and reach left to the arête.

The Uppercut *6b*
Sit-start on the jug left of centre and go straight up eliminating the big undercut on the right.

13   More nice problems up the short slab. The slabby face is climbable everywhere, with all of the ways up being short and pleasant:

3+
The leftmost line.

3
Climb about five foot in from the left.

Blister's Sister *4* ✳
The slab just left of the bobbles.

Blister Slab *4+* ✳
Mantel the mid-height hold.

4
The right-hand line.

14   **Black Nook Slab** *4*
The short slab.

15   **Black Nook Arête** *4*
Arête on the left-hand side.

16   *5*
Arête on the right-hand side.

17   **Three Pocket Slab** *6a* ★
The line of pockets up the otherwise blank slab is one of the best lower grade problems in the Peak.

18   **Parental Duties** *7b*
The pebbly slab above the starting foot-pocket of *Three Pocket Slab* (the ledge out right is not in). *James Pearson*

The ledge just right is more shrubbery than boulder problem.

19   **Big Simple Flake** *3* ✳
Climb the big flakes – the easiest way up.

20   **Sketchy Wall** *5*
The wall between the flakes and the diagonal crack is a bit worrying.

21   **The Crack** *4+*
The diagonal crack and occasional plant. Highball.

22   **Flake Crack** *4*
The flaky crack.

23   **Stretch and Mantel** *6c* ★
Undercut and stretch up the wall. Congratulations, you've got your hands on the top, just the mantel to go then. A Peak rite of passage.

24   **The Big Dyno** *7a* ★
This cunningly named problem is a) a dyno, but, more specifically, b) big. Also referred to as the *Undercut Dyno* because it starts on an undercut. *Richard Williams*

25   **Stretch Left** *6a+*
Span left to the finishing jug of *The Big Dyno* from the right arête and mantel it out.

26   **Classic Arête** *4* ★
Big holds up the arête.

The Dougless Boulder

The huge boulder in the grounds of the cottage is home to some big, green problems, including one of *Nadin's* classic slabs.

27 Particle Exchange *6c+*
Climb the crack and tentatively step left to the arête. Highball. *Mark Katz*

28 Dougless *6b+*
Climb the crack and continue over the roundedness. Highball.

29 The Rumour *7a+* ✳
The rippled slab right of *Dougless*. *Simon Nadin*

30 Sketchy Rib *6a*
The rib just right.

31 4+
Arête.

32 6a
Chips and flake up right.

33 Scratchy Scoop *6a*
The scoop left of the big blunt arête, right of the carved steps, on the opposite side of the boulder (marked on the topo plan).

Ascent of Man Area

The next problems are on the crag, up and left of the main boulders. Two routes-come-highballs climb through the pod on the wall to the left: *Apache Dawn* through the centre, and *Catastrophe Internationale* through the right-hand side. Both about E5, both about 7a+, but high with fragile pebbles and gripping top-outs.

34 Bareback Rider   *6c*   ★
The highball arête, climbed initially on its left-hand side until a rock-over gains the slab. *Ron Fawcett's* favourite E3. *Dave Jones*

35 Ascent of Man Start   *6a+*   ✳
Start low in the cave and climb to the break.

**36 Ascent of Woman Start   *6b*
The twin ribs to the break.

**37 Traverse of Man   *6a*
Start in the cave under *Ascent of Man* and traverse left all the way to the bushes.

Inertia Reel Area

The next buttress right is home to some toughies.

38 The Inertia Reel Traverse *8a+* ★
A beautifully sculptured traverse, climbed from extreme left to extreme right. *Jerry Moffatt*

39 Ant Lives *7a*
Press out the shelf to reach the break. *Nick Dixon*

40 Inertia Reel *7a+* ★
Manteling, bridging, undercutting nonsense – brilliant. More than one finger pulley has been ruptured by that undercut. *Johnny Dawes*

Turbo *7c+*
The sit-start to *Inertia Reel*. Ouch! *Rupert Davies*

41 Thud *7b*
Upside-down toe-hooking or a guns-out campus move. Start from the perfect scallop and the undercut under the roof, with your feet on the back wall and finish up *Teck Crack Direct*. It has also been done by starting matched on the undercuts, but they are quite fragile and often wet. *Paul Higginson*

42 Teck Crack Direct *6c* ★
Traverse the slopey shelf up and right, then bounce for the top. Classic.

43 Teck Crack Super Direct *7b+*
The thin seam to the finish of *Teck Crack Direct*. To start you will need to either 1) be tall, 2) grow, 3) stand on something. *Paul Higginson*

44 The Dignity of Labour *6c+*
Traverse the break left from the block, and lunge up to an intimidating finish. *Nick Dixon*

To the right is a jutting prow with a steep undercut wall to the right, peppered with little dishes.

45 A Modest Proposal *7a*
The jutting nose is approached from the leftmost of the two prows, starting at the break. A variation – *Skydivin'* – jumps to the nose from the boulder. The offwidth roof crack also goes at 6b. *Tom O'Rourke (AMP) Justin Critchlow/Paul Higginson (SD)*

46 Mushin *7c+* ★
The awesome bulge features climbing as God intended it to be – footless campussing on sloping dishes. It's worth brushing the top if you want to top-out, otherwise finish at the break and jump off like everyone else. *Ben Moon*

47 Boozy Traverse *6c+*
From the holly bush, shuffle left beneath *Mushin* to take a crux slopey section left of the crack. *Simon Panton*

The Gutter

Right of the steps leading to the *Upper Tier* is the massive roof and prow of *Valkyrie* (VS). At the bottom right of this prow is a small, well chalked cave.

48   The Gutter   *7a+*   ✳

From the back of the cave on an undercut pull out to the lip and finish up the arête and face above. The sidewall to the right and any holds right of the crack, including the large right heel pocket are not in at this grade. Using the large pocket for a heel hook out right makes it 6c+. See topo on p338.

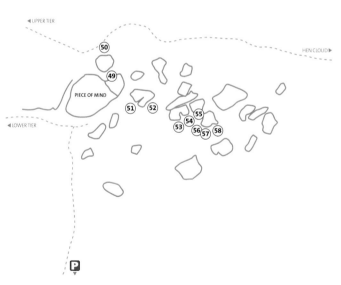

Piece of Mind Boulders

Walking right beneath the crag brings you to the boulders around the big slab at the end just out of the trees – the *Piece of Mind* circuit. We have described the best problems in this cluster of boulders – more problems exist on smaller blocks scattered down the slope, but they are small, scrittley and generally not as good.

The first set of problems is in a cluster of boulders on top of, and just to the right of the large *Piece of Mind* (E6) slab. A bit high and a bit poky, some were originally given route grades.

49   Crinkles Wall   *6c+*

The bare wall in the cubicle made by the boulders. It is on the wall facing away from the edge.

50   Annie's Egg   *6c+*

On the back of the rear-most boulder, on the side facing away from the crag, is a hanging scoop above a gap. Jump the gap (!) and climb the scoop. Originally given E4. *Nick Dixon*

10m right of *Piece of Mind* is a slabby buttress, split by a crack on its left hand side.

51   The Jams   *5+*

The high crack line.

52   The Teacup   *5*

Slab and flakes to the right of the crack

A further 10m right, at a lower level is:

53   Twisted Crack   *6b*

The crackline on the right of the overhang.

54   Off Work   *5*

The wide crack.

55   *5*   ✳

The arête just left of the gully. Reachy at the top. A good sit-start off two bumps is 7a.

56   Wildy's Arete   *5+*   ✳

The good arête, climbed on its left. 6b+ from sitting.

57   Wildy's Right   *6a*   ✳

The arête climbed on its right hand side. Worth walking over for.

58   *4*

The big slab and cracks right of the arête.

Upper Tier Boulders

The *Upper Tier* boulders are very popular and have a spread of mostly lower grade problems on very good, fine-grained rock. They dry much faster than the *Lower Tier* boulders, making them a great place to warm up before trying your project downstairs. Approach up the steps from the *Lower Tier*.

1 **Left Arête** *4*
The left arête.

2 **Rippler** *6a*
Rock up leftwards from a round hold. Sit-start at 7a.

3 *6a*
A rising left to right traverse line on the high holds. A contorted sit-start on undercuts and pinches is 6c+.

4 **The Boss** *6c* ✳
Start low and inch awkwardly up to the ledge.

5 **Grand Theft** *7c* ✳
A hard and conditions dependant traverse along the slopey lip from the left arête to finish up *The Boss*. *Justin Critchlow*

6 **Ripple Arête** *4*
The arête. A variety of sitting starts are possible.

7 *3+*
A few easy lines have been climbed on this boulder – take your pick.

8 **Crimpy Wall** *4*
The wall left of the arête.

9 **Nose Arête** *5* ✳
The slab and arête on the right is an entertaining thrutch for those watching. 4+ on the left side of the arête.

10 **Nose Scoop** *6a* ✳
Mantel onto the hanging slab from a low start. An easier line to the right is 3+.

11 **Big 'Oles** *4+* ✳
Big holes.

12 **Joe's Arête** *6a* ★
The classic arête is probably the most climbed problem in Staffordshire. It's polished, balancy and brilliant. The one-handed variation is also a must. *Joe Brown CBE*

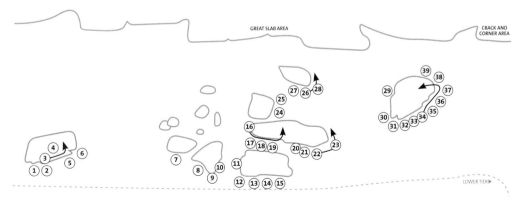

13 Pink Wall Eliminate *6c+* ✳
A frustrating eliminate right of the arête – pull up to the very slopey sidepull from a low start on the right-hand gaston and try to stay on long enough to reach the small high flakes.

14 5
Another eliminate up the bigger flakes in the centre of the face, without the holes.

15 Joe's Portholes *4+* ✳
Climb more big holes, or better still do one of these eliminates:

Mean Ol' Bastard *7b* ✳
Sit-start in the low holes and snatch up small gastons and crimps without using the big holes in the middle of the wall. *Justin Critchlow*

Apocalypse Now *7a+*
A sit-start dyno from the low side pulls to the top. *Mark Sharratt*

16 Nadin's Traverse *7a* ✳
Start on big holds on the left arête, drop down to the big glued-up hold and traverse right on flatties and slopers to finish up *Pixie*. Unsurprisingly there are several variations: finishing up *Reg* is 7a+; continuing rightwards to finish up *The Staircase* is 7a+; continuing further, staying below the top and finishing along *Cooper's Traverse* is 7b. *Simon Nadin (NT)*

17 Jug Up *5*
The juggy arête from low.

18 Glued Up *6a* ✳
Start low on the glued jug and climb the wall. The *Glued Up Dyno* (from the glued jug to the top) is 7b.

19 Reg *6c+*
An eliminate dyno starts on the sloping finger rail at chest height and slaps for the top.

20 Pixie *5*
Climb the flake.

21 The Staircase *5* ✳
Climb the staircase-esque feature from a sit-start.

22 Cooper's Traverse *6a+*
Start just right of *The Staircase* and traverse the lip rightwards until it gets easy.

23 Long Boulder Mantel *6b+*
Sit-start under the bulge and snatch upwards to glory, or the top.

>>

24 Don's Crack 5 ✳
The crack. An eliminate just right (no crack, no arête) is 6b.

25 Don's Arête 3+
The arête.

26 Winger 5
Traverse right past the breaks to finish around the nose up the back arête.

27 Wing Wong 5
Climb the wall past breaks.

28 The Beak 6a+ ★
The undercut nose from a hanging start.

Broken Wing 7a ✳
Start as for *The Beak* and swing low under the roof to finish up *Wing Wong*.

29 Slippery Groove 5
The slippery and polished groove.

30 Arête on Left 5
Climb the arête on the left-hand side.

31 Easy Groove 3+ ✳
The easy groove.

32 Flakes and Chips 4+ ✳
A good problem. Polished chips gain the high flake. 6b from a sit-start, or without the chips.

33 Bancroft's 6b 7a+ ★
The centre of the face approached from the left. Stand in the first chip, reach tile edges in the centre of the shield and then the top. *One Inch Punch* is a project direct start that attempts to slap to the tile edges from a start undercutting the rib, with feet on smears.

34 Higginson's Arm 7b+ ✳
An eliminate traverse under the roof. Start on undercuts under *Left Groove* and traverse rightwards under the roof, along the lip of the boulder to finish up *The Nose*. *Justin Critchlow*

35 Left Groove 6b ★
A classic, climbing up the right-facing groove.

36 Right Groove 6a ✳
The next groove line right.

37 Vague Arête 5
The arête, if you can call it that.

38 The Nose 6b+
Start hanging on the low break.

39 Juggy Groove 5 ✳
Climb jugs up another groove.

Great Slab Area

The bottom of the big slab behind the boulders, below the classic route *The Sloth* (HVS), is covered in lozenge-shaped pods and has now been extensively bouldered on.

40   Big Traverse   *4+*
Start on the right where the pods stop and traverse left, then up, until you get bored, scared, or run out of rock.

41   Popper   *3+*
Link the pods up the left side of the slab

42   Flap Dancer   *7b*
An eliminate: climb the wall above a small hole, without using the large pod.

43   The Lintel   *5+*
Up past the ledge. Freaky.

44   Cheesy Moon   *4*
The wall directly above the large pod.

45   Goats Gruff   *4+*
More pockets up the wall.

The next problems are under the large roof.

46   Goat's Eye   *6b+*
Start on the low pocket, move right to crimps, then climb the wall above. 6a from standing.

47   The Monodoigt   *7b+*   ✶
Use a small left-handed crimp to reach a mono. Use this to climb the wall. Nails.

48   Flake Museum   *6a*
Pull right above the low overhang and climb the wall on flatties and flakes. Bad landing.

49   Scallop   *4+*
Flakes on the right side of the wall.

Crack and Corner Area

To the right of the *Great Slab* is another buttress full of classic routes on which boulderers have been scratting round at the bottom. The buttress is defined by the classic corner crack. The first problems are left of the corner.

50   Magic Crossing   *5*
From a good flake, climb via small holds leftwards to a deep pocket.

51   Toucan   *7a*
Climb direct through the dark splodge, starting at an incut edge. Hard.

52   Lichenthrope   *7a+*   ✳
Start low on a slot left of the small cave that forms the bottom of the corner crack. Rock out left and head for a jug on small, poor holds.

53   Crack Indirect   *5+*
Start in the cave under the corner crack, gain the rail and climb the wall just left of the crack. Finish in the big pod. A weird extension falls/spans leftwards from the pod into the jug at the top of the previous problem: 6c, depending on span.

54   Crack Start   *5*
From the back of the cave, climb the corner crack.

55   Babbacombe Start   *5*   ✳
Climb the wall right of the arête using the flakes to the break. Lovely.

Polish   *7a+*
Sit-start to *Babbacombe* on ripples.

56   Sheep Shit   *7a+*
Start right of the arête on a finger rail and climb leftwards to join *Babbacombe*.

57   Sheep Shit Crack   *6c*   ✳
Start on the finger rail and head rightwards for the hanging crack.

58   Oik   *6a*
From a hanging start under the roof climb up and rightwards to the break.

EDDIE STEPHENSON ON *DIRTNAP*   **PHOTO:** SIMON WILSON

Calcutta Buttress

Continuing right from the *Crack and Corner Area* is a steep buttress that is home to a range of problems that surmount its undercut base. The problems are fingery and powerful and well worth visiting.

59 Bombay Overhang *5* ✳
The blunt left-most arête.

60 Calcutta Crimp *6c* ✳
From a jug under the roof, gain positive crimps over the lip and rock over to the break.

61 Sleeping with the Flowers *6c+* ✳
A gem of a problem that takes the right arête on ripples from a sitting start under the roof. The big block on the right is out, but a kneebar helps. 5+ from standing. Harder for the short. *Andi Turner/Justin Critchlow*

62 Dirtnap *7b* ✳
An extension to *Sleeping with the Flowers*. Once at the lip, continue leftwards to gain the break on the left side of the buttress and move up to join *Bombay Overhang*. *Simon Wilson*

63 Mistral Start *6b*
Use either a long reach, or some small ripples, to reach better edges and then a flat hold on the left.

64 Limbless Limbo Dancer *7a* ✳
From a low start under the roof, reach out to good holds and then make a big lunge to an incut hold at the top of the rib – finish at the break. *Paul Higginson*

65 Dish Grab *6b+*
From a low start, head for the good dish up and right.

66 Calcutta Rib *5+* ✳
The crisp rib.

67 Calcutta Traverse *6a+*
Traverse the juggy shelf from right to left to finish at the crack. A low start begins in the pit and adds a few harder moves on crimps onto the start – *The Black Hole Start*, 7a.

The next buttress to the right of *Calcutta Buttress* is *Pepper Buttress*. Scout up the hill just after passing this buttress to find an obvious low overhanging boulder on the left. This is *Too Drunk*.

68 Too Drunk *7a* ✳
Climb the central line on the steep face from a sit-start on the flake. Powerful moves using the rib and some slopey pockets above. Very good. *Simon Panton*

69 Drunk Enough *6c+*
The steep right arête from a sit-start. *Simon Panton*

The Cellar and Attic Area

Above and left of *Calcutta Buttress* there is a confusing maze of boulders containing a few hidden gems among some more mediocre problems. These are worth seeking out if you have ticked the more mainstream circuits, or if you fancy a bit of esoterica. After a bit of wandering to orientate yourself, it should be easy enough to find the problems. The rock, especially on the back side of the boulders, is very soft and so many problems have been omitted to prevent further damage.

70 **Stretch Armstrong** *6c+*
Hard smearing up the right side of the slab. There are loads of other problems around here, but the rock quality is not great.

71 *5+*
Reach slopey crimps on the lip from under the roof and then top-out more easily.

72 **The Squirm** *4+*
The crack and gap above.

73 **The Finger** *5+* ✻
Move left to the 'finger' after climbing the arête.

74 **Handy Wall** *4+*
The easy wall.

75 **Mounty** *4*
The bulge above the crack.

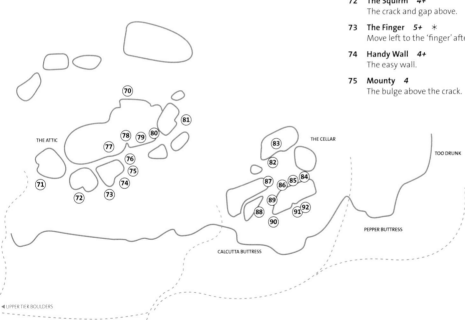

THE ATTIC

THE CELLAR

TOO DRUNK

PEPPER BUTTRESS

CALCUTTA BUTTRESS

◀ UPPER TIER BOULDERS

6 Chasm Arête   6a
Climb the arête on the left without using the sidewall on the boulder next to it.

7 Sexy Steve   6a+
A squeezed-in problem up crimps left of the crack.

8 Scrack   3+   ✳
The easy but nice crack.

9 Reachy Wall   6a
A long move is needed to get up the wall right of the crack.

0 Runnel Rouser   5
The wall to the right from the runnel.

1 Risky Runnel   5+
The runnel quickly gets scary and high. The arête to the left is 4.

2 Cellar Slab   4+
The rippled wall is climbable all over at about the same grade.

3 Easy Groove   Fun
The groove.

4 4
The left-hand line up the slab.

5 Tiny Groove   3
Climb the feature up the middle of the slab.

86 Right Slab   Fun
The easy right-hand slab.

87 Cellar Dwella   7a+
Slap to the top from sidepulls. *Justin Critchlow*

88 The Gates   7a   ✳
Climb the centre of the black slab.

89 Crinkly Wall   6a
Delicate climbing up the wall.

90 Ride My Pimp   6b
Thrutch onto the arête.

91 The Downpipe   6c   ★
The hanging pipe is a fantastic feature that begs to be climbed.

92 Pipe Entry   7a+
Not quite the hoped for sit-start to *The Downpipe*: sit-start right of the pipe, climb to the lip and reach left to the pipe to top-out. *Andi Turner*

JUSTIN CRITCHLOW ON *HIGGINSON'S ARM*   **PHOTO:** ADAM LONG

The Cube

An isolated monolith on the moorland behind the left-hand end of the *Upper Tier* is home to a beautiful highball – *The Cube* – and a host of other problems. Access is sensitive. Approach from the right, **not** from the *Skyline*. At the right side of the *Upper Tier* take the track running back from the crag past old poles and 100 metres after a small stream, a vague path runs left off this to *The Cube*. See map on p334.

1 Cube Traverse *6a+*
Traverse the three faces of *The Cube* in a round-robin style.

2 Flakes *5*
Climb flakes up the wall.

3 Cube Crack *3+*
Climb the crack.

4 Period Drama *6a*
Traverse right around the arête and up when the break finishes.

5 Jump *6c* ✳
Dynamic slapping up the arête. 7a+ from a sit-start.

6 The Cube *6b* ★
A brilliant highball, climbing the rippled face on small but always adequate holds. A hard start using a large pebble leads to easier climbing to the left side of the break. Move left and confidently pull up the upper wall. *Nick Dixon*

The Cube Direct *7b+* ✳
Climb direct up the face left of the start to *The Cube* to join that problem at the top.

The Pube *6a+*
An alternative finish to *The Cube* up the arête. The sit-start is 7b+.

7 Right Pube *6a+*
Climb the arête on the right.

8 Back Crack *5*
The crack on the far side of the block. 5+ from a sit-start.

9 Cave Exit *6c+*
An awful problem climbing out of the dirty, low cave.

10 K2 *3+* ✳
A great hand traverse with feet on the steep side.

11 4
Climb the slab from the shallow crack.

12 Summit Slab *5+* ✳
Climb direct up to the highest point of the slab.

13 Notch Slab *5*
The slab just right. The arête right is 3+.

Roaches Skyline

Effectively a northern continuation of the *Upper Tier*, the bouldering along the *Skyline* is similarly top class, and has a character all of its own, particularly at the *Far* and *Very Far Skyline*, where the rock is simply heavenly. Pick up the path from the left-hand end of the *Upper Tier* and keep going uphill. See map on p334.

Doxey's Pool

Doxey's Pool is the first area reached, to the right of the path by a small tarn. It is named after the daughter of the occupant of *Rock Hall*, who was tragically raped and drowned here. This small area is a fantastic bouldering spot with many good problems including an area classic: *The Staffordshire Flyer*. The rock is nicely featured with many sloping ripples, but it has a thin skin with soft rock underneath. Please be careful and keep brushing to an absolute minimum. Paddling in the pool itself is not to be recommended, as the bottom is full of rotting peat which is easily stirred.

1   **The Man with the Red Face**   *7a*
    Around the back of the left-hand block, climb up ripples to a delicate rock onto the slab.

2   **Left Cheek**   *6c*
    The left arête, behind the roof.

3   **Soggy Bottom Crack**   *6a*
    The crack above the puddle.

4   *6a+*
    Jump to the ledge by the crack and mantel.

5   **The Staffordshire Flyer**   *6b*   ★
    The awesome overhang is overcome using a thin rail in the roof and jugs on the lip. It's totally classic and not as hard as it looks. Unless you think it looks about 6b.

6   **The Arête**   *6c*   ✳
    A sit-start on undercuts bumps the grade to 7b.

7   **Another Nadin Traverse**   *7c*   ★
    Start as for *The Arête* (from sitting) and traverse the lip rightwards on poor slopers to gain the hanging flake on the next problem. Finish up this. Hard. *Simon Nadin*

8   **The Drowning Pool**   *7a+*   ★
    Start low on the jug, span left to a poor sloper and make a funky move to the hanging flake. Superb.

9   **Groovy Crack**   *4*
    Into the hanging crack.

10 **Chipped Wall**   *3+*
    Climb the chipped wall.

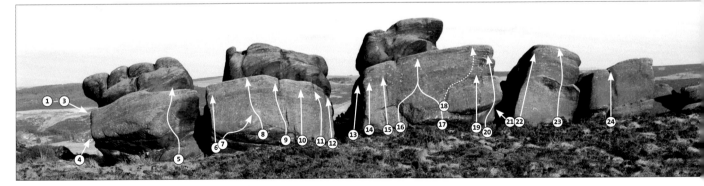

11 Flake *4+*
The flake line on the right. Starting up this problem and traversing left to *The Arête* is 5.

12 *4*
The crack and sidewall.

13 *6c*
The sloping sidewall past a pocket.

14 Arête on Left *6a+*
Climb the arête on the left. Climbed on the right it's 5+.

15 Blind Flake *5+*
An eliminate up the flake only – no arête.

16 *6c+* ✳
Start in the niche and climb up and right to gain a small pocket. Finish direct.

17 *6c* ✳
The same pocket is gained from a start further right, below the arch feature.

18 The Arch *6a+* ✳
Start as for 17, but follow the arch right.

19 Little Flake *6a+*
Direct into the flake at the end of *The Arch*. A low start on the undercuts brings the grade up to 6b+ ish.

20 Bulging Arête *6b+* ✳
Climb the arête from low undercuts.

21 *4*
The jamming crack.

22 Easy Arête *3+*
The arête.

23 Pancake *4* ★
Climb into, and out of, the big dish.

24 Li'l Crack *Fun*
The small crack to the right. The arête right is the same grade.

Far Skyline

Two separate clumps of boulders by the path, both containing some fine, isolated problems.

Chasm Boulders

Some 200m or so further on from *Doxey's Pool*, between the paths, just after the path splits. Some of the problems are in the channels between the boulders and require attention to prevent unintentional bridging onto the opposite walls.

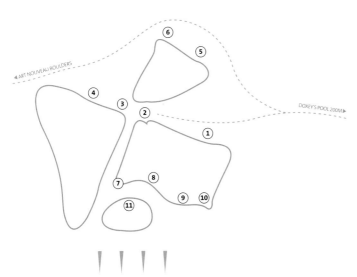

1 **Gritstone Pimple**   *6b*
A scary pull, using the pimple feature.

2 **Ramp**   *4+*
Ascend the ramp, escaping rightwards at the top.

3 **Mantel**   *4+*
A mantel.

4 **Harder Mantel**   *6a+*
Another mantel, this time harder.

5 *4*
Climb to the arête using a rounded feature.

6 **Triptych Groove**   *6c+*   ★
Climb the groove and arête from a sit-start. Good stuff. *Andi Turner/Justin Critchlow*

7 **Acne Arête**   *7a*   ✳
The hanging arête – trying hard not to bridge. A sit-start is a bit harder. *Andi Turner*

8 **Squeezer's Spots**   *6c*
The wall from sitting. *Andi Turner*

9 **Spotter's Pop**   *6b*
The wall from a sit-start on crimps.

10 **Puss in Boots**   *6c*
Another sit-start, with feet on the back.

11 **Spotter's Slop**   *7a*
Sloper to top.

Art Nouveau Boulders

Some way on from the last boulders are some more – next to the path, just before and above the route *Art Nouveau*.

12   Mono Slab   *4*   ✳
Easy slab.

13   Sidepull Wall   *7a*   ★
The wall right of the arête, via the obvious sidepulls. A good problem.

14   *3+*
The easy crack.

15   Flaky Romp   *4*
Up flakes.

16   Juggy Flakeline   *4+*
Either get some spotters or don't fall off.

17   Crack and Arête   *6a+*
As the name suggests.

18   Art Nouveau   *7b+ (E6 6c)*   ★
With innovative padding, this route might just feel like a highball. Might. To be honest, even if you don't plan on climbing it, you should go take a look if you're in the area, as it's about as breathtakingly beautiful as gritstone gets. A series of curving overlaps up a very steep slab. It's just over the edge, just on from the boulders above. *Simon Nadin*

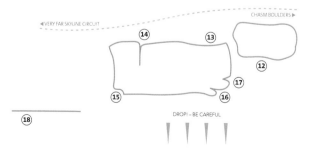

Very Far Skyline Boulders

Further still is the final bouldering hereabouts. A good little circuit of low grade problems on excellent rock. The boulders described are below the path, but there are more blocks above the path. The rock on these higher boulders is very soft, and climbing on them is very damaging, so you are requested not to.

1   **Rounded Arête**   *3*   ✳
    Delicate and good.

2   **Open Groove**   *5*   ✳
    Smear up the faint groove.

3   **Two Pocket Slab**   *5*
    Past the twin pockets.

4   **Lazy Trout**   *5+*
    Climb the highest section of the slab, to a pocket.

5   *5+*
    Climb direct to the upper arête.

6   **Max**   *6a*   ✳
    Tackle the steep arête. A sit-start from a low slot is 7a.

7   **Crack**   *3+*
    The crack.

8   **Harry Patch**   *5*
    Swing left from the crack over the bulge on pockets.

9   **Bernie**   *5+*
    The right side of the arête, 6c+ from sitting.

10 **Off Fingers Crack**   *5+*
    The thin crack.

11 **Pinkies to Perkies**   *4*   ★
    The ace splitter crack.

12 *3*
    Walk up the slab.

13 Inner Tube *6a+*
Sit-start with hands in the hole and then go for the top.

14 Wall and Rib *3*

15 Left Crack *3+*

16 Right Crack *3+*

17 Easy Ramp *3*

18 Flight Exam *5+* ★
Climb the slab, working the pocket for all it's worth.

19 The Loner *5+* ✳
Smear up and right from the pocket.

20 The Shepherd *6c* ★
Climb the thin seams up the rib.

21 Leek Hills *6b+* ✳
The right arête.

The Five Clouds

This small line of outcrops below the *Roaches Skyline* is composed of some of the best gritstone to be found anywhere. The elements have conspired to produce wonderful natural sculptures on a much finer-grained rock than that which is to be found just a few hundred metres away at the *Lower Tier*.

Access and Approach

Park on the road below the crag as you would for a visit to the main bulk of the *Roaches*. Walk through the gate towards the *Lower Tier*, but take a path immediately on the left that runs parallel with the road. The first outcrops become visible on the right after a few hundred metres. Do not take shortcuts up from the road. A footpath also drops down from the left-hand end of the *Upper Tier* to join the lower path.

Please note: there are occasional bird nesting restrictions, so respect these when in place.

cond Cloud

e don't count the first cloud, but the *Second Cloud* has a small selection of brilliant highballs.

Communist Crack   5   ★
The sickle crack that slices the buttress in two is an awesome highball if you are confident at this grade. Climbed as a layback flake it is positive and satisfying all the way.

Marxist Undertones   5+
Lunge from the hole in the centre of the wall to the ledge and top-out much more easily up the arête above. Variations: the undercuts on the right to the ledge – 6b; using the hole for your right hand to gain the ledge using a flake on the left – 6b.

Nadin's Secret Finger   7b+
Start to the left of the slab, slightly up the bank. Reach/span/jump rightwards to the finger edge in the middle of the wall, match and reach rightwards to a junction with *Finger of Fate*. *Simon Nadin*

Finger of Fate   6b   ★
An elegant highball arête, climbed on the left. The awkward sloping landing means that you get gripped much sooner than it looks like you ought to. *Simon Nadin*

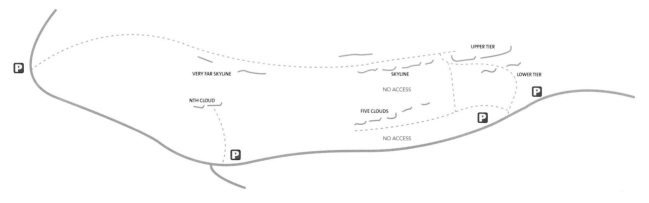

Third Cloud

The *Third Cloud* has some brilliant problems on the short wall to the left of the main face, and directly below it.

5   Persistence   *6b*   ★
The flakes at the left end of the wall make for a perfect problem. *Simon Nadin*

6   Who Needs Ready Brek?   *7c*   ★
The thin seam that winds its way across the blank face cries out to be climbed. Climb half-way up *Persistence*, paste your feet on smears, crimp down hard, and follow it rightwards to its end, some better holds, and a final pull to jugs. *Simon Nadin*

7   Icarus Upstart   *6b+*
A direct start to *Icarus Allsorts* (E4). Start with right hand in pocket on the right lip of the cave and jump for a good hold, use an undercut to gain a jug and mantel this. Step off right or continue up the highball slabby arête. *Adam Long*

8   The Pinnacle of Human Achievement   *6b*
Just right of the *Icarus* cave is a low narrow prow. Climb this from a sit-start.

ourth Cloud

e *Fourth Cloud* has a brilliant boulder beneath it that looks as though it was shaped
th a giant spoon.

Fourth Arête   *6a*
The left arête. Swinging right to the sloping shelf before the top is *Fourthright* – 6b.

Hard Arête   *7a+*   ★
The right arête is awkward to start.

Tetris   *7c*   ★
The sit-start to *Hard Arête* is a beautiful little beast. Technical and powerful moves
up the steep rib lead to a final fight with the slopey upper arête and flake.
Rupert Davies

Four Lions   *7b*   ★
Start up *Hard Arête* but swing left at the flake along the sloping shelf to finish by
the left arête. Start as for *Tetris* at 7c.

13   **Columns**   *7c+*   ★
Sit-start as for *Tetris* and make hard moves up and right to the lip, traverse right
and finish up *Thrust*. *Mike Adams*

14   **Trust**   *7a*   ★
Rock onto the hanging slab above the scooped-out lower wall. A brilliant problem.

15   **Thrust**   *7a*
Traverse the lip rightwards from the start of the last problem, to finish up the right arête.

16   **The Ugly Brother**   *7a+*
Below the main boulder is a low roof. Start on crimps under the lip and work upwards
to finish up and left on slopers. *Andy Banks*

17   **Milky Buttons**   *7b*   ★
On the main buttress above the boulder, is a lovely open scoop, with a shark's fin
block next to the landing. Make a thin rockover up the scoop. *Justin Critchlow*

JOHN COEFIELD ON *TETRIS*   PHOTO: ADAM LONG

Fifth Cloud

100m further on from the *Fourth Cloud*. The first block is a small slab, facing the *Fourth Cloud*.

18 Matchbox Arete   6a
Smear up the left side of the slab, using the arête, after a tricky start.

19 Matchbox Slab   5+   ✷
Smear up the right side of the slab.

On the left side of the cloud is a leaning square-cut pinnacle. The next problems are described clockwise starting on the front right arête.

20 Dreamer   5+
The arête, climbed on its right.

21 Ninestein   6a
The front face right of the front-left arête – escape left at about 4m or continue for an E2 tick.

22 The Darkest Cloud   8a   ★
The next arête left again, on the back of the block, gives an excellent hard problem.
Sit-start on double undercuts with a foot lock and head directly up the arête on crimps,
slopers and pinches. A good 7b from standing – *Ride The Lightning*. *Dan Varian*

23 The Imperfect Catch   7c+
The wall left of *The Darkest Cloud*. Start right hand on the sloping shelf, left hand
on an undercut. Catch an edge and continue upwards using the left arête and
right-hand pinches. *Dan Varian*

Nth Cloud

The *Nth Cloud* is somewhat separated from the other *Clouds* and it is best approached from the road via a track behind a gate. The first problems are on the short wall to the left of the two higher buttresses.

1   The Flakes   *6b*
Easy moves on positive flakes lead to an unhelpful rounded scoop above an awful landing.

2   Swivel Finger   *6b*   ✱
The arête, or massive flake, in the centre of the buttress is simply wonderful. A series of balancy barn-door moves are followed by a tricky top-out. A sit-start adds fun and maybe nudges the grade up to 6b+. *Simon Whalley/Nick Dixon*

3   Nth Power   *8a+*   ✱
The amazing wall immediately right of *Swivel Finger* is spoiled only by the large holds on the left and the proximity of the gulley. It was a long-standing project. Start on a small right hand undercut and a high left hand mono. Pull on and snatch into a high left hand gaston before your feet pop. Pull directly up the wall above. *Dan Varian*

Over towards the main crag is a tall, attractive wall, with a faint flake/crack in the upper half.

4   Crystal Voyager   *7b+*   ✱
The centre of the wall, direct to the flake/crack and poor pockets above. A fine highball. *Simon Nadin*

5   Spankosaurus Does Chicago   *6b*   ✱
The highball arête to the right is a great problem. *Nik Jennings*

Hen Cloud

Although primarily a top-notch trad climbing venue, there's just enough decent bouldering at *Hen Cloud* for it to warrant a couple of pages alongside *The Roaches*. Don't expect to come here and do tons, but if you're climbing in Staffs and fancy something different then there a handful of gems on offer, most notably *Touch*, an old school *Simon Nadin* E4, that's 7a in new money and certainly up there with the best problems of its grade in the Peak.

Access and Approach

Park in the obvious big lay-bys below the crag and approach from the farm track, and then take a choice of paths upwards.

The Aiguille

The small pinnacle at the northern toe of *Hen Cloud* is home to some fine highball problems. It's easy to spot: simply park below and wander up to it.

1   **Starlight Left   6b+   ✳**
    Climb the left-hand face using both arêtes to the break. Step right and climb the right arête to finish.

2   **Starlight and Storm   7a   ✳**
    The perfect highball arête is climbed on the right. Presumably named after the book by *Gaston Rebuffat*, who gave his name to the gaston hold – none feature on this problem. *John Allen/Martin Veale*

3   **Simon's Slab   7a+**
    The centre of the slab. *Simon Nadin*

Bachelor's Area

The first few metres of this wall offer a bunch of good problems before it gets proper big and you need a 'rope' and 'gear'. The landings are narrow, but paddable and spottable.

4   **Right Ramp   4+**
    The right-hand side of the big ramp/smile feature.

5   **Slight Crack   4+**
    The faint crack and wall just right.

6   **Left Vein   5+   ✳**
    The left-hand of the two fine vein features in the wall.

7   **Right Vein   6a   ✳**
    The taller line has a stiffer start followed by fine climbing to a tricky last move on the huge vein/tufa at the top.

8   **Stokesline   6b**
    The initially-vague crack line. The climbing eases after tricky start. *Mark Stokes*

The Poison takes the wall to the right using a big pebble but it's really more of a route (E3 6b).

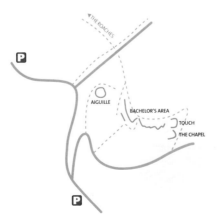

Touch

Over the back are the *Boxing Gloves*, home to *Touch* – a fine highball, one of the best in the Peak.

9   Touch   *7a*   ★
Climb the wall to a particularly vague break and use poor slopers to gain better holds above. *Simon Nadin*

If you fancy exploring there's some smaller blocks in *Hen Cloud's* 'Magic Wood' just below the *Touch* area. The pick of the bunch is:

The Chapel   *6c*
The east-facing, highball arête to the left of *Mick's Metaphor* (E1), about 25m below *Touch*. Start on the chipped arête then swing onto the rounded arête above and climb it on its right. *John McGuiness*

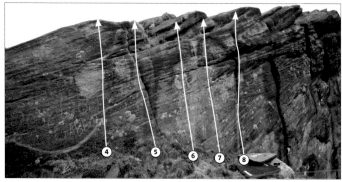

Gradbach Hill & Bosley Cloud

You know those days when you sit at *The Roaches* bathing in evening light, gazing west at the lump of a hill silhouetted in the sun to the west? Well that's *Bosley Cloud*, overlooking Congleton. We've included it as there's a couple of problems there, and we've also included the excellent *Yawning Stone* at *Gradbach Hill*, just over the back of *The Roaches*, near *Gib Torr*.

Gradbach Hill

Another of those crags you've never been to, included for the benefit of the Staffs connoisseur who's been, seen and done everything else. Worth a trip if you're in the area, as there's not a dud on the entire block. It's just over the back of the *Roaches Skyline*, easily accessible from *Newstones* & *Baldstones*, and *Gib Torr*.

Access and Approach
Most easily approached past the *Newstones* (p379) off the A53. Turn off the A53 near the Winking Man pub, signed *Gradbach* 2½. Follow the road past the *Newstones* on your right, and along a long straight. Pass minor roads on the right and the road takes a left-hand, then right-hand bend. Park on the right-hand bend at a dirt cut-in. Walk along the double track west over a stile, uphill. As the path crests a small rise and starts to descend, look out for and follow a thin, vague path right along the ridge. The *Yawning Stone* is one of the first pieces of rock reached, perched on top of the crag. See *Roaches* area map on p333.

No large groups please.

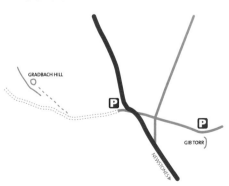

The Yawning Stone
A collection of high-ish problems, but with generally good landings.

1   **The Bitch**   *5*
    The short wall.

2   **Slim Groove**   *5*
    The groove on slopers above a slightly dodgy landing.

3   **Mishmash**   *4+*   ✻
    The arête on its left above a very dodgy landing is, thankfully, fairly steady.

4   **Woody**   *5+*
    Sit-start on a horizontal pinch in the cave and trend left to a tough mantel. Finish up the arête.

5   **The Yawn**   *4+*   ✻
    Pull over the centre of the roof and romp up the face on jugs. High.

6   **The Bishop**   *5*   ★
    Start as for the previous problem, but move right onto the arête. High. A sit-start on crimps is 6a.

7   **The Green Streak**   *7a*   ✻
    Rock into the green streak. Sit-start on crimps below at the same grade.

8   **Brown Wall**   *6b*   ✻
    Crimping up the wall to the right, from the large, oval pocket.

9   **Chunky**   *5+*
    Big holds up the right wall lead to a tough top-out.

OHN COEFIELD ON *BROWN WALL* **PHOTO:** ADAM LONG

Bosley Cloud

Although more rock here could be bouldered on, *Bosley* – the prominent bulwark visible to the west from *The Roaches* – is included for the once-mythical *Summit Arête*, a route-come-boulder problem given E5 7a in old guidebooks. These days it's a one move 6c+, with a companion problem to the left to justify the drive.

Access and Approach

As you're probably not a local, it's best to approach from the A523 Leek – Maccclesfield road. From the village of Rushton Spencer, turn onto Beat Lane and follow this for two miles to a junction. Turn right, signposted Cloudside, and follow this around the eastern side of the *Cloud* to a small parking lay-by on the right, opposite a path. Follow the path, rising diagonally right to *Summit Rocks* at the northern tip of the *Cloud*, just down from the summit.

Summit Arête *6c+* ✳
The main, north-facing arête feature. Lean in from the bank to poor holds, and slap to the jug above. Top-out direct. *Johnny Woodward*

Codfinger Workout *7b*
Gain the seam 1m left of Summit Arête and top-out direct. *Adam Long*

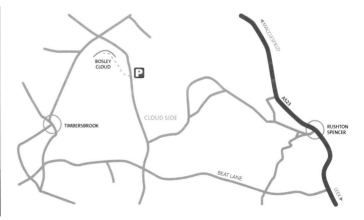

Ramshaw

One of the fiercest looking crags in the Peak District; a series of battleship prows moored against the prevailing wind. Varied climbing on character-building rock rewards the visitor, and the bouldering is significantly better than the crag's apparent lack of popularity would suggest. Much of the climbing can be described as 'real bouldering' — although the landings are generally grassy, there is no guarantee of a friendly camber. Ramshaw is not the home of the one-move wonder, several of the classic problems are high, but a few pads and spotters will make things feel that little bit more secure. A hard circuit here is a good test of all round climbing ability and will feature slabs, offwidths, steepness and even the odd E5.

The crag dries quickly and catches the early morning sun, but it also gets a good amount of shade. The varied aspect of the many scattered problems usually guarantees something will be in condition. Don't be put off by the greenness, it's often bone-dry, and easily assessable by a passenger from the road as you drive by.

Access and Approach

From Buxton, drive under the obvious spikey crag overlooking the A53, turn right just after the crag, and park in a lay-by just over the brow. Paths lead up opposite the lay-by and along the top of the crag.

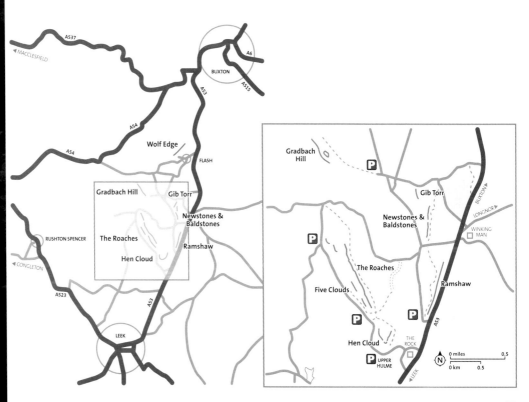

Undertaker Area

The first bouldering reached, at the left-hand end of the crag.

1 Melvyn Bragg 7b ✳
On top of the buttress is a tunnel with a wide roof crack. Butterfly, stack, leg jam and more to climb this from the back to an exit on the left wall. A specialist problem, don't expect it to feel like any other 7b you might have ever done. The rock low down where it scoops isn't in for feet. *Pete Whittaker/Tom Randall*

2 Pink Flake 5+
On the right-hand wall of the buttress. Climb the hollow flake to a scary top out.

3 Mantel 5
Mantel onto the ledge.

4 The Letter T 6a
The flake leads to a tricky top-out.

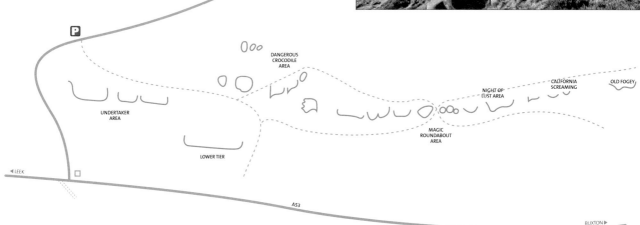

The Lower Tier

Situated at a lower level to, and in front of, the main edge, and – usefully – fairly rainproof.

Sensible Shoes   *4+*
Cross the roof at the very left-hand end.

Crab Walk Direct   *6a* ✷
The short hanging crack.

Roof Direct   *6c*
Climb the roof – requires a span.

Smoothment Traverse   *6b+*
Start at the low crack and traverse rightwards under the roof to finish up flakes where the roof ends.

Rock Climbing in Britain   *7a+*
Traverse the rising, sloping rampline from left to right, from a sit-start. Finish up the groove as for *Collywood*.

0   Roll Off   *5+*
Mantel/rock onto the ledge. A lowstart (*Tit Grip*) originally dynoed off some nipples, but then they broke off. It's unlikley to have been reclimbed in its current state. *Paul Higginson*

11   Collywood   *6c+* ✷
The counter line to *Rock Climbing in Britain*, traversing the sloping ramp leftwards from a sit-start to exit into the groove.

12   Tierdrop   *7a+* ★
Stunning. Climb up over the roof past crimps and a pinch, then lay one on for the good break from the runnel. The sit-start is 7b. *Nick Longland*

Sam's Left-Hand   *7b*
As for *Tierdrop* then reach left from the runnel to a slot then the top. *Sam Whittaker*

13   Tier's End   *5* ✷
Pull into the groove. The sit-start (as per *Tierdrop* sit-start) is a pretty good 6c+.

14   Last Drop   *5*
Climb up from the chipped rail.

15   Hemline   *7a*
A long traverse with some hard bits. Start on the far left and wander along following the line of least resistance, until the hard bit is reached passing, and finishing right of *Tierdrop*, up *Last Drop*.

To the left of, and at a slightly higher level than the lower tier, is an isolated block.

16 Midge *6a*
The double cracks on the left side of the face.

17 Cleg *4*
The easy groove on the right side of the face.

Dangerous Crocodile Area

Good quality bouldering, masquerading as a circuit. The problems lie to the right of the track. There are a few easy warm-ups scattered around the main challenges.

18 Easy Prow *3+* ✳
Flake.

19 Little Prow *6c*
From the shelf make a tricky move onto the arête and then gain the top. Easy when you know how.

20 The Scoop *4* ★
Mantel up through the superb scoop.

21 The Lurch *6b+* ✳
From the flake swing left then up, via a hidden dish.

22 Ossie's Bulge *6b+* ✳
Starting from the flake, climb straight up finishing left or, slightly harder, direct to a tricksome mantel.

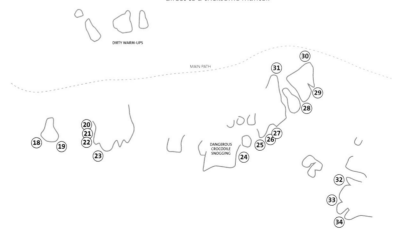

3 Ram Air 7b+ ✳
A classic of the crag. Climb up and left onto the rounded arête. Needs a few pads.
John Welford

4 Elastic Wall 6c ✳
Bounce up from the sidepull crimp to the top – hard for the short.

5 The Arête 6a
Climb the arête on either side, the right-hand side being harder.

6 5c Wall 6a ✳
Climb the crimps. It's harder if you static it and it's not 5c by any method.

7 Baby Groove 3
A pleasant groove.

8 Mansize 7c
This steep arête is a problem that should be a gritstone classic, but unfortunately its position in a damp hole, and some soft rock at the start, means that it's often dirty and ignored. A shame. Make a big move to the mansized pinch and use it as best you can. Be gentle if attempting to clean it. *John Welford*

29 Hanging Crack 5

30 Classic Mantel 5
Very short and very awkward.

31 Saian 6c ✳
At the opposite end of the block/corridor from *Mansize*, climb the rounded pillar from a broad pinch past a lovely sloper. *John McGuiness*

32 Johnny's Groove $E = mc^2$
Jump into a bridge position, top-out. Ungradeable.

33 Crocodile Slot 5
It's an offwidth, and a bit high as well – nuff said!

34 Right Slot 5
Another horror.

Magic Roundabout Boulders

The routes on the front of this buttress all have boulder problem starts for the confident. A very good bouldering area. The first problems are on the back, facing *The Roaches*.

35   Force Nine   *7a+*   ★
A superb slab problem. From the flake step left to escape or push on to the top for the full tick (E4). *Simon Nadin*

36   Be Calmed   *6b+*   ✳
From the arête swing right and mantel into the scoop. Mantelling direct is a reachy 6c+. *Richie Patterson*

37   Be Calmed Right-Hand   *6c+*
Gain the scoop from the right.

38   Magic Arête   *4*   ✳
A good problem.

39   The Finger   *3*   ✳
An isolated finger of rock between the last problem and the next problem.

40   Jamless   *5*
Much harder if you jam this perfect crack.

41   Arête on Left   *7a*
Quite high, the grade is for the gritty finale. Several mantelshelf problems exist to the left.

42   Epilogue   *7a*   ✳
Another hard and relatively high *Ramshaw* classic.

43   The Rammer   *5*   ★
The best easy problem on grit? Don't get stuck, and let someone know where you are going.

44   Monologue   *7b+*   ★
The hard arête. *Andi Turner*

45   The Pinches   *6a+*   ★
Superb arête on great holds. Tricky.

46   Practice Chimney   *Fun*
Not one of grit's best problems.

47   Dialogue   *7b+*   ✳
Hug the rock to glory. Stunning. *Andi Turner*

48   Cracked Arête   *5*
A warm-up, or a warm-down.

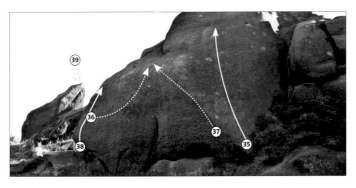

Night of Lust

Across the grassy gully, under a large pinnacle lies a steep compact wall. On the buttress to the left, *Wheel of Misfortune* (6a+) climbs a hanging prow without the sidewall.

49   Press Direct   6b
Twin seams to a bounce to the base of the groove, finishing in the crack. 7a from a sit-start.

50   Lust Left-Hand   7b   ✳
Climb the crimpy handrail rightwards to the niche. Finish up this at a jug.

51   Night of Lust Start   7a   ★
Start low on a flat jug and head up into the niche. See photo p370. Classic.

52   Runnel Entry   6c
From the same low start as *Night of Lust*, head up and right.

53   Foord's Folly Start   6a
Do battle with the crack to finish on the jug at half height. Jump off or keep going for the E1 tick.

The Far End

54   California Screaming   7b+   ★
The excellent big arête just under the next buttress. Hard climbing, getting high for its gripping finale. *Tom Briggs*

55   Shark's Fin   4   ★
Up and right of *California Screaming* is a steep overhang made famous by *Johnny Dawes* double dynoing his way up it at the start of *Stone Monkey*. The easy way up is to climb the flake, the double dyno is 6c.

Various other fun dynos can be had here from about 3–5.

56   Upstart   7c
The final buttress on the crag at the extreme right-hand end (about 60m on from *California Screaming*) has a perfect steep left arête. Climb this from a sit-start, while your spotters do battle with the pads on the awkward landing. *John Welford*

Down and right of *Upstart* is a boulder. *Ae Line* sit-starts on the steep side, joins the arête before finishing up the hanging slab into the heather – 7a. *Neil Pearsons*

Newstones & Baldstones

Newstones and *Baldstones* are really two parts of an intermittent line of outcrops spanning along a secluded ridge. Combined, they make a good day out. On its own, the *Newstones* has a great selection of easy problems and a couple of highball frighteners and its a particularly nice spot for an evening session. The eliminate potential is massive, so the problems listed are the most independent lines only.

The landings are flat and grassy at both venues and the rock is of good quality. All grit is prone to local peculiarities and *Newstones* has got a sprinkling of weird veins and protruding armour plate things that makes much of the climbing that bit different and interesting. However, under the hard skin, the rock around here is very soft, so please brush any problems with great care, or preferably not at all. Please avoid when damp.

Conditions

Both areas are exposed to adverse weather along the ridge. Both areas dry fast, but the *Fielder's Wall* area of the *Baldstones* can get a bit green if it's been wet or after an access restriction, especially on the top-outs. Nine times out of ten, however, it's fine. The rocks to the east of the *Baldstones* ridge are an important wildlife area so no climbing please. And remember; no wire brushing.

Access and Approach

Park in the lay-by opposite the house and take the small path that runs to the right of the house along to the crag. Keep going past *Newstones* to get to the *Baldstones*.

The house owner is very tolerant of climbers, so please behave and keep it so. There may be occasional access restrictions on this estate due to nesting birds – please respect any bans. Also please note that the land between the *Baldstones* and *Gib Torr* (p387) is a protected *SSSI*, so **please do not** walk directly between the two.

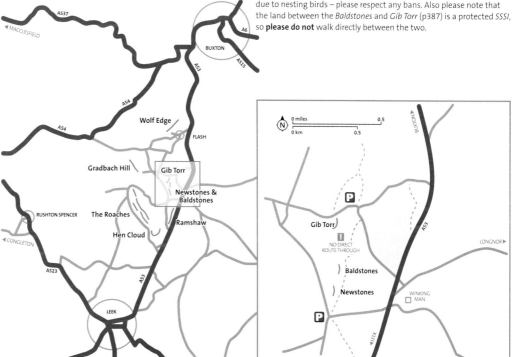

Newstones

Charlie's Overhang
Once past the house, this is the large overhang encountered on the first block.

1   **S&M**   *7a+*   ★
The flake/cracks up the left side of the wall lead to a distressing direct top-out. Finishing left is 6c+. The sit-start is 7b (direct finish).

2   **Leather Joy Boys**   *7b+*   ★
Start up *S&M* and slope or jam rightwards along the break. Really quite good. *Mark Stokes*

3   **Little Traverse**   *6a*
Starting at the same point as *S&M*, traverse right on rounded holds until they stop. Finish as you like.

4   **Charlie's Overhang**   *6b*   ★
The big roof on big holds is a classic highball. The crux is obviously where you don't want it. *Tony Barley*

5   **Moonshine**   *6a*
The steep wall right of the crack right of *Charlie's*.

6   **Praying Mantel Sit Start**   *6b*
Sit-start the low prow.

7   **Wraparound Arete**   *6c*
The steep undercut arête, from big holds on the left. A variant hard slap off poor crimps on the right to the arête is 7a+.

Upper Block
A low, rounded barrel of rock above and right of *Charlie's Overhang* contains a concentration of fun sit-starts. The problems all take independent lines but are quite tightly packed.

8   *6a*
Sit-start the steep left face.

9   *5+*
Sit-start the arête on the left side.

10   *6a+*
Sit-start and climb the wall just right of the arête using edges and a mono.

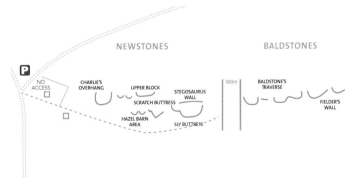

1 Varicose *6a+* ✳
Sit-start the vein feature.

2 The Grinding Sloper *6a* ✳
Sit-start the wall on slopers right of *Varicose*.

3 Easy Slab *4*
The slab left of the crack

4 *Fun*
The crack.

5 *Fun* ✳
Slab right of the crack.

6 *5+*
The right arête.

7 Uppermost Traverse *6b+*
Start right of problem 12, drop down onto the sloping shelf and then traverse left to finish up problem 8. Alternatively finish up any of the other problems – grades from 6b – 6c.

Hazel Barn Area

The outcrops below the *Upper Block* have yet more good easy stuff and one Staffordshire classic.

18 Left Twin Arête *3* ✳
Arête of the left-most (looking up) of the three blocks beneath the *Upper Block*, climbed on the left-hand side.

19 Right Twin Arête *4* ✳
The arête on the next block to the right.

20 Flake Slab *5*
The slab just right gives delicate padding. A sit start is a nice 6b.

21 The Ripple *6b+* ★
The aesthetic ripple/vein feature gives a superb problem.

22 Martin's Traverse *5*
The right-trending lower break. If you climb until halfway before breaking out up the wall above it is 6b. *Martin Boysen*

23 Crack and Arête *6a+* ✳
The overhanging arête climbed direct through the steepness, then on the right.

>>

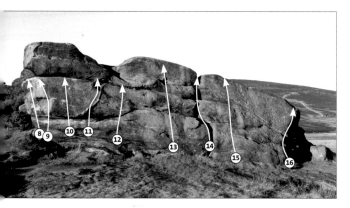

There are two routes on the face to the immediate left of the next problem. These are *Hazel Barrow Crack* (HS) and *Hazel Barn* (S). Although these are routes, they are also good highballs at 4+.

24   Hazel Groove   6b   ★
The groove line, climbed on slopers, is excellent. High at the top, but easier.

25   Nutmeg   4+
The armour plate jugs. Highball to finish direct, or scuttle rightwards.

26   Nutmeg Groove   5+   ✳
The slight groove right of *Nutmeg*. Very good.

27   Hammy   6a   ✳
From a low start on the shelf pull up to the hanging arête.

28   Mister Coconut   6a+
The sloping, undercut ledge right of *Hammy*.

Scratch Buttress

Right of *Hazel Barn* and just left of *Sly Buttress* is this scarred collection of problems. Preventing further damage may involve not climbing them.

29   5+
The eliminate left wall.

30   Scratch Crack   5
The crack and chunky flakes. The sit-start from an undercut is 6a+.

31   Scratch Arête   6c
Climb the steep arête trending left from a sit start. A bit squeezed in.

32   Itchy Groove   6b+   ✳
The groove is tricky but brilliant. See photo on p378.

33   Itchy Fingers   6a
The thin slab on the right, approached from slightly right. It merges with the previous problem a bit.

34   Bridget   4+
The slab set back on the right.

35   Puffed Up   7b   ✳
A highball problem up the steep face to the right. Climb the wall using a jam in the flared undercut at half height. Originally climbed (and best?) as a route (E3 6b). *Martin Boysen*

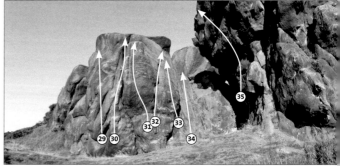

ly Buttress

6 Stallone Arête *6c+* ★
A classic steep trip on big fat slopers up the left arête.

7 Sly Stallone *6b* ★
Dyno from the finger holds in the middle of the shelf to the top. 7a if you eliminate the ramp. An extension starts up this and traverses left to finish up the arête – *Char's Traverse*, 7b.

8 The Sly Mantelshelf *5+* ✳
Traverse the vein from the left and mantel it at its highest point. Finish up the slab above. Highball.

9 Sly Super Direct *6a*
Gain the centre of the daddy vein using the mini vein that has sprouted beneath. Finish as for *The Sly Mantelshelf*. *Sly Direct* (5+) gains the same finish from the vein on the right-hand side of the wall.

0 Captain Quark *6c+* ✳
Just right of *Sly Super Direct*, use two small ripples to reach a vague pocket and thus the vein. *Rob Mirfin*

Stegosaurus Wall

Around the back is a short wall that has eroded to produce large flat plates. The bouldering is short but thuggy on holds that are so good they hurt.

41 *3+*
Sit-start the left-most tiny crack.

42 *4*
Sit-start the next crack right.

43 Tyrannosaurus Hex *5* ✳
The central line, pulling up the sides of the big plate. Sit-start.

44 Prehistoric Offwidth *3+* ✳
Sit-start the big crack.

45 Soup Dragon *4+*
Traverse the top of the block from right to left.

The Clanger *5+*
The mid-height traverse from right to left.

46 Yo Clam *4+*
15 metres or so right is a lone boulder. Start on the left arête and traverse right to gain the horizontal vein. At its end, mantel onto it and either walk back leftwards to the beginning or don't bother.

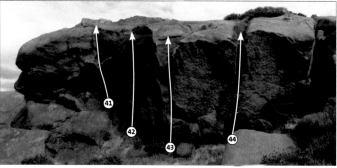

Baldstones

Continue along the ridge from *Newstones* and you will reach the *Baldstones*. Do the classic *Elephant's Ear*, get pumped on the traverse, puzzle about how to climb *Fielder's Wall* with its single hold and try the classic arête *Clever Skin* until your fingers bleed. More good rock, more good landings, more good problems.

1 **Baldy** *6a+*
Crimp up the wall from a low start, with feet on the ramp.

2 **Baldstones Dyno** *6b+* ✳
Dyno from jugs on the rail to the holds above.

3 **Throwball** *7a+*
Start low on good edges, slap for the flat holds above and finish at the ledge.

4 **Baldstones Traverse** *7a+* ★
A right to left traverse along the rail from the corner. Dip lower at the end, then finish up *Baldy*. Variations:

   a) Easy Exit *6a+*
   Finish up the flake halfway along.

   b) Muzzle *7b*
   Finish up *Throwball*.

   c) Baldstones Traverse Low *7b+*
   Stay low just after the start, traversing a line of small edges.

5 **Crank Cuffin** *7c*
Start low on the obvious hold and climb to the ledge using a gaston.
May be sandy. *Andi Turner*

Fielder's Wall

6   Indirect Arete   *7a+*
The undercut block left of *Fielder's Wall* and right of *Ray's Roof* (E7) has a little arête climbed the left-hand side. A bit artificial, but the project lip traverse into it looks quite good.

7   Indirect Arete Right   *6a*
Climb the arête on the right.

8   Ganderhole Crack   *4+*
The crack.

9   Fielder's Indirect   *5*
Climb rightwards around the rib and finish up the slab.

10   Fielder's Corner   *6a+*   ★
Classic cunningness up the groove. Or just yard on the mono.

11   Fielder's Wall   *7b*   ★
Use the large pocket to climb the wall. The top out can be a bit gritty.

12   Elephant's Ear   *4+*   ★
The super-chunky flake. If you prefer to start from sitting it's 6c.

13   Elephant's Eye   *6b+*   ★
From the (super) flake reach left into the (nice) pockets and up.

14   Clever Skin   *7a+*   ★
The classic arête on its right is not very dermatologically friendly. Snapped pebbles have made the starting pebble cluster much worse, much more painful and the problem is now harder than it was. *Martin Boysen (but named by Johnny Dawes)*

15   Clever Skin Left-Hand   *7b+*
The same arête on its left. No ear at the top. *Dave Kettle*

The Bun

The 'bun' shaped bit of rock on the right.

16   The Wart   *7a+*
Start low on a vague pocket, and mantel onto the left side of *The Bun*. 6b from standing.

There is more bouldering on some roofs further right. They stay dry in the rain, but this is their best feature. Problems from 4 – 6b can be contrived.

Remember: no access across to *Gib Torr* from here!

RUPERT DAVIES ON STALL PHOTO: DAVIES COLLECTION

Gib Torr

A gem of a crag which, despite its small size, is home to a high proportion of great problems. Many of these problems climb strong independent lines on fantastic features and grades range from 4+ to 7c+.

Conditions

The crag is shady for most of the day, so it's a good bet when the sun is out. Although the crag is often green the problems tend to stay clean. It can be a bit midgy on still late season days.

Access and Approach

Turn right off the A53 from Buxton onto a small road just before the Winking Man pub – if you pass it, you've gone too far. Follow the road around a few bends and park next to a gate on the left, where the crag is visible and signed. The walk-in will take you all of 30 seconds.

Note: there is no direct access to the *Baldstones* from *Gib Torr*.

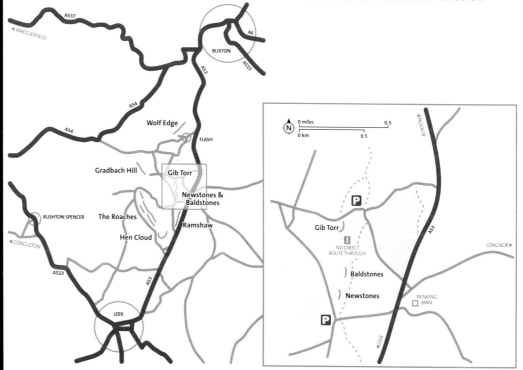

The Lower Tier

Up and right from the main bulk of the lower tier is a small green wall with two rarely climbed problems.

1   Gary's 5c   5+
Climb the arête.

2   Seams Green   6a+
Climb up small holds on the wall to the right.

The good stuff starts next to the fine arête of *Stall*.

3   Little Traverse   5
Traverse the lip of the little cave from left to right from sitting.

4   Little Mantel   6b
Mantel through the middle of the traverse.

5   Stall   7a   ★
The perfect sharp arête is climbed on the left-hand side. A technical classic. *Martin Boysen*

6   Stall Sit-Start   7c   ✳
The sit-start adds a series of dynamic and powerful slaps onto the original problem. Start matched on the finger jug left of the arête. The foot ramp is not to be used.

7   Martin's Problem   6b+
From a low start on a large hold, climb the wall above on pleasant ripples. *Martin Boyse*

8   Porridge Wall   5+
From a low start on a finger jug head for a pocket above.

9   Gibby Haines   6b+
Lunge from an uncomfortable pocket and a sloper to the big rail and top-out directly abov

10   Stayin' Alive   7b
A fierce sit-start to *Gibby Haines* using a selection of sharp edges and painful pockets. Start on the large sidepull pocket under the overhang. *John Welford*

11   Maurice Gibb   7c+   ✳
One of the biggest pure dynos in the Peak. From the rail on *Gibby Haines* launch up and left to land a jug just below the top. *Pat Rainbird*

12   Gibbering Right   6c+   ✳
In a small scoop on the left side of the large overhanging prow is an ergonomic finger hol Hang this and slap up and right to finish. An extension continues right along the lip at 7a

13   Gibbering Left   6b+   ✳
A left-hand variation starting from the same finger hold.

The Fin

14 5c Wall *5+*
The high sidewall, to the right of *The Fink*, is lovely, but the landing isn't.

15 The Fink *7a+* ✳
Climb the featured wall right of *The Fin* on big rounded slopers to a gritty top-out. The sit-start is a tough 7b.

16 The Fin *6c* ★
The undercut arête has a tricky move to gain the rounded, gritty top.

17 The Fin Sit-Start *7a+* ★
The sit-start to *The Fin* is superb. Start on a pair of low pockets and hug your way up the steep prow.

18 Left Fin *5*
Climb the big holds in the sidewall left of the *Fin*. Often choked with plants.

The Upper Tier

19 Gibbering Wreck *7b* ★
The massive roof on top of the tor is a highball classic. It was first soloed at E6, but it is now relatively safe with pads and spotters, as long as you miss the sign below if you fall off. *Andy Brown*

20 Gibb Torrture *5+*
Climb the left side of the large roof via a break and the short hanging crack. *Extended Torrture* starts as above then traverses the break to exit up the next crack to the right, 6b+.

Wolf Edge

A small, broken-up bouldering edge that is also the highest edge in Staffordshire. A little dirty at the time of writing, it does see occasional traffic and is worth a visit on a quiet day or evening. Home to a few great problems, including *Quantum Leap* and *This is My Church*.

Access and Approach

Turn off the A53 Buxton–Leek road to the small village of Flash. Fork right after 300m and park considerately in the village. Walk up the dirt lane past the last house, cross a stile and crest a hill at which point the edge is visible ahead. Stay on the left-hand track when the lane forks.

Note: parking is very limited, so if there's nowhere to park, please try another crag.

Wolf Edge is *Open Access*, however the field below *The Warren* is not. Bizarre. So, if you should be asked to leave, please do so, and let the BMC know when you get home.

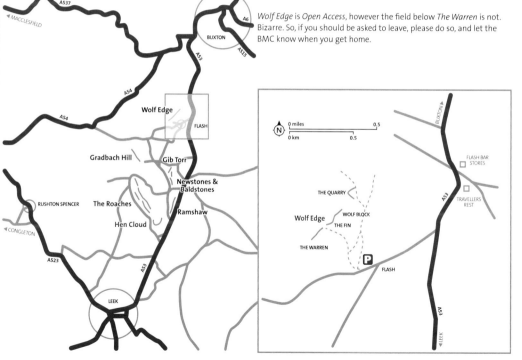

The Warren

This is the collection of rocks to the left of the track. Follow the track to the top of the hill and pass through a gate on the left. Walk along the top of the edge and drop down after 30m at the first proper rocks. The first problems are to the left of the wall and fence that bisect the crag.

1   **3+**
    The arête.

2   **5**
    The dirty sidewall.

3   **4**
    The crack.

4   **Lair   6a+**   ✳
    The face between the cracks, above the big hole.

5   **Fine Slab   4+**   ✳
    The central slab.

6   **Fine Slab Arête   3+**
    The right arête of the slab.

7   **Rock Fusion   6b**   ✳
    The rib on its right is a classy problem.

Right of the wall and fence is:

8   **Claustrophobic Arête   6a**
    The tower feels high and gritty, although it is a little escapable.

9   **Horseshoe Arête   5**   ✳
    Sit-start the sharp arête at the break with the jammed-in horseshoe.

10 **Swiss Cheesed   6a+**
    The highball arête above the walled-in area on slightly dodgy rock. Be careful.

11 **Quantum Leap   7b**   ✳
    The right arête of the big buttress, taken on its left-hand side. Classic. *Dave Kettle*

12 **Project Quantum   7a+**   ✳
    The arête on its right. The sit-start is just 7b. *Dave Kettle/John McGuiness*

Down below is a triangular boulder with:

13 **6a+**
    Seams up the face.

14 **5+**
    A left to right rising traverse from a sit-start.

15 **6a**
    Sit-start the right arête on its left.

e Fin

is the rock to the right of the track. The first problems are on the big jutting fin.

This is My Church *6c+* ★
The left sidewall of the fin, using pockets to gain a sloping pinch and sidepull, before making a move to a slopey bowl to finish. The classic of the crag. See photo on p390.

The Fin *4+* ★
The big fin, on its left. Highball.

Ear Flake *4* ✳
The ear-shaped flaked on the right wall. Highball.

6a
Sit-start the short arête. 4 from standing.

5+
The left arête.

Crumble *6b*
The centre of the block.

4+
The right arête.

Wolf Prow *5* ✳
Sit-start the fine prow.

24 **4**
Mantel the ledge.

25 **The Underground** *6b+* ✳
The tricky right arête. Also known as *Gollum*.

26 *6a* ✳
The arête just right, on its right. *The face* just right is 4+.

Wolf Block

27 **Wolf Bite** *6b* ✳
Hang the sloper on the blunt left arête and climb direct.

28 *5+*
Start the blunt right arête on the left and trend right to finish.

29 *4+*
The thin face just right of the previous problem.

30 **The Ramp** *3+* ✳
The classy ramp line. A tight line can be squeezed in to the right – 5.

The Quarry

About 200m further along is a small quarry. Approach along the edge-top path.
It's not great, but the hanging crack is worth doing at 4, as is the wall to the right at 4+.

New Mills Torrs

Hidden below the streets and viaducts of this northern mill town is a series of sheltered quarried walls by the *River Goyt*. It's a great spot for locals, or if you've been rained out of the rest of the Peak as some of the rock stays dry, sheltered by the viaducts. Many of the up problems are the starts to routes, so use your common sense as to the finish of the problem. While it may not be a classic bouldering area, the rock is good quality and it is close to the shops.

Conditions

Tucked away beneath street level, the rock is protected from the wind. Some of the rock is also sheltered from the rain below the viaduct arches. As such climbing is possible in some pretty foul weather. On the other hand the holds can get sweaty in warmer conditions and as the rain fails to touch some holds, they can get greasy. The rock itself is a fine-grained grit that can be sandy in places.

Access and Approach

The crags at the *Torrs* are situated directly under Union Road in the centre of New Mills, and access to the *Torrs* themselves is signposted around the town. Limited parking is available behind the bus terminal from where a path leads downwards to the *Torrs* – the crags are on the left. Alternatively, there is parking by the side of Hyde Bank Road and an alternative descent is posted below. From here the crags are directly opposite the bottom of the descent path.

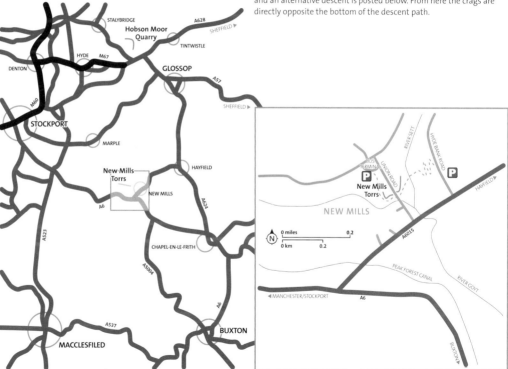

Alcove Area

The recessed wall on the left side of the crag has an easy traverse and some nice highballs.

1 Alcove Traverse 5+
Traverse the back wall onto the sidewall.

2 Porky's Wall Left-Hand 6a
Climb the highball wall left of the crack, right of the corner, to the ledge.
The easiest descent is around the back of the block.

3 Porky's Wall Right-Hand 5+
The slightly easier wall to the right, keeping left of the crack.

4 Piggy's Crack 4
The pleasant crack (VS 4c).

5 The Steeple 5
The right arête (HVS 5a).

Grim Reaper Wall

This is the wall to the left of the remains of a small stone wall.

6 Grim Reaper Traverse 6a+ ✳
A pleasant traverse on nice finger-holds. Start on the low shelf on the left and follow the rising line of holds to finish on jugs next to the small arête. Same grade in reverse.

7 Grim Reaper Direct 7b
Sit-start and climb directly into *Grim Reaper*, with a dyno or a balancy pop.
The last hold can be mucky.

8 Sandy Arête 6a+
Climb the wall right of *Grim Reaper* (left of the brick wall), using the sandy left arete. Climbing the wall without use of the left arête is a (poor) project.

Viaduct Wall

The sheltered wall under the viaduct.

9 Viaduct Crack 4+
The thin cracks and flakes to better holds. Retreat.

Viaduct Eliminate *6a+*
Reach a thin right-hand pinch right of *Viaduct Crack* and pull though to the good hold on *Viaduct Wall*. The high finish to the ledge bumps the grade to 6c+.

Viaduct Wall *6a*
Various methods can be used to gain flat holds, the diagonal rail then the small ledge. Reverse then jump off to escape. High. See photo on p394.

Honcho Left *6c*
Rock up into a left hand sidepull and use crimps to move rightwards into *Honcho*.

Honcho *6b* ✳
Starting on a positive flake left of the cracks, use a sidepull and various flatties to gain the flat jug. Jump off.

Honcho Right-Hand *6b*
Right-hand variant on *Honcho* starting just left of the arête and using a positive crimp to join *Honcho*.

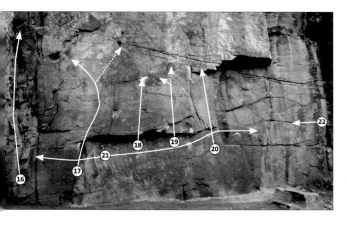

15   **Viaduct Wall Traverse** *5*
Traverse the wall in either direction

16   **Deception** *3*
Climb the cracks right of *Honcho*. Reverse or jump when you get scared.

Bionics Wall
The thin wall right of *Viaduct Wall* with a low overlap/roof.

17   **Bionics Low Left** *6c+*
Start matched on the low flake, reach the left side of the triangular hold on *Bionics Direct* and use this to reach a gritty hold up and left. Finish on holds to the left. A right-hand finish making a big move for the high ramp is 7a/+.

18   **Bionics Direct** *6a+* ✳
Probably the best problem here. Use opposing sidepulls to pop to the juggy ramp. A low start under the small roof bumps the grade to 6b and a full sitting start on low crimps gives an unpleasant 6c.

Bionic Man *7c*
An eliminate slapping to the juggy ramp from the thin left hand slot and right hand pock-mark between the sidepulls on *Bionics Direct*.

19   **Bionics Right** *6b+*
Start on a left hand undercut and right hand sidepull. Undercut to the diagonal sloper and pop leftwards to the juggy ramp. A good eliminate pulls straight though to the highest, right-hand bit of the ramp off the diagonal sloper – 7a.

20   **Hallelujah Start** *4*
Climb small flakes for 2 metres.

21   **Bionics Traverse** *7a+*
Start on jugs on the right-hand side and traverse left at a low level. Same grade when climbed in the other direction.

22   **The Full Traverse** *7a* ✳
Start at the extreme right-hand side of the crag and traverse to the extreme left-hand side via the easiest sequence, passing shrubs, stone walls and the locals.

The viaduct pillar itself can be traversed on 'natural' holds in the stonework for a pumpy workout.

Hobson Moor Quarry

A popular venue with the local Manchester and Glossop climbers. The crag features a big traverse and scores of eliminates on vertical quarried gritstone. The difficulty spans a range from very easy to very hard. The independent problems and the more popular eliminate problems are described, but for the more obscure variations grab a local.

A huge thanks to local James Hilliard for putting most of this together for us, and to Paul Worsdale for checking it.

Access and Approach

The crag is situated off the A6018 Glossop to Stalybridge road, just outside Mottram. Travelling from Glossop, turn right off the A6018 just after an obvious high-walled cutting onto Hobson Moor Road. The road doubles back to the right. Take the left fork and the quarry is obviously visible on the left side of the road after a hundred or so yards. Park in the lay-bys by the road.

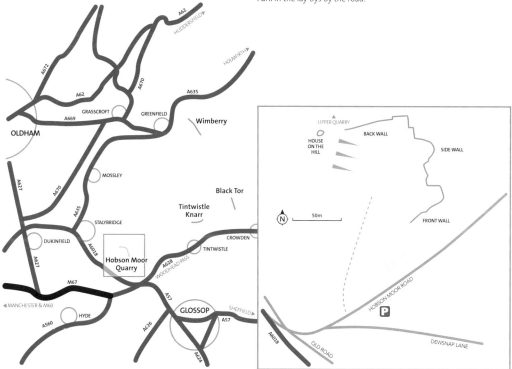

Front Wall

1　Green Slab　5
Surprisingly climbable despite its colour. Start just left of the middle using crimps directly to the top.

Side Wall

2　High Arete　5+
Above the easy slab is a good looking arête with a big drop down one side. Climb it on its left-hand side above the big ledge.

3　4
Lots of different ways to climb the easy wall just left of the arete.

4　4
Positive holds up the slab.

5　3
Easy climbing up the groove.

6　6a　✳
Climb the arete on its left-hand side using everything. Also done as an eliminate missing out all the chips and large holds (smears for feet and hands only on the arete) – 6c.

7　Triangle　6b
The rib above the triangular hole. Without the crimp up and right by jumping it's 7a.

8　6a+
Start on crimps just left of the triangular hole and climb direct using a thin slot.

9　5+
Climb the centre of the small wall on small holds. The lowest start is 6b.

10　4
From the break slap straight to the top.

11　Percy 97　6a+
Start on adequate crimps and climb the wall past the thin break and the graffiti. Some harder variations and eliminates are as follows:

a) Dyno from the start to the top, the big foothold to the left is out – 6c+.

b) Start with your left hand on the right-hand of the two good crimps and your right hand on a tiny crimp just to the right and pull on. Now move left hand to the small pocket in the break directly above and pull straight through for the top. The low break for feet is in, the seams to the sides are out – 7c. *Lee Anderson*

Dragon's Slab *5*
Mantel onto the middle of the slab beneath *Dragon's Wall*.

Pillar Arête *5*
From the large pocket do a big move out right and then finish up the arete

Pillar Face *7a*
Big moves between the big pockets. No bridging into the corner or arêtes. Hard.

Steve Phone Home Start *6b*
The wall between *Crew's Route* and *Peak Arête*, not using the arete or the crack. Start with good crimps in the break and somehow get stood up on the starting handholds.

Basic Training Start *7b+*
A desperate leg-press in the middle of the wall off undercuts to a thumb sprag, to get stood up on the slopey break. The thin crack on the right is definitely out!

ack Wall

Back Wall Traverse *6b+* ★
A popular and pumpy training traverse. Usually done from right to left finishing on the ledge.

18 **The Full Traverse** *6c*
Traverse the whole quarry whichever way you like, normally started from below problem 2 and finishing along the *Back Wall Traverse*.

19 *6b*
Sit-start on the low break, reach a small, positive sidepull pinch with your right hand, one of the selection of holds for your left and pull through to jugs. See photo on p398.

20 **House on the Hill** *7b*
Situated on the front face of the lone boulder on the hillside on the left of the quarry. Start on the lowest possible holds, snatch upwards to some more small crimps and flick to the top. The large foothold on the right is in.

21 **House on the Hill Left-Hand** *7a*
Start low just left of the middle on two crimps, make a big move out left to the arête, then a big slap to the top.

22 **Lintelatomy** *6b*
In the upper quarry, the first roof holds this little gem. Gain a hidden undercut at the back of the roof and reach out blindly to a poor pocket. This leads to better holds and a mantelshelf. Often green.

Tintwistle Knarr

The *Tintwistle Knarr* boulders did get a brief write-up in the BMC's 1990 Kinder guidebook, although it was not until 2010 that Mike Adams documented the area properly, adding most of the harder problems in the process. Due to the nature of both the approach and the landings under some of the problems the circuit could best be described as 'esoteric'. There are basically no paths, so moving between the blocks is frustrating, but there are some good problems, which warrant a visit for the dedicated explorer. The information we've included here is based on Mike's topo and we thank him for that. Other variations and link-ups have been climbed; the main problems are described.

Access and Approach

Tintwistle Knarr is located along the A628 Woodhead Road, which runs between the urban sprawl east of Manchester, and Barnsley. If heading east on the A628 Woodhead Road, look for a small parking bay on the left about 1 mile out of the village of Tintwistle, just as the road heads into trees, and opposite a reservoir access road on the right-hand side of the road. Park here – space for about 3–4 cars. Pass through the gate and zigzag up the wide track, ignoring the first two tracks into the woods. Enter the woods through the top gate over a stile and follow this steep track all the way to the main crag/quarry – don't enter the woods too early as the other tracks don't veer uphill to the climbing. The boulders are visible directly below the main crag/quarry and the approach involves a very awkward scramble down the steep, blocky scree. **Please take care!** Approach time about 30 minutes.

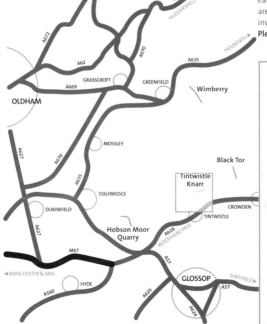

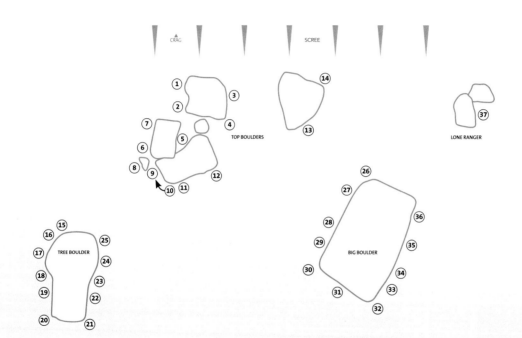

CRAG

SCREE

① ③ ② ④ TOP BOULDERS

⑦ ⑤ ⑥ ⑧ ⑨ ⑩ ⑪ ⑫

⑭ ⑬

③⑦ LONE RANGER

⑮ ⑯ ⑰ ⑱ ⑲ ⑳ ㉑ ㉒ ㉓ ㉔ ㉕ TREE BOULDER

㉖ ㉗ ㉘ ㉙ ㉚ ㉛ ㉜ ㉝ ㉞ ㉟ ㊱ ㊱ BIG BOULDER

op Boulders

e first boulders are at the foot of the scree, above the trees.

Nikita *6b+* ✳
Sit-start on an undercut and gaston and climb left past slopers to the arête.
A variant heads to the right arête, avoiding the left arête. See photo on p402.

Leon *7b*
Just right, sit-start with LH crimp and RH arête and climb the face. *Mike Adams*

La Femme Slab *5+*
The slab on the back of the block.

La Femme Fatale *7b+*
Sit-start the steep arête on its left side, with a tough mantel finish. No landing, literally.
Mike Adams

Soul Deep *6b+* ✳
The rippled wall in the pit. Variants moving to left and right arêtes are the same grade.
Sit-starts are 7b.

5
The right arête of the streaky face.

7 **5+**
The streaky face. A similar line just left is the same grade.

8 **Small Arête** *6c*
Sit-start the arête of the finger of rock.

9 **Underpass** *6c*
From the block under the roof, undercut out and pull over on decent holds.

10 **Mr Brightside** *7a*
Sit-start right of the arête and traverse low to finish around the arête.

11 **Layaway Wall** *6b*
Sit-start as before and climb the wall on layaways. The wall to the right is 4.

12 **Fire Fly** *6c+*
Sit-start on the sloping crimp and climb the wall left of the arête.

13 **Left Slab** *6a*
The left side of the tall slab, meeting the arête near the top. The right side of the slab is 5+.

14 **Back Side Arête** *6c+* ✳
Sit-start the curvy arête on its right. The slab just right is 6a.

Tree Boulder

A good quarried boulder hidden just down in the woods.

15 Overhanging Arête *6c*
Sit-start at the left side of the roof and climb right to finish up the arête.

16 Straight No Chaser *7c*
From LH pinch and RH pocket slap out to and up the arête. *Mike Adams*

17 Dream Chaser *7a+* ✳
Sit-start at the right side of the roof and climb the lip left to finish up the arête. A good problem.

18 The Groove *4+* ✳
The classy groove.

19 Pocket Slab *6b* ✳
A good line up the slab, past the small pockets. A left-hand variant is 6c.

20 Deforestation *7a*
The arête on its right, avoiding the big holds round left. Sit-start at 7b. 5 on its left.

21 The Porthole *6c+* ✳
Straight up from the good porthole. Traversing right from the porthole to finish up the vague prow is 7a.

The Enigma *8a* ✳
The sit-start to *The Porthole* off very poor holds below. *Mike Adams*

22 The Rib *6b*
The vague rib on small edges.

23 Easy Wall *5*

24 Pocket Wall *5+*
Up to and past the pocket.

25 The Hanging Arête *6a*
Sit-start the hanging arête.

Big Boulder
The biggest boulder, just out of the woods.

26 Uphill Arête *6a*
Sit-start the overhanging, uphill arête.

27 Left Wall *6c*
The wall right of the arête.

28 Seam Wall *6c+* ✳
Seams up the centre of the wall.

29 Two Pocket Wall *6b*
The right-hand side of the wall. A low R-L traverse of the face finishing up *Overhanging Arête* is 7a.

30 Right Arête *5*

31 Big Slab *3+*

32 Whispa Loudly *7a* ✳
The right side of the arête.

33 The Ramp *6c+*
Sit-start on the shelf right of the arête, climb up and rock left onto the slab.

34 The Dark Side *7a*
Sit-start at the right side of the overhang, climb up to good holds and the good flat hold on the arête. *Midnight Monster* starts as for this problem but climbs the wall, keeping right of the arête – 7b.

35 Broken Moon *7a*
The wall past the flake and layaways.

36 Acapella *8a* ✳
Sit-start at the vague arête and climb up direct. *Hard Moon* breaks off left into *Broken Moon* halfway up – 7c. *Mike Adams*

37 Lone Ranger *7c+*
60m further on is a small pit formed by two boulders. Sit-start the steep eastern face on a good RH sidepull and slap up on slopers. Feet on the main boulder only. *Mike Adams*

Black Tor

A collection of boulders, micro buttresses and the edge itself give an eclectic mix of bouldering and bilberries nestled in a beautiful moorland valley. Mike Adams documented the problems while working at the outdoor activity centre at Crowden, although it's likely that the easier problems have been done before. This is a sleepy backwater to the more popular Peak bouldering and the *Wolverine Boulder* is a great piece of Moorland Grit. The rock is in places a little raw, but the landings are generally good. Coupled with the aspect of the crag and the heather moorland above the rock, some of the problems can be green and damp, so a visit after dry weather is advisable. A quiet gritstone edge, this is a haven for wildlife, so please be considerate during the bird nesting season, and ensure dogs are kept on a lead.

Access and Approach

Park in the large car park at Crowden just off the A628 Woodhead Pass. Walk out the back of the car park, following the path alongside the campsite, and go straight ahead through the gate towards the Youth Hostel. Turn right up the track just before the bridge to the hostel and, after 100m, take the old iron gate on the left across the weir, just before the entrance to the nature reserve. Cross the weir and follow the path up the hillside to join the Pennine Way path at a T-junction. Turn right and look out for a well-defined path on the left that leads directly up to *Weasel Boulders*. Approach time about 15 minutes.

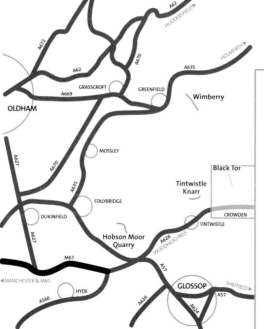

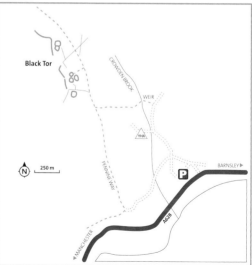

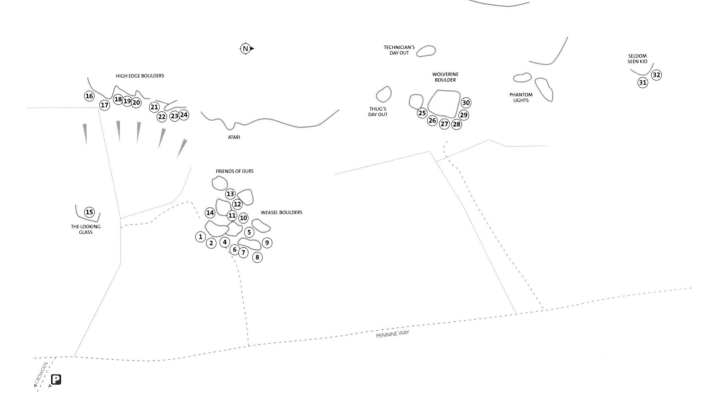

TECHNICIAN'S DAY OUT

SELDOM SEEN KID

HIGH EDGE BOULDERS

WOLVERINE BOULDER

PHANTOM LIGHTS

THUG'S DAY OUT

ATARI

FRIENDS OF OURS

WEASEL BOULDERS

THE LOOKING GLASS

PENNINE WAY

CROWDEN

Weasel Boulders

Many problems, eliminates and variations have been climbed here, the most obvious are described. Some have specified start holds. The first problems face the Pennine Way.

1   Playing With Fire   8a
Sit-start on two crimps, make a stiff pull off the floor to slap to on OK crimp and use this to get the top. Gritstone's answer to *Sway On*. *Mike Adams*

2   One Move   5+
Pop to the top from the good edge in the centre and pull over.

3   3   ✳
Climb the big slab up the side of the central boulder.

4   Angry Love   6c+
Sit-start with both hands matched on the big layaway on the face of the boulder and use a heel hook to lock to the arête. Finish up this. A variant, *Technical Love* (7b), starts as for *Angry Love* but traverses right using only low holds below the lip to finish at the right arête.

5   Magic Love   6c
On the back of the slab, sit-start LH sidepull in the cave, RH on low, crimpy pinch on the face right of the arête, and climb up to the shoulder and the top.

6   Slab Arête Left   4

7   The Left Slab   5+
Smear up the slab just left of centre. 6a just right of centre.

8   Slab Arête Right   3

9   Don't Dab Arête   6b
Around the back, sit-start RH sidepull, LH arête, and climb the arête.

The next problems are on the back of the boulders, facing the edge.

10   The Weasel   6b
Sit-start in the pit at the back of the central boulder with LH on low undercut pinch and the RH on a high edge. Pull on and use an intermediate to go for the good ledge.

11   Manchester March   5+
Sit-start at the right arête and follow this left and continue traversing left along the good ledge to finish at the left side of the boulder.

>>

12 Loves Stroll   5+
On the boulder behind the first boulder, sit-start left arête and follow the lip right around the prow to rock round on the right.

13 The Groove   6a+
Sit-start the attractive groove.

14 The Mantle   6a+
On the back of the boulder, sit-start the right arête using the big ledge on the right.

Two problems can be found in a pit slightly higher up. *Si's Problem* sit-starts on a jammed low boulder and climbs the small roof – 6a. *Friends of Ours* takes the short wall and arête just right from a sit-start with LH arête, RH low undercut – 7b+.

Up towards the chossy edge, sit-start the slab up twin arêtes before swinging around the left side to a heathery finish. This is *Atari* – 7a+.

15 The Looking Glass   7a+   ★
Just before the *Weasel Boulders* a faint track leads off to the left up a little hill to a drystone wall. Follow this to an obvious slab. This excellent problem climbs up the middle, starting just left of the arête. The right arête is a decent 6c.

High Edge Boulders
These problems are high on the left side of *Black Tor*.

16 The Mantle   6c
Sit-start up slopers and mantel out the lip.

17 Escape from Monday   7a
Sit-start the left side of the right arête. Starting up the previous problem and traversing the shelf right to the arête is 6b+.

18 Twins   6b+
Around the corner, climb the twin arêtes, staying on the left side of the right arête.

19   6a
Just right of the crack, sit-start the wall.

20 The Ill Defined   7a+
Sit-start the ill-defined arête on the right to a tricky top-out.

21   6b
Sit-start the wall on the next bit along.

2   The Fin   *6c*   ✳
Sit-start the right side of the striking fin.

3   The Wall   *6a+*
Sit-start the wall to the right.

4   Right Arête   *6b+*
Sit-start the arête right again.

Wolverine Boulder
classic lump of moorland grit with some good problems.

5   Vague Arete   *6a*
The left arête.

6   Baby Wolverine   *5+*   ★
The face just left of centre. See photo on p408.

7   Crowden Girls   *7a+*   ✳
Sit/crouch start on twin edges and slap up the vague rib. Powerful.

28   The Arête   *6c+*
Sit-start the right side of the arête. The arête on its left from the same start is 7a.

29   The Groove   *7a*
Climb the good grove, eliminating the arête and the flake.

30   One Arm   *6c*
Sit-start up the flake holds, without the blocks on the right. 5 from standing. Often dirty.

Up and left of the *Wolverine Boulder* is a big undercut block. *Thug's Day Out* starts on the left side, undercutting with feet on the slab. Lean out to and campus up edges to the lip. Traverse off left. 7b.

Directly behind *Wolverine Boulder* on the edge are some often dirty blocks. *Slap Problem* climbs the left-hand block from low – 6b. *Technician's Day Out* climbs up the right side of the arête to slopers, with a slap off a toe hook (the boulders jammed in the crack are out) – 7b. *Means to an End* climbs left of the arête off undercuts – 7a. *The Crack* is 5+.

Right of the *Wolverine Boulder* is a tall crag with a pit below. A vague line – *Phantom Lights* (7b+) – starts stood on a cleaned boulder with a choice of rubbish edges and pops to a pinch hold in the groove – holding this is the crux. Continue up slopers above and mantel using the tree.

Seldom Seen Kid
Continuing up and around the hill leads to a couple of good highballs, with heathery top-outs.

31   Seldom Seen Kid   *7c+*   ★
Climb the stunning, highball left arête of the block. Very high and hard. *Mike Adams*

32   Pennine Way Variation   *6c*   ✳
The centre of the fine slab, with a crux rockover around the lip.

Wimberry

Wimberry **is practically ignored by many Peak climbers, which is good. The circuit is just as fine as any of the classic eastern venues, but it's only half as spoilt and it's twice as quiet. The boulders are strewn down the steep hillside below the crag and they contain stacks of classic problems, many of which you probably won't have heard of. The rock is rough, but not painfully so, and of top-notch quality.**

Access and Approach

The access and approach details are described for those approaching from the west. *Wimberry* is located just off the A635 Chew Valley road on the northeast side of Manchester, just east of Greenfield. After driving through Greenfield, take a road called Bank Lane on the right, then follow it down to the obvious pay and display car park next to the reservoir. Make sure that you do pay and display – you will get a parking ticket if you don't.

To get to the boulders follow the track past the yachting club, turn right and follow the path with the stream on your left. *The Sugarloaf* is reached first, with the rest of the circuit scattered about the hillside above.

North-facing and exposed... actually the conditions are a lot better than this sounds. The boulders are quite sheltered and do not get as green as the crag itself. This exposure also means that the season lasts longer than at other venues, and with a stiff breeze good conditions can last into the summer.

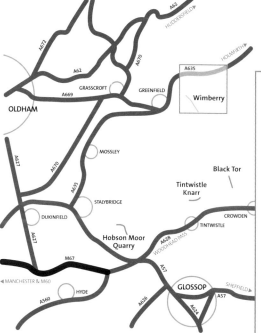

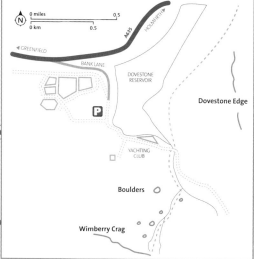

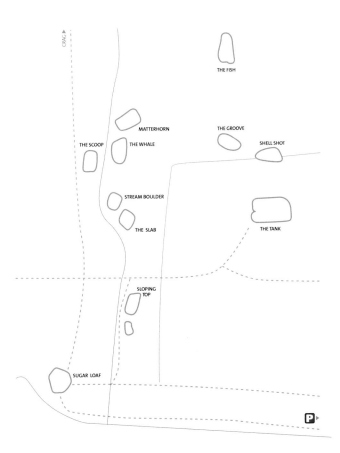

Sugar Loaf

Not the most appealing boulder on first sight, and covered with old chipped holds. Most of the stand-up starts, although good, tend to be climbing of the pulling-between-positive-chips variety. The sit starts, however, though they might not look like much on first acquaintance offer some fantastic and strange moves. The problems are described clockwise starting at the uphill face.

1 *6a+*
The blunt arête approached from the flake in the centre of the wall.

Variations:

6b
Move right from the flake via a crimp.

7b
Sit-start, with both hands on a low edge, match the rib above and layback to glory, finishing left or right as per the above problems. Unlikely, but great moves.

2 *3*
The way down, and therefore it's debatable whether it should be advertised as a way up▸

3 *4+*
Pockets, scoops and chips up the high wall.

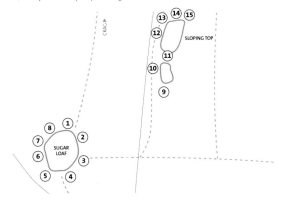

Artificial Route *4+*
The short, hanging arête and wall above on chips.

Artificial Route Sit-Start *7b*
Sit-start hanging the low, sloping boss, lock for flatties in the break using an unusual splits move, mantel and up. Harder than it looks. *Lee Anderson*

Baxter's Wall Direct *5+* ✳
The next vague arête on the left is followed on more chips.

Brush Electric *7c*
A desperate sit-start to *Baxter's Wall Direct*, directly pulling into, and using, the lip of the little roof as an undercut to reach better holds above. *Sam Whittaker*

Local Hero *6b+* ✳
The wall taken on crimps. *Baxter's Wall* starts up this and trends right to the arête – 6a+. There's also a fun eliminate dyno-ing from the large hold to the top at 7b–ish.

Local Hero Sit-Start *7c+*
Sit down, hold the little crimps, smear the foot of your choice on the rock and snatch upwards. *Lee Anderson*

Chips *5+*
The rib just left on chipped holds.

Chips Sit-Start *7a*
Sit-start the rib on a chipped, rounded dish, flick to a crimp and use a mono and/or other features to finish up *Chips*. *Lee Anderson*

4
The heavily chipped, slabby wall left again.

The next boulder up and right is *Sloping Top*. The block below this is home to two bits of fun:

6b
The undercut right arête, from a sit-start, has a great move. If you are very strict and pull on to the front face using just the undercut and exit direct, it's much harder – in the region of 7a.

4
The unfortunately chipped slab is easy.

Sloping Top

11 The Grey Road *7c*
The sit-start to the downhill face. Use a high right-hand crimpy sidepull to power up to the sloping top. Shorties may not be able to reach the starting hold from a sit-start. 6c from a standing start.

12 Slap Happy *6c* ✳
A sloping top classic. From the high right-hand hold, slap the sloping top, slap to match, but don't slap to mantel the top-out. A low (not sitting) start can be done from the flat undercut down and left – 7b+ – but only the tall need apply.

13 Fat Slapper *6b+* ✳
The featured, blunt arête.

Fat Slapper Sit-Start *7a* ✳
Sit-start on a flatty (right) and undercut (left), slap up into the stand-up. Good moves. *Paul Ingham*

14 The Slot *5*
Undercut the slot.

15 5
The wall just left, with a left-hand sidepull. The arête left again is also 5.

KIM LEYLAND ON *PROBLEM 2* PHOTO: JOHN COEFIELD

The Slab

16   The Slab   *4*
The right arête of the slab.

17   *3+*
The centre of the chipped slab.

Stream Boulder

18   *4+*
The short arête on the downhill side.

19   *4*
The wall to the left.

20   *6a*
The groove above the stream. You have got to flash this if you want to stay dry – there's no padding out the landing of this one.

Further up the stream, on the right, is a block with a neglected gem on it. Sit-start on the right, on slopes under the steepness, slap up to a final slopey exit above the worrying slope above the stream. 7a+.

The Tank

21   Stateside   *7c*   ✳
Steep laybacking up coarse but thin sidepulls, trending rightwards. The grade is earned by not using the chips. *Miles Gibson*

22   Elephant's Pinch   *6c*
The wall between *Stateside* and *Elephant's Bum* using a nice fat pinch for your left hand.

23   Elephant's Bum   *5*   ✳
Up to, then using the rounded crack feature.

24   Elephant's Slab   *6c*   ✳
The slab left of the crack, right of the arête. There are two variations depending on whether you start with your left or with your right hand on the obvious pebble.

   7b
A hard sit-start to the slab off the chipped pocket, again with two variations on the pebb

25   *4*
Chips just left of the arête.

26   *4*
Wall with flakes.

27   *4+*
Leftwards-slanting crack.

28   Think Tank   *6b+*   ★
The leftwards-rising line of flakes, from the right arête on the downhill face, is a classic
See photo on p421.

Left again is an old project dyno. Holding the hold seems to be the issue rather than hitting The first ascent still awaits.

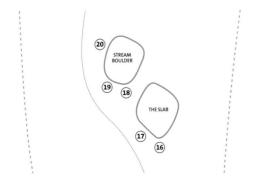

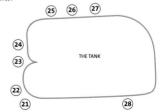

Shell Shot

29 Flakes of Concern   7a
The high wall on the downhill face via flakes. Some of the flakes are not beyond suspicion so take care.

30 Shell Shot   4
The downhill arête.

31 Shell Shock   4
The slab just right.

32 The Cannon   6a
A bit eliminate – up to flakes right again.

The Groove

The next small boulder up and left of *Shell Shot*.

33 The Groove   6b   ✳
The lovely short groove from a sit start.

34 Groove Traverse   7a
Right to left traverse along the top of the boulder from the right (not quite on the arête) to finish up *The Groove*. *Lee Anderson*

The Whale

35 4+
The stream-facing crack line.

36 6b+   ✳
The bulging wall just left is very good – for full local approval make sure that you don't use the crack for your feet.

37 5+
Pockets and wall. The problem is quite good, but much better is the eliminate – no pockets, just the right-facing big rounded flake/blob. Now try and pull on. Starting at 6b, you get an extra grade for every two seconds you stay off the floor up to a theoretical limit of 7a+ if you top it out up the scoop.

7b
Traverse leftwards from the crack to finish up the pockets, staying low on slopers. Good conditions essential. *Sam Whittaker*

The Scoop

38 Steve's Wall   7a+   ✳
The downhill-facing wall starting just left of the arête and trending left across the slab on pebbles. *Steve Fisher*

39 5+
The left side of the scoop.

40 5+
Direct up the wall above the scoop.

41 The Scoop   4   ✳
Into the scoop and out of it on the right. Nice.

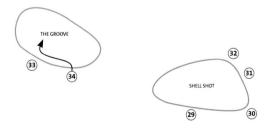

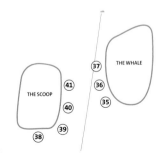

Matterhorn

A big, proud boulder, home to a famous highball slab.

42 *6a*
The arête on the left-hand side. Good climbing.

43 **Winsome** *7a* ★
A Chew Valley classic up the worryingly high slab on pebbles. Keep on that line – the problem goes straight up, not leftwards onto the good foot and handholds.
John Allen

44 **West's Route** *5+* ✳
Climb the features and overlap just left of centre.

45 **The Nipple** *6a*
The arête on the right-hand side.

46 *6a*
An eliminate up the black slab at the back.

47 *4*
Chips up the wall to the left.

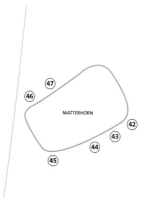

The Fish

48   Fish Arête   *6c+*   ★
The stunning arête and rib are perfect grit features. Climb them with a flowing sequence to a final slap for the top.

Fish Arête Sit-Start   *7b+*   ★
The sit-start adds more moves slapping up the arête and rib, which can only be a good thing. Totally classic.

49   The Groove   *6c*   ✳
A standing start (right hand in the groove, left on crimp) to climb the short hanging groove. A great problem. Starting a move lower on the slopey crimps in the vague break and slapping into the groove above is 7b.

50   You're Joking!   *7b*
From the slopey crimps in the vague break slap to the top. *Adam Long*

51   *6b*
Mantel out the overhanging lip.

52   *6a+*
From a low start on a sloping shelf, move right onto better shelves and then the top. Satisfying.

53   Fish Traverse   *7a*   ✳
Traverse leftwards on features below the top from the same low hanging start as the previous problem to finish up the next problem. *Sam Whittaker*

54   Fish Dish   *6b+*   ✳
A good little sit-start on the short rib leads to slopey dishes and the top.

6c+
Traverse into the previous problem from the low handrail to the left.

55   Dark Matter   *7c*   ✳
A fantastic hard problem. Starting on the low handrail, slap out to a pair of terrible slopers, do a tricky move to bring your other hand out, and then go for the top. The problem is independent but the slopers are very close to those on the similar problem just right, so make sure that you keep on the line. *Lee Anderson*

56   The Coarse Traverse   *7a*   ✳
Sit-start on the left-hand side of the large overhang and traverse the lip rightwards, footless or with heels, to finish up the vague nose.

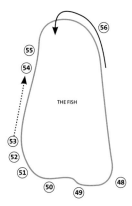

Miles' Slab

Walk parallel with the main crag back towards the parking on the same level as the *Shell Shot* boulder for about 150m and you will happen upon this well-hidden slab, just up from the northwest corner of the woodland.

57   Miles' Slab   *7b+*   ★
A cunning slab test piece that's more involved than the usual grit padding and pebbles lark. Jump into the high foot-scoop and contrive a sequence upwards using the dish and mono. *Miles Gibson*

58   *6c*
The left-hand side of the right arête.

Rail Trail

At the far right of the crag, above the route *Northern Ballet* (E3), is this low roof, high above the valley.

59   Rail Trail   *7a*
Sit-start on the right-hand side of the roof at the small arête and hand traverse the crimpy, slopey rail leftwards all the way round the roof to finish by rocking over onto the slab opposite the start. A good and unusual problem. Finishing up the first arête at the nose is 6b+. *Jon Fullwood*

DAN CHEETHAM ON *RAIL TRAIL*   **PHOTO: JON FULLWOOD**

LIMESTONE AREA

STONEY MIDDLETON
TIDESWELL DALE
CASTLETON
RUBICON
RAVEN TOR
BLACKWELL DALE
ALPORT AREA
HARBOROUGH ROCKS
THE TUBE – DOVE DALE

Stoney Middleton

Stoney is not included because it's a great place to climb, but because of its important history. When you first encounter the vertical slickness and finger strength building gloss of *Minus 10*, the stench of *Carl's Wark* and the impossible number of problems revolving around one, glued-on hold in *Tom's Roof*, you may wonder why you're here.

But *Stoney* is the spiritual home of hard Peak bouldering and it played a key role in pushing climbing standards in the 1980s. Thanks to the forefathers of UK bouldering: *Proctor, Allen, Moffatt, Stokes* and *Kirton*, we're left with a crag as rich in history as it is in polish. Back in the late 1970s/early 1980s there were no such things as climbing walls, and training merely consisted of lifting some weights and a doing few pull-ups. Then along came a few climbers who thought that bouldering around on the limestone of *Stoney* would be good conditioning for the routes they aspired to.

Almost every problem at *Stoney* is an eliminate, which means that despite all the listed problems being hard, there's good sport to be had at all grades by doing your own thing. Please bear in mind that eliminate grades are much more approximate than normal because there are no alternative sequences to suit different people. So if you're told not to use that hold, and to do the next bit like this, just remember that this is where training (and modern climbing) was born.

The majority of the problems included are old test-piece classics from the 1980s and 1990s, researched and remembered by Andy Harris. To these a few new problems and variations have been added – yes, *Minus 10* still has devotees. There's also the relatively-recently developed *Tom's Cave*, further up the road, and not to be confused with *Tom's Roof* (although it will be).

Nowhere are the conditions as reliable as they are at *Stoney*. If the grit is dripping and *Raven Tor* and *Rubicon* are sopping wet, chances are that *Stoney* will still be dry. If you're lucky you might even get to experience the elusive 'sticky damp', the most hallowed of all conditions when grades drop and gravity seems to loosen its grip.

Access and Approach

Parking is in the large lay-by on the A623 at the western edge of Stoney Middleton, almost opposite the Café/Bistro/Indian Restaurant. 150m up from the car park is a track on the right directly below *Garage Buttress*. Follow this for 200m and you'll find *Tom's Roof* after a 10m scramble up the gully, just before *Bitter Fingers* wall. For *Minus 10*, continue for another 100m and turn right. *Carl's Wark* is on the lower tier another 30m further off the main path, just drop down left on either side.

See the *Tom's Cave* section for approach information.

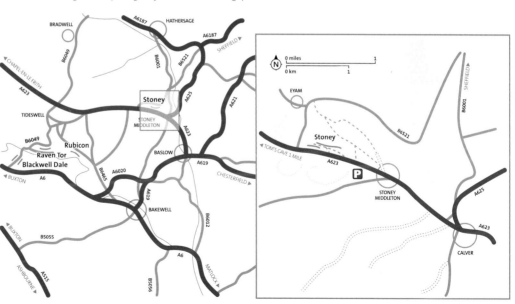

Tom's Roof

Tom's Roof was perhaps the world's first climbing 'cellar', trained on before the in-house training boards were built by Pollitt, Moon and Moffatt. It might be surprising to learn that this grotty cave is where Jerry trained for those hard, game-changing early ascents in America. *Tom's Roof* may also lay claim to the world's first glued-on hold. Around 1975, the late, great Tom Proctor stuck on that classic edge in the centre of the roof. A builder by trade, Tom covered the hold in Araldite and then held it in place with a scaffolding pole – thus creating the most solid hold at Stoney.

The holds

A	Lower sidepull	L	Flat hold in roof
B	Upper sidepull	M	Small edge
C	Big fat undercut/jams	N	Pinch
D	Pocket at base of rib	O	Small slot
E	Classic, slick, glued-on edge	P	Large flake
F	Poor pinch on lip of roof	Q	Low edge
G	Square pinch	R	Foot jam
H	Big slick jug	S	Low foothold/toe-lock
I	Crumbling slot and jug	T	Pinch in roof near lip
J	Undercut pinches	U	Triangular pinch
K	Edge in roof		

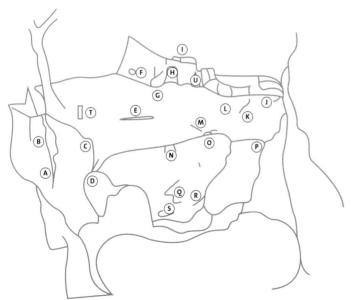

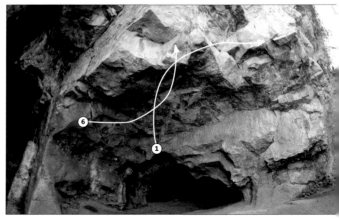

les is rules, so follow your left hand (LH) and right hand (RH), and go footless when
d to do so. On first acquaintance with the place you may become confused,
there appears to be only one hold.

Tom's Original   *7a*   ✳
(RH–C, LH–C), RH–E, LH–E, RH–H, LH–H, RH–J, LH–J. Feet anywhere.

The Womb   *6c*
Jam out from the back of the hole to D, and then add a finish of your choice.

Punker Bunker   *7a+*
(LH–C, RH–C), RH–E, LH–E, RH–H, LH–H. Feet anywhere but the side wall.

Armbandit   *7c*
(LH–B, RH–A) RH–E, LH–Q, RH–K, LH–I, RH–I. Feet anywhere.

Power Allowance   *7b*   ✳
(RH–C, LH–C) RH–E, LH–E, RH–G, right foot toe jam H, RH–E, LH–C, RH–C.
Feet anywhere but side wall.

RRY MOFFATT IN *TOM'S ROOF*   **PHOTO:** HEINZ ZAK

6   **Swing Thing**   *7b*   ✳
(LH–B, RH–A) RH–E, LH–E, footless, RH–H, LH–H Feet on back wall only. There and back is 7c.

7   **Quintesscence**   *8a*
(LH–B, RH–A) LH–T, RH–F, footless, LH–H, RH–H. Feet on back wall only. Jerry was so
desperate to repeat this Kirton nasty that he stripped down to his underpants and took
off his rock boots in an effort to lose weight.

8   **Pete's Power Pull**   *7c*   ✳
(LH–C, RH–C) LH–E, footless, RH–H, LH–H. Doing it, then reversing it, is 7c+/8a.

9   **Rack and Ruin**   *7c*
(LH–small pocket right of D, RH–pinch rib right of D) RH–E, LH–Q, RH–L, LH–I, RH–H,
LH–H. Feet back wall for 1st move, then side wall.

10   **Jerryatricks**   *7c+*   ✳
Link the following problems without getting off; *The Womb, Swing Thing, Tom's Original*
in reverse, and *Power Allowance*. Pumped?

11   **Jerry's Problem**   *7c+*   ✳
Often done incorrectly, so read carefully. (LH–C, RH–C) RH–E, LH–E, footless, RH–little
crimp directly below left-hand slot I, LH–left-hand slot I, RH–large jug I.

12   *7c*
(LH–B, RH–A) RH–E, LH–E, footless, RH–U, LH–L, LH–H, RH–H. Feet on back wall only.

13   *7c*
(LH–Q) RH–O, LH–E, RH–E, footless, LH–B, LH–A. Feet on S and back wall.

14   **Figure of 8**   *7b+*
(LH–C, RH–C) RH–E, LH–Q, RH–U, LH–E, RH–C, LH–C. Feet back wall and S.

Minus 10

Don't worry about the polish, just think how well you'll be climbing when you learn to use it. This is technical stuff indeed and the grit will feel twice as grippy after a few sessions here.

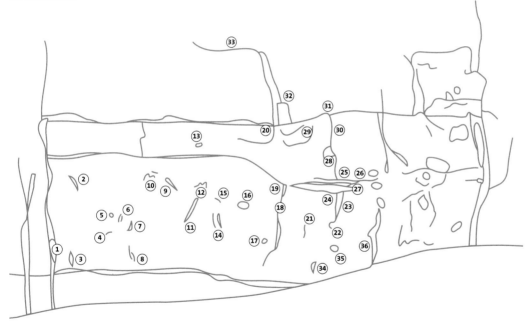

The holds

1 Chockstone/jug
2 Sidepull
3 Sidepull
4 Edge
5 Small, shallow pocket
6 Vague fin
7 Crimp
8 Slopey sidepull
9 Small ramp
10 Spikey edge
11 Sidepull
12 Edges
13 Sharp pocket
14 Sidepull/pinch
15 Edge
16 Smear
17 Perfect three finger pocket
18 Sidepull
19 Polished foothold in break
20 Quartzy edges
21 Vague sidepull
22 Undercut dish
23 Large, slopey sidepull
24 Thin seam
25 Good edge
26 Quartzy crimp
27 Slopey edge
28 Crimpy sloper
29 Quartzy edges
30 Good, smooth sidepull
31 Juggy ledge
32 Good edge in groove
33 Juggy ledge

Quent's Dyno   7b   ★

From the jug (1), and crack, launch for the big jugs at the start of the *Upper Break*. The original method had prescribed footholds: left foot on the polished edge of the crack, right foot on a group of tiny spiky bits, midway between the floor and the break – 7c.

Not Ned's Problem   7b+

Sit-start with hands in the break. Move left hand up to (3), right to (4), left to (2) and through to the break with your right hand.

Harris Problem   7b+

Start with left hand on (3), right on (4). Reach a small edge/sidepull 15 inches or so above hold (5) with your left and go to the break with your right hand. Feet on smears only.

Variant   7c+

Go through to the top break with your right hand instead of the lower one to finish.

White Ladder   7c

Start with left hand on (4) and right hand on (8). Move right hand to small crimp above and right of (6), left hand to good edge up and left, finish on the pointy, triangular bit on top break.

The JABP   7c

Done and named by Moffatt after a rumour that John Allen had done it. He hadn't. Use the small shallow pocket (5) with the left and pinch the vague fin (6). Pull on, feet anywhere and reach the next break with your right. As fingery as it gets.

6   7b+

Starting on sidepulls (3 & 8) with feet low, pull on, right foot in break and balance over to ramp (9) with left. Match this and reach to sharp pocket (13) with right and leap for the top break (33).

7   7a+

Use pocket (17) with left and gaston (21) with right. Egyptian feet up onto small edges above the low break. Reach edge (28) and crank through for the edge in the groove (32), using poor edges for your feet. Feet on smears below 2nd break and lurch over for (33) with right.

8   Easy Dynos

Using pocket (17) with left and undercut (22), dyno to break using small edges above the low break for feet. A great introduction to dynoing.

9   One Arm Bandit   7b   ✳

With your left in (17) and your right behind your back, dyno for the jug (31) with your left! Can be done with the other hand at the same grade.

10   Kirton Dyno   7a+   ✳

Start with your right on (19), left in the break and toe in (17), leap for (33).

11   Sean's Problem   7b+   ★

Left on (34), right on (36) and feet in the low break, reach the shallow dish (38) and crimp (24) (thumb around side edge). Feet up on tiny edges (no break for this move) and reach over to edge (28) with right, and incut (32) with left. Feet on smears below 2nd break and lurch over for (33) with right. Superb. Using sidepull (23) instead of edge (24) is 7c. Even better.

12   Zippy's Sidepull   7b+

Left on (34), right on (36) and feet in the low break. Get top of sidepull (23) with your right and put toe in shallow pocket (35). Lurch for jug (31).

13   Lucian's Undercut   7a

Easier version of the previous problem. Using undercut (22) instead of (23). Peculiarly, Lucian knows nothing about this problem.

14   6c+

Left on (34) and right on (36) reach up to scoop (22) with your right. Reach up to (19) then (30) and (33).

The holds

17 Perfect three finger pocket
18 Sidepull
19 Polished foothold in break
20 Quartzy edges
21 Vague sidepull
22 Undercut dish
23 Large, slopey sidepull
24 Thin seam
25 Good edge
26 Quartzy crimp
27 Slopey edge
28 Crimpy sloper
29 Quartzy edges
30 Good, smooth sidepull
31 Juggy ledge
32 Good edge in groove
33 Juggy ledge
34 Sidepull
35 Polished dish
36 Sidepull
37 Poor smear (no more resin, please)
38 Poor crimp

39 Crozzly crimp
40 Sharp undercut
41 (Right-hand) thin horizontal edge
42 Pinch
43 Big, fat sloper
44 Poor, three finger sloper
45 Jugs behind block
46 Round, smooth sidepull
47 Sloping dish
48 Big sidepull
49 Undercut in roof
50 Pinch on lip of roof
51 Sloper
52 Juggy block
53 Flatty above sidepull
54 Slopey gaston
55 3 downward sloping edges – always
    use lowest, poorest edge as per
    foothold eliminator!

For the following three problems please refer to our handy foothold eliminator to ensure the full tick. We hope that you've not been using the wrong footholds all this time?

15   Zippy's Problem   7b+   ★
Start with left on edge (36), right on pinch (42) and outside edge of left foot on (41). Up to sloper (44) with left, swap feet on (41). Reach the sloper (47) with your right (no holding the good bit at the back). Now place left foot on foothold (55), slap up for sidepull (48) and reach the top (52) with right foot on pinch (42). Sorry.

Variant 1   7b+
As above but instead of reaching sidepull (48), reach pinch (50) then right hand to (53) with toe on smear (43).

Variant 2   7c
Miss out ledge (53) by dynoing for jug (52).

16   7c
As for problem 12 to sloper (47). Swap feet on edge (41), reach ripple (54) with left. Right foot on smear (43), grunt to pinch (50) with right and flick to edge (51) then footless to jug (52).

17   Pinch 2   7c+ (8a+)   ✳
Ben Moon growling in slow mo. *Stuart Cameron* not doing it. You got it! Once the hardest eliminate around and the highlight of the video *One Summer*. There is a massive variation in grade depending on who you ask and exactly how they did it.

Start with left on edge (36), right on pinch (42) and outside edge of left foot on (41). Up to sloper (44) with left, swap feet on (41). Left toe onto smear (37) and dyno with right for pinch on lip (50). Right foot up to smear (43) and dyno again for edge (51) with left. Then the top (52).

>>

18 Nasty Traverse 7c+
Start with left on edge (36), right on pinch (42) and outside edge of left foot on (4). Up to crozzly crimp (39) with left, swap feet and left foot to small edge above low break. Right hand to poor crimp (38) and fall into crimp (24 – thumb around side edge). Finish as for *Sean's Problem*. Nasty.

19 The Double Double 6c ✳
Classic 70s double dynoing. From the good flakes (45) and edge (46), dyno to opposing sides of the block (48) and the side below (53). Then the jug (52).

20 Young American 7a+ (Originally B2) ★
Done by visiting American Christian Griffith (he of thong fame), hence the name. Dyno straight from (45) and (46) to (52) with feet on (43) and edges to the left. Classic!

21 Megatron 7a+ ✳
Dyno from edge A to jug B. *Megatron Turbo* double dynos to jug B, no change in grade.

There are three left to right traverses; two along the obvious upper and middle breaks, while a tricky traverse takes a line of holds below the middle break. You can use whatever footholds you like:

The Upper Break 5

The Middle Break 6b
It starts off fine, but you may struggle with the final moves. Pumpy.

The Wall Traverse 6c+
Quite awkward passing *The JABP*.

George's Wall

In between *Tom's Roof* and *Minus 10* is this clean little wall.

1   **George's Wall Dyno**   *7b*
Big dyno from the jug in the low break to the break. Dynoing to the large sloper below the break is *Quentin Fisher's* much harder dyno – 7c.

2   *6a+*
The vague groove.

Carl's Wark

A bit smelly and lonely, but it has some good routes, some OK problems and a classic limestone traverse.

3   **Carl's Wark Traverse**   *7b*   ✳
A low-level traverse, starting from the crack and heading right on a variety of pockets and edges, to finish up the flakes to the break, that being the start to *Bubbles Wall* (E3 6a). Keeping low on poor pockets to rejoin the higher traverse as it passes the start of *Au Revoir Mono Doigt* is 7c.

4   **More Air than Chocolate**   *6a*
Climb pockets on the left-hand side of the wall, trending right to a groove.

5   **Au Revoir Mono Doigt**   *7b*
Old school bouldering and quite hard. Climb the highball centre of the wall.

6   **Soapsuds Traverse**   *6b+*
Situated to the right of the main wall is the *Soapsuds* wall – ironically it's a bit dirty. Start on the left and make an awkward move into the crack, climb it, traverse the second break back left and climb down to the start.

Tom's Cave

A small, roadside limestone cave that looks scruffy and uninviting. Don't be put off – it is home to some very good, steep and hard problems.

Conditions

Like most Peak limestone the cave seeps and can take a while to dry. Once dry it stays that way even after prolonged rain, although it does suffer condensation in high humidity.

Access and Approach

The cave is situated by the side of the A623. Approached from Stoney Middleton, the cave is on the right-hand side of the road after the sweeping right-hand bend, about a mile out of Stoney. It's clearly visible from the road, just after a lay-by on the right (and the parking for sport climbing venue *Horseshoe Quarry*), and directly opposite one on the left. Park in either.

1 **5+**
Warm up on wobbly jugs on the right side of the cave. Various eliminates possible.

2 **Hannibal** *7c* ★
Athletic climbing on good holds. Sit-start on the right wall of the cave then traverse the lip leftwards to a big span to a jug. Pull up to finish on higher jugs.
Dawid Skoczylas

3 **Titus** *7c*
Jump to the lip jug on *Hannibal*, pull up, and follow the lip leftwards to finish at the tree. *Dan Varian*

4 **King Cannibal** *7c+*
Link *Hannibal* into *Titus* for the full lip job. *Dan Varian*

5 **Hannibal Corner** *7b+*
Sit-start as for *Hannibal* but finish straight up the corner from the juggy crimp.

6 **Andronicus** *8a+* ✳
A big line through the roof that is both powerful and technical. Reach big undercuts in the back of the cave and span out to the fin and other assorted unhelpful holds. Finish up jugs above the niche.
Dawid Skoczylas

7 **Tamora** *8a+*
Sustained climbing, linking *Andronicus* into *Titus*.
Dan Varian

8 **6a**
A sit-start problem up the left wall, starting at the small side cave.

9 **7a**
Traverse the back wall of the cave, far left to far right.

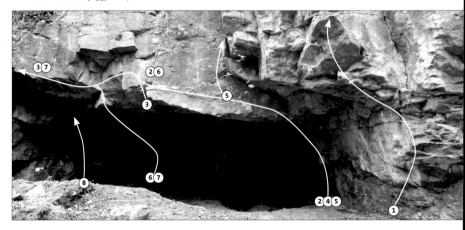

Tideswell Dale

A minor buttress of compact limestone, developed by Robin Mueller and Dawid Skoczylas. Like most Peak limestone, you'll get more out of a visit if you're operating into the 7's, and if you're a regular at 7c+ then *Infinite Suspense* is worth seeking out. The rock quality is variable, from the average and occasionally snappy, through to good. The crag faces north and so is shady for most of the day, getting the smallest amount of sun in summer. **Note:** the nettles can get quite high in mid summer.

Access and Approach

Easiest approached heading south on the B6049 from the village of Tideswell. Approx. ½ mile out of Tideswell, look for a parking area in the trees on the left, signed *Tideswell Dale Picnic Site*. Pull in and park here (pay and display). Walk south on the broad footpath out of the car park for about 800m, passing through a gate, and take the left-hand path when it forks just out of the trees by a big wooden mouse thing(!). Just before the main path veers back right to rejoin the lower path, break left on a smaller path up steps. The crag is just right of this path after 20m.

Freda's Buttress

1 Freda Mind 5+
The wall to jugs.

2 Freda Direct 6b
The fingery groove from the pockety-flake, past the undercut to high jugs. A good problem.

3 Infinite Suspense 7c+ ✳
A hard problem using some nice holds. Undercut up to the sloper in the groove with your left hand and get the wide pinch with your right. Now slap to a poor edge and finish on jugs.

4 Skylarkin 7a+
Start left hand undercut and right hand undercut/sidepull and dyno to the jug rail up and right.

5 E.T. Bone Home 7a
From undercuts gain a thin, pockety left hand crimp, make a hard move to a sloping edge in the groove and finish on jugs as for *Skylarkin*.

6 More Glee in the Jungle 6a
Climb direct to jugs from from big undercuts.

7 Pedal to the Nettle 6c
Sit-start at the back, reach out to the obvious flat hold on the lip and pull up to finish.

8 Bum Note 5+
Low jugs to the break. The warm up.

9 Scroll 7a
From the start of *Bum Note*, make a couple of moves up and traverse left to finish up *More Glee in the Jungle*

Space Invaders 7b
As for *Scroll*, but finish up *E.T. Bone Home*.

Cipple's Crab 7a+
Again, as for *Scroll*, but continue all the way left across the buttress to finish at a no-hands rest at the extreme left.

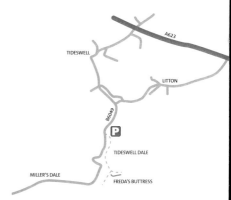

Castleton Area

Two small venues near Winnats Pass in Castleton, with a limited number of steep, hard limestone problems. *Odin Cave* is a proper cave, headtorches can be usefull on a dull day. *The Arch* is a steep wall overlooking Castleton. All of the problems were put up by *Robin Mueller* and *Dawid Skoczylas*.

Access and Approach

For *Odin Cave* take the A6187 west out of Castleton towards Winnats Pass, but do not turn off left to Winnats. Continue up the dead-end road towards Mam Tor and park at the end near the bus turning circle. The cave can be seen on the left side of the road.

For *The Arch*, park further down the dead-end road at Treak Cliff Cavern. Walk up to the show cave entrance with the tourists, then on past the entrance without them on the public footpath. Turn left up the hill next to a large hole and the crag should come into view.

Odin Cave
Essentially a one-problem venue, although a super project into *The Dark Room* still exists, plus a couple of others. The ground can be wet and very muddy so a tarpaulin is useful. The rock can also be affected by condensation in humid weather.

The Dark Room   *8a*   ✳
An atmospheric 3D trip through the dark roof of the cave. Sit-start at the back of the cave at the left end of the groove in the cave roof. Climb rightwards along the groove and finish on an obvious jug.

Short Circuit   *7a+*
The warm up. Sit-start on large holds at the back of the cave, climb to the finish of *The Dark Room*.

The Arch
A small arch of limestone, hidden on the hillside between the Blue John and Treak Cliff *Cavern* show caves.

1   **Grass Dynamique**   *7b+*
Start on the slab at the back of the left side of the arch, reach high undercuts and make a big move round the lip, a hard move to bring your hand out and another tricky move to finish on the jug above.

2   **Cry of the Beholder**   *7a*
Start undercutting from a big pocket in the back left of the large undercut hole on the right side of the arch and climb straight up to jugs.

3   **Sight Beyond Sight**   *7b+*
Start undercutting from a big pocket in the back right of the large undercut hole, use a pocket and crimp to get a flat hold then jugs.

4   **Dot the Eyes**   *6c*
Sit-start and traverse the lip left to the finishing jug of *Sight Beyond Sight*.

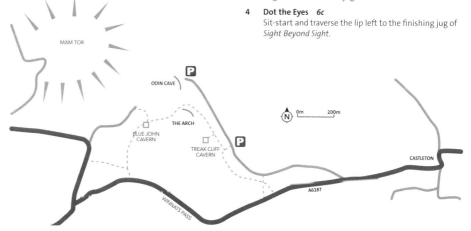

Rubicon

Rubicon is a hardcore limestone bouldering venue. Like its soul brother *Raven Tor*, a little further up *Miller's Dale*, the climbing is steep, polished, powerful and fingery.

Rubicon is riddled with eliminates. However, the best problems here are mostly independent, and so it is these problems that are described. If you want endless eliminates then bag a local or make some up for yourself.

Access and Approach

Rubicon is situated in Water-cum-Jolly, behind the big mill at the bottom of the village of Cressbrook. Park on the side of the road and follow the path next to the mill, past D's Brew Stop and cross the wooden footbridge on the right. *Rubicon* will then be directly in front of you. You will be sharing the dale with many walkers and the occasional fisherman, so be on your best behaviour.

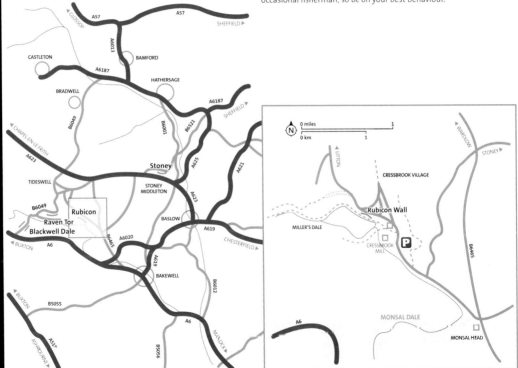

Traverses Area

The first area reached is the most popular. It has some pumpy training traverses and a few good up problems. The potential for eliminates is unlimited.

1   5

The standard warm-up traverse. Start at the extreme left of the bay and join the conga shuffling right on big holds. Or set the cat amongst the pigeons and do it the other way.

2   7a

Traverse the edges below the ledge/shelf next to the path, from the hole leftwards to good flakes.

3   5+

Flakes and pockets up to the ledge.

4   6b+ ∗

Traverse the lowest line of slots through the alcove. It can be done either way, but right to left is nicest. A classic.

5   6a ∗

The middle traverse line.

6   5+ ∗

The top traverse line.

7   6b

From the jugs in the middle of the traverse lines, trend up and right to the break on edge

8   6b

As above but trend left.

9   6b+

Climb small crimps and pockets up the right side of the groove.

10   Debris Groove   6a ∗

The right side of the prow.

11   Toenail Pie   5 ∗

Haul up jugs past the sign to the break.

12   6a+

Climb diagonally through the bulge.

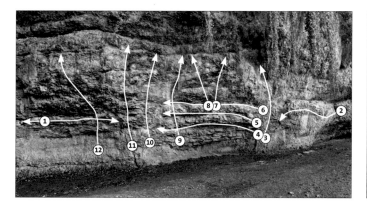

Kudos Wall

This small, steep wall has a concentration of hard, fingery and powerful problems.

3 A Bigger Prize   7a   ✳
The wall right of *A Bigger Splash* from a sit-start. *Andy Banks*

4 A Bigger Splash   7a+   ✳
From the jugs on the right-hand side of the wall, climb up and left to more jugs using painful flakes and crimps.

5 The Press   7b+   ★
Press off the opposing gastons to a sharp crimp, and then up for the jug.

   a) Kneeling Start   7c+ (easy)
   Start *The Press* from the rail.

   b) Low Right Sit-Start   7c+ (hard)
   Sit-start *The Press* under the start of *A Bigger Splash*.

   c) Low Left Sit-Start   8a (hard)   ★
   Sit-start with hands in the low slot down and left (hard for the grade).

   d) Rich's Link   8a+
   Link *Low Left Sit-Start* into *Kudos* by reversing *Kudos Traverse* from *The Press*. *Rich Simpson*

6 A Bigger Splash Direct   7b   ✳
Use *The Press* gaston as a layaway for your right hand and a small undercut for your left – then slap into the jug.

   a) Kneeling Start   7b+
   Start from the rail.

   b) Low Right Sit-Start   7c   ✳
   Start under *A Bigger Splash* and traverse left into the stand-up.

   c) Tsunami   8a   ★
   The low left sit-start with hands in the low slot down and left. *John Welford*

   d) Dancing Fish   8a
   Finish *Tsunami* by slapping out left to the sidepull jug. Finish up *A Bigger Tail*. *Mike Adams*

7 The Pinch   7b+
An eliminate. Start with both hands matched on the poor slopers and pinches below the undercut on *A Bigger Splash Direct*. Pull on, and slap into the big sidepull jug up and left. *Ned's Problem* slaps from the pinch to *The Press* jug –7c. *Ned Feehally*

18 A Bigger Tail   7a   ★
Jump to good edges, swing right and pull up more edges to gain the high jugs. Link from *Kudos* sit-start at 7b+.

19 Johnny G   7c
From an awkward thin slot under the overlap (right hand) and a shallow scallop just above the overlap (left hand) slap to the big edges on *A Bigger Tail*. Finish up this. *Dan Varian*

20 A Bigger Belly   8b
The fierce sit-start to *Johnny G* from a poor right hand crimp, and an even worse left hand one. *Dan Varian*

21 Kudos   7b   ✳
Start on the jugs on the left of the wall, pull up to sidepulls using a pocket and pull left and match the flakes to finish. *'Kudos Easy Way'* takes the lowest sidepull with the left hand and the higher on the right with your right before slapping up, while *'Kudos Hard Way'* takes the lower side pull with the right hand and rocks out to the flake. Both are approximately the same grade. A sit-start is 7b+.

22 Kudos Traverse   7b   ✳
Start as for *Kudos* but traverse right to finish on the finishing jugs of *The Press*. There and back is 7c.

23 Rather Grim   7c+ (before broken holds)
Reach the flakes at the end of *Kudos* from the left via small edges. Holds have snapped since it was climbed.

24 A Miller's Tale   6b+   ✳
Climb into the big hole from a sit-start. 6b from standing.

25 Piranha Start   7a
Just left of the tree, yard up drilled monos to a flake.

To the left are various routes, the starts of which can be bouldered out, but to prevent excessive polish they are not described. The pick of the bunch is the starting groove of *Caviar* – 7b. Further left still, the wall slabs out to give a long traverse line.

26 The Dragon Flight Traverse   6a+   ✳
Traverse the slabby face on polished holds in either direction.

Raven Tor

Raven Tor is where finger strength was invented, the original laboratory of power. The problems are steep and powerful, polished and often painful, but ultimately rewarding. The bouldering at *Raven Tor* was historically used as training for the routes, so many of the problems are eliminates that have been devised to maximise power and even some of those that follow natural lines have accepted 'rules'. If this seems like an unnecessary throwback to a period of bouldering when difficulty was sought rather than avoided, then feel free to climb the problems however you like; but if you wish to climb the problems as they were historically done then read on – every problem is described in pedantic detail.

Raven Tor stays dry in the rain and is shady in the morning and late evening. Although the grades start at about 5+, you will not get much out of a visit unless you climb at least 7a.

Access and Approach

Raven Tor is situated in Miller's Dale just off the B6049 road between Tideswell and the A6. From the A6, drive down the hill on the B6049, around a few bends and under the big railway bridge. Take the next turn on the right to the Angler's Rest pub. From Tideswell the turning is on the left, at the bottom of the hill, after passing the Youth Hostel on the left. In Miller's Dale, drive past the Angler's Rest and continue for half a mile – the crag is on the left.

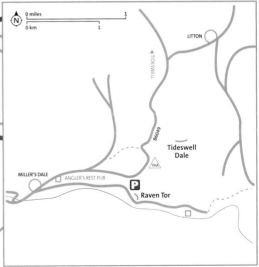

The Cave

Home to some excellent burly problems that, despite being through a roof, mostly still manage to feature the Tor hallmark – the sharp crimp.

1   Ben's Roof   *7c+*   ★

An endurance problem that is both powerful and painful in equal measure. Sit-start on low side-pulls in the back right-hand side of the cave, cross the cave leftwards to the side wall on scoops and crimps and then exit on undercuts, slopers and yet more crimps to finish below the top roof. *Ben Moon*

An extension start has been climbed starting way back in the cave, feet on the back wall, hands in a slopey undercut pod – 8a.

2   Too Hard for Mark Leach   *6c*   ✳

The exit to *Ben's Roof* from a low start on jugs.

3   Keen Roof   *8b*   ★

The central line. Start on good holds in the middle-left of the cave and climb to the pod in the centre of the roof. Hard moves punch out from here to the lip. Finish on the jugs under the next roof. The finish on its own from the lip is 7a+. *James Pearson*

Keen Roof Extension *(8b)* adds a slightly harder start to *Keen Roof*. Start left hand on the *Ben's Roof* start holds, and right hand on a sidepull crimp. Slap out to the pod, match and finish up *Keen Roof*. *Nacho Sanchez*

4   Hook   *7c*

Climb straight up from the good lip hold on *Keen Roof* on small crimps, avoiding better holds out left. *Dawid Skoczylas*

5   Cave Problem   *7b+*   ★

Start on a slot in the middle of the cave on the right, pull out to a crimp and an undercut on the lip and then pull rightwards to the finishing jug on the *Weedkiller Traverse*. Various extensions, links and variations have been done:

Cave Problem Sit-Start *(7c)* From holds at the back of the roof and climb out via a crimp and an undercut. Makes a great problem even better.

Tumbleweed *(7c+)* Link the *Cave Problem* sit-start into *Basher's Problem*. *Robin Mueller*

Let's Get Ready to Rumbleweed *(8a)* follows *Tumbleweed* but finishes up *Basher's* right-hand finish. *Andy Banks*

Fat Lip *8b* ★
A significant problem. Start as for *Cave Problem* (stand-up) and traverse the lip into the finish of *Keen Roof*. *Steve McClure*

Chimes Start *6b*
From the flat jug, pull up good holds to the jug below the roof.

Converter *7c*
Sit-start on painful pockets on the small tufa arête at the back of the roof. Gain a right-hand pinch and an uncomfortable undercut pocket in the roof and slap the lip. Finish up *Chimes Start*. *Dawid Skoczylas*

The Weedkiller Traverse *7b* ★
Start on large holds just right of the pillar and traverse the lip of the cave leftwards on the lowest line of slots and edges to finish up *Chimes Start*. Footless it is 7c (after hold growth). *Perverse Reverse* (7b) reverses the problem from as high as you can reach. *Killerweed* does it there and back – 7b+. See photo on p444.

10 Basher's Problem *7a* ★
Cross the roof from the back wall on undercuts to slots on the traverse, gain pockets above and finally the flat jug up and left. A slightly harder, right-hand finish climbs to a collection of better holds around the thin break 1m right of the normal finishing jug – 7a+.

11 High Green *7b*
Start as for *The Weedkiller Traverse* but reach into a high line of pockets after a couple of moves and follow these left to finish up *Basher's Problem*.

12 8a+
A big link with a lot of climbing. Start on *Weedkiller Traverse*, reverse *Cave Problem* down to damp jugs at the bottom of the roof, and traverse left into *Ben's Roof*. Finish up this. *Steve McClure*

The Pinches Wall

Tens of eliminates have been contrived on this tiny but incredibly versatile section of rock. Grades are meaningless on this wall because many problems don't even involve moving your feet and once wired they are more about body position than pulling. The problems are listed from easiest to hardest, the easiest being about 6a, and the hardest about 8a+, but take these grades with a pinch of salt.

For each problem the handholds are described in sequence with the starting holds in brackets, but you can use any* footholds unless otherwise stated.

Generally speaking this means the low, polished ones. If you find a funky method that makes the problem much easier you're cheating.

1	(L1, R1) R11, L8, L14, R14.
2	(L1, R1) R11, L14, R14.
3	(L1, R1) R13, L14.
4	(L1, R1) L8, R14, L14.
5	(L1, R1) L7, R11, L14, R14.
6	(L1, R1) L7, R12, L14, R14.
7	(L1, R1) L9, R14, L14.
8	(L15, R15) L20, R22, L22.
9	(L1, R1) R6, L8, R14, L14.
10	(L1, R1) R10, L14, R14 (feet high on C).
11	(L1, R1) R8, L22, R22.
12	(L1, R1) L14, R14 dyno.
13	(L1, R1) R4, L8, R14, L14.
14	(L15, R15) R slots, L11, R23, L14, R14.
15	(L1, R1) L11, R foot A, R14, L14. (Static)
16	(L15, R15) R7, L8, R14, L14.

17	(L1, R1) R4, L9, R14, L14.
18	(L1, R1) R2, feet A and B, R14, L14.
19	(L1, R1) L3, R12, R14, L14.
20	(L15, R15) R7, L9, R14, L14.
21	(L1, R1) R7, L21, R22, L22.
22	*The Bear Claw* (L15, R15) R16, L18, R19, L20, R22, L22 (feet low and on dish out left – no heels, no ledge).
23	(L15, R15) R16, L19, R7, L8, R11, L13, pocket, continue right to finish up *A Little Extra Start.*
24	(L15, R15) R16, L19, R7, R14, L14.
25	(L1, R1) L5, R7, L9, R14, L14.
26	(L1, R1) L17, R7, L9, R14, L14.
27	*Malc's One Armer* (L9) – do a one arm pull up. No jumping off the floor.

The holds

1	Big rippled sidepull	13	Sharp flatty
2	Slopey undercut/thumb sprag	14	Jugs
3	Very poor sloper/pinch	15	Jugs
4	Bobbly pinch/crimp	16	'Bear claw' pinch
5	'Concept' edge	17	Poor pinch
6	Poor sloper/crimp and good thumb sprag	18	Poor rounded pinch
7	Pinch	19	Poor edge/slot
8	'Matchbox' edge	20	Slopey sidepull
9	Poor slopey crimp	21	Very small edge
10	Sidepull/pinch	22	Jugs
11	Good, big, flat hold	23	Highest small slot
12	Sloping 3 finger drag		

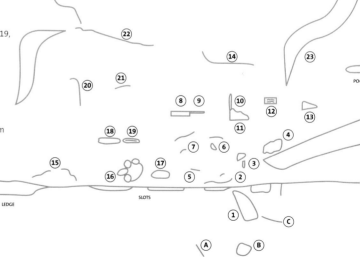

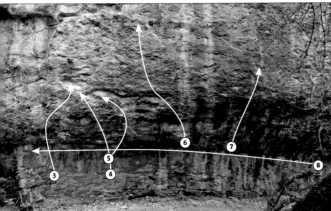

A Little Extra Area

1   **The Rib**   *6b+*
The vague, undercut rib just left of *Pinches Wall*, to jugs.

2   **Verbal Abuse Start**   *6a+*   ✳
The highball groove to jugs.

3   **A Little Extra Direct Start**   *7a*   ★
From slots under the bulge span out to the greasy flat hold (mono optional) and lock or pop to the jug out right. Share to finish or continue to the next jug (better, but same grade). A left-hand variant takes the crimp with your right hand and rocks left to the slots.

4   **Undercuts to Crimp**   *7b+*
A powerful eliminate. Start once again on slots under the bulge, match a pair of undercuts and make a big move to the high diagonal crimp and slap left to the jug from here. Climbing the same problem but using the sloper instead of the diagonal crimp is 7c (*Undercuts to Sloper*).

5   *7c*
Another eliminate. From the same slots reach out and use the fingery edge/pocket hold to get the crozzley sidepull above and finish on the jug.

6   **Pump up the Valium**   *7c+*
A start from a high left hand pinch and a poor right hand undercut allows a stiff pull to gain a crozzley side-pull. Crimp up the highball wall above to jugs. Start on stacked mats to reach the pinch. *Dan Varian*

7   **Hooligan Start**   *8a+*
Slap for a crimp from a tiny left hand undercut and a barely adequate right hand pinch. Once at the crimp another hard crossover move up and right gains a further crimp allowing the flakes above to be reached. The grade is for pulling on before going for the edge. *Steve Dunning*

8   **Ben's Traverse**   *8a*   ✳
Traverse left from the start of *Out of My Tree* to the *Pinches Wall*. Contorted, tenuous, powerful and in need of weeding. In reverse it's harder and called *Pocketrocity*, 8a. *Ben Moon (BT), Andy Harris (P)*

Powerband Area

1 Boot Boys Start *6c* ✳
Big undercuts and sidepulls left of the pillar are used to gain the big glue-covered jug. Continue up and right to the good hold below the groove in a highball stylee for *Out of My Boots* (7a+).

2 Out of My Tree Start *7b* ✳
The steep wall above the pillar is climbed by twisting your fingers into the painful and greasy slots. Finish on the jug. *Andy Pollitt*

3 Pump Up the Power *7c+* ★
The vague, hanging white groove on small but positive crimps. The hard section is only finished when you move out left onto a good flatty at 15ft. F8a+ (route grade) if you take a rope. *Ben Moon*

4 The Steve Miller Band *7c*
Climb *PUTP* to the lip and traverse left to finish on the *OOMT* jug. *Steve McClure*

5 Rattle and Hump Start *7a+* ★
Any which way up to the big jug two metres up, from the good square pocket. All methods are powerful and fingery. Starting on the slots on the right, rather than the bigger holds above the vague pillar and eliminating the heel-toe is 7b. 7c+ footless.

6 Powerhumps *7b* ✳
An extension to the *Rattle and Hump Start*, starting on the first two slots of the *Powerband*. The harder (and better) method is to go straight up from the two higher slots to the pair of crimps rather than traverse left to the start of the stand-up – 7b+.

7 Powerband *7c* ★
Start on the right-most pair of twin slots and traverse all the way left to the pillar. You must stay high on pinches through the middle section rather than dropping down low into a mono (*Powerless*), and the finishing sequence – the crux – drops down to the undercuts on the pillar from the painful, high two-finger pocket. A rite of passage. *Jerry Moffatt*

For hunters of *Raven Tor* esoterica, there is *Under the Powerband* – climb the last section of the Powerband by keeping low and palming off the roof.

Strict Blueband *7c+*
Reverse *Powerband*, keeping high over the middle section (no use of undercut vertical slot or the big square pocket) and finish without the final pocket on the higher line of slots.

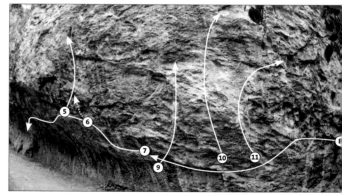

Staminaband *8a* ★

An extension start to *Powerband* from under *Super High Intensity Body Building*. Start on the flake and traverse left, with a hard sequence using the low slot and the sloper, into undercuts and then into *Powerband*. The big high pocket just after the start is out. *Ben Moon*

Staminahumps *7c+ (hard)* ✳

Staminaband into *Powerhumps* (the hard way).

Influx *8a*

Sit-start on the undercuts on *Staminaband*, and climb the left facing rib above finishing at the high edge. The big holds out right are eliminated at this grade. *Dawid Skoczylas*

Kristian's Problem *7b*

Stand start just right of *Influx* and use both sides of the rib and edges to finish on a small crimp on the route *Wild in Me*.

Wild in Me Start *6c*

Use an edge to span right to finish on the sidepull jug. Slightly harder from sitting.

12 Boy Band *7c*

The low level R-L traverse starting on the large jug right of *Saline Drip* and finishing at the start of *StaminaBand*. *Andy Harris*

Links:

BB into SB (aka *Stamina Boys*) 8b (F8c+/9a route grade). *Steve McClure*
PB into PUTP (aka *Pump Up the Powerband*) 8a+
SB into PUTP (aka *Pump Up the Stamina*) 8b/+ (F8c+ route grade). *John Gaskins*
SB into OOMT (aka *Out of Stamina*) 8a+ (do not step left to rest on the plinth). *Rupert Davies*
SB into BT (aka *Should be Band*) 8a+. *Andy Harris*

13 Saline Drip *7a* ✳

Climb the fingery wall to jugs, on the other side of the tree to the right of the start of *Staminaband*, starting either direct or slightly right. Reverse or jump. 7a+ from sitting.

14 4+

The central weakness on good but slightly suspect holds. There are other straight up problems on this wall on suspect rock in places.

JAMES PEARSON ON *KEEN ROOF* **PHOTO:** JOHN COEFIELD

ANDY BANKS ON *PAINT IT BLACK*   PHOTO: DAVE PARRY

Blackwell Dale

This small valley leading down from the A6 to Miller's Dale contains a number of small steep limestone craglets that stay wet throughout most of the winter but provide good, shady and difficult bouldering in the summer, on mostly excellent rock. Grades vary from 6b to 8a+ but, as is the case with most limestone bouldering in the Peak, the quality starts from about 7a.

There is also a bit of further bouldering across the road but we've chosen not to include it as it's on private land, an SSSI further down and you have to hop a barbed wire fence to get to it. Details on the internet for anyone keen.

Access and Approach

All crags are situated on either side of the B6049 just before it joins the A6. Parking is available in a bay next to *Beginner's Wall* or under *Sean's Roof* – two very obvious lay-bys on the left side of the road as you drive uphill.

The climbing on *Ovine Buttress* and *Black and Decker Buttress*, opposite *Beginner's Wall*, has not been included for access reasons.

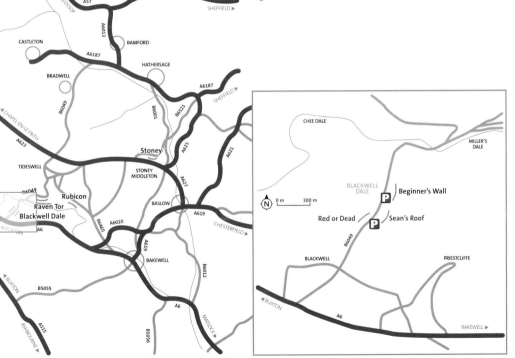

Beginner's Wall

Although bouldered on for many years, the base of this small buttress has now been fully developed with some very good problems.

1 A Bit on the Side *7a*
From a sitting start on the left-hand side of the low broken ledges, move out left to good holds, then back right to share on high central edges.

2 Recreational Violence *8a+*
From the same start as the previous problem, climb the grey streaked wall direct via a small crimp (taken with the left hand) to finish on the same holds as the previous problem. *Dawid Skoczylas*

3 Recreational Violence Left-Hand *8a*
This time, take the crimp with the right hand and go left to another, then go to the top. Stay right of the good holds on problem 1. *Dan Varian/Ned Feehally*

4 The Love of Money Start *7b* ✳
The vague arête feature that forms the start of the route.

5 Aurora *7c*
The wall to the right, on sidepulls and crimps to finish on high edges.

6 *7a*
From a low start, climb to the left-hand end of the ledge.

7 Man of Steel *7b* ✳
From the large ledge, climb up to the spiky jug, staying right of the crack. *Neil Travers*

8 Swing Time *7a* ★
Start as for *Man of Steel*, but move out right to the sidepull jug, then back left to finish on the spiky jug. *Neil Travers*

9 It's a Traversty *7b+*
Link *Swing Time* into the finish of *Neil's Wall*. *Neil Travers*

10 Advanced Training *7c+*
Sit-start on small pockets, pull up to a shallow vertical slot with a crimp above it and then into *Swing Time*. Finish as for *Man of Steel*.

11 Mike's Problem *7c+*
Pull on with poor crimps ('footholds' to the lay man) and slap for the *Swing Time* sidepull jug. Finish up this. *Mike Adams*

Neil's Wall *7b+* ★

A Peak classic. From two small crimps, slap upwards to finish on a vague ledge system at 2m. The sitting start is 7c. Originally done backhanding both start holds, they can also be pinched, ensuring grade opinions vary, so don't be surprised if it feels easier or harder. *Neil Travers*

Neil's Wall Right-Hand *8a*

Climb direct to the right-hand slot via a big pull on a small crimp and toe hooks out right. *Mike Adams*

6b

Climb the groove on the far right to a jug.

Hall of the Mountain King *(7a+)* can be found in a cave down the road and left of *Beginner's Wall*. Potentially ruined by cavers, it starts on the left wall at a mono and jug. Easy moves lead to undercuts, a perfect handjam, and a tricky exit to jugs up and left.

Sean's Roof

Although it can seep badly after wet weather, this charming, scruffy little cave is home to some of Peak lime's best, modern problems. The problems to the left are a bit lowball but have some good moves. See topo overleaf.

1   Sean's Roof   8a+   ✳
The central (bolted) line through the roof is highball and hard. It just about scrapes in as a boulder problem, but is perhaps more logically climbed with a rope (F8b+). *Jerry Moffatt (first soloed by Mark Leach pre-pads)*

2   Paint It Black   7c   ★
Climb the prow on the left side of the cave from a sit-start on the low rail. Span the roof to finish on vegetated holds around the lip. Classic. See photo on p452. *Andy Banks*

3   Byker Groove   7c
Sit-start the groove from the left end of the rail and crimp powerfully upwards passing a sloper to finish on a square-cut jug around the lip. Hard. *Andy Banks*

DY BANKS ON *WHAT WOULD JERRY DO?*   **PHOTO:** DAVE PARRY

DAVE NORTON ON *RED OR DEAD*   PHOTO: JOHN COEFIELD

4 Push Me Pull You *6b+*
Start on the jug and climb diagonally rightwards to jugs. An eliminate start on poor edges right of the starting jugs is 7a+. *Robin Mueller/Dawid Skoczylas*

5 Don't Jump *6c*
Start on jugs under the bulge, pull to a jug then sloping edges and make a hard move to jugs. *Robin Mueller/Dawid Skoczylas*

6 Fudge *7a*
From the same start, pull direct up the wall to finish on a jug over the lip.
Robin Mueller/Dawid Skoczylas

7 My Friend Flicka *7b+*
Start on two poor crimps either side of the thin crack and use the small hold in the crack to flick for good holds. *Robin Mueller/Dawid Skoczylas*

8 Twice a Slice *6b*
Start in the low break and pop to the higher holds. *Robin Mueller/Dawid Skoczylas*

9 Orange Si *7b*
From a lie-down start on a left hand crimp and right hand good sidepull, reach twin crimps and pop to a left hand dish. Finish above. *Robin Mueller/Dawid Skoczylas*

10 Somebody's Head *7a*
Another lying down start. From the lowest holds on the lip of the hole reach crimps and the protruding jug above. *Robin Mueller/Dawid Skoczylas*

11 Uno *6a*
Sit-start the bulge left of the crack. The crack from a sit-start is 6b.
Robin Mueller/Dawid Skoczylas

12 Back in Black *7a*
Slightly further down the road from *Sean's Roof*, and set back a little, is a small amphitheatre that promises much but delivers little. On the left is a low roof. Climb the centre of the roof from jugs at the back to blocky holds just under the lip by bridging on the plinth to the right. Turn the lip, pull up to jugs and tickle the tree to finish. *Andy Banks*

d or Dead
next problems are found in the attractive bay opposite *Sean's Roof*.
en dry when other stuff is wet.

6b
Climb the juggy ledge to the break.

Free Range Abattoir   7a+   ✶
Sit-start and climb direct from the slopey ledge. A low start from the break down and right, under the roof, is 7b+. *Andy Banks*

Red or Dead   7a+   ★
A great problem. Sit-start the slopey ledge, move right to a pocket and then up. The low start from the break under the roof is *Any Hole's A Goal*, 7c. *Andy Banks*

4 **Top Shop**   *7b+*
A right-hand start to *Red or Dead*, traversing left from a flat hold at various heights.
Low: follow pockets to the big crimp, continue up.
Middle: gain the crimp above twin pockets with right hand, then left hand and up.
High: take the same crimp with left hand, then up with right hand, then up.

5 **Deranged Abbott**   *7b*
The right-hand start finishing up *Free Range Abbatoir*. *Robin Mueller*

6 **What Would Jerry Do?**   *7a+*   ★
He'd warm up on this traverse, then he'd climb *Sean's Roof*. Can be done either way at the same grade. See photo on p455. *Jerry Moffatt*

7 **A Lack of Colour**   *7b*   ✶
From just right of centre, climb straight up the groove to finish on jugs at the top of the crag. Highball. *Dan Varian*

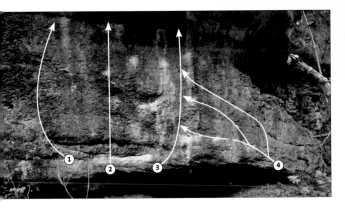

Alport Area

Spitting distance from the gritstone of the *Cratcliffe Area* are two limestone venues that could not be more different. Situated in a beautiful spot by the river, *Rheinstor* provides good – but high – limestone bouldering at amenable grades. The rock is solid – unusually good for Peak limestone – and is peppered with small pockets, giving a fingery feel to many problems. Many of the problems are the starts (and often the cruxes of) routes and they finish by escaping at the top (high!) break line – reverse and jump off. There is some polish. The crag faces west so is in the shade in the morning and in the sun in the afternoons.

Nuda's Tartan, by comparison, is a collection of steep, shady bulbous limestone bulges giving interesting and powerful problems at higher grades. The rock is rough, grippy limestone with tufa features and pockets. Some of the problems are pretty three-dimensional and require the full gamut of climbing techniques for success. Steep? Yes. Straight pulling? No.

Access and Approach

Alport is a few miles south of Bakewell, not far from the A6. Turn off the A6 onto the B5056 in the direction of Youlgreave. Don't turn left towards *Cratcliffe* and Birchover, but instead continue along the road by the river into Alport.

Rheinstor is a couple of hundred metres southwest of Alport village and is easily visible from the road to Youlgreave. Park in the village and follow the path across the river. The crag is unmissable to the left of the path.

Nuda's Tartan is on the right just as you enter Alport, by a turn-off on the right (a minor lane – Dark Lane). Park in the village and walk back round to the crag. As there have been access issues here in the past (now resolved thanks to the BMC) please keep visits to single parties, don't park next to the crag, and don't damage walls or vegetation. Take your litter home too. Thanks.

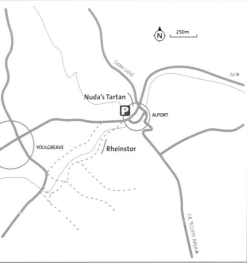

Nuda's Tartan

A strange collection of steep problems, on limestone quite different to that at the traditional Peak venues. The first problems are on the obvious steep roof to the left. The right-hand section is often wet.

1   The Meltdown   7b   ✳
Sit-start the rising lip and traverse it all the way right to finish at jugs.

2   Nuda's Tartan   7b+
Start back right of the bulbous pillar, and make a few moves across the roof to join *The Meltdown* about half-way along. The line is a little vague. *Iain Farrar*

3   Tarantula   7c
Start at the right-hand side of the bulbous pillar and climb the roof, joining the traverse about two thirds of the way along. Another vague line. *Mark Evans*

4   Submission   6c+
Lean out from the bulbous pillar at the back, and use a pocket and undercut in the roof and a monster toe-hook to reach holds at the lip. Swing up and right to finish as for *The Meltdown. Ben Humphris*

5   Dave's Roof   7a+   ✳
Bridge up the back wall right of *Submission* and cross the roof from an undercut at the back, a slot and a pinch in the roof to the jug pocket at the lip. Finish straight up or as *The Meltdown*. It's possible to span straight to the lip, but holding the swing without hitting the tree would be hard. *Dave Parry*

6   Slap Happy   6b+
Sit-start and follow good holds to a large pinch. Finish at high jugs. *Mark Evans*

7   The Scenic Route   7a
Start up *Slap Happy* and traverse left from the jugs to the far left arête and rock onto the slab to finish. No footledges. Also good in reverse, finishing up the high line of jugs. *Dave's Extension* extends the right to left version, starting deep in the first, right-hand cave on a large sidepull, and avoiding the footledge – 7a+. *Robin Mueller/Dawid Skoczy*

8   Slot Machine   7a+
Sit-start as for *Slap Happy* then move into hand/arm jams and traverse right to finish at the top of Iron Flag. *Mark Evans*

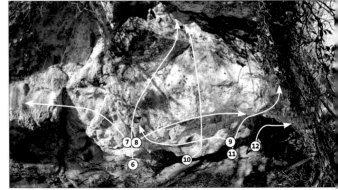

Enigma 7b+
A sit-start right to left traverse on low painful pockets (often wet) using tufa flows for helpful leg jams. Finish up *Slap Happy*. *Ben Humphris*

Calorie Count 7c
Sit-start at the back of cave and move directly out through pockets and jams to finish at high jugs. *Mark Evans*

Iron Flag 7b+
Sit-start the crack feature. Often wet. *Bobby Digital* reverses *Enigma* into *Iron Flag* – 7c. *Mark Evans*

Stumped 7c+
A strange problem that's hard to grade. From the back of the cave move through the roof above the old tree stump, using foot and hand jams, to finish over the lip on jugs. *Mark Evans*

nty of potential for hard link-ups.

Rheinstor
A lovely spot by the river, perfect for an evening's highballing on gnarly pockets (!). The problems are described from left to right.

13 Le Crepscule 5+ ✳
The groove is polished but still gives good climbing.

14 6b
Climb the wall to the flake, pulling on pockets.

15 Wizard of Aus 6b+
The wall to the right, with a crux to gain the high flake.

16 Meridian 6c ✳
The fingery wall to the break. See photo on p458.

17 Ron's Route 6b+ ✳
More fingery-ness up the wall just left of the big low pocket.

18 Mjollnir 6a+
The faint scoop to the break. High.

19 Valhalla 5
The high wall past two possible threads.

20 Asgard 4+
The wall below the faint rampline.

21 Loki 4+ ✳
The wall to the pocket, just left of the fence.

Middle Break Traverse 6c
Traverse the vague, thin middle break/seam in either direction.

Rheinstor Traverse 7a
Traverse at a low level, in either direction.

JOHN COWBELON ??? Peak Bouldering

Harborough Rocks

Harborough is a rare beast: a limestone climbing venue where the grades are low, the rock is good, and the climbing is great. Throw into that mix excellent grassy landings and a south-facing aspect, and you have all the ingredients for a fun, relaxing day out. The rock is actually dolomitic limestone with a profusion of pockets uncommon on limestone elsewhere.

Spoilt only slightly by the factory at the foot of the crag, *Harborough* is a good place for beginners and low-grade climbers to come and refine their craft on 'proper' problems, with 'proper' holds. As *Harborough* has been climbed on for years, some of the more popular lines are polished, although there's a lot less sheen than you might expect and there's often a decent, rough foothold just to the side of the more obvious polished one. Some of the lines straddle the line between highball and route, but with positive holds and flat landings, you might be more inclined to push yourself here than at other venues.

We haven't attempted to describe every single line; instead we've singled out the better 'bouldering' lines, leaving you to discover the rest for yourself.

If you enjoyed it here, look up the nearby *Brassington Rocks* too.

Access and Approach

The crag is best approached from the A6 near Cromford, just south of Matlock. Turn off the A6 onto the A5012 at Cromford, and immediately turn right again – this confusingly keeps you on the A5012. Follow the road for several miles and turn left in Grangemill onto the B5056 towards Longcliffe. Turn left in Longcliffe towards Brassington and look for a left turn just as the road starts to descend into the village. Turn left here and the crag is visible on the left after about 1km. Park just past the factory in the lay-by and approach the crag by the footpath next to the factory, across the *High Peak Trail*.

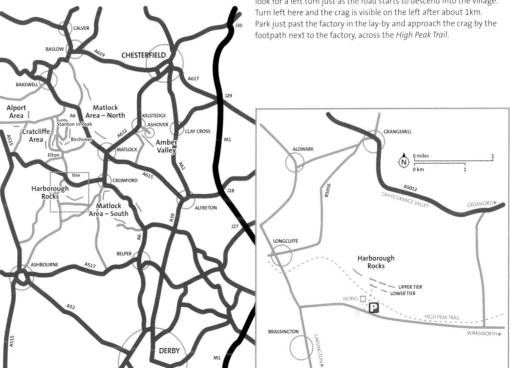

The Upper Tier

The buttresses on the Upper Tier are taller, feature more cracks and are a bit more polished than the Lower Tier. The first problems can be found on the steep, vertical wall below the prominent steeple at the left-hand end of the crag. Tall lines that might feel strenuous and a little high.

1   **Cave Buttress Arête**   *Fun*
     The easy-angled, well featured arête down and left of the cave, climbed on its right.

2   **Introductory Wall**   *Fun*
     The wall right of the previous problem.

3   **The Swarm**   *8a+*
     From the right-hand sidewall of the cave, climb the roof at right angles to the crack, finishing matched in the crack. Impressive stuff. *Mark Evans*

4   **The Arête**   *5+*
     The blunt arête on chips. Avoid the good holds left of the chips.

5   **Cracks**   *6a*   ✳
     The cracks right of the arête are tricky higher up.

6   **Jug**   *5+*   ✳
     The centre of the wall, with the crux passing the jug rail halfway up. See photo on p462.

7   **4+**
     A tight line up the wall to the right, just left of the crack (the crack isn't actually much help anyway).

8   **Concave Wall**   *4*
     The curvy wall right of the crack has plenty of good holds. *Steeple Arête* climbs the easy-angled arête to the right – 3.

9 Bow Ridge *3+*
The blunt arête on the right of the descent path.

10 Bow Corner *3+*
The blocky groove is good, although sadly the landing isn't.

11 Bow Shaped Wall *5+* ✳
The cracks up the left-hand side of the wall give out handholds, but not so many footholds.

12 Bow Arête *4*
The juggy, easy angled wall just left of the arête.

13 *4*
The arête started front on.

The pocketed wall to the right offers some fun, easier problems. The next described problems are about 60m to the right.

14 Shorty *4+*
The short arête.

15 Mantel Wall *4*
Up the short wall from a pocket.

16 Cracked Wall *5+* ✳
The steep cracks at the left-hand side of the wall.

17 Overhanging Crack *5* ✳
The concave wall is climbed on great pinches formed by the cracks, and has a steep finish.

18 The Arête *4* ★
The tall arête is a classic of the crag.

19 Blinkers *5+*
The thin crack just right of the arête.

20 Legs Over *4+* ✳
The centre of the wall has a tricky start and eases immediately.

The Lower Tier

The problems on the Lower Tier are shorter, less polished and a bit more crozzly. Many other easy and fun problems could be climbed, on good holds above good landings. Described left to right, the first problems are on a low bulge by a tree.

21 Left Bulge *5+*
Sit-start the left-hand side of the bulge.

22 Right Bulge *5* ✳
Sit-start the right-hand side of the bulge from a layaway and undercut. Variations and eliminates possible, including starting up *Right Bulge* and traversing the lip left into *Left Bulge*.

The next problems are on a series of walls 20m to the right.

23 Cracked Arête *3*
The cracked, bulging arête.

24 Slab Wall *5* ✳
The clean, slabby wall is not quite as tricky as it looks.

25 Flake Mantel *3*
Mantel up past the sharp flake.

26 Cod Eye Wall *5+* ✳
Crank up the wall from the double pockets.

The final problems are on some low buttresses around the corner.

27 Sharp Bulge 5
Sit-start the bulge and climb it on sharp holds.

28 4 ✳
Sit-start the left-hand side of the wall.

29 Flake Sitter 4+
Sit-start the wall left of centre past a small flake.

30 3
The wall just right of the vague crack, from a sit-start.

The Tube – Dove Dale

Located some distance further southwest of the traditional limestone bouldering centres of the central Peak, *The Tube*, near Dove Dale, offers very steep bouldering on good, clean white limestone. Developed by Graham and Dan Warren, the crag actually sits high on the north side of Hall Dale, with fine views south down Dove Dale itself. The reason for the name will become apparent on first visit – a unique tubular cave with two entrances/exits. Although there are 'warm-up' problems, the crag is only really worth a visit for climbers operating at 7a and above, with the grade spread extending up to 8a thanks to the powerful *Metal Slug*. *Ringpull* is a good 7a, with horizontal climbing on big holds; *Dawn Raider* is the classic of the crag, and potentially one of the best problems of its grade on Peak limestone; while *Creep* could be the longest roof problem in the Peak District.

Access and Approach

The crag is actually located in Hall Dale, just before it joins up with Dove Dale. It is unfortunately rather hidden, high on the south-facing hillside, and so may not be found straight away on a first visit. Although the crag is on access land and can be approached from Stanshope, we've described the approach from Milldale as it's a bit nicer and it avoids crossing, and potentially damaging, the farmer's fences and walls.

From the A515 Buxton–Ashbourne road, turn off just north of Tissington, signed to Milldale and Alstonefield. Follow the road into the bottom of the valley and turn left down to Milldale. Park in the car park just west of the main village.

Walk south on the western bank of the river (right-hand side, looking down the valley) on the footpath that starts adjacent to the toilets in the centre of Milldale. Follow this over several stiles for about 800m until the impressive *Raven's Tor* is visible up on the right. Bear right up to the crag and follow the path along the base of the crag. At the far end of the crag is a fence corner. Bear diagonally right up the steep hillside until almost at the wall at the top. Contour around the hill passing an old broken wall until a rocky knoll is reached. The cave is about 50m below this, and slightly to the right (looking down), just as the hillside steepens and the bushes become more dense. (The crag can be approached by contouring around from the fence corner, but this may be more difficult on a first visit.)

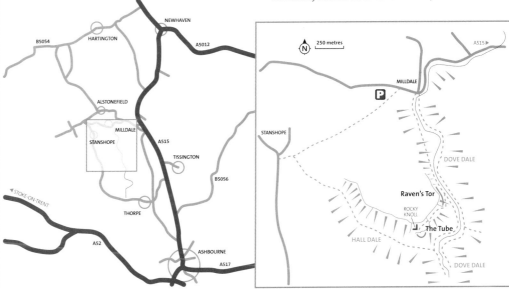

The Tube

The problems are described from left to right, starting at the higher, smaller cave entrance.

1   **Doug Hnuts** *7a+*
Sit-start and traverse the low lip from right to left. Finish as for *Ringpull* without the side wall.

2   **Ringpull** *7a* ✳
A good roof problem. At back, centre left is a broad pillar with jugs at its left-hand side. Sit-start here and climb out the left-hand side of the roof to an obvious 'ring' hold at the lip. Rock to small holds in the face to finish. No side wall: it's a bit easier with, but superior without.

3   **Dan's Other Roof Problem** *7a+*
A parallel line to *Ringpull*, starting to the right in the crack, without the footledge. At the lip swing left to finish as for *Ringpull*.

4   **The Crack** *6b*
From the pillar, climb the roof crack to jugs around on the front face. Everything is in for feet.

5   **Metal Slug** *8a* ✳
From the rectangular, vertical slot at the right-hand side of the cave, climb diagonally across the roof to reach, and finish at, the crack.

6   **Creep** *7c+* ✳
Sit-start at sidepulls at the right-hand side of the cave, and climb the long roof to finish up *Ringpull*. The obvious footledges by the pillars are out of bounds.

7   **Obelisk** *7a+*
From the lip, climb up and left to the vague groove feature above the hole. Finish at the break above. The problem avoids the bigger holds and crack to the right at the grade – using these is *Obelisk Right-Hand*, 6c.

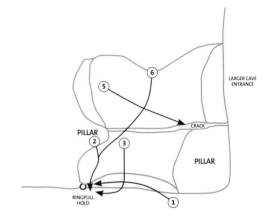

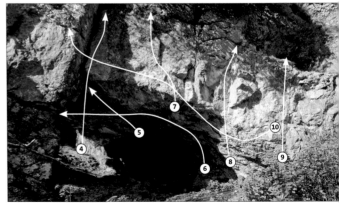

8 **Little Brown Groove** *6b*
The brown groove just right of the arete, from a sit-start.

9 **Warm Up** *5*
Climb straight up to the ledge from the flat hold on the right of the crag.

10 **Dawn Raider** *7c* ★
From the start of *Warm Up*, traverse left on low holds (veering higher here is 7b+), then power up the arête and traverse the lip to finish on jugs on the pillar, left of the crack. Classic.

11 **Dawn Raider into Obelisk** *7c*
Link *Dawn Raider* into *Obelisk*.

12 **Creep Extension** *8a*
From the start of *Dawn Raider*, traverse into *Creep*. Sustained!

DAN WARREN ON *CREEP* **PHOTO:** ROBIN MUELLER

Graded List

Every climber's favourite thing: a graded list. The following is a list of some of the Peak's best problems at each grade in approximate order of difficulty.

8b+
Voyager Sit-Start

8b
Staminaband/Pump up the Power
Brad Pit Sit-Start
The Ace
Fat Lip
Keen Roof
Voyager
A Bigger Belly
Close of Business

8a+
Stanton Deliver
Tamora
The Nth Power
Hooligan Start
Superboc
Sean's Roof
8 Ball
The Bed of Procrustes
Andronicus
Inertia Reel Traverse
Whippet
Out of Stamina
Super Size Me

8a
The Pessimist
Pink Lady
The Press – Low Left Sit-Start
Hats for Youths
Careless Torque
The Darkest Cloud
Ben's Extension
Chequers Groove
The Dark Room
Westwood
Influx
Blind Drunk
Ben's Traverse
Full Power

The Enigma
Little Rascal Sit-Start
Staminaband
Tsunami
Help the Young Sit-Start
Solomon's Seal
Blazing 48s
The Joker
Westworld

7c+
The Press – Low Right Sit-Start
Infinite Suspense
Jumpers for Trousers
Raw Deal
Walk on By
Pump Up The Power
Darkstar
The Imperfect Catch
Tumbleweed
The Golden Egg
Master Kush
Seldom Seen Kid
Blind Ali's Date
Slingshot
River of Life
Local Hero Sit-Start
Blind Fury
My Orange
Creep
Turbo
Jerry's Problem
Low Rider
Columns
Mushin
Left-Hand Man Direct
Warchild
Three Hundred Pounds of Musclin' Man
Maurice Gibb
Sweet Release
Ben's Roof
Western Eyes

7c
The Leotard Legend
Brad Pit
The Seeker
Salle Goose
The Brazilian
Byker Groove
Courtesy of Jonboy

Spring Voyage
Jerry's Traverse (Stanage)
Who Needs Ready Brek?
My Buddy the Apple
Higher Ground
My Prune
Zaff Skoczylas
Great White
Ben's Wall (Curbar)
Hurricane
Brad's Wall
Grand Theft
Cave Problem Sit-Start
Blind Fig
Barry Sheene
Hannibal
Powerband
Culpeper's Practice
Brass Monkeys
Les Grand Doigts
Another Nadin Traverse
Stall Sit-Start
Ladies Wall
The Terrace
Zorev
White Ladder
The DT's
Neil's Wall Sit-Start
Dark Matter
Dawn Raider
Quine
Little Pig
Tetris
Paint it Black
Green Room Slap Sit-Start
The Green Man
The Golden Path
Sole Power
Stateside
Ben's Wall (Robin Hood's Stride)
Mossatrocity

7b+
Miles' Slab
The Eastwood Traverse
West Side Story
Famous Grouse
Cave Problem
Shit
Powerhumps (Hard Way)
Point Break

Old King Cascade
Zippatrocity
The Press
Le Musée Imaginaire
Deliverance
Guplets on Toast Sit-Start
Blind Ali
The Dove From Above
Zippy's Sidepull
Leather Joy Boys
California Screaming
Basic Training Start
Left-Hand Man
Blind Date
Storm
HMS Daring
Giza
Boba Fett
Goosecreature
The Rib
Fish Arête Sit-Start
Rocket Man
Swingers Party
Sean's Problem
The Beast
Stump Hole Cavern (first bit)
Back in the YMCA
Flatworld
Monologue
Dick Williams

7b
Simple Simon
Happy Campus
Cheeks n Beaks
The Art of White Hat Wearing
Spare Rib
Big Al Qaeda
The Buckstone Dyno
Fielder's Wall
Desparête
The Gritstone Treaty
The Bus Stop Mantel
Captain Hook
Beneath the Breadline
Sean's Arête
All Sit Down
P Crack
Jorge
Jerry's Traverse (Cratcliffe)
Burning Lark Sunset

A Bigger Splash Direct
One Arm Bandit
Powerhumps (Easy Way)
Suavito
Melvin Bragg
Wright's Traverse
Little Gem
Spike
T-Crack
Swing Thing
Andle Stone Wall
Green Death Super Direct
Kidneystone
Superbrook
Pig Heart Boy
Out of My Tree Start
Rambeau
Brigadoon
Milky Buttons
Kudos
Stottie
Zaff's Problem
My Apple
Pogle's Wood Sit-Start
For a Few Beagles More
The Meltdown
A Case of Mistaken Identity
Yoghurt Hypnotist
Boyager
Hats for Clowns
Slabotomy
Mark's Roof
Weedkiller Traverse
Electrical Storm
Zippy's Traverse
Soft on the G
Quantum Leap

7a+
Rattle and Hump Start
Red or Dead
Velvet Crab
Monomantel
Tierdrop
Ten Inch Zombies
Krush Regime
The Ripper
Wright's Unconquerable
Green Room Slap
Fact Hunt
Inertia Reel

PHOTO: KEITH SHARPLES

THE FOUNDRY

0114 2796 331
www.**foundry**climbing.com

45 Mowbray Street Sheffield S3 8EN

**Bouldering • Leading • Top rope
Café • CragX climbing shop
Instruction**

6c+

Bin Laden's Cave
Brad's Arête – The Presence of Absence
Beauty
Diamond Slab
Mark's Roof Left-Hand
Mono Seam
Sleeping with the Flowers
Soft Top Beetle
Pepper Mill
Thing on a Spring
Stallone Arête
Iain's Prow Right-Hand
The Sheep
A Fearful Orange
Fish Arête
The Porthole
Summit Arête
This is My Church
Back Side Arête
Gibbering Right
The Lark Ascending
Triptych Groove
G-Thang Sit-Start
Rocket Ride
Ape Drape
Collywood
Captain Quark

6c

Fallen Archangel
The Fin (Gib Torr)
Scratchy Bun Left
Teck Crack Direct
Banana Finger Direct
The Chapel
Bristol Dreaming
Renegade Bulge
The Downpipe
Safe Bet
Pogle's Wood
Jump
Soft Groove
Bunny Wailer
Universal Squab
Not To Be Taken Away
Life in a Radioactive Dustbin
Stretch and Mantel
Razor Roof
Acid Reign
Slap Happy

Left Pine
The Shepherd
Hot Ziggerty
Brain Dead
Cottaging
Boot Boys Start
Walnut Whip (Secret Garden)
Adults Only
Saian
Elastic Wall
Breadline
Eyes to the Skies
The Walnut
7 Ball
Steep Traverse
The Art of Japan

6b+

Golden Days
Chip Shop Mantel
Ossie's Bulge
Friends and Relations
The Bookend
Starlight Left
Pagan Cross
Runnel Rib
The Ripple
Baldstones Dyno
Think Tank
K Kole Arête
Conan the Librarian
Honeypot Wall
Local Hero
A Miller's Tale
Arête Problem
Elephant's Eye
Right Pine
Chaste
Back Wall Traverse
Harold
Seventy Degrees
Golden Arête
Curving Arête
Cool Running
G-Thang
Fish Dish
Trench Flakes

6b

D.I.Y.
Lean, Green, Bean Machine

Dolly
Sly Stallone
Freda Direct
Persistence
Nicotine Stain
Finger of Fate
Like Pommel
Spankosaurus Does Chicago
Push
Cummerbund
It Hurts
Tiger
A Beagle Too Far
Ousal High Traverse
Alternative Three
Honcho
Remergence
The Staffordshire Flyer
Brown Wall
Miss Sunshine
Stepped Arête
Cracker Block
Sitting Duck
Swivel Finger
Technical Master
My Crazy Head
The Cube
Rhododendron
Hazel Groove
New York New York
Lintelatomy
Charlie's Overhang
Rock Fusion
Seismic Start
Bullworker
Oedipus Traverse
Pothole Slab

6a+

Thomas the Tanked Up Engine
Bionics Direct
The Pinches
Blazes
Glory Days
Nasal Arête
Dobb Egg
All Quiet on the Eastern Front
Fielder's Corner
Crack and Arête
The Arch (Roaches)
The Dragon Flight Traverse

Got Milk
Eggs Arête
The Grasshopper
The Beak
The Dragon's Den
Original
Ascent of Man Start
Leggit
Varicose
Between the Bars
Crash Test

6a

Mating Toads
Moai
Love Handles
Debris Groove
Sprung
Viaduct Wall
Neutral Milk Hotel
Wall End Grab
Tufa
Harland Globetrotter
Wildy's Right
Fat World
5c Wall (Ramshaw)
Violence
Outlook Roof
Right Vein
Lurcher Direct
Birch Tree Arête
Long John
Three Pocket Slab
Joe's Arête
Banana Finger
Cottonmouth
Crescent Arête
Wobbly Wall
My Left Foot

5+

The Celtic Cross
Roo
Jug
Chicken Ninja
Sublime Indifference
Tody Boy
The Hourglass
The Lone Slab
Calcutta Rib
Foie Gras

Joe's Original
Sidepull Arch
Cleo's Edge
Baby Wolverine
Stingray Arête
Cod Eye Wall
Useful Slab
Microbe
Seconds Out
West Wall
Baxter's Wall Direct
Diamond Slab Left
Flight Exam
Pockets Wall (Stanage)
Nutmeg Groove
Fab Arête
The Wafer
Trevor
Wildy's Arête
Slanty Man
Ace in the Hole

5

Buckstone Groove
Horseshoe Arête
Tody Bear
Nunn's Eliminate
Mini Prow
The Chant
Chieftain
Stepped Arête Right-Hand
Pocket Wall (Churnet)
Wolf Prow
Len's Areet
The Rammer
Seamstress
The Bishop
Gripple Nipple
Angle Arête
Beagles About
The Big Slab
Perfect Porthole Problem
The Shearing
Elephant's Bum
Bombay Overhang
Curbar Corner
Toenail Pie
Communist Crack
Pert Bloke
Issue 53
Corpse Crack

Index